CONTENTS

Cover Picture: *The Old Rectory, Norwich, Norfolk (page 1*

Key to symbols 2

How to use this guide 3

Johansens 1998 Awards for Excellence 4

Introduction from Chippenhall Hall, Eye, Suffolk *(see page 64)*
Winner of the Johansens 1998 Most Excellent Country House Award 6

Introduction from Kingston House, Near Totnes, Devon *(see page 160)*
Winner of the Johansens 1998 Most Excellent Value for Money Award 8

Johansens Recommended Country Houses and Small Hotels in England 11

Johansens Recommended Country Houses and Small Hotels in Wales 187

Johansens Recommended Country Houses and Small Hotels in Scotland 203

Johansens Recommended Country Houses and Small Hotels in Ireland 237

Johansens Recommended Country Houses and Small Hotels in the Channel Islands 255

'Mini Listings' of Johansens Recommended Traditional Inns, Hotels & Restaurants (published in full in the Johansens Recommended Traditional Inns, Hotels & Restaurants Guide 1999) 262

Maps of the British Isles showing all Johansens Recommendations 263

Indexes 270

Johansens Guides Order Forms and Guest Survey Reports 277

FOREWORD BY THE EDITOR

Guests and hoteliers alike recognise the truth of Shakespeare's famous saying "All the world's a stage". Every guest knows, that however delicious the food and comfortable the beds, it is the personal performance of the staff and the way everything is presented that provides true excellence.

At Johansens we consistently inspect and select for recommendations in our guides...your guides...hotels, country houses, restaurants and traditional inns which attain the high standards which you and we are looking for. But you the guests, an increasingly discerning readership, are the essential judges of quality. Our thanks go to the many thousands of you who have sent us Guest Survey Reports. Your comments have helped us with the compilations of our 1999 editions. There are for example fifty new entries in our Hotels guide replacing a similar number no longer included for various reasons as Johansens recommendations. We need your reports, especially if our recommendations ever fail to come up to your expectations. The report forms are at the back of all guides. Keep sending them to us.

A new development which will interest readers is the Johansens Internet site, enabling guests to view the details of and communicate by e-mail with our recommended hotels – http://www.johansens.com

All of us at Johansens wish you very many happy visits to our recommendations this year.

Rodney Exton, Editor

KEY TO SYMBOLS

Symbol	English	Français	Deutsch
12 rms	Total number of rooms	Nombre de chambres	Anzahl der Zimmer
MasterCard	MasterCard accepted	MasterCard accepté	MasterCard akzeptiert
VISA	Visa accepted	Visa accepté	Visa akzeptiert
AMERICAN EXPRESS	American Express accepted	American Express accepté	American Express akzeptiert
	Diners Club accepted	Diners Club accepté	Diners Club akzeptiert
	Quiet location	Un lieu tranquille	Ruhige Lage
	Access for wheelchairs to at least one bedroom and public rooms	Accès handicapé	Zugang für Behinderte

(The 'Access for wheelchairs' symbol ( ) does not necessarily indicate that the property fulfils National Accessible Scheme grading)

Symbol	English	Français	Deutsch
	Chef-patron	Chef-patron	Chef-patronn
	Licensed	Avec Licence	Schankerlanbnis
en famille	Guest and Hosts usually dine together	Table d'Hôte	Mit der Familie essen
M 20	Meeting/conference facilities with maximum number of delegates	Salle de conférences – capacité maximale	Konferenzraum-Höchstkapazität
8	Children welcome, with minimum age where applicable	Enfants bienvenus	Kinder willkommen
	Dogs accommodated in rooms or kennels	Chiens autorisés	Hunde erlaubt
	At least one room has a four-poster bed	Lit à baldaquin dans au moins une chambre	Himmelbett
	Cable/satellite TV in all bedrooms	TV câblée/satellite dans les chambres	Satellit-und Kabelfernsehen in allen Zimmern
	Fax available in rooms	Fax dans votre chambre	Fax in Schlafzimmern
	No-smoking rooms (at least one no-smoking bedroom)	Chambres non-fumeur	Zimmer für Nichtraucher
	Lift available for guests' use	Ascenseur	Fahrstuhl
	Indoor swimming pool	Piscine couverte	Hallenbad
	Outdoor swimming pool	Piscine de plein air	Freibad
	Tennis court at hotel	Tennis à l'hôtel	Hoteleigener Tennisplatz
	Croquet lawn at hotel	Croquet à l'hôtel	Krocketrasen
	Fishing can be arranged	Pêche	Angeln
	Golf course on site or nearby, which has an arrangement with the hotel allowing guests to play	Golf sur site ou à proximité	Golfplatz
	Shooting can be arranged	Chasse / Tir	Jagd
	Riding can be arranged	Équitation	Reitpferd
H	Hotel has a helicopter landing pad	Helipad	Hubschrauberlandplatz
	Licensed for wedding ceremonies	Cérémonies de mariages	Konzession für Eheschliessungen

Published by
Johansens Limited, Therese House, Glasshouse Yard, London EC1A 4JN
Find Johansens on the Internet at: http://www.johansens.com
E-Mail: admin@johansen.u–net.com

Publishing Director: Peter Hancock
P.A. to Publishing Director: Carol Sweeney
Editor: Rodney Exton
Copy Editor: Yasmin Razak
Regional Inspectors: Christopher Bond, Geraldine Bromley, Robert Bromley, Julie Dunkley, Martin Greaves, Joan Henderson, Marie Iversen, Pauline Mason, John O'Neill, Mary O'Neill, Fiona Patrick, Brian Sandell
Production Manager: Daniel Barnett
Production Controller: Kevin Bradbrook
Senior Designer: Michael Tompsett
Designer: Sue Dixon
Copywriters: Norman Flack, Martin Greaves, Yasmin Razak, Jill Wyatt
Sales and Marketing Manager: Laurent Martinez
Marketing Executive: Emma Woods
Sales Executive: Babita Sareen
P.A. to Managing Director & regional editorial research: Angela Willcox

Managing Director: Andrew Warren

Johansens is a member company of Harmsworth Publishing Ltd, a subsidiary of the Daily Mail & General Trust plc

ISBN 1 86017 583X

Printed in England by St Ives plc
Colour origination by Catalyst Creative Imaging

Distributed in the UK and Europe by Johnsons International Media Services Ltd, London (direct sales) & Biblios PDS Ltd, West Sussex (bookstores). In North America by general sales agent: ETL Group, New York, NY (direct sales) and Hunter Publishing, New Jersey (bookstores). In Australia and New Zealand by Bookwise International, Findon, South Australia

HOW TO USE THIS GUIDE

If you want to find a Country House or Small Hotel in a particular area you can:

- Turn to the Maps on pages 263–269
- Search the Indexes on pages 270–274
- Look for the Town or Village where you wish to stay in the main body of the Guide. This is divided into Countries. Place names in each Country appear at the head of the pages in alphabetical order.

The Indexes list the Country Houses and Small Hotels by Countries and by Counties, they also show those with amenities such as fishing, conference facilities, swimming, golf, etc.

The Maps cover all regions. Each Country House and Small Hotel symbol (a green square) relates to a property in this guide situated in or near the location shown.

Red Triangles show the location of Johansens Recommended Traditional Inns, Hotels & Restaurants. If you cannot find a suitable Country House or Small Hotel near where you wish to stay, you may decide to choose one of these establishments as an alternative. They are all listed by place names on page 262.

The prices, in most cases, refer to the cost of one night's accommodation, with breakfast, for two people. Prices are also shown for single occupancy. These rates are correct at the time of going to press but always should be checked with the hotel before you make your reservation.

We occasionally receive letters from guests who have been charged for accommodation booked in advance but later cancelled. Readers should be aware that by making a reservation with a hotel, either by telephone or in writing, they are entering into a legal contract. A hotelier under certain circumstances is entitled to make a charge for accommodation when guests fail to arrive, even if notice of the cancellation is given.

All guides are obtainable from bookshops or by Johansens Freephone 0800 269397 or by using the order coupons on pages 277–288.

JOHANSENS AWARDS FOR EXCELLENCE

RECOMMENDED COUNTRY HOUSES & SMALL HOTELS

The 1998 Johansens Awards were presented by Penny Junor at the Johansens Annual Dinner held at The Dorchester on November 3rd 1997. It was a happy occasion for everybody especially for the host hotel, winner of the Most Excellent London Hotel Award.

For the first time ever awards were made to Johansens Recommended Hotels – Europe. Their merits were recognised by large numbers of guests who reported to us their views on the hotels where they stayed.

Johansens guests were also the initial selectors of the winners of the 1998 Most Excellent Country House and the Most Excellent Value for Money Award.

Barbara Sargent and Tanya Hardy of Chippenhall Hall receiving the Country Houses and Small Hotels Award.

Elizabeth Corfield of Kingston House receiving the Most Excellent Value for Money Award.

The Most Excellent Country House Award went to Chippenhall Hall at Fressingfield in Suffolk, a highly reputed, family run, small establishment in a listed Tudor building with a very popular restaurant.

The Most Excellent Value for Money Award was given to Kingston House near Totnes in Devon, not only a most enjoyable place in which to stay, but in addition a fine 18th century mansion of immense historic interest.

Congratulations to these winners and thank you to everyone who sent in Guest Survey Report forms.

Each year we rely on the appraisals of Johansens guests, alongside the nominations from our team of inspectors, as a basis for making all our awards. The other award winners of 1998 were:

Johansens Most Excellent City Hotel Award:
The Royal Crescent, Bath, Somerset

Johansens Most Excellent Country Hotel Award:
Arisaig House, Inverness-shire, Scotland

Johansens Most Excellent London Hotel Award:
The Dorchester, Park Lane, Mayfair

Johansens Inn Award for Excellence:
The Inn at Whitewell, Clitheroe, Lancashire

Johansens Most Excellent Restaurant Award:
The Sea Crest, St Brelade, Jersey

Johansens Most Excellent Service Award:
Gilpin Lodge, Lake Windermere

Johansens – Europe: The Most Excellent Waterside Hotel:
Il Pellicano, Porto Ercole, Italy

Johansens – Europe: The Most Excellent Country Hotel:
Château des Vigiers, Monestier, France

Johansens – Europe: The Most Excellent City Hotel:
The Königshof, Munich, Germany

INTRODUCTION

From Chippenhall Hall, Fressingfield, Eye, Suffolk
Winner of the 1998 Johansens Most Excellent Country Houses and Small Hotels Award

In 1992, after all our grown up children had left Chippenhall, we decided to turn the family home into a small Country House Hotel. Starting from scratch, the major initial problem was how to become known. Fortunately we became involved with Johansens, which has proved to be by far our most outstanding, successful, responsive and prestigious advertising medium. Although Barbara has achieved ETB Highly Commended and AA Premier Selected status, above all, it has been her dream to win the Johansens Country Houses Award for Excellence.

Like many other country houses in Johansens, the manor at Chippenhall has a very long history. The present heavily timbered structure is of the medieval to early Tudor period, but its origins date from Saxon times and several mentions in the Domesday Book show the Viking influence on the spelling such as Cibberhald, Cybenhalla and Ciphenhalla. Obviously the manor is a listed building and some period films have been made here. If the reader enjoys the warmth, character and comfort of heavily beamed rooms with inglenook log fires, these features are to be enjoyed at Chippenhall and the Johansens Country Houses guide itself also probably represents one of the best concentrated collections of similar period style buildings inside one cover.

Since we began operating Chippenhall as a Country House, we have always regarded ourselves as professional hotel managers. We simply do our best to ensure that our guests enjoy the warmth and character of the house, its very peaceful location, our food and wines served in a dinner party atmosphere. We believe that this style is the hallmark of a Johansens Country House and which typifies so many of us in the guide.

Finally it pleases us immensely that the Johansens Award for 1998 is now in Suffolk, which is to many unknown, but it is a beautiful, unspoilt and still very rural community.

Jakes Sargent

WELL... DE GUSTIBUS NON EST DISPUTANDUM
HILDON
AN ENGLISH
NATURAL MINERAL WATER
OF EXCEPTIONAL TASTE
GENTLY CARBONATED
Composition in accordance with the results of the officially recognized analysis 26 March 1992.
Hildon Ltd., Broughton, Hampshire SO20 8DG, ☏ 01794-301 747
"FOR BEST BEFORE DATE SEE CAP"
Bottled at source, Broughton, Hampshire
750mle

INTRODUCTION

From Kingston House, Near Totnes, Devon
Winner of the 1998 Johansens Most Excellent Value for Money Award

Kingston House is delighted to have received The Most Excellent Value for Money Award 1998. We thank our guests for being so appreciative of the house, our mouth watering dinners and extensive wine list, and for appreciating that we do offer excellent value for money. We are delighted to be associated with Johansens with their beautifully produced guides, high standard of professionalism and ability to reach people all over the world with word of Kingston House and its pleasures.

Here at Kingston, we aim to make each stay a very special and unique experience, gathering together many good things. Firstly a remarkably authentic and beautiful early 18th century English Country House, bedrooms furnished in period with superbly comfortable beds; total peace and quiet; no passing roads, and most importantly wonderful food fusing the centuries using the best local ingredients with fresh vegetables, fruits and herbs grown at Kingston for much of the year. The gardens are recreated in keeping with the period and continue to improve year by year with several garden openings for charities.

When we bought the estate in 1985, it was in desperate need of restoration. The project has evolved. We now have nine cottages in the listed courtyard buildings, all with four poster beds in the master bedrooms, and we have guests to stay in the house, something we greatly enjoy and satisfyingly our guests do too.

We look forward to many more pleasurable and rewarding years in association with Johansens.

Michael & Elizabeth Corfield

"FOR BEST BEFORE DATE SEE CAP"
Bottled at source, Broughton, Hampshire

WELL… DE GUSTIBUS
NON EST DISPUTANDUM

HILDON

AN ENGLISH
NATURAL MINERAL WATER
OF EXCEPTIONAL TASTE

DELIGHTFULLY STILL

Composition in accordance with the results of the officially
recognized analysis 26 March 1992
Hildon Ltd., Broughton, Hampshire SO20 8DG. ☎ 01794-301 747

750 ml℮

Bottled at source, Broughton, Hampshire
"FOR BEST BEFORE DATE SEE CAP"

Photograph reproduced with the kind permission of the ETB

Johansens Recommended Country Houses & Small Hotels in England

Castles, cathedrals, museums, great country houses and the opportunity to stay in areas of historical importance. England has so much to offer. Whatever your leisure interests, there's a network of around 560 Tourist Information Centres throughout England to give you friendly, free advice on places to visit, entertainment, local facilities and travel information.

English Heritage
Keysign House
429 Oxford Street
London W1R 2HD
Tel: 0171 973 3396
Offers an unrivalled choice of properties to visit.

Historic Houses Association
2 Chester Street
London SW1X 7BB
Tel: 0171 259 5688
Ensures the survival of historic houses and gardens in private ownership in Great Britain.

The National Trust
36 Queen Anne's Gate
London SW1H 9AS
Tel: 0171 222 9251
Cares for more than 590,000 acres of countryside and over 400 historic buildings.

Regional Tourist Boards

Cumbria Tourist Board
Ashleigh
Holly Road
Windermere
Cumbria LA23 2AQ
Tel: 015394 44444
England's most beautiful lakes and tallest mountains reach out from the Lake District National Park to a landscape of spectacular coasts, hills and dales.

East of England Tourist Board
Toppesfield Hall
Hadleigh
Suffolk IP7 5DN
Tel: 01473 822922
Cambridgeshire, Essex, Hertfordshire, Bedfordshire, Norfolk, Suffolk and Lincolnshire.

Heart of England Tourist Board
Woodside
Larkhill Road
Worcester
Worcestershire WR5 2EF
Tel: 01905 763436
Gloucestershire, Hereford & Worcester, Shropshire, Staffordshire, Warwickshire, West Midlands, Derbyshire, Leicestershire, Northamptonshire, Nottinghamshire and Rutland. Represents the districts of Cherwell and West Oxfordshire in the county of Oxfordshire.

London Tourist Board
6th floor Glen House
Stag Place
London SW1E 5LT
Tel: 0171 932 2000
The Greater London area
(see page 13)

Northumbria Tourist Board
Aykley Heads
Durham DH1 5UX
Tel: 0191 375 3000
The Tees Valley, Durham, Northumberland and Tyne & Wear

North West Tourist Board
Swan House
Swan Meadow Road
Wigan Pier, Wigan
Lancashire WN3 5BB
Tel: 01942 821222
Cheshire, Greater Manchester, Lancashire, Merseyside and the High Peak District of Derbyshire

South East England Tourist Board
The Old Brew House
Warwick Park
Tunbridge Wells
Kent TN2 5TU
Tel: 01892 540766
East and West Sussex, Kent and Surrey

Southern Tourist Board
40 Chamberlayne Road
Eastleigh
Hampshire SO5 5JH
Tel: 01703 620006
East and North Dorset, Hampshire, Isle of Wight, Berkshire, Buckinghamshire and Oxfordshire

West Country Tourist Board
60, St David's Hill
Exeter
Devon EX4 4SY
Tel: 01392 425426
Bath and NE Somerset, Bristol, Cornwall and the Isles of Scilly, Devon, Dorset (Western), North Somerset and Wiltshire

Yorkshire Tourist Board
312 Tadcaster Road
York YO2 2HF
Tel: 01904 707961
Yorkshire and North & North East Lincolnshire

ARROW MILL HOTEL AND RESTAURANT

ARROW, NEAR ALCESTER, WARWICKSHIRE B49 5NL
TEL: 01789 762419 FAX: 01789 765170

OWNERS: The Woodhams Family

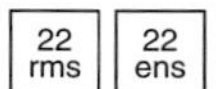  

S: £65
D: £84–140

Once a working flour mill, Arrow Mill is proud of its listing in the Domesday Book, when it was valued at three shillings and sixpence. Since Norman times standards and inflation have risen. Today it remains a historic and charming building, although it offers its guests the most modern and comfortable accommodation.

Its rustic charm, enhanced by log fires and exposed beams, is complemented by a spectacular yet secluded riverside setting. Creature comforts are plentiful in the individually furnished bedrooms and panoramic views take in the mill pond, River Arrow and surrounding countryside.

A highly trained team of chefs uses only market-fresh ingredients in maintaining their uncompromising standards. The Millstream Restaurant incorporates the original working floor of the mill, with its wheel still driven by the flowing stream. It offers an à la carte menu and carefully selected wine list to satisfy the most discriminating palate. Similarly high standards are assured by the luncheons from the Miller's Table.

Residential conferences, business meetings, hospitality days and product launches can all be accommodated. **Places of interest nearby:** Stratford-upon-Avon, Warwick Castle and the Cotswolds are all nearby. Arrow Mill is closed from 26 December for two weeks. **Directions: Set back from the A435 1 mile south of Alcester.**

For hotel location, see maps on pages 263–269

Appleton Hall

APPLETON-LE-MOORS, NORTH YORKSHIRE YO6 6TF
TEL: 01751 417227 FAX: 01751 417540

OWNERS: Mike and Barbara Clarke

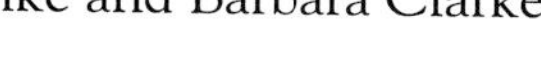

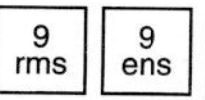

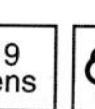

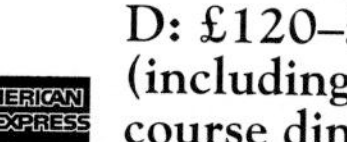

**S: £60–£65
D: £120–£130
(including 5 course dinner)**

Appleton Hall is in the centre of the pretty Yorkshire village of Appleton-le-Moors – which is on the southern side of the North Yorkshire Moors National Park. The hotel is surrounded by beautiful landscaped gardens where guests can sit and relax or wander at their leisure. The elegant refurbished rooms assure visitors they have come to a peaceful and comfortable country house where Mike and Barbara and their staff guarantee a high standard of service and hospitality.

The nine en suite bedrooms are all fully equipped to provide the modern necessities – two have their own lounges. One of the rooms has a four-poster bed.

There is a small well-stocked cocktail bar to pass the time before dinner. The delectable five-course table d'hôte menu changes daily and is accompanied by a comprehensive selection of wines. Special breaks available.

Places of interest nearby: The moors are a walkers' and bird-watchers' paradise, or visit Harrogate and York, returning to inviting log fires on chilly afternoons.

Directions: Leave A1 at Thirsk turning, taking the A170, signposted Scarborough. After passing through Kirkbymoorside the village is on the left.

For hotel location, see maps on pages 263–269

ARUNDEL (Burpham)

BURPHAM COUNTRY HOUSE HOTEL

OLD DOWN, BURPHAM, NR ARUNDEL, WEST SUSSEX BN18 9RJ
TEL: 01903 882160 FAX: 01903 884627

OWNERS: George and Marianne Walker

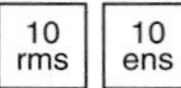

S: from £40
D: £82–£98

This charming Country House Hotel set in the heart of walking country nestles in a fold of the Sussex South Downs – just perfect for a 'Stress Remedy Break'.

The ten en suite bedrooms have all been tastefully refurbished with direct-dial telephone, colour television, hairdryer, radio/alarm clock and tea/coffee making tray. A lovely old world garden with a croquet lawn surrounds the hotel.

Drinks before dinner can be enjoyed by the open fire in the comfortable Cocktail Lounge. A good wine list is available with most countries represented. The Hotel has a full residential and restaurant licence. Swiss born Marianne Walker has won a well-deserved Rosette from the AA for her culinary skills and a constantly changing menu using only the finest ingredients is presented in the Rösti room. The Hotel has recently been awarded a Highly Commended Certificate by the English Tourist Board.

Special breaks are offered throughout the year. Golf, riding, fishing and sailing are all readily available in the locality. Racing at Goodwood and Fontwell.

Places of interest nearby: Burpham has a beautiful and historic Norman church, while Arundel, with its Wildfowl Sanctuary and renowned Castle, is three miles away. The coast lies within six miles. **Directions: The Hotel is signposted on the A27 east of Arundel railway bridge. Turn off here and follow this road for 2½ miles.**

For hotel location, see maps on pages 263–269

The Beeches Farmhouse

WALDLEY, DOVERIDGE, NR ASHBOURNE, DERBYSHIRE DE6 5LR
TEL: 01889 590288 FAX: 01889 590559 E-MAIL: beechesfa@aol.com

OWNERS: Barbara and Paul Tunnicliffe
CHEF: Barbara Tunnicliffe

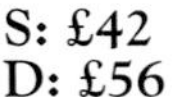

S: £42
D: £56

The Beeches Farmhouse Hotel and Restaurant was opened in 1986 by Barbara and Paul Tunnicliffe. It is situated on the dairy farm which Paul's family has worked for 50 years. Located in the Derbyshire Dales, The Beeches is surrounded by lots of things to see and do, whatever your age or interests. Families are most welcome: children love staying on the farm, where they can feed the many pet animals. For executives there are spacious en suite rooms with direct dial telephones and access to the fax.

At the heart of The Beeches' popularity is Barbara's splendid cooking. Like the dishes she demonstrates at the BBC Good Food Show, Barbara's menus feature bold country recipes. Specialities include local boneless beef rib with port, Guinness and pickled walnuts and casserole of spiced lamb with apricots and miniature herb dumplings. Vegetarian and fresh fish dishes are also offered. Everything is freshly prepared with seasonal ingredients. **Places of interest nearby:** Sudbury Hall, Calke Abbey, Tutbury Castle, the Potteries museums and Alton Towers. **Directions: The nearest motorways are the M6, junction 15 or M1 junction 24. Once on the A50, exit at Doveridge. Travel North to Waldley for two miles.**

CHAPEL HOUSE

FRIARS' GATE, ATHERSTONE, WARWICKSHIRE CV9 1EY
TEL: 01827 718949 FAX: 01827 717702

OWNERS: Chapel House (Atherstone) Ltd
MANAGING DIRECTOR: David Arnold

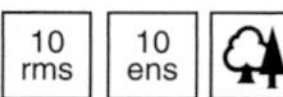

S: £47.50–£62
D: £65–£75

Chapel House was the dower house of the now demolished Atherstone Hall, home of the Bracebridge family since the early 18th century. The oldest part of the house dates from about 1720 and subsequent additions were made until 1879. Many original features have been retained and others carefully restored so that the house, now furnished in traditional style, retains the elegance of an earlier age. Chapel House is discreetly tucked away in the corner of Atherstone's market square within a well-tended, walled garden that still is a particularly attractive feature of the property.

Awarded its second AA Rosette in 1997, Chapel House has acquired an enviable reputation for high quality, imaginative food and an excellent selection of wines. Chefs Adam Bennett and Gary Thompson use only the very best ingredients and their particular specialities are fish and game. Special dietary needs can be catered for by prior arrangement. Closed on Christmas Day and Boxing Day. Chapel House is just 25 minutes from the centre of Birmingham and is convenient for those visiting the NEC. **Places of interest nearby:** Bosworth Battlefield, Tamworth Castle, Arbury Hall, Lichfield and Coventry Cathedrals and the many industrial museums of the Midlands. Also close is the Belfry Golf Centre. **Directions: On the A5 about 8 miles south-east of the M42 junction 10. Chapel House is in the market square beside the church.**

For hotel location, see maps on pages 263–269

PETTY FRANCE

DUNKIRK, BADMINTON, SOUTH GLOUCESTERSHIRE
TEL: 01454 238361 FAX: 01454 238768 E-MAIL: hotel@pettyfrance.telme.com

OWNERS: Bill Fraser

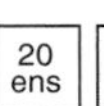

S: £69–£99
D: £89–£119

Built in warm Cotswold stone and set in beautiful countryside, this 18th century country house has been transformed into a delightful private hotel. The owner calls the elegant surroundings 'pleasure gardens', the only sport being croquet!

Bill likes to welcome new arrivals personally and his staff are equally hospitable.

Reflecting the Georgian era are the spacious, flower filled, public rooms. The restaurant has a sophisticated menu based on local produce. Vegetarians are not forgotten and the cheeses often include Cheddar-Denhay from Dorset and Little Rydings goats' milk cheese. The fine wine list provides a choice of further pleasures.

The charming bedrooms are either in the main house or in the old stable block. The latter have more privacy and character, but are smaller. All have en suite shower rooms or private bathrooms, as well as telephone and television.

There is a small air-conditioned conference room, accommodating up to 25 people equipped with modern display equipment. Murder mystery weekends can be arranged.

Places of interest nearby: Well located for businessmen, close to Bristol, Bath, Gloucester and Cheltenham. Golf, riding, tennis, squash and fishing are available **Directions: From the M4, Junction 18, take the A46. Head North for five miles; Petty France is just off the main road on the left.**

BAKEWELL (Rowsley)

EAST LODGE COUNTRY HOUSE HOTEL

ROWSLEY, NR MATLOCK, DERBYSHIRE DE4 2EF
TEL: 01629 734474 FAX: 01629 733949

OWNERS: Joan and David Hardman
CHEF: Mark Allday

15 rms | 15 ens 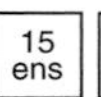    SMALL HOTEL

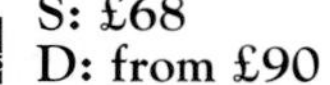

S: £68
D: from £90

This graceful 17th century lodge on the edge of the Peak District was originally built as the East Lodge to Haddon Hall, the Derbyshire seat of the Duke of Rutland. Converted to a hotel in the 1980's, East Lodge is now owned and run by Joan and David Hardman and their attentive staff. It is AA 3 star and ETB 4 Crowns Highly Commended.

The attractive lounge with log fire, charming restaurant and spacious hall offers high levels of comfort combined with a warm and relaxed atmosphere. The 15 en suite bedrooms are tastefully furnished, each having its own distinctive character. Imaginative lunches and dinners are served daily in the excellent AA Rosetted restaurant with lighter meals available in the lounge. A wide selection of fine wines is on offer.

Set in 10 acres of attractive gardens and surrounded by rolling Derbyshire countryside, East Lodge provides a tranquil setting for relaxing breaks, conferences and corporate activity/team building events.

Places of interest nearby: Peak district National Park, which boasts some of the country's most spectacular walks. The famous stately homes, Chatsworth House and Haddon Hall, are within two miles. Bakewell, Buxton, Matlock and Crich are a short drive away. **Directions: Set back from the A6 in Rowsley village, three miles from Bakewell. The hotel entrance is adjacent to the B6012**

60 M

For hotel location, see maps on pages 263–269

THE PEACOCK HOTEL AT ROWSLEY

ROWSLEY, NR MATLOCK, DERBYSHIRE DE4 2EB
TEL: 01629 733518 FAX: 01629 732671

OWNERS: Jarvis Hotels plc
MANAGER: Roger Hudson
CHEF: Phil Black

S: £85–£100
D: £145–£160
(including dinner)

Once the Dower House to Haddon Hall, this superb 17th century country house is now a marvellous hotel with gardens leading down to the River Derwent.

When first a hotel in 1820 it attracted bathers who plunged into the nearby River Wye! Fishermen are spoilt here. There are 12 rods on the River Wye and two on the Derwent. Tickets are available and the Head Keeper offers advice and tuition. Fish caught will be cooked by the hotel or put in the freezer. The dedicated can enjoy the Angler's Picnic, brought to the riverside. Walkers get a delicious picnic in a thermally insulated knapsack.

The hotel is beautifully furnished throughout, with antiques and flowers in abundance. The bedrooms are extremely comfortable and thoughtfully equipped.

Resident and non-resident diners can enjoy an apéritif in the delightful bar or lounge before dining in one of the three rooms, two of which feature furniture by "Mousey" Thompson. Both lunch and dinner are served in traditional style and smoking during food service is discouraged. A special diet can be catered for with prior notice. Special rates may be available on weekdays at certain times of the year. There are excellent facilities for small meetings in a delightfully furnished room.

Places of interest nearby: Haddon Hall, Chatsworth, Crich Tram Museum. **Directions: M1/exit 28, head for A6. Rowsley is midway between Matlock and Bakewell.**

For hotel location, see maps on pages 263–269

WAREN HOUSE HOTEL

WAREN MILL, BAMBURGH, NORTHUMBERLAND NE70 7EE
TEL: 01668 214581 FAX: 01668 214484 E-MAIL: enquiries@warenhousehotel.co.uk

OWNERS: Peter and Anita Laverack
CHEFS: Jean Francois Perocheau and Lee Irving

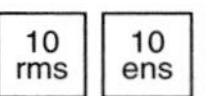
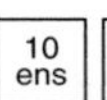

10 rms | 10 ens | SMALL HOTEL

S: £55–£67.50
D: £114–£135
Suite: £155–£185

"To visit the North East and not to stay here, would be foolish indeed". So says one entry in a visitors book that is filled with generous and justified praise for this delightful traditional country house which lives up to all its promises and expectations and beyond. The hotel is set in six acres of gardens and woodland on the edge of Budle Bay Bird Sanctuary overlooking Holy Island and two miles from the majestic Bamburgh Castle.

The owners, Anita and Peter, do not cater for children under 14, so they are able to offer a rare commodity of peace and tranquillity even during the busy summer months. Throughout the hotel, the antique furnishings and the immaculate and well-chosen décor evoke a warm, friendly and charming ambience.

Seated in the candlelit dining room, surrounded by family pictures and portraits, guests can select dishes from the daily changing menu and wines from over 250 bins. There is a boardroom for executive meetings. Dogs by prior arrangement. Special short breaks available all year.
Places of interest nearby: The Farne Islands are just a boat trip away, while Bamburgh, Alnwick and Dunstanburgh Castles along with Holy Island are nearby. Waren House is open all year. **Directions: There are advance warning signs on the A1 both north and south. Take B1342 to Waren Mill. Hotel (floodlit at night) is on south-west corner of Budle Bay just two miles from Bamburgh.**

For hotel location, see maps on pages 263–269

Apsley House

141 NEWBRIDGE HILL, SOMERSET BA1 3PT
TEL: 01225 336966 FAX: 01225 425462 E-MAIL: apsleyhouse@easynet.co.uk

OWNERS: David and Annie Lanz

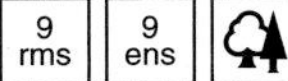

S: £45–£65
D: £60–£100

One mile from the centre of Bath, this elegant Georgian house was reputedly built for the Duke of Wellington in 1830 and is set in a delightful garden.

The hosts, David and Annie Lanz, greet guests with a warm welcome into their home, with its magnificently proportioned reception rooms which have been refurbished in great style and comfort including the addition of two new rooms opening onto the garden. A quite delicious breakfast is the only meal served, although drinks are available. David and Annie will recommend local restaurants and inns which visitors will enjoy.

The bedrooms are invitingly romantic with lovely drapery and delightful en suite bathrooms. Televisions almost seem to intrude in this timeless décor. Private parking available. **Places of interest nearby:** There is so much to see and do in Bath, the centre of which is just a 25 minutes stroll from Apsley House. The magnificent architecture includes the Assembly Rooms, mentioned so often in Jane Austen's and in Georgette Heyer's historical novels, the Royal Crescent and the Roman Baths. Fascinating museums, the thriving theatre and excellent shopping all add to ones enjoyment of this lovely city. The Cotswolds, Mendip Hills, Stourhead, Stonehenge, Avebury and Longleat are within driving distance. **Directions: The hotel lies one mile west of the centre of Bath, on the A431 which branches off A4, the Upper Bristol Road.**

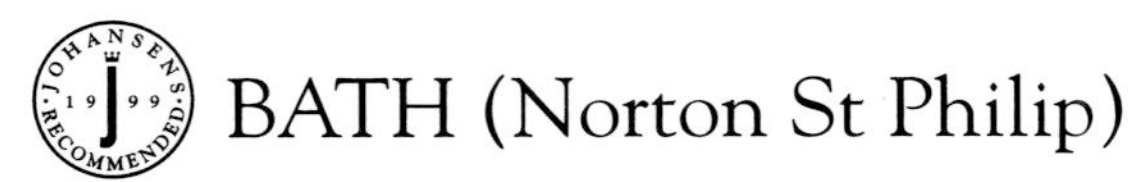

BATH LODGE HOTEL

NORTON ST PHILIP, BATH, SOMERSET BA3 6NH
TEL: 01225 723040 FAX: 01225 723737 E-MAIL: walker@bathlodge.demon.co.uk

OWNERS: Graham and Nicola Walker

7 rms | 7 ens

S: from £45
D: £55–£95

The Bath Lodge Hotel, originally called Castle Lodge, was built between 1806 and 1813 as one of six lodges added to a former gentleman's residence known as Farleigh House. This splendid building, with its towers, battlements, portcullis and heraldic shields, is redolent of Arthurian romance and offers guests a delightful setting in which to escape the stresses and strains of modern life.

The rooms, which are superbly decorated and furnished, are beautifully located and have many castellated features within them. Three rooms overlook the magnificent natural gardens with their cascading stream and the adjacent deer forest. The main entrance hall, lounge and conservatory all contain oak beamed ceilings, natural masonry and large log burning fireplaces. All the rooms are furnished in keeping with this unique building.

An excellent breakfast is served at the hotel. A five course dinner is available Friday and Saturday evenings. Alternatively there are many restaurants locally and in Bath. The hotel has a no-smoking policy, but guests may smoke in the conservatory area.
Places of interest nearby: Stonehenge and Longleat. Bath Lodge is an ideal location for enjoying the tourist attractions of the World Heritage City of Bath itself. Wells and Bristol are also both within easy reach. **Directions: From Bath take the A36 Warminster road. Bath Lodge is on your left after approximately seven miles.**

For hotel location, see maps on pages 263–269

Bloomfield House

146 BLOOMFIELD ROAD, BATH, SOMERSET BA2 2AS
TEL: 01225 420105 FAX: 01225 481958 E-MAIL: bloomfield-house.co.uk

OWNERS: Bridget and Malcolm Cox

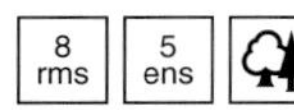

S: from £45
D: £65–£105

This elegant country house, Grade II listed, was commissioned in 1800 by a notable Mr Henshaw, later to become Lord Mayor of Bath. It nestles in a tranquil location in grounds that afford magnificent views over the city.

Bloomfield House is one of the most comfortable and relaxing country houses in the area and is furnished with handsome antiques, hand-woven silk curtains and French chandeliers.

The main bedrooms feature canopied or four-poster beds, including "The principal bedroom of the Mayor and Mayoress of Bath (1902/3)". Remote control colour television, direct dial telephone and tea/coffee making facilities are available in all bedrooms. There is ample parking.

A comprehensive list of restaurants and menus is available at Bloomfield House from which guests may choose their evening meals. Bloomfield House is a strictly non-smoking house.

Riding, golf, swimming, sauna and leisure facilities are available locally by arrangement.

Places of interest nearby: The Cotswolds, Castle Combe, Stourhead, Stonehenge and Longleat. **Directions: From the centre of Bath take the A367 Wells road for 1/4 mile towards Exeter. Fork right after The Bear Pub; Bloomfield House is on the right before the third road junction.**

For hotel location, see maps on pages 263–269

Duke's Hotel

GREAT PULTENEY STREET, BATH, SOMERSET BA2 4DN
TEL: 01225 463 512 FAX: 01225 483733

OWNERS: Caparo Hotels Ltd
MANAGER: Theresa Vickery

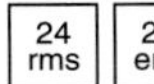

S: £55–£70
D: £70–£100

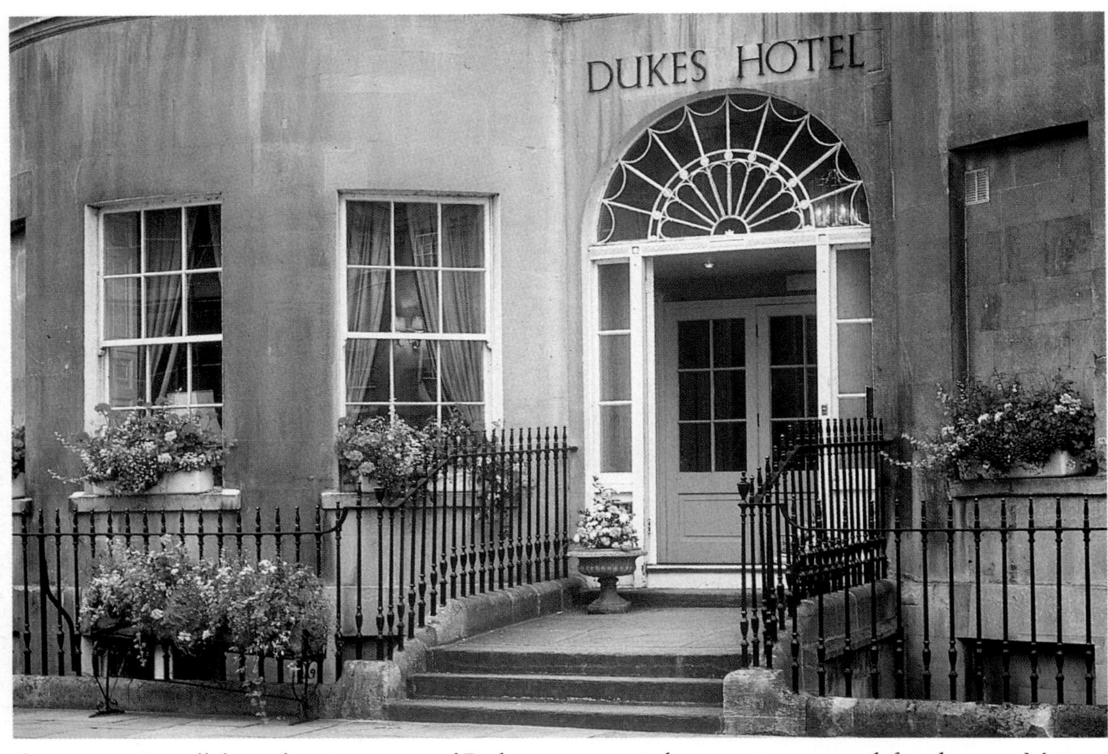

Set just a few minutes' stroll from the city centre of Bath, Duke's Hotel is a late 18th century Grade I listed building which has been extensively restored. It stands in Great Pulteney Street, Europe's most elegant Georgian boulevard. Mouldings, cornices and many other original features of the time have been retained as a mark of its architectural importance.

Internal refurbishment and modernisation has created elegant and comfortable accommodation throughout. The bedrooms have been carefully and individually furnished to a high standard and include every modern comfort.

Breakfast is a generous meal, complemented by the hotel's own marmalade and freshly-squeezed orange juice, while a varied menu is prepared for dinner. Main courses may include tempting dishes such as chicken breast with apricot and apple sauce; grilled fillet of lemon sole with a citrus juice and an orange and mint couscous salad; and warm salad of vegetables with garlic and onion, surrounded by pine nuts and tomato coulis. A good selection of reasonably-priced wines have been chosen to complement any meal.

Places of interest nearby: Among the many places to visit in the city are the Roman Baths, Pump Room, Assembly Rooms and a number of museums. **Directions: From M4, junction 18, take A46 to Bath. Turn right into London Road, left at lights, over Bathwick Bridge, then right into Great Pulteney Street.**

For hotel location, see maps on pages 263–269

Eagle House

CHURCH STREET, BATHFORD, BATH, SOMERSET BA1 7RS
TEL: 01225 859946 FAX: 01225 859430 E-MAIL: jonap@psionworld.net

OWNERS: John and Rosamund Napier

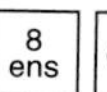 

 S: £36–£46
D: £48–£76

Three miles from Bath lies the charming conservation village of Bathford. Behind a high stone wall, wrought-iron gates and elegant façade, this Georgian home, designed by John Wood, stands in $1^1/_2$ acres of grounds, giving far-reaching views of the surrounding countryside.

The eight bedrooms, including some large family rooms, all have private facilities, colour television, hairdryers and tea and coffee-making facilities. Cots and extra beds can be provided upon request. There is a spacious drawing room, where meetings for up to 12 people can be held, and a second, smaller lounge. Although dinner is not served at Eagle House, the owners, John and Rosamund Napier are always glad to help with reservations for tables in one of Bath's many good restaurants. For exercise there is a new lawn tennis court.

Set in a walled garden adjacent to the main house is a cottage with two bedrooms, two bathrooms, sitting room and kitchen, which can be occupied for stays of two nights or more. It offers complete privacy with views across the valley. **Places of interest nearby:** The beautiful city of Bath, Castle Combe, the National Trust village of Lacock, the Cotswolds, Longleat House, Avebury and Stonehenge. **Directions: From the A4 take the A363 towards Bradford-on-Avon. After 150 yards, veer left up Bathford Hill. Take first right into Church Street; Eagle House is 200 yards on the right.**

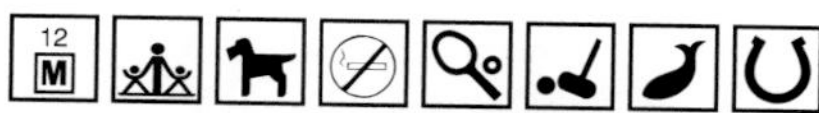

For hotel location, see maps on pages 263–269

OLDFIELDS

102 WELLS ROAD, BATH, SOMERSET BA2 3AL
TEL: 01225 317984 FAX: 01225 444471 E-MAIL: info@oldfields.co.uk

OWNERS: Berkeley and Moira Gaunt

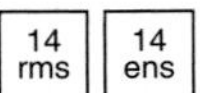
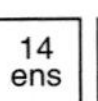

S: £48–£60
D: £58–£80

Oldfields is a large, elegant Victorian house built of the honey-coloured stone for which the city of Bath is famous. Superbly positioned just 10 minutes walk from the city centre, it has a private car park for the use of guests.

Although the house is equipped with every modern feature to ensure that visitors experience maximum comfort and convenience, it retains many of the elaborate cornices and artistry of its original character.

The bedrooms are beautifully furnished with rich fabrics and antiques and offer a full range of amenities. Ideal for the less mobile, two rooms are situated on the ground floor with level entry. Oldfields is a totally non smoking hotel.

Guests can choose between a traditional English breakfast or the lighter continental alternative offered by an extensive buffet. Unlimited supplies of tea and coffee are available and newspapers are provided for those with time to linger. Bath is full of excellent restaurants, many within a fifteen minute walk of Oldfields. Outdoor pursuits such as hot-air ballooning, golf and horse-riding can be arranged.

Places of interest nearby: Within Bath itself are the famous Roman baths and pump room, the Book Museum and No 1 Royal Crescent. The city is also the perfect centre from which to explore the Cotswolds, Glastonbury and Wells Cathedral, east to Stonehenge and Salisbury, west to Bristol and South Wales. **Directions: From the M4 junction 18 follow the signs to Bath city centre, then take the A367 Wells Road.**

For hotel location, see maps on pages 263–269

PARADISE HOUSE

HOLLOWAY, BATH, SOMERSET BA2 4PX
TEL: 01225 317723 FAX: 01225 482005 E-MAIL: paradise@aspleyhouse.easynet.co.uk

OWNERS: David and Annie Lanz

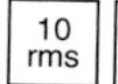 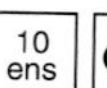 

  S: £45–£65
D: £60–£110

In the peaceful grounds of this early 18th century mansion house, guests could be forgiven for forgetting that they are only seven minutes' walk from the Roman Baths, Pump Room and Abbey in the centre of the beautiful Georgian city of Bath.

Situated in a quiet cul-de-sac, Paradise House has been carefully modernised and restored to a high standard to enhance its classical elegance. Ornate plaster ceilings and a marble fireplace adorn the public rooms; where the décor is essentially a fusion of antique and contemporary furniture and soft pastel fabrics. The new garden room is glorious, featuring a sumptuous four-poster bed. The large walled garden, with its fish pond and rose covered pergola, is a delightful sun-trap affording a panoramic vista of the city and surrounding landscape, where guests may enjoy a game of boules .

The new owners, David and Annie, extend a friendly welcome to all their guests and are on hand to offer advice on the many nearby attractions. Although neither lunch nor dinner is served, details of over 85 local restaurants are provided. Garage parking is available.

Places of interest nearby: Wells, Glastonbury and Stonehenge are within easy reach. The city is also notable as a fashionable shopping centre and home of the arts. **Directions: Enter Bath on A4 London Road. Turn left onto A36. Take first left after viaduct onto A367 Exeter Road. Go left at Day and Pierce and down hill into Holloway cul-de-sac.**

For hotel location, see maps on pages 263–269

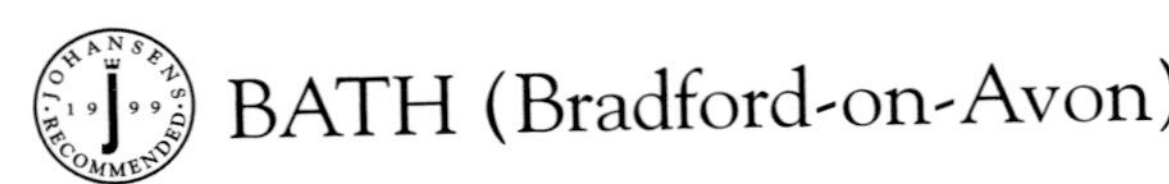

BATH (Bradford-on-Avon)

WIDBROOK GRANGE

TROWBRIDGE ROAD, BRADFORD-ON-AVON, WILTSHIRE BA15 1UH
TEL: 01225 864750/863173 FAX: 01225 862890

OWNERS: John and Pauline Price

S: £62–£95
D: £95–£115

According to the ancient rent books, Widbrook Grange was built as a model farm in the 18th century amid eleven acres of idyllic grounds, traversed by a stream. No longer a farm, Widbrook still reflects its agricultural heritage. Together resident owners John and Pauline Price have converted the Grange with skill and care to combine contemporary comforts with a traditional ambience.

All of the bedrooms, whether a spacious four-poster room or one that is petite and cosy, are well appointed with facilities and antique furnishings. Some of the bedrooms are in the recently converted 200-year old stone barn which forms the courtyard. Evening dinner is available Monday to Thursday in the spacious antique furnished dining room and there are also many excellent restaurants locally about which your hosts can advise you. The Manvers suite, with its oak table and carver chairs has been designed for board meetings, seminars and private functions.

Widbrook boasts a superb indoor heated swimming pool and gymnasium. There is an arrangement with nearby Kingsdown Golf Club. Riding and fishing can also be arranged.

Places of interest nearby: Longleat House and Safari Park, Bath, Avebury and Stonehenge. **Directions: From Bradford-on-Avon take the A363 Trowbridge Road, the Grange is on the right after the canal bridge.**

For hotel location, see maps on pages 263–269

WOOLVERTON HOUSE

WOOLVERTON, NR BATH, SOMERSET BA3 6QS
TEL: 01373 830415 FAX: 01373 831243

OWNERS: Noel and Marina Terry

S: £40–£50
D: £55–£80

This early 19th century house, built originally as a rectory for the 'United Parishes of Woolverton & Rode', has been sympathetically converted and restored to become an elegant English country house. It is set in over 2½ acres of grounds and commands scenic views over the 'glebe lands' on which the parson traditionally had grazing rights.

Today Woolverton House has been developed by its present-day hospitable owners into a retreat where the emphasis is on heritage, history and nature. The gardens are full of colour and also include a narrow gauge steam railway.

All the bedrooms are pleasantly decorated and furnished with private bathrooms en suite. They are fully equipped with colour television, direct dial telephone, hospitality tray, trouser press, hairdryer and minibar. Both the dining room and drawing room have log fires in the cooler months and the conservatory bar is pleasant all year.

The restaurant is beautifully furnished in excellent taste with food and wines to match.

Places of interest nearby: There is plenty to explore in the historical and agricultural history of this area – most within a 20 mile radius. Major attractions include Bath, Longleat, East Somerset steam railway, Cheddar Caves, Wookey Hole and Rode Tropical Bird Gardens. **Directions: From M4 exit 17 take A350 and then A361 for Woolverton – or on A36 halfway between Bath and Warminster.**

DANNAH FARM COUNTRY GUEST HOUSE

BOWMAN'S LANE, SHOTTLE, NR BELPER, DERBYSHIRE DE56 2DR
TEL: 01773 550273/630 FAX: 01773 550590

OWNERS: Joan and Martin Slack
CHEF: Joan Slack

S: £45–£55
D: £70–£110

Set amid undulating countryside high above the Ecclesbourne Valley, Dannah Farm is part of the Chatsworth Estates on the edge of the Peak District. This is an exceptional farmhouse conversion so it is not surprising that in addition to being Highly Commended by the ETB (3 Crowns) and AA Premier Selected, the hotel won the 1993 National Awards for Excellence and Innovation and the 1994 Best of Tourism Award for the East Midlands. As the Georgian farmhouse is still part of a 128-acre working farm, guests and their children will discover plenty of activity within the grounds.

Four-poster, twin-bedded, double and single rooms are offered, all overlooking rolling pastures. There are two residents' lounges and large, safe gardens.

The restaurant has rapidly earned a fine reputation. Aromas of freshly baked bread, home-made soups and piquant sauces escaping from the kitchen whet the appetite for dinner, which is served with good wines in relaxed surroundings and is by arrangement. **Places of interest nearby:** The countryside is criss-crossed with footpaths with walks in all directions. Dannah Farm is optimally placed to enjoy the many attractions of the area – Chatsworth, Haddon Hall, Dovedale and water sports at Carsington. **Directions: From Derby take the A6 Matlock road. At Duffield turn left onto the B5023 towards Wirksworth. At the traffic lights at Cowers Lane turn right onto the A517 towards Belper, then take the first left to Shottle. Bowman's Lane is 100 yards past the crossroads.**

For hotel location, see maps on pages 263–269

THE MANOR HOUSE

NORTHLANDS, WALKINGTON, EAST YORKSHIRE HU17 8RT
TEL: 01482 881645 FAX: 01482 866501 E-MAIL: the manor-house-hotel@compuserve.com

OWNERS: Derek and Lee Baugh
CHEF: Derek Baugh

   S: £70–£80
D: £85–£120

This delightful, 19th century house with decorated chimneys soaring majestically skywards stands serenely on the wooded flanks of the rolling Yorkshire Wolds. Surrounded by three acres of tree-lined grounds which overlook paddocks and parkland it is the perfect retreat for those seeking relaxation, comfort and excellent food. The house has been the RAC small hotel of the North on two occasions.

The seven spacious, en suite bedrooms – one in an adjoining cottage – provide superb views over the countryside. Each is individually furnished and decorated to the highest standard and guests will find themselves pampered with unexpected and useful personal comforts.

Chef-patron Derek Baugh, formerly of The Dorchester, provides a distinctive, imaginative style of cuisine, awarded two AA Rosettes. All meals are served with flair and the wine list is extensive. On summer evenings, diners can enjoy their evening meal in the cool elegance of the conservatory which overlooks the south facing terrace and lawns.

Places of interest nearby: Horse riding, clay pigeon shooting, rambling, hunting and golf are close by while Beverley, York and Doncaster racecourses are within easy reach. North Yorkshire Moors, the rugged coastline, the walled city of York with its magnificent Minster, enchanting villages and numerous stately homes. **Directions: From Walkington on B1230, turn left at the traffic lights (following the brown hotel signs), then left and left again for the hotel.**

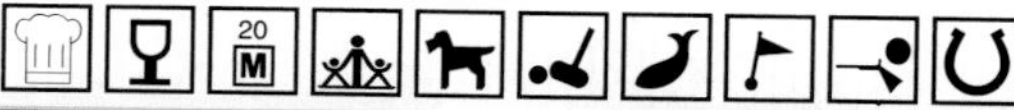

For hotel location, see maps on pages 263–269

Bibury Court

BIBURY COURT, BIBURY, GLOUCESTERSHIRE GL7 5NT
TEL: 01285 740337 FAX: 01285 740660 E-MAIL: @biburycourt.co.uk

OWNERS: Jane Collier, Andrew and Anne Johnston
MANAGER: Simon Gould

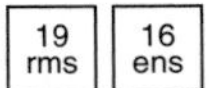
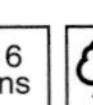

S: from £67
D: from £90
Suite: £130

Past visitors to Bibury Court are reputed to have included Charles II and during the reign of George III, the Prince Regent. This gracious mansion dates from Tudor times, but the main part was built in 1633 by Sir Thomas Sackville, an illegitimate son of the 1st Earl of Dorset. After generations of illustrious owners, it became a hotel in 1968.

The great house is set on the outskirts of Bibury, which William Morris called "the most beautiful village in England". As a hotel, it is run on country house lines with one of the main objectives being the provision of good food and wine in informal and pleasurable surroundings. Log fires during the cooler months add to the comfort of guests.

There are some lovely panelled rooms in the house, many containing antique furniture. Many of the bedrooms have four posters, all have private bathrooms and for those who like greater privacy there is the Sackville suite.

Trout fishing is available in the Coln, which forms the southern boundary of the hotel's six acres of grounds and there are golf courses at Burford and Cirencester. Water sports and riding are available nearby. The hotel is closed at Christmas.

Places of interest nearby: Bibury Court is ideally placed for touring the Cotswolds, while Stratford, Oxford, Cheltenham and Bath are all within easy reach.

Directions: Bibury is on the B4425, seven miles from Burford and seven miles from Cirencester.

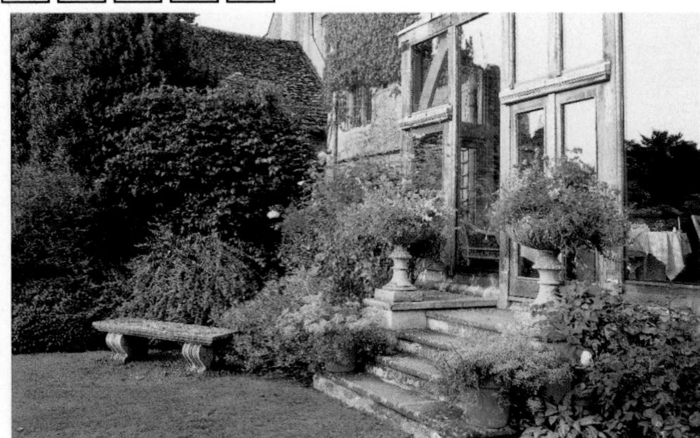

For hotel location, see maps on pages 263–269

YEOLDON HOUSE HOTEL

DURRANT LANE, NORTHAM, NR BIDEFORD, DEVON EX39 2RL
TEL: 01237 474400; FAX: 01237 476618

OWNERS: Kevin and Sue Jelley
CHEF: Kevin Jelley

10 rms | 10 ens | SMALL HOTEL

S: £40–£55
D: £75–£95

Kevin and Sue Jelley have achieved a special quality at Yeoldon, a distinguished and attractive country house standing in beautiful grounds in the village of Northam, birthplace of J.H.Taylor, England's only winner of 5 Opens. Visitors are charmed by the hotel's refreshingly casual atmosphere and its blend of Victorian grandeur with today's comforts.

A rich green and terracotta colour theme enhances the Yeoldon's relaxing ambience. Deep, soft sofas and armchairs in the inviting lounge are so comfortable that guests may find it difficult to leave them for pursuit of the hotel's surrounding charms. The bedrooms are beautifully decorated in country style and have panoramic views over the expansive lawned gardens which slope gently down to the River Torridge and the estuary beyond.

A wide choice of cuisine is served in the elegant restaurant where chef Kevin Jelley takes pride in his à la carte dinner menus. He uses local produce whenever possible and bakes his own bread and biscuits daily. **Places of interest nearby:** Bideford, Arlington Court, Rosemoor Gardens, Tapeley Park, Lundy Island and the picturesque village of Clovelly. **Directions: From the M5, exit at junction 27 and follow the A361 to Barnstaple and then the A39 to Bideford. At Torridge Bridge roundabout turn right onto the A386 towards Northam and then take the third turning on the right.**

For hotel location, see maps on pages 263–269

Biggin Hall

BIGGIN-BY-HARTINGTON, BUXTON, DERBYSHIRE SK17 0DH
TEL: 01298 84451 FAX: 01298 84681 E-MAIL: 100610.1573@compuserve.com

OWNER: James Moffett

S: £30–£45
D: £45–£70

Centrally situated in the Peak district National Park, Biggin Hall is a 17th century, Grade II listed property set in eight acres of grounds. Situated 1,000 feet above sea level, the air may particularly benefit insomnia and asthma sufferers. Visitors come here for the peace and quiet and to enjoy the landscape with its dry-stone walling, deep wooded valleys, heather-clad moorlands and historic market towns and villages. Walkers will appreciate the many uncrowded footpaths nearby.

The rooms of this house feature massive oak timbers and antiques, with one containing a superb four-poster bed. One of the sitting rooms has an open log fire where guests can enjoy a convivial atmosphere. A recently converted 18th century stone building, comprising four self-contained studio apartments and two-roomed suites, each with a private bathroom, is situated 30 yards from the main house. The traditional farmhouse cooking puts emphasis on free-range produce, wholefoods and natural flavours. Dogs are accommodated in the apartments only. **Places of interest nearby:** Chatsworth, Bolsover Castle, Kedleston Hall, Alton Towers, American Adventure Theme Park, Buxton, Ashbourne and Bakewell. **Directions: This country house is situated at the end of Biggin Village, which is off the A515, nine miles from Ashbourne and ten miles from Buxton.**

20 M 12

For hotel location, see maps on pages 263–269

Lower Brook House

BLOCKLEY, NR MORETON-IN-MARSH, GLOUCESTERSHIRE GL56 9DS
TEL/FAX: 01386 700286

OWNER: Marie Mosdale–Cooper

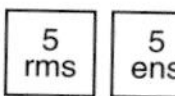 

S: £50–£85
D: £50–£85

Lower Brook House has been skilfully created from a well-built detached property dating back to the 17th century and it epitomises the traditional Cotswold stone house of its period. It is quietly situated in the village of Blockley, famous in the 1700s for its silk trade. Standing within attractive gardens Lower Brook House offers a warm welcome to those in search of good hospitality and comfortable accommodation.

The hostess takes great care to ensure that guests' requirements are swiftly attended to. The five en suite bedrooms have antique furnishings and plenty of interesting bric-à-brac. One of the rooms has a four-poster bed and all have tea and coffee facilities, a colour television, hairdryer and fluffy towelling robes.

Memorable breakfasts are enjoyed along with unlimited amounts of fresh and cooked fruits. Evening meals will be provided by prior arrangement and there are a number of places that serve excellent food in the local area. **Places of interest nearby:** Blockley is a short drive from Cheltenham, Oxford and Stratford-upon-Avon. As well as being a good point for day trips around the picturesque local villages – perhaps to hunt for antiques, Blockley is the perfect location to peruse the Moreton market every Tuesday. **Directions: As you enter the village from Moreton-in-Marsh, Lower Brook House can be found on your right.**

For hotel location, see maps on pages 263–269

QUARLTON MANOR FARM

PLANTATION ROAD, EDGWORTH, TURTON, BOLTON, LANCASHIRE BL7 0DD
TEL: 01204 852277 FAX: 01204 852286

OWNERS: Pauline and Philip Davies
CHEF: Pauline Davies

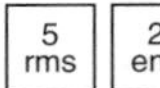

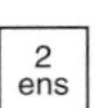

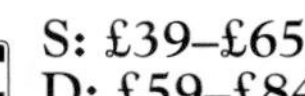

S: £39–£65
D: £59–£84

Standing in its own 20 acres at the heart of rural Lancashire's hill country this sprawling 17th century stone-built farmhouse is the essence of peace and tranquillity. It is ideally suited to those seeking the friendliness and warmth of homely, family accommodation. It has built up an excellent local reputation for its food. Huge open fireplaces, heavy oak beams, antique furnishings and wholesome farmhouse cooking add to the hotel's charm. Guests enjoy sumptuous five-course set dinners around a large table in the galleried dining hall or in the conservatory with its panoramic views over the countryside and hills. Business meetings are welcome. Two double-bedded rooms and a twin share two bathrooms. The main bedroom is en suite and has a huge four-poster bed. With another four-poster in the three room en suite ground floor family suite which can sleep six in total. All bedrooms are non-smoking. Original member of the Green Globe Sustainable Tourism initiative.

Places of interest nearby: Manchester, The East Lancashire Railway, Jumbles Country Park and Turton Tower. **Directions: From Bolton take A676 (A56) towards Burnley. After two miles turn left at traffic lights into Bradshaw Road and after one-and-a-half miles turn left at crossroads. Turn right at the Edgworth crossroads into Broadhead Road, then turn right again into Plantation Road and then 1 mile to the end.**

For hotel location, see maps on pages 263–269

Cross Lane House Hotel

CROSS LANE HEAD, BRIDGNORTH, SHROPSHIRE WV16 4SJ
TEL: 01746 764887 FAX: 01746 768667 E-MAIL: m.hobbs@virgin.net

OWNERS: Ann and Mike Hobbs
CHEF: Ann Hobbs

S: £42.50
D: £55

Situated just a mile from the heart of the historic town of Bridgnorth, this delightful 17th century house, under the hospitable ownership of Ann and Mike Hobbs, is a haven of peace, quiet and comfort amidst the beauty of Shropshire's open countryside.

The hotel is surrounded by two acres of mature gardens from these and from the windows of the house there are stunning views over the Severn Valley.

Although ancient in origin, with an ornate William IV tiled entrance hall, impressive inglenook fireplace and exposed beams throughout, Cross Lane House offers every modern comfort for the discerning guest.

All bedrooms are en suite and most have roll topped Victorian cast iron baths with overhead showers. The restaurant is small and intimate with Ann serving up excellent wholesome traditional dishes complemented by a carefully chosen wine list. Diets can be catered for. Golf, riding, fishing and shooting facilities are a short drive away. Smoking is not permitted within the hotel.

Places of interest nearby: Ironbridge, the birthplace of the industrial revolution, Shrewsbury, the Coalport China Museum, the Severn Valley Railway, the Midland Motor Museum and the Aerospace Museum at Cosford.

Directions: Cross Lane House is on the B4373 Bridgnorth-Broseley road, one mile north of Bridgnorth.

For hotel location, see maps on pages 263–269

The Granville

124 KINGS ROAD, BRIGHTON, EAST SUSSEX BN1 2FA
TEL: 01273 326302 FAX: 01273 728294 E-MAIL: granville@brighton.co.uk

OWNERS: Mick and Sue Paskins
CHEF: Alison Lynch

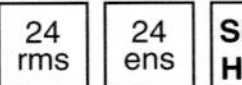 

24 rms | 24 ens | SMALL HOTEL

   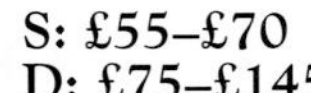

S: £55–£70
D: £75–£145

You only have to take one step through the front door to realise, and appreciate, that this Regency sea front property is a place for the style aware. Proprietor Sue Paskins believes that a hotel stay should be memorable and has furnished The Granville with flair and elegance to offer guests something unique. Situated in the heart of Brighton overlooking the sea and the splendid Edwardian West Pier, her creation is both lavish and original in its furnishings, decor and outlook.

The majority of the 24 en suite bedrooms are not large but they are quite distinctive and have sumptuous bathrooms. Many have fabulous sea views. Among them is the romantic, pale pink and white Brighton Rock Room, the opulent Noel Coward Room with its art-deco bathroom, the huge late-Victorian four-poster bed and marble fireplaces of the Balcony Room and the Marina Room with a water bed.

Apart from breakfast, the cuisine served in Trogs Restaurant is vegetarian, comprising imaginative and substantial dishes. Meals are complemented by an excellent range of organic wines.The atmosphere is convivial with beautifully laid tables. **Places of interest nearby:** The delights of Brighton, including the Royal Pavilion, the famous Lanes, theatres and cinemas. Glyndebourne, Arundel, Chichester and Lewes are within easy reach. **Directions: The Granville is on the north side of Kings Road opposite the West Pier.**

For hotel location, see maps on pages 263–269

Collin House Hotel

COLLIN LANE, BROADWAY, WORCESTERSHIRE WR12 7PB
TEL: 01386 858354 FAX: 01386 858697

OWNER: Tricia and Keith Ferguson
CHEF: Antony Icke

7 rms | 6 ens | SMALL HOTEL

S: from £68
D: from £92

Believed to have formerly been the home of a wealthy wool merchant, Collin House is a 16th century Cotswold stone house standing in 2 acres of grounds, encompassing gardens, meadows and orchards set amid rolling countryside. It has been carefully restored to retain its original character, with oak beams, inglenook fireplaces where log fires burn on cool evenings, antique paintings and furnishings.

Each of the bedrooms is individual in style and is decorated and furnished to a high standard. All rooms have private bathrooms and two have four-poster beds. Collin House has an air of friendly informality, thanks largely to the enthusiasm of the new owners Tricia and Keith Ferguson, who aim to create an ambience akin to that of a weekend house party.

Collin House has long held a reputation for good English cooking served with flair and the candlelit restaurant, with its exposed timbers, mullioned windows and views over the gardens, provides the perfect setting. A balanced choice of delicious dishes is offered by the à la carte menu while an exceptional variety of imaginative bar and garden meals is served at lunchtime. Recommended by many accommodation and good eating guides. Closed for five days at Christmas.
Places of interest nearby: The Cotswolds, renowned for its picturesque villages and National Trust properties. Stratford-upon-Avon and Cheltenham are also within easy reach.
Directions: Collin House is 1 mile north-west of Broadway on the A44; turn right at the roundabout into Collin Lane.

For hotel location, see maps on pages 263–269

BROADWAY (Willersey)

THE OLD RECTORY

CHURCH STREET, WILLERSEY, BROADWAY, GLOUCESTERSHIRE WR12 7PN
TEL: 01386 853729 FAX: 01386 858061 E-MAIL: beauvoisin@btinternet.com

OWNERS: Liz and Chris Beauvoisin

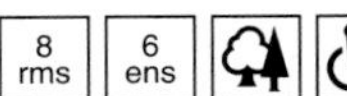

S: £50–£80
D: £65–£98

Built of mellow Cotswold stone, the 17th century Old Rectory at Willersey quietly tucked away at the end of a lane, opposite the 11th century church. With a backdrop of the Cotswold hills and a dry stone wall surrounding the delightful garden, this is truly an idyllic spot. A mulberry tree, reputed to have been planted in the reign of Elizabeth I, is laden with fruit each year and often supplies the breakfast table.

A superb breakfast is served in the elegant dining room, with log fires in winter. The immaculate bedrooms have all had new bathrooms installed, each one subtley stencilled and colour washed. Each room has colour television, tea and coffee making facilities, radio alarms, hairdryers and Crabtree and Evelyn toiletries. The combination of four poster beds and tranquillity make this an ideal place for honeymooners. Non smoking throughout!

The Bell Inn for lunch or dinner and many other fine restaurants are only minutes away. An ideal base from which to tour the Cotswolds with walks straight from the house and maps and picnics provided. Horse riding and bicycle hire locally. Broadway golf course is only 1 mile away.

Places of interest nearby: Cheltenham, Stratford, Warwick Castle. Blenheim Palace, Snowshill Manor, Hidcote Gardens. **Directions: From Broadway take B4632 (Stratford Road) for 1½ miles. At Willersey turn right (opposite the duck pond) into Church Street, the Rectory is at the end of the road and the private car park is at the rear of the property.**

For hotel location, see maps on pages 263–269

THATCHED COTTAGE HOTEL & RESTAURANT

16 BROOKLEY ROAD, BROCKENHURST, HAMPSHIRE SO42 7RR
TEL: 01590 623090 FAX: 01590 623479 E-MAIL: ThatchedCottageHotel@email.msn.com

OWNERS: The Matysik Family

5 rms | 5 ens | SMALL HOTEL

S: From £70
D: £90–£155

This enchanting thatched cottage was built in 1627 and only became a hotel in 1991. The Matysik family has over 111 years of hotel experience between them and this is reflected in the careful transformation that has taken place.

Set in one of the prettiest villages in the heart of the New Forest, modernisation for the comfort of guests has not detracted from its original charm. The individually decorated double bedrooms each have a special feature for example, a four-poster bed, Turkish steam shower or open hearth gas fireplace. A cosy beamed lounge is idyllic for pre/after-dinner drinks. An elegant tea garden is presented with lace table cloths and sun parasols. Memorable services include a superb late breakfast, Champagne cream tea and gourmet wicker hampers. In the evening, exquisite culinary delights are freshly prepared by the culinary team on show in their open country kitchen. The table d'hôte menu offers luxurious ingredients harmoniously combined with flair and imagination. "A dining experience difficult to surpass" set in a unique and relaxing ambience by romantic candlelight. An authentic Japanese celebration menu can be prearranged.

Places of interest nearby: Home of Lord Montagu and his National Motor Museum, Rothschild's Exbury Gardens and the yachting town of Lymington. Activities include wild mushroom hunting, riding, sailing and golf. **Directions: M27, Jct1, drive south on A337 through Lyndhurst, in Brockenhurst turn right before level crossing.**

Whitley Ridge Country House Hotel

BEAULIEU ROAD, BROCKENHURST, NEW FOREST, HAMPSHIRE SO42 7QL
TEL: 01590 622354 FAX: 01590 622856 E-MAIL: whitleyridge@brockenhurst.co.uk

OWNERS: Rennie and Sue Law

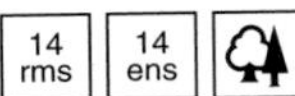

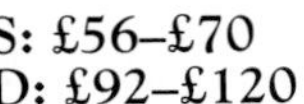

S: £56–£70
D: £92–£120

Whitley Ridge, once a royal hunting lodge, was built in Georgian style in the late 18th century. In more recent years the house has undergone extensive refurbishment, enhancing the appeal of its original Georgian features.

The bedrooms are individually decorated and most have lovely views over open Forest. The public rooms are elegantly furnished with and log fires burning on cooler evenings.

The Restaurant has two AA Rosettes for good food, offering a table d'hôte menu, which changes daily, together with a high standard of à la carte choices, plus a well balanced and imaginative vegetarian menu. The wine selection includes those wines from traditional areas and also interesting choices from further afield.

You are invited to relax in the grounds or enjoy a game of tennis. In addition, some of the best woodland walks in the country are directly accessible from the gardens. Whichever pastime you choose, Whitley Ridge is the perfect setting for a restful holiday. Your hosts Rennie and Sue Law welcome guests for a very pleasant stay.

Places of interest nearby: A number of stately homes, including Broadlands and Wilton House, are within easy reach. Lord Montagu's Motor Museum, Buckler's Hard and historic Stonehenge are also within driving distance.

Directions: M27 junction 1. Situated on the B3055, Brockenhurst – Beaulieu.

For hotel location, see maps on pages 263–269

The Priory

TOLLGATE, BURY ST EDMUNDS, SUFFOLK IP32 6EH
TEL: 01284 766181 FAX: 01284 767604 E-MAIL: reservations@prioryhotel.co.uk

OWNERS: Eagle Hotels
CHEF: Kevin Wood

S: £65–£95
D: £85–£105

Now under new management, The Priory is a charming country house, situated on the edge of the historic town yet close to the magnificent Suffolk landscape. Retaining the serene atmosphere of bygone times, the interior is furnished in a stylish manner with soft fabrics and elegant furnishings.

The bedrooms are located in either the main building or in the garden rooms and offer a blend of comfortable décor with the latest modern facilities. Most afford breathtaking views across the beautiful grounds and lawns, particularly the Honeymoon Suite.

Awarded an AA Rosette for the traditional English and modern European cuisine, the restaurant offers an à la carte menu and is renowned for its enthusiastic yet professional service and excellent presentation. The hotel's modern conference facilities are well-equipped and contain flip-charts, overhead projectors and screens. Special weekend breaks are available throughout the year, excluding the Christmas period. The Priory is an AA 3 Star, ETB 4 Crowns Highly Commended hotel.

Places of interest nearby: An exciting afternoon may be spent watching the horse-racing at Newmarket or visiting Bury Cathedral and Abbey gardens with its spectacular flower festival. The city of Cambridge is a delight to explore with its historic colleges, cobbled streets and the renowned Fitzwilliam museum. **Directions: From the A14, signed Bury St Edmunds, follow the A1101 to Mildenhall for ½ mile.**

For hotel location, see maps on pages 263–269

CAMBRIDGE (Melbourn)

Melbourn Bury

MELBOURN, CAMBRIDGESHIRE, NR ROYSTON SG8 6DE
TEL: 01763 261151 FAX: 01763 262375

OWNERS: Anthony and Sylvia Hopkinson

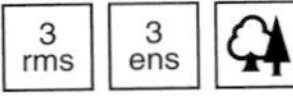

   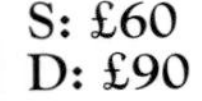

S: £60
D: £90

Set in extensive grounds with a lake and wildfowl, Melbourn Bury is an elegant manor house. It has had only two ownerships since the 1500s. The first owners were the Bishops of Ely and then in 1850, the property was purchased by the ancestors of Sylvia Hopkinson.

Gracious reception rooms are furnished with antiques and fine paintings, while the en suite bedrooms are comfortable and have charming views of the gardens. Fresh flowers and log fires are extra touches which guests will appreciate. Adjoining the library is a 19th century billiard room with a full-size table.

Delicious home cooking encompasses traditional English recipes and continental dishes prepared in cordon bleu style. Dinner is by prior arrangement.

Lunches and dinners for up to 22 persons seated; more can be accommodated buffet-style – small conferences, receptions and exhibitions. Closed at Christmas and Easter.

Places of interest nearby: Cambridge, Duxford Air Museum, Audley End, Ely, Wimpole Hall and Hatfield House. **Directions: Off A10, 10 miles south of Cambridge, 3rd turning on left to Melbourn; 2 miles north of Royston, 1st turning on right to Melbourn. Entrance is 300 yards on left after the turning. Look for the white gate posts and lodge cottage.**

For hotel location, see maps on pages 263–269

Crosby Lodge Country House Hotel

HIGH CROSBY, CROSBY-ON-EDEN, CARLISLE, CUMBRIA CA6 4QZ
TEL: 01228 573618 FAX: 01228 573428 E-MAIL: crosbylodge@crosby–eden.demon.co.uk

OWNERS: Michael, Patricia and James Sedgwick
CHEF: James Sedgwick

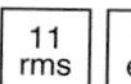

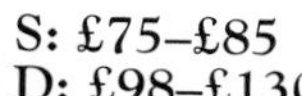

S: £75–£85
D: £98–£130

Crosby Lodge is a romantic country mansion that has been converted into a quiet efficient hotel without spoiling any of its original charm. Grade II listed, it stands amid pastoral countryside close to the Scottish Lowlands and the Lake District.

Spacious interiors are elegantly furnished and appointed to provide the maximum of comfort. The personal attention of Michael and Patricia Sedgwick ensures that a high standard of service is maintained. All of the bedrooms are beautifully equipped, most with antique beds and half-testers. Two bedrooms are situated in the converted courtyard stables overlooking the walled garden and in these rooms guests are welcome to bring their pet dogs.

In the restaurant, extensive menus offer a wide and varied choice of dishes. Traditional English recipes are prepared along with continental cuisine. Tables are set with cut glass and gleaming silver cutlery and in keeping with the gracious surroundings, gentlemen are requested to wear a jacket and tie for dinner. Crosby Lodge, with its spacious grounds, is a superb setting for weddings, parties, business and social events. Closed 24 December to 20 January.
Places of interest nearby: Hadrian's Wall, Carlisle Cathedral and Castle and nine miles from Lanercost Priory, the Scottish Borders. **Directions: From M6 junction 44 take A689 Brampton road for three miles; turn right through Low Crosby. Crosby Lodge is on the right at High Crosby.**

Aynsome Manor Hotel

CARTMEL, GRANGE-OVER-SANDS, CUMBRIA LA11 6HH
TEL: 015395 36653 FAX: 015395 36016

OWNERS: Tony, Margaret, Chris and Andrea Varley
CHEF: Victor Sharratt

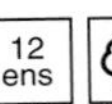

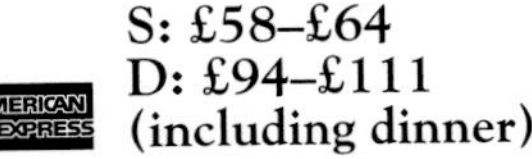

S: £58–£64
D: £94–£111
(including dinner)

In the beautiful Vale of Cartmel, with views of the priory and beyond to the village of Cartmel itself, stands Aynsome Manor, once the home of Wiliam Marshall, Earl of Pembroke. It is an ideal retreat for anyone seeking peace and quiet. Guests can stroll around the grounds or, in cooler months, relax by log fires in the lounges.

The elegant candlelit dining room is the perfect setting in which to enjoy a five-course dinner. The restaurant has an excellent reputation for its home cooking, from delicious home-made soups such as apple, celery and tomato, to main courses such as roast breast of pheasant with smoked bacon and an orange and chestnut sauce. Fresh, local produce is used wherever possible. A high tea is provided for children under five as they are regrettably not allowed in the restaurant for dinner. There are 12 bedrooms, 2 of which are in Aynsome Cottage, across the courtyard.

Places of interest nearby: Aynsome Manor is a perfect base for touring the Lake District. Lake Windermere is 4 miles away. In summer, Holker Hall organises ballooning and vintage car rallies. There is horseracing in Cartmel on Whitsun and August bank holidays and 5 golf courses nearby. Closed January. **Directions: Leave M6 at junction 36 and take the A590 signposted Barrow-in-Furness. At end of dual carriageway (12 miles) turn left into Cartmel. The hotel is on the right.**

For hotel location, see maps on pages 263–269

Easton Court Hotel

EASTON CROSS, CHAGFORD, DEVON TQ13 8JL
TEL: 01647 433469 FAX: 01647 433654 E-MAIL: stay@easton.co.uk

OWNERS: Gordon and Judy Parker

S: from £70
D: £128–£138
(including dinner)

Easton Court is a 15th century, Grade II listed, thatched Tudor house with many historic connections, particularly literary ones. Both Evelyn Waugh – who wrote *Brideshead Revisited* here – and Patrick Leigh Fermor found inspiration in this rural setting amid the glorious Devon countryside. The sensitive restoration of the hotel has removed none of its old-world charm and period features such as exposed granite walls, oak beams and a great inglenook fireplace, complete with bread oven, have been retained. For those with a literary bent, there is a superb library housing a fascinating collection of old tomes.

The eight tastefully furnished bedrooms have lots of interesting nooks and crannies and offer wonderful rural and moorland views. The menus in the attractive restaurant vary with the seasons and special diets can be catered for by prior arrangement. Special breaks available. **Places of interest nearby:** Dartmoor's mystery and grandeur lie 'on the doorstep' of the hotel, offering an endless variety of breathtaking walks, while Exmoor, Lynton and the rugged North Devon coast are a short journey away. Castle Drogo, Fernworthy Reservoir and Exeter are among the many other local places of interest. Closed January. **Directions: From Exeter, take the A30. At the first roundabout take the A382 signposted Moretonhampstead.**

CHELTENHAM (Charlton Kings)

CHARLTON KINGS HOTEL

CHARLTON KINGS, CHELTENHAM, GLOUCESTERSHIRE GL52 6UU
TEL: 01242 231061 FAX: 01242 241900

OWNER: Trevor Stuart
MANAGERS: Cassie Fuller and Aran Hayes
CHEF: Aran Hayes

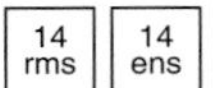

S: £51–£77.50
D: £64–£98

Surrounded by the Cotswold hills, on the outside of Cheltenham but just a few minutes by car to the heart of town stands Charlton Kings Hotel. If you seek instant peace and solitude follow the footpath running alongside the hotel into the beautiful Cotswold countryside. The famous 'Cotswold Way' escarpment walk passes just half a mile away.

The hotel is attractively furnished with an accent on light woods and pastel colouring. All rooms are en suite, some are reserved for non smokers. The Restaurant is fresh and inviting offering space and privacy for those all important business meetings or perhaps an intimate dinner for two? An à la carte menu is supplemented by a daily table d'hôte, using the finest fresh produce. The bar and conservatory are open throughout the day for snacks and refreshments. A full Sunday Roast Lunch is served 12–2. **Places of interest nearby:** Cheltenham Spa – famous for its architecture festivals and racing also has plenty to offer in the way of theatres, restaurants and a distinguished selection of shops. To the North, East and South lie charming Cotswold Villages, too numerous to mention, and to the West the Forest of Dean, Wye Valley, Malvern Hills and much more. **Directions: The hotel is the first property on the left coming into Cheltenham from Oxford on the A40 (the 'Welcome to Cheltenham' Boundary Sign is located in their front garden!).**

For hotel location, see maps on pages 263–269

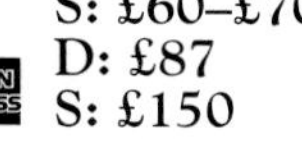

HALEWELL

HALEWELL CLOSE, WITHINGTON, NR CHELTENHAM, GLOUCESTERSHIRE GL54 4BN
TEL: 01242 890238 FAX: 01242 890332

OWNER: Mrs Elizabeth Carey-Wilson

 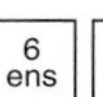  

S: £60–£70
D: £87
S: £150

This enchanting manor house is built of warm honey-coloured Cotswold stone. It is the home of Elizabeth Carey-Wilson who has made it a charming venue for guests seeking to stay within the ambience of a private house. The skillful restoration reflects both her affection for Halewell and consideration for those staying with her.

The guest rooms are individual. Two have adjoining rooms so families can be together and a ground floor room has been designed for disabled guests.

Meals are en famille, prepared by the hostess, at one long and lovely table. Breakfast is seldom before 9 o'clock and early children's meals are provided, as the traditional dinner is around 8 o'clock accompanied by good wine. Lunches and more exotic meals can be found in the attractive pubs close by.

Guests use the Sitting Room which has a games table and after dinner appreciate joining Mrs Carey-Wilson in her private drawing room, The Solar, with its unusual vaulted ceiling. Within the grounds are delightful terraced gardens, a stretch of the River Colne for fishing and a large trout lake, in addition to an outdoor swimming pool.

Places of interest nearby: The Cotswolds offer fine walking and there is an old Roman villa within 2 miles walk. Cheltenham has its races and festivals and Blenheim and Sudeley are in easy reach. **Directions: Leave A40 at South Andoversford (A436). Take first left to Withington village, then second right and second entrance on the left.**

For hotel location, see maps on pages 263–269

Crouchers Bottom Country Hotel

BIRDHAM ROAD, APULDRAM, NEAR CHICHESTER, WEST SUSSEX PO20 7EH
TEL: 01243 784995 FAX: 01243 539797

OWNERS: Drew and Lesley Wilson
CHEF: Drew Wilson

S: £45–£70
D: £65–£105

Crouchers Bottom Country Hotel is situated just ½ mile from the Yacht Basin and 2 miles from the centre of Chichester. Surrounded by fields, it offers fine views of the Cathedral, Goodwood and the South Downs and aims to create a relaxed and informal atmosphere for its guests.

There are sixteen luxury en suite bedrooms located in the converted coach house and barn with a full range of amenities, including a telephone, colour television, hairdryer and tea and coffee-making facilities. The 12 ground floor rooms open out onto a large patio with a lovely view of the garden and its pond with resident waterfowl. One of the twin-bedded rooms is particularly suitable for wheelchair users. Free-range hens provide the eggs of a full English breakfast, while dinner promises an interesting selection of freshly prepared dishes which changes daily. The area provides guests with a plentiful choice of activities, including boating around Chichester Harbour and visiting the City, with its cathedral, Roman walls, Festival Theatre, art gallery and museum.

Places of interest nearby: The famous Mary Rose can be seen in Portsmouth, where there are also a number of Maritime museums. Goodwood House and Arundel Castle are both within easy reach. **Directions: From the M27, junction 12, take the A27 to Chichester and then the A286 south towards The Witterings. Crouchers Bottom Hotel is on the left.**

For hotel location, see maps on pages 263–269

WOODSTOCK HOUSE HOTEL

CHARLTON, NEAR CHICHESTER, WEST SUSSEX PO18 0HU
TEL: 01243 811666 FAX: 01243 811666

OWNERS: Michael and Elizabeth McGovern

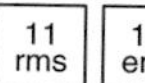

S: £38.50–£55
D: £66–£92

Nestling below the heights of Charlton Forest in the middle of West Sussex downland, Woodstock House is a perfect example of the small country house hotel. In summer the sun shines all day on its secluded courtyard garden. It was built in the 18th century but the public rooms, which include a bar and two sitting rooms, enjoy a modern feeling of spaciousness.

The dining room, however, retains a more traditional, atmosphere in which the high standard of cooking – set by Mrs McGovern – can be savoured to the full. The 11 bedrooms, all en suite, are comfortable and well-equipped with television and tea-making facilities. One bedroom offers a four-poster bed.

The hotel could not be better placed for offering outside interest from racing at Goodwood, golf at Goodwood and Cowdray Park golf clubs, sailing at Itchenor, Bosham and Dell Quay and Chichester Sea School and yacht basin, bathing at East and West Wittering and the Chichester Festival Theatre.

Places of interest nearby: There are historic houses in the area: Goodwood, Petworth, Parham and Uppark and Arundel Castle. The gardens of Wakehurst Place and Sheffield Park are well worth a visit, also nature reserves at Kingsley Vale and Pagham Harbour. **Directions: From M27 take A27 north of the Goodwood Estate. Charlton can be approached from A285 or A286.**

For hotel location, see maps on pages 263–269

CHIPPING CAMPDEN (Broad Campden)

THE MALT HOUSE

BROAD CAMPDEN, GLOUCESTERSHIRE GL55 6UU
TEL: 01386 840295 FAX: 01386 841334

OWNERS: Nick and Jean Brown
CHEF: Julian Brown

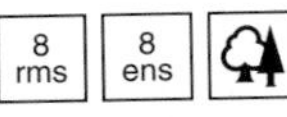

S: £49.50–£77.50
D: £72.50–£98.50
Suites: £92–£115

Nick and Jean Brown have achieved a blend of warm, relaxed and yet professional service, welcoming guests as part of an extended family. The idyllic surroundings of The Malt House, a beautiful 17th century Cotswold home in the quiet village of Broad Campden, further enhance the congenial atmosphere.

Rooms, including residents' sitting rooms, combine comfortable furnishings with antiques and displays of fresh flowers. Most bedrooms overlook the wide lawns which lead to a small stream and orchard beyond. All of the recently refurbished rooms are individually decorated and have an en suite bathroom. The Windrush Suite has an 18th century four-poster bed and a family suite is also available.

Dinner is served five days a week. The proprietors' son Julian is a highly accomplished chef who uses many ingredients from the kitchen gardens to prepare a table d'hôte menu, accompanied by a choice selection of wines. The English breakfasts are equally good.

The Malt House has earned a Highly Commended award from the English Tourist Board and most deservedly 2 Rosettes for its food and Premier Select 5Q from the AA. **Places of interest nearby:** Hidcote Manor Gardens (N.T), Chipping Camden Church, The Cotswolds, Cheltenham, Stratford-upon-Avon, Oxford and Bath. **Directions: The Malt House is in the centre of the village of Broad Campden which is just one mile from Chipping Campden.**

For hotel location, see maps on pages 263–269

MYND HOUSE HOTEL & RESTAURANT

LITTLE STRETTON, CHURCH STRETTON, NR SHREWSBURY, SHROPSHIRE SY6 6RB
TEL: 01694 722212 FAX: 01694 724180

OWNERS: Janet and Robert Hill
CHEF: Janet Hill

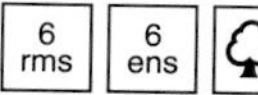

D: £60–£80
Suite: £80–£110

In the main street of the idyllic village of Little Stretton at the base of the NT Longmynd, this Edwardian village house is run by a husband and wife team and is the perfect retreat for those wishing to spend a few days or a short break in the country.

Comfort is an important criterion in the two lounges and the intimate bar as guests often frequent these rooms and recline with a book during the afternoons or enjoy a pre-dinner drink in the evenings. The bedrooms, many with glorious views across the valley, are individually furnished and well-equipped.

Awarded an AA Red Rosette and an RAC Merit Award, the restaurant offers a fixed price four or five-course menu comprising traditional recipes and using the finest local produce. Guests may choose a wine to accompany their meal from a selection of 500 vintages including some excellent Chiantis and an impressive list of half-bottles. Those wishing to explore the surrounding landscape can choose from the six well-described walks starting from the hotel.

Places of interest nearby: There are many distractions within easy reach such as Acton Scott Historic Farm museum, the Marches and the Ironbridge Gorge museums. The area is also renowned for its churches. Antique shops may be found in Ludlow and Bridgnorth whilst several music and arts festivals take place within the area. **Directions: Little Stretton is signposted off A49, 1½ miles south of Church Stretton.**

TUDOR FARMHOUSE HOTEL & RESTAURANT

HIGH STREET, CLEARWELL, NR COLEFORD, GLOUCESTERSHIRE GL16 8JS
TEL: 01594 833046 FAX: 01594 837093

OWNERS: Colin and Linda Gray
CHEF: Dean Wassell

12 rms 12 ens SMALL HOTEL 

  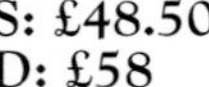 S: £48.50 D: £58

Tudor Farmhouse is an idyllic haven away from the hustle and bustle of everyday life. A cosy, friendly 13th century stone-built hotel in the centre of the historic village of Clearwell on the peaceful fringe of the Forest of Dean. Clearwell's history dates from Roman times and the village is dominated by the huge ramparts of a fine Neo Gothic castle.

Owners Colin and Linda Gray take pride in the standard of comfort and hospitality at Tudor Farmhouse, whose features include massive oak beams and original panelling. There is a large, roughstone inglenook fireplace in the attractive lounge providing warmth and cheer in winter. A conservatory looks onto the landscaped garden and 14 acres of fields. The bedrooms have been refurbished in traditional style. Those in the house are reached by a wide, oak spiral staircase. Others are in converted stone cider makers' cottages quietly situated in the garden and include three family suites.

The candlelit restaurant, awarded a red Rosette, with its open stonework and exposed beams is the ideal setting in which to enjoy unhurried evening meals.

Places of interest nearby: The Forest of Dean and Wye Valley, Offa's Dyke, Tintern Abbey, Monmouth and Ross on Wye, spectacular Symonds Yat, Raglan and Chepstow Castles. **Directions: From M4 join M48 taking junction 2 to Chepstow then follow A48 and B4231.**

Foxdown Manor

HORNS CROSS, NR CLOVELLY, NORTH DEVON EX39 5PJ
TEL: 01237 451325 FAX: 01237 451525

OWNERS: Bob Wood and Shirley Greaves

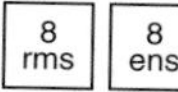

S: from £50
D: from £100

Deep in the heart of the North Devon countryside the sixteen acres of woodlands and gardens that surround Foxdown Manor provide a most rare and peaceful setting.

The garden is a sun-trap. Along the western walls that house the pool, sauna and Jacuzzi, figs, vines and roses grow in abundance. Nearby are a Victorian walled garden, croquet lawns and putting greens alongside a free-running trout stream.

This idyllic setting is the home of Bob Wood and Shirley Greaves who along with their friendly staff provide every comfort for their guests in a traditional way. The day rooms, too, are traditional in style and comfort, the drawing rooms' bay and French windows affording wonderful views of the surrounding countryside.

All the bedrooms have private facilities, colour televisions, telephones, beverage trays and baby listening. Several have four-poster beds and a feature of the bridal suite is its 18th century full canopy four-poster with a barley twist oak frame. Fresh seasonal fare is prominent on the dinner menu: fish from the local market, supremes of free-range chicken and noisettes of Devon lamb.

Places of interest nearby: Beautiful countryside walks, Hartland Point, Clovelly Bay and Exmoor all lie within easy reach. **Directions: From junction 27 of the M5 (28 miles), Foxdown Manor is six miles west of Bideford on the A39.**

ABBOTS OAK

GREENHILL, COALVILLE LE67 4UY
TEL: 01530 832 328 FAX: 01530 832 328

OWNERS: Bill, Audrey and Carolyn White

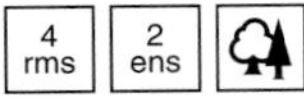

S: £50–£60
D: £60–£85

This Grade II listed building is on the edge of Charnwood Forest, with 19 acres of gardens, woodland and unusual granite outcrops where guests can stroll or play croquet and tennis. Being in the heart of Quorn country, stables are available for visitors' horses in the hunting season.

Inside is the most spectacular carved oak panelling and stained glass – indeed the staircase goes to the top of the tower from where it is possible to look out over five counties.

The house has four bedrooms available for the use of guests, two of which are en suite. There is a gorgeous drawing room and elegant dining room. Dinner is served en famille by candlelight. The menu is therefore not extensive and the wine list short but good. After dinner enjoy a game of snooker in the superb billiard room. This establishment is not suitable for young children.

Places of interest nearby: Mid-week it is ideal for businessmen with meetings in Loughborough or Leicester. There is excellent golf nearby and shooting can be arranged. Further afield are Stratford-upon-Avon, Warwick Castle and Rutland Water. **Directions: From the M1, take the A511 towards Coalville. At the first roundabout, take the third exit to Loughborough. At the traffic lights, turn left. Abbots Oak is 1¼ miles opposite the Bulls Head pub. From the A42, take the A511 towards Coalville. At the fourth roundabout take the first right, then right at T-junction. Abbots Oak is 50 yards on the right.**

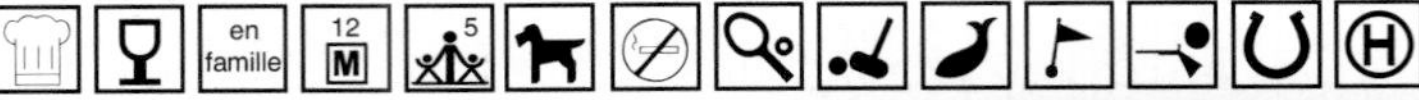

For hotel location, see maps on pages 263–269

ASHELFORD

ASHELFORD, EAST DOWN, NEAR BARNSTAPLE, NORTH DEVON EX31 4LU
TEL: 01271 850469 FAX: 01271 850862

OWNERS: Tom and Erica McClenaghan
CHEF: Erica McClenaghan

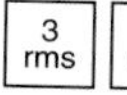  

S: £60
D: £80–£95

North Devon has over 850 square miles of heritage countryside and coast that are classified as one of the last remaining tranquil areas in England. Ashelford stands in over 70 acres of superb pasture and woodland facing south at the head of its own valley with views beyond the National Trust's Arlington Court to Exmoor.

Formerly a 17th century farmhouse, Ashelford has retained its sense of history with a wealth of oak beams, slate floors and log fires. Owners Tom and Erica McClenaghan offer peace, seclusion and cosy informality where a visitor's comfort is their greatest concern.

Privacy is enhanced by enchanting, warmly decorated and well-appointed bedrooms, each having en suite facilities and extras that include a refrigerator with fresh milk, orange juice and spring water. The lounge and dining room are comfortable and welcoming with superb meals prepared from local produce.

The 8 inch reflectory telescope will delight those wishing to observe the planets and stars. Golf, fishing, riding and carriage driving can be arranged. The residence has an outside bath with hot and cold water for well-behaved dogs after they have completed one of the many nearby walks with their owners! **Places of interest nearby:** The R.H.S. Rosemoor Gardens, Dartington Glass, Arlington Court. **Directions: From Barnstaple take A39 towards Lynmouth. After Shirwell village take second turning on left and follow signs to Churchill. Ashelford is on the right.**

For hotel location, see maps on pages 263–269

Coombe House Country Hotel

COLEFORD, CREDITON, DEVON EX17 5BY
TEL: 01363 84487 FAX: 01363 84722 E-MAIL: coombehs@eurobell.co.uk

OWNERS: David and Pat Jones
CHEF: Bill Denton

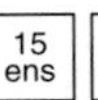  

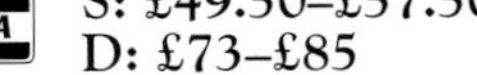

This elegant Georgian manor is listed as a protected building of historic interest and certainly the Cellar Bar has over 700 years of history – reputedly it sheltered Cromwell's men in the Civil War. Now these elegant buildings which offer relaxation in lovely landscaped grounds are being thoughtfully refurbished and up-graded by their caring and welcoming owners.

There are 15 bedrooms in all, the spacious Superior rooms at the front of the house enjoying restful views over the grounds and surrounding countryside with well-equipped bathrooms en suite; the six Standard en suite rooms are equally pleasant but their differing quality is reflected in the price structure.

The restaurant was once a ballroom added on in Victorian times and it provides a gracious, elegant atmosphere in which to enjoy the daily-changed cuisine and wines from the informative list. The grounds provide facilities for those who wish to play tennis, or indulge in croquet. For the more adventurous golf, shooting and riding can all be arranged.

Places of interest nearby: The city of Exeter with its cathedral and university, the Taw and Torridge valleys, Dartmoor, Exmoor and a number of National Trust properties. **Directions: From Exeter join A377 and pass through Crediton. After approximately 1½ miles further on the hotel is signposted**

For hotel location, see maps on pages 263–269

PEAR TREE LAKE FARM & EQUESTRIAN CENTRE

BALTERLEY, NEAR CREWE, CHESHIRE CW2 5QE
TEL: 01270 820307 FAX: 01270 820868

OWNERS: Duncan and Claire Douglas

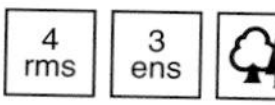

S: £35–£40
D: £40–£50

This attractive farmhouse has been totally upgraded and transformed under the new ownership of Duncan and Claire Douglas to provide very comfortable and homely accommodation. The farm buildings have been similarly improved and used to create an impressive Equestrian Centre. Duncan was an international event rider.

All four bedrooms, situated in the house, feature soft furnishings and attractive décor. The room with the four-poster bed, the large pine double room and the twin room all offer en suite facilities. The cosy sitting room boasts an open fire during the cold winter months and is the ideal place to sit, relax and enjoy a quiet drink.

In true farmhouse tradition, guests dine around one table in the candlelit dining room. From two to five-course dinners feature tempting dishes such as salmon and ginger cakes with a sweet red pepper sauce and mixed pepper relish and pork tenderloin pan-fried and flambéed in Calvados and finished with cider, cream and sage. The Equestrian Centre includes training stables, a riding school for all levels, show jumps, a cross-country course and two all-weather arenas. **Places of interest nearby:** The area is ideal for outdoor pursuits and opportunities for hunting, shooting and fishing abound. **Directions: From M6, junction 16, take A500 towards Crewe, turn left at second roundabout towards Keele. After ½ mile turn left at Broughton Arms and the farm is ½ mile on the left.**

Bel Alp House

HAYTOR, NR BOVEY TRACEY, SOUTH DEVON TQ13 9XX
TEL: 01364 661217 FAX: 01364 661292

OWNERS: Jack, Mary and Rachael Twist

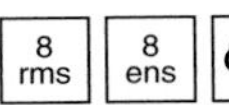

S: £65–£75
D: £130–£160

Peace and seclusion are guaranteed at the Bel Alp House with its spectacular outlook from the edge of Dartmoor across a rolling patchwork of fields and woodland to the sea, 20 miles away.

Built as an Edwardian country mansion and owned in the 1920s by millionairess Dame Violet Wills, Bel Alp has been lovingly restored and the proprietors' personal attention ensures their guests' enjoyment and comfort in the atmosphere of a private home.

The set dinner is changed nightly, using only the best local produce and the meals are accompanied by a well-chosen and comprehensive wine list.

Of the eight en suite bedrooms, two still have their original Edwardian basins and baths mounted on marble plinths and all bedrooms have views over the gardens.

An abundance of house plants, open log fires and restful colours complements the family antiques and pictures to create the perfect environment in which to relax. Awarded an AA Rosette.

Places of interest nearby: Bel Alp is ideally situated for exploring Devon and parts of Cornwall. Plymouth, famed for Drake and the Pilgrim Fathers, Exeter with its Norman cathedral and National Trust properties Castle Drogo and Cotehele Manor House are all within an hour's drive. **Directions: Bel Alp House is off the B3387 Haytor road, 2½ miles from Bovey Tracey.**

For hotel location, see maps on pages 263–269

Broome Court

BROOMHILL, DARTMOUTH, DEVON TQ6 0LD
TEL: 01803 834275 FAX: 01803 833260

OWNERS: Jan Bird and Tom Boughton

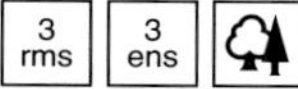

S: £40
D: £60–£80

Tucked away on a hill, Broome Court overlooks three copses and is surrounded by an area of outstanding natural beauty. The undulating South Devon countryside is on view from many of the farmhouse building windows, creating an idyllic location in which to relax and unwind. In the bedrooms, which are charming in their tasteful simplicity, every essential amenity is supplied.

A hearty breakfast is served in the old farmhouse kitchen and daily changing dinner menus make use of local fish, pork, beef, lamb and game. The south-east wing of Broome Court is occupied by The Granary, self-catering accommodation which boasts every facility needed to ensure a comfortable stay. Dartmouth Golf and Country Club, just a five minute drive away, has an 18-hole Championship Course and offers Broome Court residents reduced green fees. Opportunities for walking and riding abound.

Places of interest nearby: The picturesque and historic port of Dartmouth is within five minutes' drive and offers an abundance of leisure activities. Slapton Ley Field Centre/Nature Reserve is within easy reach, as is the rugged charm of Dartmoor. **Directions: On approaching Dartmouth from Totnes, take the second turning on your right from Norton Park.**

NONSUCH HOUSE

CHURCH HILL, KINGSWEAR, DARTMOUTH, DEVON TQ6 0BX
TEL: 01803 752829 FAX: 01803 752829

OWNERS: Patricia, Geoffrey and Christopher Noble
CHEF: Christopher Noble

5 rms | 4 ens

S: £57.50
D: £75

Nonsuch House stands high on a south-facing hill overlooking the ancient seaport of Dartmouth, the River Dart and out to sea. The Nobles, formally owners of the award-winning Langshott Manor, near Gatwick, have ensured the same high standards of hospitality, service, food and value for money continue at their new charge.

This Edwardian house offers comfort to all who stay – whether it be seafarers, walkers or holiday-makers looking for peace and tranquillity. The bedrooms are beautifully appointed and all enjoy fine sea and river views. Log fires blaze in the Dining Room and the Saloon and guests can also enjoy the conservatory and terrace. A set menu is offered each evening using the very best and freshest of local produce.

A short walk down to the waters edge will bring you to the vehicular and passenger ferries for the five minute crossing to Dartmouth and its many charms.

Places of interest nearby: Many National Trust properties and Heritage Coastal walks abound. Visiting Dartmoor and boat trips up the river to the medieval town of Totnes are other pastimes. **Directions: From Exeter or Plymouth on A38. Take Dart Valley exit A384 to Totnes then A385 to Paignton. Then A3022 to Brixham, A379 to Dartmouth/ Kingswear and onto B3205 to Kingswear. After 1½ miles, take left turn onto Higher Contour Road and you will find Nonsuch House ½ mile on, below a hairpin bend.**

For hotel location, see maps on pages 263–269

Prince Hall Hotel

TWO BRIDGES, DARTMOOR, DEVON PL20 6SA
TEL: 01822 890403 FAX: 01822 890676

OWNERS: Adam and Carrie Southwell

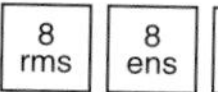   

S: £59.50–£72.50
D: £119–£129
(including 4 course dinner)

Set high in the heart of Dartmoor National Park, Prince Hall is a unique and peaceful, 18th century country house hotel. Once the summer residence of Lord and Lady Astor, it commands spectacular views over the the West Dart River to rolling open moorland, an idyllic setting for walking, bird-watching or simply just relaxing.

Prynse Hall, as the hotel was originally called, is one of the ancient tenements of Dartmoor and a dwelling has stood on the site since 1443.

The Hall is comfortably furnished. Attractive fabrics, interesting pictures, shelves of books and roaring log fires in winter add to the warm welcome. Each of the spacious, en suite bedrooms, individually decorated, has its own particular character and offers all modern comforts.

In the delightful restaurant with its granite stone walls and charming ambience, great care and attention is taken with the four course table d'hôte daily changing menu. Quality local produce, including local venison and lamb, Brixham fish and salmon and trout from the River Dart is used. Dogs are welcome free of charge. Closed January. **Places of interest nearby:** Buckland Abbey, houses and gardens such as Castle Drogo, Knightshayes and Killerton, Iron Age and prehistoric sites. **Directions: From Exeter take the A38 to Ashburton and follow the signs for Two Bridges and Princetown. Prince Hall is on the left on the B3357 one mile before Two Bridges.**

For hotel location, see maps on pages 263–269

CHIPPENHALL HALL

FRESSINGFIELD, EYE, SUFFOLK IP21 5TD
TEL: 01379 588180/586733 FAX: 01379 586272

OWNERS: Barbara and Jakes Sargent

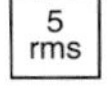

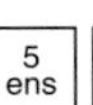

S: £62–£68
D: £68–£72

The present manor is a listed Tudor building, although its origins date from Saxon times and is referred to in the *Domesday Book* as Cybenhalla. Secluded at the end of a long leafy drive, the hall enjoys a setting of rural tranquillity amid seven acres of lawns, trees, ponds and gardens.

Every evening, by arrangement, a superb candlelit dinner is prepared by the hostess and served in convivial surroundings. Proprietors Barbara and Jakes Sargent pride themselves in offering a fine choice of reasonably priced wines from the cellar to complement your meal. A seat beside the copper-canopied inglenook fire in the Shallow End bar room is the ideal place to enjoy pre-dinner drinks.

The house is heavily-beamed throughout, including the en suite bedrooms which are named after relevant historical associations. During the summer, guests can relax by the heated outdoor swimming pool which is set in the rose-covered courtyard. With attentive service, good food and wine, it is not surprising to learn that Chippenhall Hall won the Johansens 1998 Country Houses and Small Hotels Award and is ETB Highly Commended and AA Premier Selected.

Places of interest nearby: Snape Maltings, Minsmere Bird Sanctuary, the Otter Trust at Earsham and the towns of Bury St Edmunds and Norwich. **Directions: One mile outside Fressingfield on the B1116 to Framlingham.**

For hotel location, see maps on pages 263–269

YALBURY COTTAGE HOTEL

LOWER BOCKHAMPTON, DORCHESTER, DORSET DT2 8PZ
TEL: 01305 262382 FAX: 01305 266412 E-MAIL: yalbury.cottage@virgin.net

OWNERS: Heather and Derek Furminger
HEAD CHEF: Russell Brown

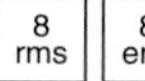 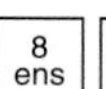 

 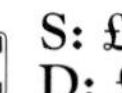 S: £49 D: £74

Yalbury Cottage Hotel is a lovely thatched property dating back about 300 years. Family run, it offers guests a warm welcome and a friendly, personal service in an atmosphere of peace, relaxation and informality.

The eight spacious bedrooms are attractively decorated and furnished, all having well appointed bathrooms en suite. Each offers a full range of desirable extras, including colour television, hairdryer and tea and coffee making facilities.

A comfortable lounge, complete with large inglenook fireplace and low, beamed ceilings, is the perfect place to relax before dinner. The proprietors pride themselves on the high standard of cuisine served in the attractive dining room. A good variety of imaginative dishes is always available, for example, oven-baked fillet of hake with a lime and coriander salsa, pastry case filled with ratatouille topped with a herb crust served with mushroom sauce, lamb cutlets topped with a tarragon mousse with red wine jus. A selection of carefully chosen wines is available to complement any meal.

Places of interest nearby: Thomas Hardy's birthplace, Athelhampton House, Parnham House, Abbotsbury Swannery, Corfe Castle and Sherborne Castle. Yalbury Cottage is an excellent centre from which to explore Dorset, with its superb walking country, pretty villages and magnificent coastline. **Directions: Lower Bockhampton is one mile south of A35 between Puddletown and Dorchester.**

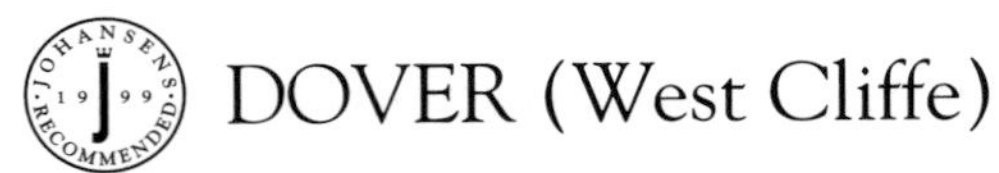

DOVER (West Cliffe)

WALLETT'S COURT

WEST CLIFFE, ST MARGARET'S-AT-CLIFFE, DOVER, KENT CT15 6EW
TEL: 01304 852424 FAX: 01304 853430 E-MAIL: WallettsCourt@Compuserve.com

OWNERS: Chris, Lea and Gavin Oakley

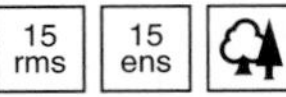  

S: £65–£100
D: £75–£130

This listed Grade II house, recorded in The Doomsday Book as 'The Manor of Westcliffe', was transformed by the Oakley family who discovered it in ruins in the late 70s. The result is a charming property, enveloped in a relaxing atmosphere and set in extensive and recently landscaped grounds.

The beautifully appointed bedrooms are comfortable and well-equipped with an array of modern conveniences. They are located in either the main house or the recent Barn conversion, which also features an indoor swimming pool and leisure facilities.

The attractive restaurant, awarded 3 AA Rosettes, offers an imaginative menu with a Jacobean flavour. The dishes change every month to incorporate the fresh seasonal produce. Try the Huntsman's Platter, local monkfish, Kentish lamb and syllabub. The extensive wine list includes a good selection of half-bottles, all acceptably priced. Breakfast is another feast, with farm eggs, sausages made by the nearby butcher and home-made preserves. Fitness enthusiasts may use the steam room, sauna, spa pool, tennis courts and croquet lawn.

Places of interest nearby: Guests enjoy walking on the cliff tops to St Margaret's Bay, exploring the Cinque Ports and playing golf on the nearby championship courses. **Directions: From A2 roundabout immediately north of Dover take A258 signposted Deal. After one mile turn right and the Court is on the right.**

THE WOODVILLE HALL

TEMPLE EWELL, DOVER, KENT CT16 1DJ
TEL: 01304 825256 FAX: 01304 825256

OWNER: Mr A.D.M. Allen
MANAGERS: Sue and Roger Westoby

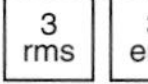

Suites: from £95

The owners justifiably boast that this is one of the most beautiful small hotels in England. One cannot believe that this magnificent residence, built in 1820 for Henry Colman (of mustard fame) and set in 25 acres of secluded parkland, a short drive from Dover and the Channel Tunnel.

The accommodation is superb, three spectacular suites which are all furnished most luxuriously in the greatest detail. Awarded 'Best Small Hotel' by the Welcome to Kent Scheme.

The ambience throughout the entire house reflects the gracious Georgian era, with silver and highly polished antiques, oil paintings and marvellous flowers. Welcoming and friendly hospitality is of the highest standard. Guests enjoy immaculate service and fine food beautifully presented with interesting wines and champagnes. Dinner is served either in the dining room or in the suites.

Places of interest nearby: When not enjoying the extensive grounds with its ancient woodland guests can visit nearby nature reserves, Dover Castle and Hellfire Corner, the Battle of Britain Museum, the Old Town Gaol, the White Cliffs Experience and Walmer Castle, or, further afield, Canterbury Cathedral. **Directions: Take A2 from Dover and at the second roundabout turn left. At the bottom of the hill turn right towards Lydden. Continue for one mile and Woodville Hall is on your right just before the "Z" bend.**

For hotel location, see maps on pages 263–269

ASHWICK COUNTRY HOUSE HOTEL

DULVERTON, SOMERSET TA22 9QD
TEL: 01398 323868 FAX: 01398 323868

OWNER: Richard Sherwood
CHEF: Richard Sherwood

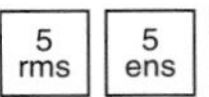

S: £75–£85
D: £130–£154
(including dinner)

This small, charming AA Red Star Edwardian Country House stands in six acres of beautiful grounds above the picturesque valley of the River Barle within Exmoor National Park. Sweeping lawns lead to large water gardens where guests can relax in summer shade and breathe in sweet floral scents. Ashwick House offers old world hospitality. Its atmosphere is sunny with flowers in summer and elegantly cosy with candlelight and log fires in winter.

The baronial style hall with its long, broad gallery and cheerful log fire, the restaurant opening onto a terrace where breakfast is served and the comfortably furnished lounge offer a peaceful sanctuary not easily found in today's busy world. All the spacious bedroom suites are pleasantly decorated.

Chef-patron Richard Sherwood presents quality cuisine using fresh local produce. Shooting and riding facilities are close by.

Places of interest nearby: Dunster's Norman Castle and 17th century Yarm Market, Exmoor Forest, many National Trust houses and gardens. **Directions: From the M5, exit at junction 27 onto the A361 to Tiverton. Take the A396 north until joining the B3222 to Dulverton and then the B3223 signposted Lynton and Exford. After a steep climb drive over a second cattle grid and turn left to Ashwick House.**

For hotel location, see maps on pages 263–269

OAK LODGE HOTEL

80 VILLAGE ROAD, BUSH HILL PARK, ENFIELD, MIDDLESEX EN1 2EU
TEL: 0181 360 7082

OWNERS: John and Yvonne Brown

S: £79.50
D: £89.50–£125

Oak Lodge is just nine miles from central London with excellent road and rail connections and conveniently placed for each of the capital's five airports. The hotel is small but it offers a very generous welcome which encompasses charm, courtesy and old-fashioned hospitality.

Each en suite bedroom is highly individual, imaginatively furnished, and with all the facilities found in larger rooms.

Traditional English cuisine, complemented by an exceptionally good wine list, is served in the intimate restaurant which overlooks and opens out onto a delightful evergreen garden. For after-dinner relaxation a pianist regularly entertains guests in a romantic Noel Coward style in the hotel's elegant lounge.

Enfield has excellent shopping facilities and preserves the atmosphere of the country town it once was. There are many fine old houses, particularly in Gentlemen's Row, where the 19th century author Charles Lamb lived.

Places of interest nearby: Forty Hall, built in 1632 for Sir Nicholas Raynton, Lord Mayor of London, now a cultural centre and museum, Capel Manor, St Albans cathedral and the ruins of a Roman amphitheatre. **Directions: From the M25, exit at junction 25 onto the A10 south. Turn right at the tenth set of traffic lights into Church Street, then right again at the next traffic lights into Village Road. Oak Lodge is 200yards on the right.**

For hotel location, see maps on pages 263–269

CHALK LANE HOTEL

CHALK LANE, EPSOM, SURREY KT18 7BB
TEL; 01372 721179 FAX: 01372 727878 E-MAIL: chalklane@compuserve.com

OWNERS: McGregor Hotels Ltd
CHEF: Nicholas Arnold

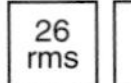   

   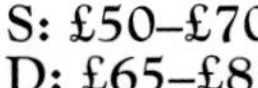

S: £50–£70
D: £65–£85

This delightful country house is hidden away from the hustle and bustle of modern life in the conservation area that is old Epsom. It has recently come under the management of Steven McGregor, who has a lifetime of experience in top quality hotels. His appointment heralds a total refurbishment programme that will guarantee an excellent standard of accommodation throughout.

Discerning gastronomes will be delighted by the imaginative and beautifully-presented cuisine on offer. A good range of starters includes such irresistible offerings as hot roasted red pepper and goats cheese tart, Provençal-style vegetable and seared lamb fillet terrine and hot smoked Scottish salmon on a potato pancake with lemon on dill. A choice of nearly a dozen main courses includes mouth-watering dishes like Thai style monkfish curry with bok choi and jasmine rice, Scotch rib eye steak with crunchy leeks, French fries and port wine sauce and roasted salmon fillet with a red wine risotto scented with thyme and served with green asparagus. Vegetarians are also superbly catered for.

Places of interest nearby: This is an ideal location for horse-racing enthusiasts – the course at Epsom Downs is just minutes' away. Wisley, Hampton Court and Richmond.

Directions: M25, junction 9. Take A24 Dorking Road, turn right into Woodcote Road, left into Avenue Road and right into Worple Road. Take a left into Chalk Lane – the hotel is situated on the right.

For hotel location, see maps on pages 263–269

RECTORY HOUSE

FORE STREET, EVERSHOT, DORSET DT2 0JW
TEL: 01935 83273 FAX: 01935 83273

OWNERS: Denis and Angela Carpenter
CHEF: Angela Carpenter

5 rms | 5 ens

MasterCard VISA S: £40–£50 D: £70–£90

Rectory House is a charming, 18th century listed building standing serenely in a quiet, unspoilt village surrounded by an area of natural beauty made famous by the novels of Thomas Hardy. Denis and Angela Carpenter give all their guests a genuinely friendly welcome, encouraging them to relax as if in their own home. On warm summer days and evenings the colourful garden with its huge beech tree for shade is popular with visitors seeking a secluded spot for a coffee, a cool drink or a quiet read.

Antique furniture, deep pile rugs and vases of fresh flowers abound throughout the hotel. Three of the five bedrooms are situated by the garden. All are en suite, tastefully decorated and furnished and have every comfort. The cuisine is highly regarded with chef Angela Carpenter using fresh local produce to create a distinctive brand of international cooking.

The unspoilt countryside and its coastline, 12 miles south, make for limitless exploration and bring to life the setting of the Hardy novels. Golf is available at Chedington Court and there is fishing, riding and sailing at Sutton Bingham. Closed December–January.
Places of interest nearby: Sherborne Castle, the Cerne Giant, Parnham House, Yeovilton Air Museum and the gardens at Mapperton House, Kingston Maurward, Hooke Park and Forde Abbey. **Directions: Leave the A37 for Evershot halfway between Dorchester and Yeovil.**

The Mill at Harvington

ANCHOR LANE, HARVINGTON, EVESHAM, WORCESTERSHIRE WR11 5NR
TEL: 01386 870688 FAX: 01386 870688

OWNERS: Simon and Jane Greenhalgh

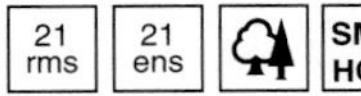

S: £59
D: £96

From the first glimpse of Simon and Jane Greenhalgh's elegant brochure one is aware that The Mill at Harvington is going to be very special. This delightful small country house hotel set on the bank of the Avon is in the heart of England with easy access to the West, The Cotswolds, Wales and, of course, Shakespeare country.

From inside the welcoming and graceful reception rooms, which are brightened by big open fires in the winter, there are views over the extensive gardens and the river.

The high standards of hospitality and service are evident. The en suite bedrooms whether in the main building or the superb recent annexe extension are beautifully furnished with all the modern comforts including hairdryers, mineral water, colour television, tea and coffee facilities.

A modestly priced but excellent wine list accompanies the appetising menu which makes maximum use of local and seasonal produce, fish and game (there are also light lunches on the Terrace), reflecting the owners' belief that dining well must be high on the agenda for a successful visit. Guests take away memories of spectacular countryside, superb meals, immaculate service, charming surroundings and perfect hosts. **Directions: The Mill can be reached by a roadbridge over A46 opposite Harvington village, off the Evesham to Bidford road.**

For hotel location, see maps on pages 263–269

THE LORD HALDON HOTEL

DUNCHIDEOCK, NR EXETER, DEVON EX6 7YF
TEL: 01392 832483 FAX: 01392 833765

OWNERS: Michael and Simon Preece

SMALL HOTEL

S: £48–£56
D: £68–£95

Ideally situated amid rolling Devon countryside between the historic cathedral town of Exeter, Dartmoor and the coast stands this imposing country house.

The present building is a fragment of the huge mansion that once stood in this marvellous location, built in 1737. However, the beautiful views planned by Capability Brown can still be enjoyed, as can the peace and tranquillity of this quiet part of Devon.

All the bedrooms are decorated in an individual style, the majority enjoying picturesque rural views and there are family rooms and four-poster suites for the romantic at heart.

Meals are served in the AA Rosetted Chandelier Restaurant, a superb setting to enjoy the freshest of seasonal produce. Special diets can be catered for and picnics provided on request. A member of Relais Du Silence.

Places of interest nearby: The Maritime Museum at Exeter, Haldon Forest, (designated SSSI) perfect for ornithologists and photographers, and the moorland beauty of Dartmoor, are all just a short drive away from the hotel. **Directions: Exit junction 31 of the M5 onto A30 and leave this dual carriageway at the first available exit signed Marsh Barton and Exeter. Take the first exit at the roundabout signed Ide and then follow local signs for Ide and Dunchideock.**

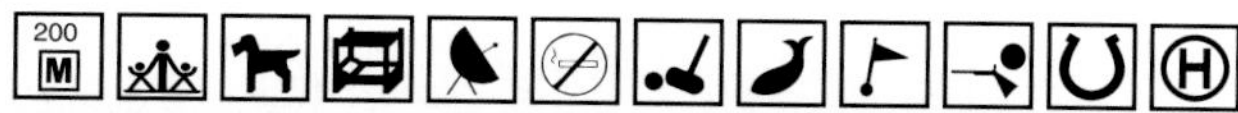

For hotel location, see maps on pages 263–269

The Crown Hotel

EXFORD, EXMOOR NATIONAL PARK, SOMERSET TA24 7PP
TEL: 01643 831554/5 FAX: 01643 831665 E-MAIL: bradleyhotelsexmoor@easynet.co.uk

OWNERS: Mike Bradley and John Atkin
CHEF: Eric Bouchet

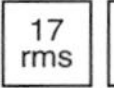

S: £37–£67
D: £74–£110

This coaching inn, almost three hundred years old, in the Exmoor National Park is surrounded by wonderful countryside, from coastline to valleys, streams and moorland, populated with red deer, ponies, amazing birdlife and salmon.

The hotel has been completely refurbished, to the highest standards of elegance and comfort. Guests can enjoy its comfort in every season – its coolness in summer, its warmth in winter.

The bedrooms, all en suite, have been beautifully decorated and are well-equipped with modern necessities.

There is a lively bar, patronised by the locals, for drinks or informal meals ordered from the extensive menu, or guests may prefer an apéritif in the lounge before entering the delightful dining room for a beautifully presented evening meal from the seasonal menu. Good wines complement the meal. After dinner guests may wish to stroll in the water garden. Special breaks available throughout the year.

Places of interest nearby: Fly fishing (and tuition) in local rivers, riding over the moor and clay pigeon shooting can be arranged. Order a packed lunch and walk the moor or visit Lynmouth and Porlock. **Directions: Exit M5, junction 27. Drive eight miles down the A361, then take the A396 to Wheddon Cross, where Exford is signposted.**

For hotel location, see maps on pages 263–269

THE BEACON COUNTRY HOUSE HOTEL

BEACON ROAD, MINEHEAD, SOMERSET TA24 5SD
TEL: 01643 703476 FAX: 01643 707007 E-MAIL: Beacon@globalnet.co.uk

OWNERS: David and Gina Twist
CHEF: Keith Wearing

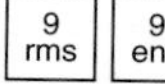

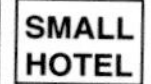

S: £58–£98
D: £86–£96
suite: £136

An elegant Edwardian country house hotel perched high above the coastline, embraced by its own 20 acres of land, gardens, orchard, livery and home farm, nestling peacefully amid the rolling countryside, the hotel has direct access onto Exmoor and the Coastal Path, yet is only minutes from Minehead town centre.

All bedrooms are en suite, individually decorated, some with sea view and all overlooking the landscaped gardens and countryside beyond. There are two attractive lounges with open fireplaces, a domed glass conservatory and a stylish restaurant and bar serving superb food and drink. Riding, golfing, hiking, cycling, fishing, sailing, sightseeing and shopping are all close by. The hotel is highly reputed for its friendly staff and thoughtful personal service.

Places of interest nearby: The Beacon Country House Hotel is an ideal base for touring Exmoor and the West Country. **Directions: From M5, turn off to Bridgewater at Jct23 then take A39 to Minehead. At Minehead follow signs into the Town Centre. Turn right at T-junction onto The Parade, take second left into Blenheim Road, then first left into Martlet Road. Proceed uphill and turn straight across at the memorial into Burgundy Road. Carry on round the hairpin bend and follow Beacon Road to the end. The hotel is on the right with its own car park.**

For hotel location, see maps on pages 263–269

VERE LODGE

SOUTH RAYNHAM, FAKENHAM, NORFOLK NR21 7HE
TEL: 01328 838261 FAX: 01328 838300

OWNERS: Major and Mrs George Bowlby

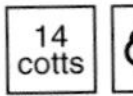  

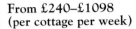

  From £240–£1098 (per cottage per week)

Fourteen spacious, and beautifully decorated self-contained cottages are scattered in seclusion throughout 8 acres of woodlands, paddocks and sweeping lawns surrounding impressive Vere Lodge, a Grade II listed building dating from 1798 and former dower house to Raynham Hall. Some are conversions of old outbuildings, others recently built. All have every home comfort.

Families are particularly well catered for. The grounds are a paradise for children with a playground, a toddlers' play area and unusually tame rabbits, hens, peacocks, dogs, goats, a donkey and a pony to stroke, feed and enjoy.

A grass tennis court and croquet lawn cater for the sports enthusiast and a leisure centre with a 38-foot-long swimming pool, sauna, solarium, table tennis, pool table, sun patios, lounge and an occasional bar serving drinks and alfresco snacks are in a corner of the grounds so as not to intrude upon the peace and seclusion of Vere Lodge. Fresh free-range eggs and a selection of mainly home-cooked frozen foods can be obtained in the leisure centre and there is a launderette. Three night breaks are available. **Places of interest nearby:** Norfolk's long sandy beaches, Blickling Hall, Holkham Hall, Sandringham. Riding and fishing can be arranged. **Directions: From Swaffham take A1065 towards Fakenham. After 11 miles enter South Raynham: 100 yards past the village sign turn left. Vere Lodge is the white house 400 yards ahead.**

For hotel location, see maps on pages 263–269

TRELAWNE HOTEL – THE HUTCHES RESTAURANT

MAWNAN SMITH, NR FALMOUTH, CORNWALL TR115HS
TEL: 01326 250226 FAX: 01326 250909

OWNERS: Paul and Linda Gibbons, Anthony and Jenny Bond
CHEF: Nigel Woodland

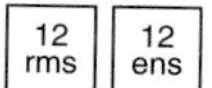  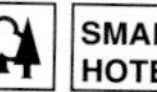

S: £55–£80
D: £95–£155
(including 4 course dinner)

A very friendly welcome awaits guests, who will be enchanted by the beautiful location of Trelawne Hotel, on the coast between the Rivers Fal and Helford. Large picture windows in the public rooms, including the attractively decorated, spacious lounge/bar, ensure that guests take full advantage of the panoramic vistas of the ever-changing coastline.

The bedrooms are charming, many with views of the sea. The soft colours of the décor, the discreet lighting and attention to detail provide a restful atmosphere, in harmony with the Wedgwood, fresh flowers and sparkling crystal in The Hutches Restaurant, which has been awarded 2 AA Rosettes.

The menu changes daily and offers a variety of inspired dishes, including local seafood, game and fresh vegetables. Recreational facilities include an indoor heated swimming pool and a games room. Trelawne Hotel offers its own golf package at no less than ten fine courses. 'Slip Away Anyday' spring, autumn and winter breaks. Closed January. **Places of interest nearby:** The Royal Duchy of Cornwall is an area of outstanding beauty, with many National Trust and English Heritage properties to visit and a range of leisure pursuits to enjoy. **Directions: From Truro follow A39 towards Falmouth, turn right at Hillhead roundabout, take exit signposted Maenporth. Carry on for 3 miles and Trelawne is at the top overlooking Falmouth bay.**

FENNY DRAYTON (Leicestershire)

WHITE WINGS

QUAKER CLOSE, FENNY DRAYTON, NR NUNEATON, LEICESTERSHIRE CV13 6BS
TEL: 01827 716100 FAX: 01827 717191

OWNERS: Ernest and Josephine Lloyd

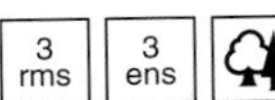

S: £50–£60
D: £75–£85

This lovely family home provides peaceful and informal accommodation with spacious and traditionally furnished rooms. The well appointed bedrooms all offer private facilities, colour television and views of the luxuriant garden.

Breakfast and dinner are served on some of the finest collections of china and crystal, in fact Josephine's collection is so vast that you could quite easily not see the same china twice during your stay and all this is in the elegant dining room overlooking the garden. Afterwards, guests are invited to relax in the library or the conservatory and to enjoy the use of the Steinway grand piano or go through to the billiard room and play on a full sized billiard table.

The surrounding villages and towns offer plenty of entertainment including music, opera, ballet, theatre and exhibitions. For the active, there are golf courses and opportunities for fishing, canal trips and indoor skiing. **Places of interest nearby:** Fenny Drayton is an excellent centre from which to visit Stratford-upon-Avon, Warwick, Kenilworth and Leicester, with their ancient castles, historic houses, museums and art galleries. Close by is the village of Twycross with its zoo housing a famous collection of primates. **Directions: On the A444 from Nuneaton, turn left into George Fox Lane (becoming Old Forge Road) and right into Quaker Close.**

For hotel location, see maps on pages 263–269

STANHILL COURT HOTEL

STANHILL ROAD, CHARLWOOD, NR HORLEY, SURREY RH6 0EP
TEL: 01293 862166 FAX: 01293 862773

OWNERS: Antonio and Kathryn Colas

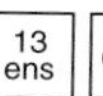

S: from £95
D: £110–£150

Built in 1881 in the Scottish Baronial style, Stanhill Court Hotel is set in 35 acres of ancient wooded countryside and offers spectacular views over the North Downs. It boasts an original Victorian walled garden and amphitheatre available for concerts or corporate presentations and events.

The hotel is traditionally furnished to provide an intimate, warm and comfortable atmosphere, with rich pitch pine panelling evident throughout the hall, minstrels gallery and barrel roof. There is a wide choice of bedrooms, all decorated and furnished to the same high standards and offering a full range of facilities.

A superb à la carte restaurant offers a menu which is international in flavour and complemented by an excellent range of regional and vintage wines. A choice of vegetarian dishes is always included and old style, friendly personal service is guaranteed.

Versatile conference facilities include small meetings rooms and a choice of five function rooms. Stanhill Court is also an excellent venue for wedding receptions, family celebrations and social gatherings.

Places of interest nearby: Leonardslee, High Beeches, Nymans and Wakehurst Place. **Directions: Charlwood is north west of the airport and reached off the M23/A23 via Hookwood or Lowfield Heath. Go through Charlwood and follow signs towards Newdigate.**

THE CORMORANT HOTEL

GOLANT BY FOWEY, CORNWALL PL23 1LL
TEL: 01726 833426 FAX: 01726 833026

OWNERS: George and Estelle Elworthy

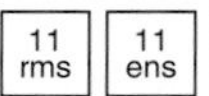

S: £44–£57
D: £92

The Cormorant Hotel stands high above the beautiful Fowey Estuary with magnificent views over the shimmering waters and the Cornish countryside. A warm, friendly and inviting atmosphere pervades the hotel which is enjoying gradual artistic refurbishment.

There are 11 entirely individual bedrooms, all en suite and with colour television, radio, direct dial telephone and extensive views over the estuary and creeks. Guests can relax in an extremely comfortable lounge which has full length picture windows and a log fire in winter. The bar is small and welcoming. Guests can also enjoy lounging on the terrace near the hotel's heated swimming pool which has a sliding roof for opening on hot summer days.

This corner of Cornwall is a living larder of wholesome produce all made use of by enthusiastic chef-patron George Elworthy and served in a pretty candlelit restaurant. A choice of long and imaginative menus is offered.

Places of interest nearby: Miles of walking along the coastline, quaint fishing villages, Lanhydrock House and gardens, Trelissick garden and many National Trust properties. Fishing, riding and golf can be arranged locally.

Directions: From Exeter, take A30 towards Bodmin and then B3269 towards Fowey. After six miles turn left at a staggered junction to Golant. Bear right as you approach the estuary and continue along the water's edge. The hotel is on the right.

For hotel location, see maps on pages 263–269

White Moss House

RYDAL WATER, GRASMERE, CUMBRIA LA22 9SE
TEL: 015394 35295 FAX: 015394 35516

OWNERS: Peter and Susan Dixon

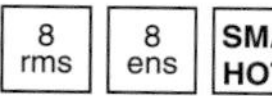

S: £80–£95
D: £130–£190
(including 5-course dinner)

Set in a fragrant garden of roses and lavender, White Moss House was once owned by Wordsworth, who often rested in the porch here between his wanderings. Built in 1730, it overlooks beautiful Rydal Water. Many famous and interesting walks through fells and lakeland start from the front door. Guests have free use of the local leisure club and swimming pool and free fishing on local rivers and lakes.

It has been described by a German gourmet magazine as 'probably the smallest, most splendid hotel in the world'. Proprietors Peter and Susan Dixon have created an intimate family atmosphere with a marvellous degree of comfort and attention to detail.

The seven bedrooms in the main house and the two in the Brockstone Cottage Suite are individually furnished, and most have lake views. Chef Peter Dixon has won international acclaim for his culinary skills including 2 AA Rosettes and a Red Star. The restaurant is deservedly famous for food prepared with imagination and style – 'the best English food in Britain', said *The Times* – and offers an extensive wine list of over 300 bins. Special breaks available. Closed December, January and February.
Places of interest nearby: Dove Cottage and Rydal Mount (Wordsworth's houses) are both one mile away. **Directions: White Moss House is off the A591 between Rydal Water and Grasmere, on the right as you drive north to Grasmere.**

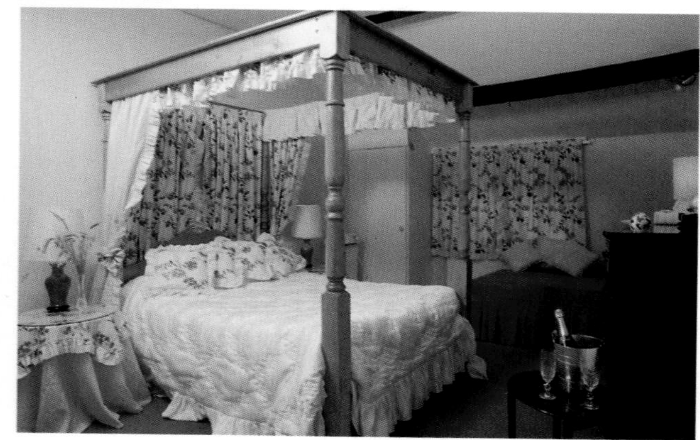

For hotel location, see maps on pages 263–269

The Old Rectory

GREAT SNORING, FAKENHAM, NORFOLK NR21 OHP
TEL: 01328 820597 FAX: 01328 820048

OWNERS: Rosamund and William Scoles

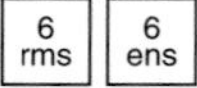  

S: £69.50
D: £87–£95

The Old Rectory, a former manor house, stands in $1^1/_2$ acres of walled gardens amid the unspoilt countryside of North Norfolk. It is believed to date back to 1500, when it was the seat of Sir Ralph Shelton. The house was originally hexagonal and the south east façade has stone mullioned windows bordered with frieze designs in terracotta tiles. Development and restoration work during the Victorian era account for its present day appearance.

The timeless tradition of the Old Rectory's décor and furnishings creates an ambience of bygone days, with fresh flowers adding a homely touch to the surroundings. Each bedroom has a private bathroom, colour television and direct dial telephone.

Full English breakfast is served in the dining room and luncheon hampers are provided on request. Traditional English cuisine is a speciality.

For those who like to be cosseted, without the restrictions associated with traditional hotel service, the Sheltons cottage apartments are available. These are serviced and self contained providing guests complete privacy in delightful surroundings, ideal for family use. The house is closed from 24–27 December.

Places of interest nearby: Norfolk coast, nature reserves, Sandringham and Walsingham. **Directions: Great Snoring is 3 miles north-east of Fakenham from the A148 King's Lynn–Cromer road.**

For hotel location, see maps on pages 263–269

Sandringham Hotel

3 HOLFORD ROAD, HAMPSTEAD VILLAGE, LONDON NW3 1AD
TEL: 0171 435 1569 FAX: 0171 431 5932

OWNERS: Linda and Peter Long

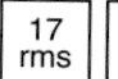  

S: £70–£85
D: £115–£130
Suite: £140

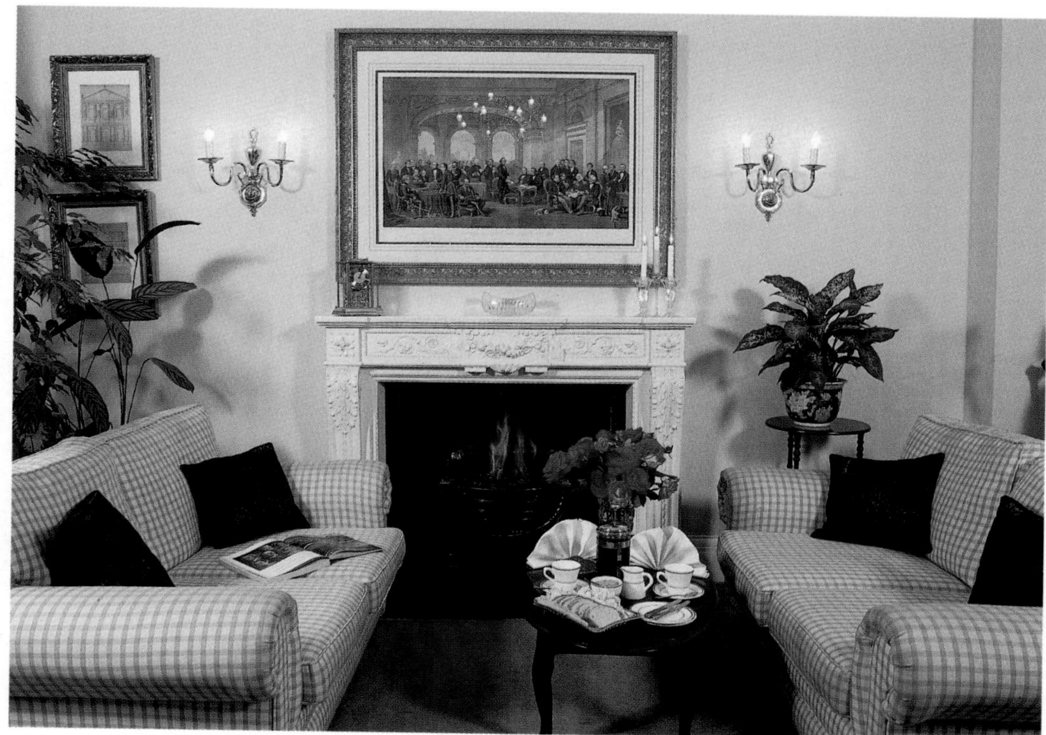

Just minutes' walk from the heart of Hampstead Village, Sandringham Hotel is tucked away in a quiet residential side street. This lively, cosmopolitan London suburb is a historic haunt of artists and writers, containing these days a wealth of restaurants, bars, galleries and boutiques.

Yet to the rear of this friendly and welcoming hotel is somewhere to relax. The walled garden is a charming oasis with its miniature pool and abundant greenery: here is the ideal spot to unwind after a day's work or sightseeing.

In less clement weather the stylish and serenely comfortable lounge with its open hearth and draped bay window provides a more than adequate alternative.

The bedrooms are cosy with rich fabrics and soft furnishings, comfortable beds and gold-tapped bathrooms. One room at the top of the house enjoys views as far distant as London's Millennium Dome, while the quietest bedrooms and an informal breakfast room overlook the garden.

The hotel has no restaurant, but tea, coffee and other refreshments are available and there is a multifarious choice of dining venues within walking distance.

Places of interest nearby: London's West End with its theatres and attractions is only 15 minutes by Underground on the Northern Line. **Directions: From Hampstead Underground station, turn uphill into Heath Street. The fourth turning on the right leads into Holford Road.**

HAMPTON COURT (Hampton Wick)

CHASE LODGE

10 PARK ROAD, HAMPTON WICK, KINGSTON-UPON-THAMES, SURREY KT1 4AS
TEL: 0181 943 1862 FAX: 0181 943 9363

OWNERS: Nigel and Denise Stafford-Haworth

11 rms | 11 ens | SMALL HOTEL

S: from £62
D: from £71

Chase Lodge is situated in Hampton Wick, adjacent to Bushy Park, in a conservation area of outstanding architectural and historical merit. Indeed, it is an ideal touring centre for places of historical interest such as Kew Gardens, Hampton Court Palace, Richmond Theatre and Royal Windsor.

Its proximity to so many major events makes Chase Lodge a popular choice for good accommodation. The Wimbledon Tournament, the Oxford and Cambridge Boat Race, racing at Kempton, Epsom, Ascot and Sandown, rugby at Twickenham and summer regattas at Kingston and Richmond are among the attractions within easy reach.

Originally built in 1870, Chase Lodge is a very successful small hotel, run with style and personality by proprietors Nigel and Denise Stafford-Haworth. The interiors have been designed to a high standard with well-chosen items of furniture and striking fabrics. The bedrooms, although not large, are beautifully appointed.

Private parties and functions can be accommodated. **Places of interest nearby:** Hampton Court, Windsor Castle and Richmond Park. **Directions: From the centre of Kingston take the A308 towards Hampton Court. Just after Kingston bridge is the Hampton Wick roundabout; take the White Hart exit into High Street (A310), the left at The Forresters into Park Road.**

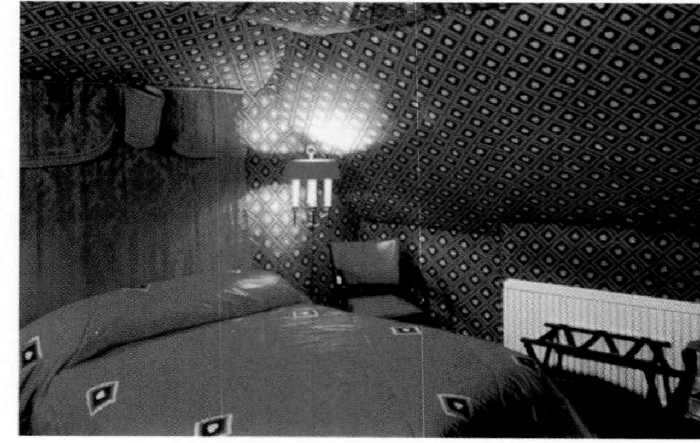

For hotel location, see maps on pages 263–269

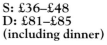

Grove House

HAMSTERLEY FOREST, NR BISHOP AUCKLAND, CO DURHAM DL13 3ML
TEL: 01388 488203 FAX: 01388 488174 E-MAIL: X0V47@dial.pipex.com

OWNERS: Helene Close

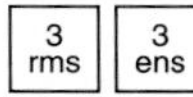

S: £36–£48
D: £81–£85
(including dinner)

Grove House nestles at the heart of a beautiful garden in the middle of glorious Hamsterley Forest. Two small rivers run, on each side of the property, through 5,000 acres of old oaks and moors. It is an idyllic situation. Peaceful, quiet and historical, the house was built in 1830 as an aristocrat's shooting box and it exudes grandeur. There are fine furnishings and fabrics, stylish décor and open fires. The bedrooms, two doubles with en suite bathroom, a twin with en suite shower and toilet – have full facilities and are extremely comfortable. This is a non smoking house.

Helene prepares five-course evening meals from the best fresh ingredients. Often on the set menu are venison and pheasant direct from the forest. Grove House is unlicensed so guests are invited to take their own wine.

Those requiring total seclusion can stay at the adjoining, fully fitted, three-bedroomed Grove Cottage which has a large patio and a hillside rock garden.

Places of interest nearby: Bowes Museum, Raby Castle, High Force waterfall, Killhope Wheel, Beamish Open Air Museum and Durham Cathedral. **Directions: From A1(M) turn off onto A68 and just over two miles after Toft Hill turn left, through Hamsterley Village until the sign for "The Grove". Follow road to right, then left and continue until right hand turn sign for Hamsterley Forest. Grove House is three miles further on.**

For hotel location, see maps on pages 263–269

THE WHITE HOUSE

10 PARK PARADE, HARROGATE, NORTH YORKSHIRE HG1 5AH
TEL: 01423 501388 FAX: 01423 527973 E-MAIL: whitehouse–hotel@demon.co.uk

OWNER: Jennie Forster

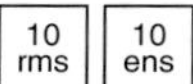

S: £70–£95
D: £95–£140

The White House enjoys a splendid location overlooking the Stray, 200 acres of parkland just a few minutes from the town centre. You will discover a unique residence in which luxury and comfort have blended with informality creating a relaxed atmosphere. The en suite bedrooms are individually furnished with designer fabrics and antiques together with full facilities.

The Venetian Room Restaurant offers a wide variety of exquisite and original dishes, with a very fine wine list.

Some of the many awards the hotel has achieved recently are 'Which?' County Hotel of the Year, A.C.E. Best Small Hotel, AA two Rosettes for cuisine, RAC Restaurant and Hospitality awards.

A perfect hotel for a private house party or wedding, where attention to detail is a foregone conclusion.

Places of interest nearby: Harrogate is a spa town with its own Turkish bath, beautiful parks and gardens and numerous shops including antiques. Other attractions include Fountains Abbey, Harewood House and the Yorkshire Dales. **Directions: The White House is situated on The Stray and is set back from the A59. Request a map when booking for detailed directions.**

For hotel location, see maps on pages 263–269

Rookhurst Georgian Country House Hotel

WEST END, GAYLE, HAWES, NORTH YORKSHIRE DL8 3RT
TEL: 01969 667454 FAX: 01969 667454

OWNER: Iris Van der Steen

S: £60
D: £100–£120
(including dinner)

Nestling in the midst of Wensleydale, the front gate of this part-Georgian, part-Victorian country house opens onto the 250 mile-long Pennine Way. Visitors to Rookhurst are welcomed as friends by proprietress Iris Van der Steen. The cosy oak-beamed Georgian bedrooms and more spacious Victorian bedrooms are furnished with half-tester or four-poster beds: the Bridal Suite and master four-poster rooms are particularly ornate. Smoking is not permitted in the bedrooms or the dining room.

Iris specialises in traditional home-cooked English dishes, made with fresh produce. Dinner in the restaurant is a candle-lit ceremony.

A wood-burning stove creates a snug atmosphere in the sitting room and bar, where guests can relax with a drink. The hotel is closed during January. Special break rates available.

Places of interest nearby: Rookhurst makes an ideal base for exploring Herriot country – the Yorkshire Dales are a delight for both serious walkers and strollers. Nearby is the Carlisle to Settle railway and you can be collected from Garsdale Station. Just round the corner is the Wensleydale Creamery, and in Hawes the Upper Dales folk museum. **Directions: Take A684 Sedbergh–Bedale road. At Hawes take Gayle Lane to Gayle. At the top of the lane turn right and the hotel is 300 yards further on the right.**

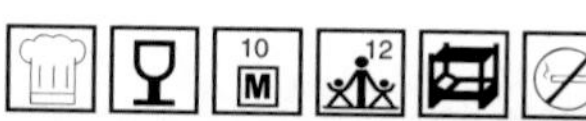

For hotel location, see maps on pages 263–269

RYEDALE COUNTRY LODGE

NUNNINGTON, NEAR HELMSLEY, YORK, NORTH YORKSHIRE YO6 5XB
TEL: 01439 748246 FAX: 01439 748346

OWNERS: Peter and Gerd Handley
CHEF: Robert Thomson

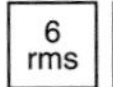 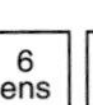  

S: £40–£45
D: £70–£76

Ryedale Country Lodge is set in four acres of lawned gardens and offers a setting of complete tranquillity. New owners, Peter and Gerd Handley, have totally refurbished the property, creating comfortable and cosy accommodation. There are six prettily decorated bedrooms and an intimate lounge where an open fire burns in the cool winter months.

Breakfast is served in the conservatory, which looks out over the countryside to the Vale of Pickering. In a dining room full of antique furniture, delicious cuisine is served, with a choice of eight mouth-watering starters and an excellent selection of meat and vegetarian main courses. Dishes are complemented by an extensive and imaginative wine list. The surrounding area is renowned for its sporting facilities, with seven great racecourses and 20 superb golf courses. Trout fishing is available to guests and horse-riding can also be arranged.

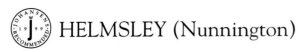

Places of interest nearby: The charming market town of Helmsley is just 5 miles away, beyond which lie the coastal towns of Whitby and Scarborough. The house is 30 minutes from York and 15 minutes from North York Moors National Park. Guests can stroll down to the nearby river and there are many lovely local walks. Castle Howard and Nunnington Hall are also close by. **Directions: Ryedale Country Lodge lies 1 mile west of Nunnington Village, which is south-east of Helmsley and north of York.**

For hotel location, see maps on pages 263–269

Nansloe Manor

MENEAGE ROAD, HELSTON, CORNWALL TR13 0SB
TEL: 01326 574691 FAX: 01326 564680

OWNERS: The Ridden Family

  S: £45–£59
D: £75–£120

This enchanting Georgian manor stands in romantic Daphne du Maurier country and guests are instantly aware they are coming to somewhere very special, as they approach the house along the tree lined drive.

Discovering Nansloe is serendipity – peaceful, surrounded by verdant, rural countryside, the hotel is owned (and managed) by the Ridden family, who have personally added so much to its warm ambience.

The bedrooms have lovely views across the Loe Valley. Each differs from the next, all are spacious and luxurious, with curtains and covers in gorgeous fabrics.

The drawing room has a fine Victorian fireplace, a welcome sight on cool evenings. It is charmingly furnished, big bowls of fresh flowers adding colour; the overall effect is relaxing – the ideal spot for a traditional Cornish tea or apéritif, in summer enjoyed alfresco on the croquet lawn.

The two AA Rosette restaurant is famed for its inspired menus, featuring local specialities including fish fresh from the sea, and the cellar contains excellent wines.

Places of interest nearby: Helston, Falmouth, St Ives and many gardens. Golf and sailing. Special breaks are available. **Directions: The Manor is situated the end of a well signed drive some 300 yards from junction of A394 from Falmouth and A3083 to the Lizard.**

The Bowens Country House

FOWNHOPE, HEREFORDSHIRE HR1 4PS
TEL: 01432 860430 FAX: 01432 860430

OWNERS: Carol and Tony Hart

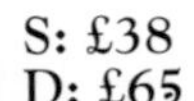

S: £38
D: £65

Surrounded by 1½ acres of mature garden and the outstanding natural beauty of the peaceful Wye Valley, this stone-built 17th century renovated farmhouse provides every modern comfort while retaining its bygone charm and character. It stands on the eastern edge of the village of Fownhope, nestling beneath wooded slopes, once the sites of Iron Age hill forts, of which there are many in the area. The fish filled River Wye meanders through meadows south of the village.

The hotel's cosy lounge opens onto the garden and features a magnificent inglenook, discovered during recent alterations. The en suite bedrooms, including four on the ground floor, offer every up-to-date facility and superb views over the garden and the village's 11th century church.

Traditional English cuisine is served in the compact dining room. Tucked away in the garden are a putting green and grass tennis court. Golf, riding, canoeing, fishing and horse racing are within easy reach. Half-board breaks are available all year round.

Places of interest nearby: Hereford, Ross-on-Wye and the beauties and attractions of the Wye Valley, the Malverns, Brecon Beacons and The Marches.

Directions: From the M50, exit at junction 4 and join the A449 towards Ledbury. After approximately 2½ miles turn onto the B4224 to Fownhope.

THE STEPPES

ULLINGSWICK, NR HEREFORD, HEREFORDSHIRE HR1 3JG
TEL: 01432 820424 FAX: 01432 820042

OWNERS: Henry and Tricia Howland

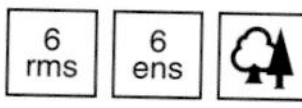

S: from £45
D: from £80

A Grade II listed 17th century yeoman's house, The Steppes is located in Ullingswick, a *Domesday Book* hamlet set in the Wye Valley. The gleaming whitewashed exterior conceals a host of original features. Cobble and flag-flooring, massive oak timbers and an inglenook fireplace were part of the ancient dairy and cider-making cellars, which form the splendid cellar bar and lounge.

Winner of the Johansens 1996 Value for Money Award", the ambience of the house has been applauded by *The Sunday Telegraph*, *The Guardian* and *The Independent* newspapers – all of which praise the enthusiasm and hospitality of owners Henry and Tricia Howland and, in particular, Tricia's cooking. The candlelit dinners are compiled from medieval recipes, revived local dishes, Mediterranean delicacies and French cuisine. The interesting breakfast menu is complemented by generous service. Exceptionally high standard en suite accommodation is provided in either the Tudor Barn or Courtyard Cottage, both located within the grounds. Closed for two weeks before Christmas and three weeks after New Year.

Places of interest nearby: River Wye (salmon fishing), Black Mountains, Malvern Hills (Elgar's birthplace), Welsh Marches, Gloucester and Worcester. Riding can be arranged. **Directions: A mile off A417 Gloucester–Leominster, signed Ullingswick.**

For hotel location, see maps on pages 263–269

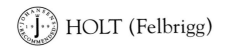

FELBRIGG LODGE

AYLMERTON, NORTH NORFOLK NR11 8RA
TEL: 01263 837588 FAX: 01263 838012.

OWNERS: Jill and Ian Gillam

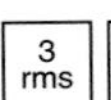 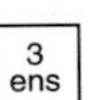 

S: £65
D: £90
Suite: £110

Jill and Ian Gillam have created this charming Lodge with the aim of providing the highest possible standards of accommodation in North Norfolk in a setting of total quiet and relaxation. Evoking an informal and welcoming ambience, the Lodge provides complete freedom for guests to mix with others or to seek solitude. Here time has stood still. Nothing disturbs over 70 different species of birds and other wildlife amongst rolling lawns and specimen trees and shrubs.

Felbrigg Lodge enjoys an unrivalled position just outside the Felbrigg Hall estate, a 17th century house owned by the National Trust. Approached by a long drive, the eight acres of grounds are totally secluded. The rooms, which are all at ground level, are situated around the gardens to take the greatest advantage of the view and landscape. All are sumptuously decorated with flair and imagination and have luxurious en suite bathrooms. Full English breakfasts and candlelit dinners are served in the converted stables. Jill is an enthusiastic cook and uses the best local produce.

Guests may relax in the privacy of their own rooms, wander at leisure through the gardens, play croquet, take afternoon tea in the summer house or swim in the heated indoor pool. A small, well-equipped gym is provided for the more energetic. **Places of interest nearby:** Felbrigg Hall, Blickling Hall and Holkham Hall. The cathedral city of Norwich is worth a visit whilst the North Norfolk coast is just 2km away. **Directions: Please ring the Lodge for detailed directions and brochure.**

For hotel location, see maps on pages 263–269

UNDERLEIGH HOUSE

OFF EDALE ROAD, HOPE, HOPE VALLEY, DERBYSHIRE S33 6RF
TEL: 01433 621372 FAX: 01433 621324 E-MAIL: underleigh-house@btinternet.com

OWNERS: Barbara and Tony Singleton
CHEF: Tony Singleton

5 rms 5 ens

S: From £44
D: From £64
Suite: £94

Underleigh House is set on a hillside, less than 2 miles from the centre of the ancient Saxon village of Hope in the glorious Peak District National Park. Every bedroom in the house has either a countryside view or one over the lovely award-winning garden which in summer displays colourful tubs and baskets, roses and honeysuckle. There is a newly created suite under the old beams. A full range of modern amenities makes guests feel at home, including a colour television, tea/coffee making facilities and a resident teddy bear! Underleigh has a 5Q Premier Award from the AA.

Breakfast and evening meals are served in "house party" style around the scrubbed top kitchen table or the oak refectory table in the stone flagged dining hall. There is a choice of a hearty English breakfast or, for the smaller appetite, a continental breakfast, while an interesting and daily changing menu has a wide selection of classical and adventurous dishes available for the evening.

Half day pony treks start from the Edale centre and there is an abundance of golf courses. Cycle hire centres cater for those who wish to enjoy the scenery on wheels.

Places of interest nearby: Chatsworth, Haddon and Hardwick. The historic villages of Hope, Castleton, Hathersage and "Plague" Eyam are within a five mile radius.

Directions: From Hope take turning opposite church to Edale, 1 mile on where road bears right take left lane. Underleigh House is 1/3 mile on right.

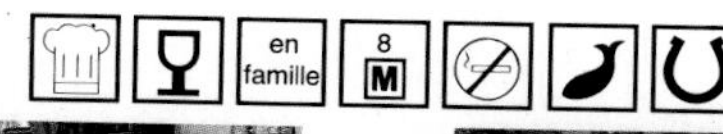

For hotel location, see maps on pages 263–269

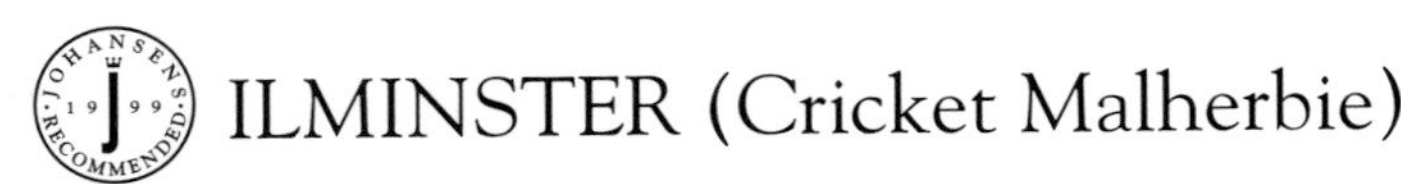

The Old Rectory

CRICKET MALHERBIE, ILMINSTER, SOMERSET TA19 0PW
TEL: 01460 54364 FAX: 01460 57374 E-MAIL: malherbie@aol.com

OWNERS: Michael and Patricia Fry-Foley, Ruth Parker

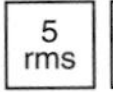  

 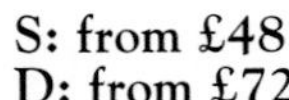

S: from £48
D: from £72

Set in the tiny hamlet of Cricket Malherbie, The Old Rectory is a delightful country house with Strawberry Hill Gothic windows, a thatched roof and weathered hamstone walls. The flagstoned hall leads guests through to the enchanting sitting room, adorned with exquisite carved oak beams and exuding a tranquil atmosphere.

The five bedrooms are peaceful and furnished in a very tasteful manner, some with Gothic windows and all overlooking the gardens. Well-equipped and offering every possible comfort, the rooms include en suite bathrooms and showers. This is a totally non-smoking property.

The dining room is beautifully presented with large shuttered windows affording views of the lawns on both sides of the house. Guests sit at the grand table in dinner-party fashion and indulge in the daily-changing four-course menu. Produce from the vegetable garden and local fish and game feature highly in the inspired dishes.

Places of interest: Those with an interest in architecture will be pleased with the location as Bath, Stonehenge, Wells and Glastonbury are ideal destinations for day trips. Monacute House, Barrington Court and Yeovilton Air Museum are all close by. **Directions: The nearest motorway is M5. Exit at junction 25, join A358 towards Chard at A303 roundabout take the Chard exit again onto A358. Drive through the village of Donyatt, turn left for Ilminster and then right for Cricket Malherbie.**

For hotel location, see maps on pages 263–269

Rylstone Manor

RYLSTONE GARDENS, SHANKLIN, ISLE OF WIGHT PO37 6RE
TEL: 01983 862806 FAX: 01983 862806

OWNERS: Neil Graham and Alan Priddle
CHEF: Neil Graham

   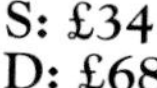

S: £34
D: £68

Neil Graham and Alan Priddle are the proud new owners of this hidden gem uniquely located in four and a half acres of tranquil gardens on the fringe of Shanklin. Just two minutes' walk away through the gardens are the promenade and beach and the manor enjoys stunning views out across Shanklin Bay.

An atmosphere of comfort and relaxation is engendered in the stylish day rooms where afternoon tea and a good book are just the thing on inclement days.

In the restaurant, Neil prepares a nightly table d'hôte menu with an eagle eye on the best available produce and an expert's touch in its preparation. Poached fillet of salmon, roast loin of lamb and breast of duck are served with imaginative, simple sauces.

Both the restaurant and bedrooms are designated non-smoking; no children under 15 are taken; and dogs are not permitted. Rylstone Manor is truly a haven of peace.

Places of interest nearby: For the more active, water sports, fishing, riding and golf can all be arranged. In addition to being a walkers' paradise, the island has many other manor houses and gardens to visit. Nearby are the thatched cottages of Shanklin Old Village, Queen Victoria's Osborne House, Carisbrook Castle and Rylstone Gardens Countryside Centre.

Directions: Just off the A3055 Sandown to Ventnor road in Shanklin Old Village, follow signs directly into Rylstone Gardens.

For hotel location, see maps on pages 263–269

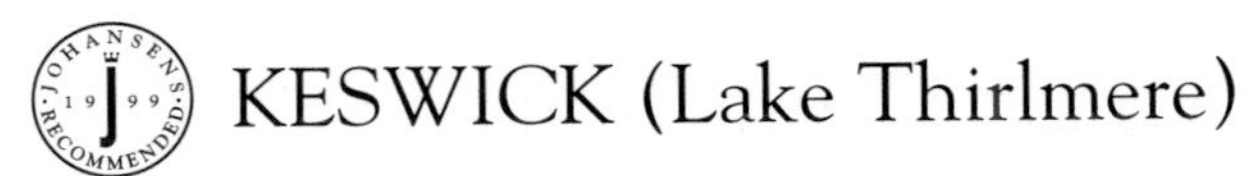

DALE HEAD HALL LAKESIDE HOTEL

THIRLMERE, KESWICK, CUMBRIA CA12 4TN
TEL: 017687 72478 FAX: 017687 71070 E-MAIL: stay@dale–head–hall.co.uk

OWNERS: Alan and Shirley Lowe and family

 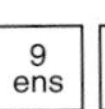 

S: £82–£99
D: £105–£170
(including 5 course dinner)

On the edge of Thirlmere, "the lake in the hollow", with only the sound of the birds breaking the silence stands Dale Head Hall. It is a truly scenic gem. At the foot of Helvellyn, almost completely surrounded by lush woodlands, this glorious 16th century house reigns alone on the shores of the lake and must surely command one of the most tranquil settings in the Lake District. Hosts Alan and Shirley Lowe and family, having restored the 16th century authenticity of the house, now offer exceptional accommodation and service. The hotel was deservedly runner-up for the Johansens 1995 Most Excellent Country House Hotel.

Bar and lounge are both delightful, sharing views over lake and mountains. The oak panelled dining room is the ideal place to enjoy the hotel's superb cuisine (Michelin; Good Food Guide; 2 AA Red Rosettes; RAC Restaurant Award). The bedrooms are extremely welcoming, warm and spacious and have all the things that you will expect to find, plus those little extras that make your stay so very special. Dale Head is one of those wonderful secrets which you would like to keep for yourself.

Places of interest nearby: All the splendours of the Lake District: Helvellyn is on the doorstep and Borrowdale is close by. **Directions: On the A591, halfway between Keswick and Grasmere. The hotel is situated along a private driveway overlooking Lake Thirlmere.**

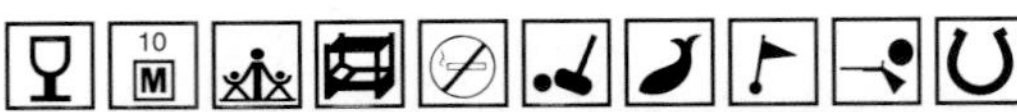

For hotel location, see maps on pages 263–269

SWINSIDE LODGE HOTEL

GRANGE ROAD, NEWLANDS, KESWICK, CUMBRIA CA12 5UE
TEL/FAX: 017687 72948

OWNER: Graham Taylor

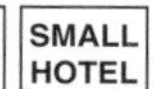

S: £73–£85
D: £128–£160
(including dinner)

Swinside Lodge, situated at the foot of Catbells, is a Victorian lakeland house, surrounded by hills, valleys and woodland, and close to the shores of Derwentwater.

The house has seven attractive en suite bedrooms, each offering a high degree of comfort and equipped with colour TV, radio, hairdryer, tea making facilities plus a wealth of extras. Begin your day with a hearty Cumbrian breakfast and later return to the comfort of the charming sitting rooms before enjoying your four-course dinner in the intimate candle-lit dining room. Menus change daily and a typical meal could include fillet of cod on a bed of salad of crushed potatoes with a dill vinagrette, a delicious soup with home-baked rolls followed by pan-fried breast and stuffed leg of guinea fowl with a red wine and shallot sauce with freshly cooked vegetables. A choice of puddings or a variety of British farmhouse cheeses is followed by coffee.

An AA Red Star hotel with 2 Rosettes for food and ETB 3 Crown De Luxe, Swinside Lodge is non-smoking and unlicensed but guests are welcome to bring wine of their own choice. Closed December to January.

Places of interest nearby: Keswick Pencil Museum, Castlerigg Stone Circle, Wordsworth's birthplace, excellent walks from the house. **Directions: M6 junction 40 take the A66 bypassing Keswick – over main roundabout – take second left. Go through Portinscale towards Grange; hotel is two miles further on the right.**

THE WHITE HOUSE

CHILLINGTON, KINGSBRIDGE, DEVON TQ7 2JX
TEL: 01548 580580 FAX: 01548 581124

OWNERS: Rob and Jenny Robson

8 rms | 8 ens | SMALL HOTEL

MasterCard VISA S: £45–£60 D: £70–£110

Standing in lawned and terraced gardens in rural South Devon, The White House has an atmosphere reminiscent of a quieter and less hurried age. A period Grade II listed building of great charm, the hotel is an ideal base for exploring the countryside and coastline.

To the west is the busy market town of Kingsbridge and the Salcombe Estuary famous for its sailing. To the north are Totnes, Dartington and the wild expanses of Dartmoor. Historic Dartmouth, Torquay and the English Riviera are to the east and south is the spectacular South Hams coastline with its rugged cliffs, sandy beaches and quiet coves.

The White House offers the utmost comfort with well-proportioned bedrooms, two of which are spacious suites. Guests can relax in the elegant Brockington Room and Doctor Smalley's Drawing Room which opens onto the south-facing terrace and garden. The Bar Lounge is another comfortable meeting place.

The Copper Beech Restaurant makes a delightful setting for enjoying appetising cuisine prepared by the chef who makes the maximum use of local and seasonal produce. **Places of interest nearby:** Kingsbridge, Totnes, Salcombe, Dartmouth, numerous picturesque villages and several National Trust properties. **Directions: Leave Totnes on the A381 to Kingsbridge and then turn left onto the A379 Dartmouth road to Chillington.**

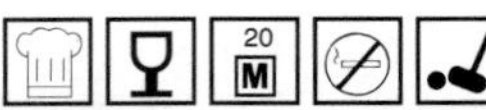

For hotel location, see maps on pages 263–269

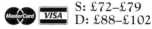

Hipping Hall

COWAN BRIDGE, KIRKBY LONSDALE, CUMBRIA LA6 2JJ
TEL: 015242 71187 FAX: 015242 72452

OWNERS: Ian and Jocelyn Bryant

7 rms | 7 ens

S: £72–£79
D: £88–£102

Hipping Hall is a 17th century country house set in three acres of walled gardens on the Cumbria/North Yorkshire borders, so an ideal centre from which to tour both the Lake District and Yorkshire Dales. Having just five double rooms and two cottage suites, this is an especially suitable venue for small groups wanting a place to themselves – families or friends celebrating an anniversary, golfing parties, corporate entertaining etc – and these house parties (available throughout the year) are a feature of Hipping Hall's success.

But from March to November it is mostly individual guests who enjoy the comfort and informality of staying with Ian and Jocelyn. The well-equipped bedrooms are largely furnished with antiques and all have attractive bathrooms. Guests help themselves to drinks from a sideboard in the conservatory before dining together at a large table in the Great Hall in a very informal dinner party style. Dinner is a set five course menu (including vegetarian dishes by prior request), served with three wines (optional) selected by Ian for that particular menu. All dishes are freshly prepared by Jocelyn, whose cooking draws so many people back to Hipping Hall.

Places of interest nearby: The Lake District, The Yorkshire Dales, The Settle to Carlisle Railway, Brontë country, Sizergh Castle. **Directions: Hipping Hall lies on the A65, two miles east of Kirkby Lonsdale towards Settle & Skipton, eight miles from M6 junction 36.**

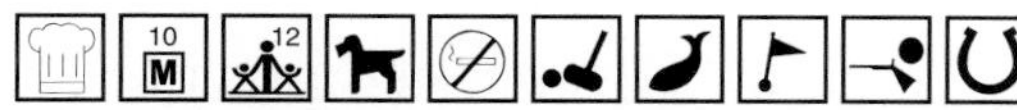

LAVENHAM PRIORY

WATER STREET, LAVENHAM, SUFFOLK CO10 9RW
TEL: 01787 247404 FAX: 01787 248472 E-MAIL: tim.pitt@btinternet.com

OWNERS: Tim and Gilli Pitt

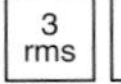  

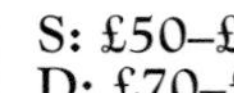

S: £50–£60
D: £70–£90

The magnificent timber-framed Priory was originally a 13th-century hall house and the home of Benedictine monks. Over succeeding centuries it passed through a number of illustrious families, including the Earls of Oxford. Although considerable alterations have been made through the ages, The Priory retains many original features. Ceilings are high and mullioned windows, exposed beams, flagged and oak boarded floors abound.

The Priory stands as a historical and intriguing bridge between past and present, a comfortable family home with modern furnishings and amenities.

At its heart is the heavily beamed Great Hall with a massive Tudor inglenook fireplace and a solid Jacobean staircase leading to the principal bedchambers decorated with Elizabethan wall-paintings. The bedrooms are spacious and comfortably furnished.

Guests can enjoy summer breakfast or a quiet drink in the sheltered herb garden surrounded by three acres of grounds. Dinner is by arrangement.

Places of interest nearby: Medieval Lavenham, the market town of Sudbury, birthplace of painter Thomas Gainsborough and many National Trust properties.

Directions: From Bury St Edmunds join A134 towards Sudbury then A1141 to Lavenham. From Colchester join A134 signed Sudbury. Take by-pass, signed Long Melford, right onto B1115 which becomes B1071 to Lavenham.

For hotel location, see maps on pages 263–269

Lower Bache House

KIMBOLTON, NR LEOMINSTER, HEREFORDSHIRE HR6 OER
TEL: 01568 750304

OWNERS: Rose and Leslie Wiles

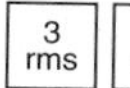

S: £31.50
D: £53

A Johansens award winner 4 miles from historic Leominster, Lower Bache is an oasis for nature lovers in 14 acres of a gentle Herefordshire valley. This substantial 17th century stone farmhouse has been restored by Rose and Leslie Wiles. While retaining its exposed stone walls, wealth of oak beams and flagstone flooring, it incorporates all the comforts of modern living. ETB Highly Commended. An annexe of three en suite bedrooms is furnished in a charming cottage style. Each bedroom has its own private sitting room. Water colours, original prints, plants, books and ornaments create an atmosphere of quality and comfort. With its vaulted ceiling and original cider mill, the dining room is unique. Rose and Leslie are acclaimed gourmet cooks: the four-course set menu is superb value. Bread, ice-cream and preserves are all home-made; fish, game and poultry are smoked on the premises and most of the vegetables are grown organically in the garden. The breakfast menu offers an exceptional choice including laverbread, kedgeree, sautie bannocks, floddies and scrambled eggs with smoked salmon. Organic wines are also available.

Places of interest nearby: The Marches, Ludlow, Hereford, Worcester and Hay-on-Wye. 13 golf courses and 3 race courses are situated within 25 miles. **Directions: Kimbolton village is 2 miles north-east of Leominster (which is off the A49). Lower Bache is signposted at the top of the hill on the Leysters road A4112.**

For hotel location, see maps on pages 263–269

LIFTON (Sprytown)

The Thatched Cottage Country Hotel and Restaurant

SPRYTOWN, LIFTON, DEVON PL16 0AY
TEL: 01566 784224 FAX: 01566 784334 E-MAIL: victoria@thatchedcott.u-net.com

OWNERS: Garth and Rita Willing and Victoria Bryant and Janet Purr

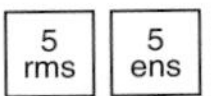

S: £42.50–£55.50
D: £85–£111

Nestling on the edge of Dartmoor in 2½ acres of landscaped gardens, The Thatched Cottage Country Hotel & Restaurant is just 1 mile from the Saxon village of Lifton. The bedrooms are situated in a converted coach house a few yards from the main thatched house. All rooms are decorated in a charming cottage style and have lovely views of the surrounding countryside.

The 16th century thatched cottage houses the restaurant, where a leisurely breakfast is served until 10am. The restaurant has been awarded two stars and a rosette by the AA for food and service. The menu which changes regularly plus an extensive wine list offers a varied and imaginative choice for the gourmet.

The lounge, with its inglenook fireplace, comfortable armchairs and cosy atmosphere, is the ideal place to enjoy apéritifs, after-dinner coffee, liqueurs and petits fours.

The premises are unsuitable for very young children. **Places of interest nearby:** Well-placed for exploring Exmoor, Bodmin Moor and Dartmoor. This is an area rich in sites of historical, architectural and archeological interest. **Directions: From Exeter, follow the A30 for about 35 miles. Leave the A30 at Stowford Cross. At the top of the slip road at the T-junction turn left (the hotel is signposted) and travel to Sprytown Cross, straight across, the hotel drive is 100 yards on right.**

For hotel location, see maps on pages 263–269

WASHINGBOROUGH HALL

CHURCH HILL, WASHINGBOROUGH, LINCOLN LN4 1BE
TEL: 01522 790340 FAX: 01522 792936 E-MAIL: washingborough.hall@btinternet.com

OWNERS: David Hill and Margaret Broddle

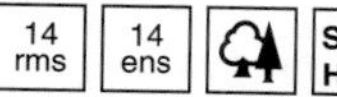

S: £56.50–£69
D: £79.50–£91.50

This listed Georgian Manor House is set in three acres of secluded grounds, containing many mature trees and some wonderful displays of fuchsias and begonias. There is also a large lawned area where guests can play croquet.

The individually and prettily furnished bedrooms offer a full range of modern comforts, with some having a four-poster bed, some a spa bath.

A good selection of real ales is served in the bar, while the Wedgwood Dining Room overlooks the garden and provides the perfect setting for a meal. The imaginative menu caters for all tastes and is complemented by an extensive list of carefully selected wines. RAC Restaurant Award and RAC Hospitality, Comfort and Restaurant Award. Guests at Washingborough Hall have access to the Canwick Golf Club and hard tennis courts.

Places of interest nearby: The city of Lincoln is just two miles away and has a magnificent 11th century cathedral and castle. A short drive away is the beautiful rolling countryside of the Lincolnshire Wolds with many unspoilt villages and market towns to visit. Aircraft buffs should head for The Battle of Britain Memorial Flight, The Aviation Heritage Centre and The Newark Air Museum.

Directions: From Lincoln take the B1188 towards Branston and then turn left onto the B1190 towards Bardney. Turn right (approx two miles) opposite telephone box. The Hall is 200 yards on the left.

For hotel location, see maps on pages 263–269

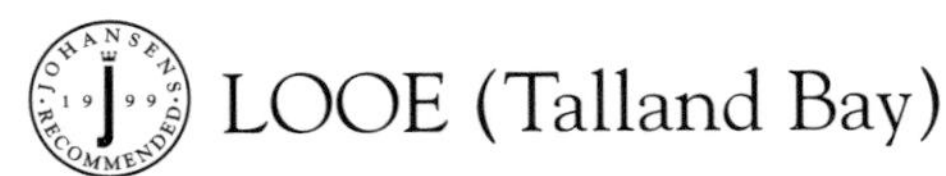

Allhays Country House

TALLAND BAY, LOOE, CORNWALL PL13 2JB
TEL: 01503 272434 FAX: 01503 272929 E-MAIL: allhayscountryhouse@BTinternet.com

OWNERS: Brian and Lynda Spring

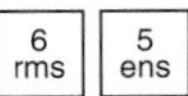

S: £30–£39.50
D: £60–£79

Set in its own gardens, just a few minutes' walk from the sea, Allhays stands on a gently sloping hillside overlooking Talland Bay. Situated between Looe and the fishing village of Polperro, it lies on a spectacular stretch of rugged coastline, much frequented by smugglers for many years. As a quiet retreat, Allhays is as attractive to those who wish to relax in comfort as it is to guests with a more energetic holiday in mind. Allhays is closed from 24 December to 7 January.

The bedrooms, most of which offer magnificent views, have a radio alarm, tea/coffee making facilities and electric over-blankets for the out-of-season months. Until the arrival of summer, a log fire blazes in the lounge where drinks are served from the bar.

This corner of Cornwall is a living larder of wholesome produce – early vegetables, dairy cattle, Cornish cream, farmhouse cheese, garden herbs, soft fruits and fresh seafood are all made use of by chef-patronne, Lynda Spring. Food is cooked with an Aga in the traditional way, using recipes that have become an integral part of West Country life and she has been awarded an AA Rosette for her cuisine.

Places of interest nearby: Miles of walking along National Trust coastline, quaint fishing villages and the smugglers museum of Polperro. Water sports, riding and golf can be arranged locally. **Directions: From Looe take the A387 signposted to Polperro. After approximately 2 miles you will see Allhays signposted on the left-hand side.**

For hotel location, see maps on pages 263–269

Coombe Farm

WIDEGATES, NR LOOE, CORNWALL PL13 1QN
TEL: 01503 240223 FAX: 01503 240895

OWNERS: Alexander and Sally Low

S: £28–£36
D: £56–£72

Coombe Farm was originally part of a large estate and the house was built in 1928 for a nephew of the landowner. It enjoys magnificent views down an unspoilt wooded valley to the sea and is set in 10½ acres of lawns, meadows, woods, streams and ponds.

A warm, friendly and relaxed atmosphere pervades the house, which has been carefully furnished with antiques and paintings. Open log fires in the winter months add to the sense of comfort and cosiness. All the bedrooms offer lovely country views and are cheerfully decorated and centrally heated.

A full English breakfast is served at Coombe Farm and in the evening a four-course dinner is available in the lovely candlelit dining room. The traditional menu is changed daily and vegetarians are well catered for.

There are over three acres of lawns where guests are invited to soak up the sun, play croquet or swim in the heated outdoor swimming pool and there is a snug stone outhouse for snooker and table tennis. The farm is closed to guests from 1 November to 1 March.

Places of interest nearby: Coombe Farm is ideal for visiting all parts of Cornwall and most of Devon – The Coastal Path, fishing villages, old smuggling coves and beaches. Dartmoor and Bodmin Moor, many superb National Trust houses and gardens. **Directions: B3253 just south of Widegates village, 3½ miles east of Looe.**

THE OLD MANOR HOTEL

11-14 SPARROW HILL, LOUGHBOROUGH, LEICESTERSHIRE LE11 1BT
TEL: 01509 211228 FAX: 01509 211128 E-MAIL: bookings@oldmanor.com

OWNER: Roger Burdell

  S: £65–£85
D: £75–£140

Overlooking the ancient churchyard of All Saints parish church at the heart of old Loughborough, the Old Manor Hotel is a treasure trove of history. A former manor house, it was rebuilt in the 1480s and later remodelled by Edward, First Lord Hastings of Loughborough, Lord Chamberlain to Queen Mary Tudor, in the mid 16th century. Today it is a lovely little hotel, full of interesting furnishings and superb fabrics. Alongside many antiques, some of the fine furniture has been beautifully made by the owner.

The Old Manor has undergone many alterations and renovations over the centuries. Today it has all modern comforts but retains a number of original features. These include extensive exposed beams and timberwork, particularly in the beautifully furnished bedrooms. The décor is individual, rich and earthy throughout with an emphasis on comfort and an atmosphere of total friendliness. The Old Manor is an entirely non-smoking house.

Although recently developed into a hotel the building has been a restaurant in the ownership of Roger Burdell for more than 15 years. His menus are thoughtfully planned. The food is simple but innovative with an Italian influenced style.

Places of interest nearby: Charnwood Forest, with some of the oldest rock formations in the country, Bardon Hill and Beacon Hill which provide spectacular views. **Directions: Exit M1 at Jct23 and take A512 Ashby Road into Loughborough centre. Sparrow Hill is at the junction with Church Gate.**

For hotel location, see maps on pages 263–269

Delbury Hall

DIDDLEBURY, CRAVEN ARMS, SHROPSHIRE SY7 9DH
TEL: 01584 841267 FAX: 01584 841441 E-MAIL: wrigley@delbury.demon.co.uk

OWNERS: Patrick and Lucinda Wrigley

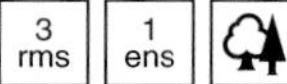

S: £50
D: £85–£95

Delbury, built in 1753 and probably Shropshire's most beautiful Georgian mansion, faces south across water meadows to medieval Ludlow, with a backdrop of the Clee Hills and the Wenlock Edge. Approached through 80 acres of landscaped parkland, the house is in a tranquil setting, surrounded by flower-filled gardens and overlooking a lake with ornamental ducks.

Delbury is a family house with bedrooms available for guests, one with a four-poster, one with a half-tester, all with private bathrooms (one en suite) and all recently restored to a high standard. The large entrance hall has the original oak staircase, leading up to a first floor gallery on three sides and there is a large drawing room and sitting rooms for guests' use.

Guests dine at one large table in the dining room, where Patrick, an enthusiastic cook, who has completed an advanced course at Leith's School of Food and Wine in London, serves the finest home produced food; smoked salmon from the house smoker, home cured prosciutto, fresh vegetables from the walled garden, eggs and hand-churned butter.

Places of interest nearby: Ludlow Castle. Offa's Dyke (built centuries ago to fend off the Welsh), Stokesay Castle, a 13th century manor house five miles away, and the Severn Valley Steam Railway. **Directions: On the B4368 between Craven Arms and Much Wenlock.**

For hotel location, see maps on pages 263–269

Overton Grange Hotel

OVERTON, LUDLOW, SHROPSHIRE SY8 4AD
TEL: 01584 873500 FAX: 01585 873524

OWNERS: Grange Hotels Ltd, Christine Ward
MANAGER: Ignacio Gonzalez
CHEF: Claude Bosi

16 rms 16 ens

S: £55
D: £81–£92

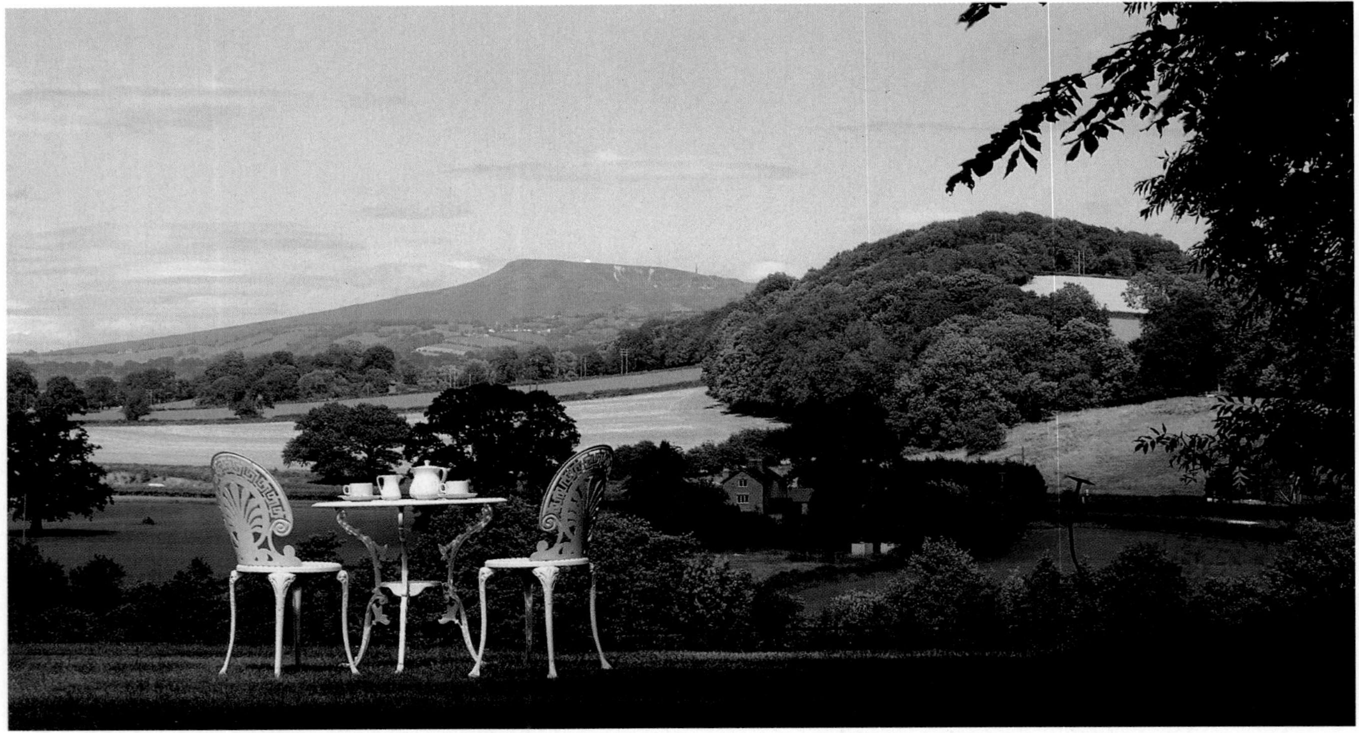

The setting of Overton Grange Hotel, which stands in 2½ acres of peaceful gardens overlooking the scenic Shropshire countryside, would be hard to rival for guests seeking to relax and refresh their spirits. A genuinely friendly and courteous staff delivers a first class personal service.

Most of the generously sized and elegant bedrooms offer excellent views over the landscape and have been individually designed with the highest standards of comfort in mind. Similar attention to detail has been paid in the spacious and attractive public rooms. For a quiet drink there is a choice of location – the cosy cocktail bar or the conservatory, which opens out onto the gardens and patio.

A comfortable oak-panelled restaurant is the setting in which to enjoy the gastronomic delights of the chef – pan-fried sea bass with braised carrots, rack of pork with Maracaire potatoes and vegetable chips and pineapple and prune fritters with Armagnac ice cream.

Sporting facilities such as tennis, swimming, fishing, golf and riding are all available within the local area.

Places of interest nearby: The hotel is only 1½ miles from the centre of the beautiful country town of Ludlow with its impressive castle and interesting museum. Stokesay Castle and Berrington Hall are also within easy reach. **Directions: From A49, exit 2 miles South of Ludlow, take B4361 Ludlow-Richard Castle road. The hotel is about ¼ mile along this road.**

130 M

For hotel location, see maps on pages 263–269

Little Offley

HITCHIN, HERTFORDSHIRE SG5 3BU
TEL: 01462 768243 FAX: 01462 768243

OWNERS: Martin and Lady Rosemary French

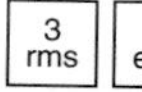  

 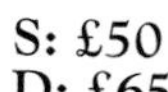

S: £50
D: £65

Set in 800 acres of farmland in the Chiltern Hills, Little Offley, not a hotel but a beautiful 17th century country house, affords wonderful views over the garden and surrounding countryside. One complete wing of the house has been set aside for guests and it provides a quiet haven comprising a large drawing room with a listed carved fireplace, dining room and 3 double bedrooms with bathrooms. The rooms are spacious and comfortable and there is an outdoor swimming pool available for guests' use in summer.

Accommodation is offered on a bed-and-breakfast basis. Lunch and dinner for larger groups can be provided, as can meetings, small exhibitions and receptions. Alternatively, there are 4 pubs – all of them with excellent restaurants – in the nearby village of Great Offley, $1^1/_2$ miles away. Guests may leave their car at the house when flying from Luton Airport. No children under 12.

Places of interest nearby: Little Offley is an ideal touring base from which to visit Hatfield House, Luton Hoo and Whipsnade Zoo, Woburn Abbey and Cambridge. The nearest town is Hitchin, which has large open-air markets on Tuesdays and Saturdays. London is 30 minutes by train. **Directions: Take A505 Luton–Hitchin road. At Great Offley, turn off for Little Offley.**

For hotel location, see maps on pages 263–269

MOOR VIEW HOUSE

VALE DOWN, LYDFORD, DEVON EX20 4BB
TEL: 01822 820220 FAX: 01822 820220

OWNERS: David and Wendy Sharples
CHEF: Wendy Sharples

S: £45–£55
D: £78–£102

This small country house was built in 1869 and has offered hospitality to the traveller throughout its life. In the early years, the Victorian writer Eden Phillpotts was a regular visitor and it was here that he was inspired to write his most successful play, "A Farmer's Wife", and also "Widdicombe Fair". The property faces Dartmoor from the front, while to the rear are spectacular views across the Devon and Cornwall countryside. Wonderful vistas of the landscape are lit by the setting sun.

Always putting their guests' comfort first, the Sharples family has created a friendly hotel with a genuinely relaxing ambience. Awarded AA 5'QQQQQ. The reception rooms reflect the cheery glow of open fires and tasteful furnishings are a feature throughout. A Victorian decorative theme characterises the well-appointed bedrooms.

Sparkling crystal, bone china and gleaming silver in the dining room ensure that each meal is a special occasion. The daily four-course dinner menu embodies traditional country-style recipes using the finest local seasonal meat, fish and game, complemented by sound, sensibly priced wines.

Places of interest nearby: Lydford Gorge and Castle, Tavistock, Clovelly and Exeter. **Directions: From Exeter take A30 Okehampton bypass to Sourton Cross. Then take A386 signposted to Tavistock; Moor View's drive is situated four miles along on the right.**

For hotel location, see maps on pages 263–269

Thatch Lodge Hotel

THE STREET, CHARMOUTH, NR LYME REGIS, DORSET DT6 6PQ
TEL: 01297 560407 FAX: 01297 560407

OWNERS: Christopher and Andrea Worsfold
CHEF: Andrea Ashton-Worsfold

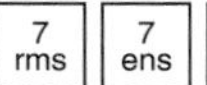
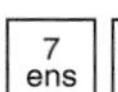

D:£75–£85
Four Poster/Half-Tester:£96

A former 14th century Monks Retreat for nearby Forde Abbey. Charmouth is internationally renowned for its Jurassic fossil-strewn beach. To the east is Golden Cap, the highest cliff on the south coast rising 617ft high, and to the west Lyme Regis, with its romantic Cobb which featured both in 'The French Lieutenant's Woman' and Jane Austen's 'Persuasion'.

Thatch Lodge itself makes its own unique contribution to an Area of Outstanding Natural Beauty – thatched roof, pink cobb walls, hanging baskets, oak beams, antiques, walled garden and a 200 year old vine. Each of the bedrooms has its own character, some have four poster and half tester beds. Luxury toiletries, crisp sheets, courtesy tray, television and thoughtful extras add to your comfort. E.T.B. 3 Crowns Highly Commended. Totally non-smoking.

An outstanding feature of the 'Thatch' is the dining. Andrea, a qualified chef, cooks to order, using the freshest seasonal produce, resulting in a meal that will delight the eye and the palate. The Daily Mail comments "I have never tasted a soufflé as good/delicious/perfect". Awarded two AA Rosettes for outstanding cuisine.

Places of interest nearby: Dorset Heritage Coast, Thomas Hardy Trail, Abbotsbury Swannery and subtropical gardens, Athelhampton House, BBC's 'Harbour Lights' location. Golf, tennis, riding, fishing, bird-watching and walking. **Directions: Charmouth is off the A35, two miles east of Lyme Regis.**

NEWSTEAD GRANGE

NORTON-ON-DERWENT, MALTON, NORTH YORKSHIRE YO17 9PJ
TEL: 01653 692502 FAX: 01653 696951

OWNERS: Pat and Paul Williams

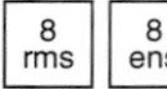

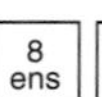

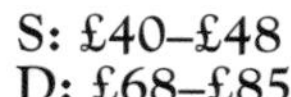

S: £40–£48
D: £68–£85

Enclosed in 2½ acres of gardens and grounds, Newstead Grange is an elegant Georgian country house with wonderful views of the Wolds and Moors. Resident owners Paul and Pat Williams extend a warm welcome to their guests, who are assured of personal attention.

The Grange maintains the quality and style of a country house restored. It has antique furniture and original features including working shutters and fine fireplaces. Open fires are lit in cooler months in one or both of the lounges. Bedrooms, all individual in character, have period furniture, paintings and prints. The Celebration Room contains an antique mahogany half-tester bed. Menus are prepared from the extensive organic kitchen garden and the best local produce, recognised by the AA Rosette award for fine food. Wines are selected to complement the food. Special diets are catered for.

Newstead Grange is an entirely non-smoking house. ETB Highly Commended. Closed end of October to early March. Special break rates available.

Places of interest nearby: The ancient market town of Malton, York, the North York Moors National Park and the East Coast. Stately homes (including Castle Howard), abbeys, scenic walks and drives. **Directions: Follow signs out of Malton and Norton-on-Derwent to Beverley. Newstead Grange is on the left, ½ mile beyond the last houses and at the junction with the Settrington Road**

For hotel location, see maps on pages 263–269

The Manor Farmhouse

DETHICK, MATLOCK, DERBYSHIRE DE4 5GG
Tel: 01629 534246

OWNERS: Harold and Ruth Groom

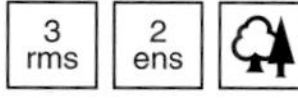

S: £30
D: £50

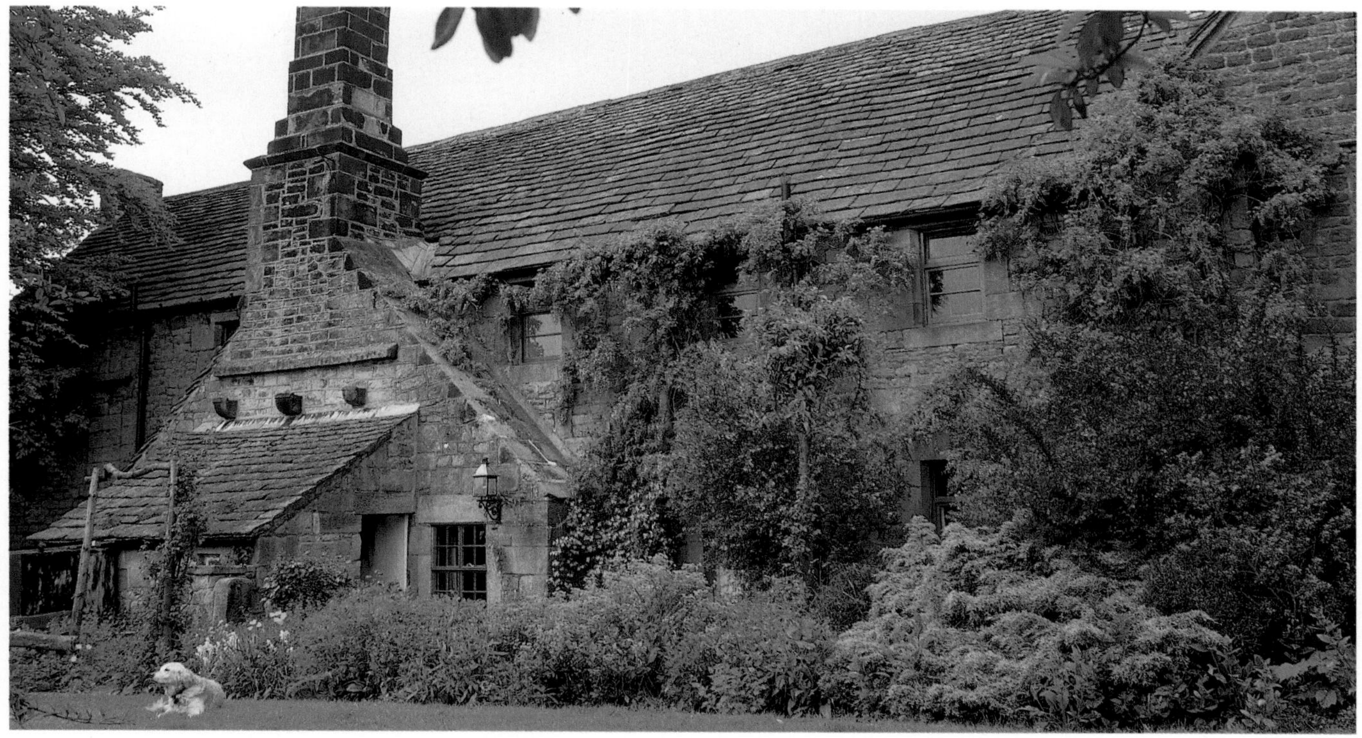

In the unspoilt hamlet of Dethick at the gateway to the beautiful Peak District, The Manor Farmhouse provides an ideal setting for relaxing breaks. It is surrounded by rolling Derbyshire countryside with enchanting walks, elegant stately homes and picturesque villages. Partly Tudor it has connections with Anthony Babington, whose misguided plot to assassinate Queen Elizabeth I cost him his own head. The house featured in Alison Uttley's book "A Traveller in Time" and often features in the 'Peak Practice' TV series.

Guests will find a friendly welcome and an informal atmosphere. With its stunning views and lovely garden it is perfect for those seeking seclusion.

There are three charming bedrooms, including two en suite with television. All have central heating and are comfortably furnished. English or Continental breakfast is served in a pretty room, with separate tables. There is a cosy upstairs sitting room with television. Evening meals can occasionally be provided by arrangement. Closed at Christmas.

Places of interest nearby: The Peak National Park, Matlock, the Heights of Abraham, the stately homes of Chatsworth, Hardwick Hall, Haddon Hall and the Crich Tramway Museum. **Directions: From the M1, exit at junction 28. Take A38 to Alfreton and then A615 towards Tansley and Matlock. Dethick is signposted left before Tansley.**

For hotel location, see maps on pages 263–269

Sheriff Lodge Hotel

THE DIMPLE, DIMPLE ROAD, MATLOCK, DERBYSHIRE DE4 3JX
TEL: 01629 760760 FAX: 01629 760860

OWNERS: Beverley-Anne and Peter Watmore

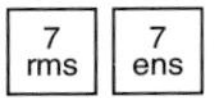 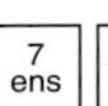  

 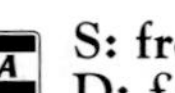 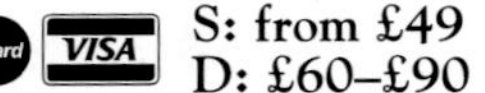

S: from £49
D: £60–£90

This charming 19th century stone-built town house still retains elements of its 17th century past. The base of Sheriff Lodge dates from 1750, whilst the rest of the house has been carefully restored and beautifully refurbished by the owner.

Once a thirteen room guest-house, it is now an opulent hotel with seven sybaritic bedrooms with en suite facilities. Each centrally heated room offers direct dial telephone, colour television, radio and many other amenities.

The Inglenook Restaurant takes its name from the main feature of the room, an exquisite fireplace. The menu comprises traditionally English dishes and country fayre and the wine cave offers a variety of wines. The uncompromising standard of service complements the extremely competitive prices.

The leisure pursuits of the Peak District include fishing, climbing and rambling.

Places of interest nearby: The area is surrounded by a variety attractions such as the amusement park Alton Towers and several National Trust properties. Chatsworth, Haddon Hall and Hardwick Hall are all located close by. **Directions: The nearest motorway is the M1, junction 26. Take the A610 to Ambergate, then travel north on the A6 to Matlock. From Bakewell Road take the first right up Dimple Road. The hotel is ½ mile on the left.**

For hotel location, see maps on pages 263–269

Periton Park Hotel

MIDDLECOMBE, NR MINEHEAD, SOMERSET TA24 8SN
TEL: 01643 706885 FAX: 01643 706885

OWNERS: Richard and Angela Hunt

   SMALL HOTEL

   S: £65 D: £96

As you climb the winding drive through the woods, rhododendrons and azaleas to this Victorian country house hotel on the edge of the Exmoor National Park, it is not hard to see why Periton Park is described as a place "where time stands still". Richard and Angela Hunt run the hotel in an efficient and friendly way ensuring that, while their guests are staying with them, they will be carefully looked after. All the rooms are spacious and well proportioned, enlivened with warm autumn colours to create a restful atmosphere.

The wood panelled restaurant, with its double aspect views over the grounds, is the perfect place to enjoy some of the finest food on Exmoor. Menus change with the seasons to reflect the best of West Country produce – fresh fish, local game, delicately cooked vegetables, local cheeses and Somerset wine.

Exmoor is for country lovers with miles of varied, unspoilt, breathtaking landscape. A perfect retreat from the trials of everyday life. Riding is available from stables next to the hotel. Shooting is also available in season. **Places of interest nearby:** Dunster Castle and Gardens, Knightshayes, Rosemoor, Selworthy, Arlington Court and Exmoor. **Directions: Exit M5 junction 24. Take the A39 towards Minehead. Follow signs to Porlock and Lynmouth. Hotel is on the left hand side.**

For hotel location, see maps on pages 263–269

Millers House Hotel

MIDDLEHAM, WENSLEYDALE, NORTH YORKSHIRE DL8 4NR
TEL: 01969 622630 FAX: 01969 623570 E-MAIL: hotel@millershouse.demon.co.uk

OWNERS: Judith and Crossley Sunderland

7 rms | 6 ens  SMALL HOTEL

S: £39–£75
D: £78–£93

The peaceful village of Middleham nestles in the heart of the Yorkshire Dales and the Millers House Hotel is a perfect base from which to explore James Herriot country. This elegant Georgian house has been decorated in period style, including a magnificent, fully canopied four-poster bedroom. A recent addition is an attractive conservatory. Voted Hotel of the Year runner up in the Yorkshire and Humberside Tourist Board White Rose Awards.

The restaurant has won an AA Red Rosette for the last few years. Extensive use is made of fresh local produce, complemented by a fine selection of sensibly priced wines. Especially popular are the gourmet wine-tasting weekends.

Close by is Middleham Castle, once the seat of Richard III. The village is now better known as a racehorse training centre and guests can combine enjoyment of the glorious views across Wensleydale and Coverdale with watching racehorses exercising on the moorland gallops. Racing breaks with a day at the races and a visit to a training yard are also popular. Millers House is open for Christmas and New Year breaks and is available for house parties.

Places of interest nearby: Bolton and Richmond Castles, Jervaulx Abbey, Aysgarth Falls, York, Harrogate and several golf courses. **Directions: Approaching from A1 take the A684 to Bedale and Leyburn; the left turning immediately before Leyburn takes you to Middleham. Millers House Hotel is in the centre of the village.**

For hotel location, see maps on pages 263–269

BURLEIGH COURT

MINCHINHAMPTON, GLOUCESTERSHIRE GL5 2PF
TEL: 01453 883804 FAX: 01453 886870

OWNERS: Ian and Fiona Hall

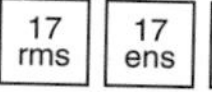

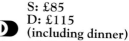

S: £85
D: £115
(including dinner)

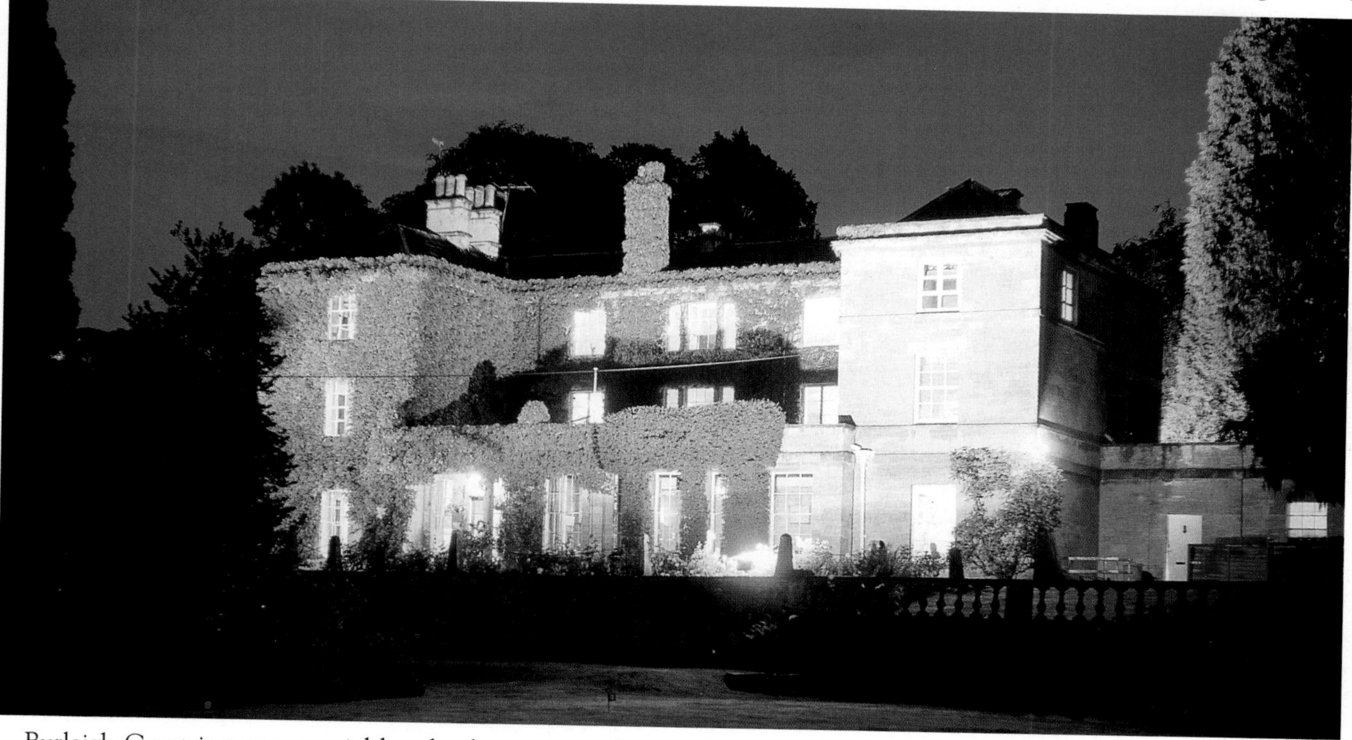

Burleigh Court is a very special hotel, where a warmth reminiscence of an era long forgotten greets all guests from the moment they arrive at this beautiful 18th century Gentleman's Manor House. Situated amidst 3.5 acres of lovingly restored landscape gardens with terrace, pool and hidden pathways, every visitor is beguiled into enjoying all the pleasures of a tranquil Cotswold life.

All of the 17 individually decorated bedrooms are full of character and recreate the atmosphere of staying in a family home with friends. Indeed the house is still owned and operated by a close-knit family. In the dining room the thoughtfully prepared dishes offer an ideal blend of traditional cooking, with simplicity, freshness and purity. Many of the herbs and salad vegetables are home-grown.

Places of interest nearby: Burleigh Court's setting in an area of outstanding natural beauty near Minchinhampton and Rodborough Commons affords the ideal location for touring the Southern Cotswolds, the Regency Spa towns of Bath and Cheltenham a short distance away and the picture postcard Cotswold villages on the doorstep.

Directions: Leave Stroud on the A419, heading towards Cirencester. 2½ miles outside Stroud take a right turn, signposted Burleigh and Minchinhampton, about 500 yards along this road there is a sharp left turn signposted Burleigh Court, the house will be on your right after a further 400 yards.

For hotel location, see maps on pages 263–269

WIGHAM

MORCHARD BISHOP, NR CREDITON, DEVON EX17 6RJ
TEL: 01363 877350 FAX: 01363 877350
FROM USA TOLL FREE: 1 800 805 8210

OWNERS: Stephen and Dawn Chilcott

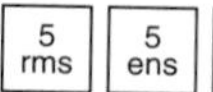
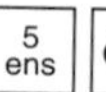

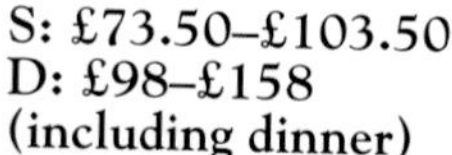

S: £73.50–£103.50
D: £98–£158
(including dinner)

Wigham is a 30-acre organic farm (currently in conversion to Soil Association Symbol) which supplies its kitchen with fresh lamb, beef and pork, eggs and dairy products. A picturesque, 16th century, thatched Devon longhouse adjoins this farm, providing comfortable accommodation. Good honest home cooking, complemented by an excellent wine list, are hallmarks of this delightful country house.

After dinner, guests may take coffee in the lounge. Please note Wigham is a no-smoking house.

Proprietors Stephen and Dawn Chilcott have created a warm and welcoming atmosphere at this charming retreat. The interiors are characterised by low ceilings, exposed beams, massive fireplaces and original wall panelling. The bedrooms are individually furnished in cottage style and have pretty, co-ordinated fabrics. In the honeymoon suite there is a rustic four-poster bed. All the bedrooms are en suite and have a television, video and direct dial telephone. For further entertainment there is a snooker lounge with a 7-foot table, a heated outdoor swimming pool with a barbecue and a well-equipped 'honour' bar.

Places of interest nearby: Exmoor, Dartmoor, Exeter, Tiverton and Barnstable. **Directions: From Morchard Bishop, take the road marked Chawleigh–Chumleigh, fork right after ¾ mile, and ¾ mile further on, on the right, is a small private road marked Wigham.**

ESHOTT HALL

MORPETH, NR NEWCASTLE-UPON-TYNE, NORTHUMBERLAND NE65 9EP
TEL: 01670 787777 FAX: 01670 786000 E-MAIL: eshott@btinternet.com

OWNERS: Ho and Margaret Sanderson

2 rms | 2 ens

S: £45–65
D: £70–95

Owned by the sixth generation of Sandersons, Eshott Hall is a private Georgian house and home, designed by Trollope. This listed building, used as a set for television costume dramas, sits in 32 acres of park and woodland where red squirrels and wild deer roam.

Built by Willaim the Conquerer, the hunting lodge and castle are this private estate's oldest monuments. The beautiful 17th century Hall is furnished with a touch of elegance and features spacious public rooms adorned with interesting paintings and antiques. The two bedrooms are well-appointed and have en suite facilities.

Guests dine in the charming dining room and indulge in the varied menu and excellent choice of wines. Fresh and seasonal produce is used in the fine, traditional cuisine. Private parties and small weddings can be held at the Hall, which is also frequented by clients for meetings and seminars. **Places of interest nearby:** The breathtaking Northumbrian Heritage Coastline is ideal for rambling and enjoying the surrounding landscape and there are extensive walks and nature trails around the grounds. A number of historic properties are within easy reach such as the castles at Alnwick and Bamburgh. Guests may peruse the shops in Newcastle's famous Metro shopping centre, situated in the city centre just 20 miles away. **Directions: Leave A1, 6m north of Morpeth and 9m south of Alnwick, turning east at the sign for Eshott. The Hall gates are about one mile on the left.**

see maps on pages 263–269

THE CORNISH COTTAGE HOTEL & GOURMET RESTAURANT

NEW POLZEATH, NORTH CORNWALL PL27 6UF
TEL: 01208 862213 FAX: 01208 862259

OWNERS: Derek and Marion Faulkner
CHEF: Martin Walker

S: £48–68
D: from £96

The Cornish Cottage Hotel is conveniently located close to the sandy West Country beach and overlooking the coastal village of New Polzeath. The hotel has recently undergone an extensive refurbishment at the request of its new owners.

Comfort is quintessential and the bedrooms, many with coastal and sea views, are furnished in a tasteful fashion. All rooms have en suite bathrooms or showers, colour televisions and refreshment trays.

The widely acclaimed Gourmet Restaurant, holder of the AA rosettes for fine cuisine, boasts an inspired choice of dishes to satisfy the most discriminating palate. The table d'hôte menu and à la carte meals are enhanced by the local produce and freshly caught fish and lobster.

The private outdoor swimming pool is available to guests only during the summer months. Guests may cycle along the Camel trail, visit the many famous golf courses or enjoy beautiful coastal walks and rambles along the beach. The area is a haven for water sports enthusiasts, with windsurfing, surfing and sailing at Rock and water-skiing in the nearby Camel estuary.

Places of interest nearby: There is an abundance of National Trust properties and gardens nearby and the hotel itself is set in National Trust land. **Directions: From Exeter, take the A30 to Bodmin followed by the A389 Wadebridge. Then the B3314 to New Polzeath.**

For hotel location, see maps on pages 263–269

For hotel location, see maps on pages 263–269

NORWICH

THE BEECHES HOTEL AND VICTORIAN GARDENS

4–6 EARLHAM ROAD, NORWICH, NORFOLK NR2 3DB
TEL: 01603 621167 FAX: 01603 620151 E-MAIL: beeches.hotel@paston.co.uk

OWNERS: Keith and Elisabeth Hill

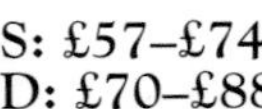

S: £57–£74
D: £70–£88

With three acres of English Heritage Victorian Gardens, this hotel offers discerning guests a warm welcome and exceptionally high standards of comfort in a relaxed, informal atmosphere. The two separate Grade II listed Victorian mansions have been beautifully restored, extended and attractively decorated and are collectively known as the Beeches.

When the houses were built in the mid-1800s, an idyllic Italianate garden was created in the deep hollow it overlooks. In 1980, this 'secret' garden, now known as The Plantation Garden, was rediscovered. It is being restored to its former glory and guests are free to wander through this enchanting and extraordinary reminder of our Victorian heritage with its ornate Gothic fountain and amazing terraces. All bedrooms feature charming individual décor, separate modern facilities and are non smoking.

A varied selection of tempting dishes is cooked to order and served in the Bistro Restaurant which overlooks a delightful patio garden. Residents and diners can enjoy a pre-dinner drink in the comfortable lounge bar.

Places of interest nearby: The city of Norwich, with its castle containing a famous collection of the Norwich school of painting and its fine cathedral, the Norfolk coast and Broads. **Directions: From the A11 take the inner ring road west and turn onto the B1108 (Earlham Road) to the city centre. The hotel is near the Roman Catholic cathedral.**

For hotel location, see maps on pages 263–269

Catton Old Hall

LODGE LANE, CATTON, NORWICH, NORFOLK NR6 7HG
TEL: 01603 419379 FAX: 01603 400339 E-MAIL: catton.old.hall@netcom.co.uk

OWNERS: Roger and Anthea Cawdron

5 rms | 5 ens

S: £42.50–£48
D: £60–£95

Catton Old Hall was built in 1632 and has been sympathetically restored to its former glory. It lies just 2½ miles north east of Norwich city centre and within easy reach of the airport. The Hall, once a farmhouse, retains a wealth of oak beams and one of the largest inglenooks in Norwich. Now the family home of Roger and Anthea Cawdron, it provides luxurious accommodation for its guests. The en suite bedrooms are spacious, tastefully decorated and furnished to the highest standards. The dining room and lounge have a homely atmosphere and are ideal places in which to enjoy quiet comfort.

Full English breakfast is served at the Hall and evening meals are available if booked in advance. A typical evening meal might be a choice between breast of Barbary duck, cooked in blackberry and blueberry sauce laced with Crème de Mûre, or fillet of beef Wellington, a steak with a mushroom and onion farce wrapped in crisp pastry served with a rich port and thyme jus.

A full range of office facilities is available and arrangements can be made to visit local sporting events. **Places of interest nearby:** The ancient cathedral city of Norwich, with its 12th century castle, fine museums and many other historic buildings. Also the Norfolk Broads and the long sandy beaches on the Norfolk coastline. **Directions: 2½ miles north east of Norwich centre. Lodge Lane is just off Spixworth Road.**

For hotel location, see maps on pages 263–269

NORWICH (Coltishall)

THE NORFOLK MEAD HOTEL

COLTISHALL, NORWICH, NORFOLK NR12 7DN
TEL: 01603 737531 FAX: 01603 737521

OWNERS: Don and Jill Fleming
RESIDENT BEAUTY THERAPIST: Nicki Fleming

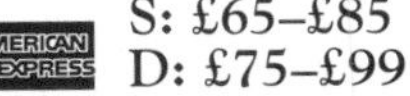

S: £65–£85
D: £75–£99

This elegant Georgian manor house, dating back to 1740, sits on a quiet edge of the Norfolk Broads, standing in 12 acres of lovely gardens and rolling lawns which sweep down to the River Bure. Guests can stroll down to the water to catch a glimpse of a kingfisher or heron and enjoy the variety of birdlife. The new owners have added a host of personal touches to create a homely atmosphere, the fragrance of fresh flowers pervades the hotel.

The delightful restaurant, overlooking the gardens and the river, offers a constantly changing menu thoughtfully selected by the chef to utilise the abundance of local produce, which includes fish caught off the Norfolk coast, game from the local estates, vegetables and herbs from the gardens. An extensive wine list has been carefully selected. Relax with a drink before dinner in the bar, where a log fire burns in winter and French windows open onto the old walled garden in the summer. Those wishing to be pampered will enjoy 'Nicki's Beauty Spot', the hotel's own salon offering a range of health and beauty treatments. Sport facilities include a well-stocked fishing lake, off-river mooring and a 60ft pool. Situated only 7 miles from the centre of Norwich and 12 miles from the coast, the Norfolk Mead is well-situated for both business and leisure. **Directions: On reaching Norwich take outer ring road to B1150 signposted North Walsham. After Horstead/ Coltishall bridge, bear right on the B1354, signposted Wroxham. Entrance signposted on right just before church.**

For hotel location, see maps on pages 263–269

Channel House Hotel

CHURCH PATH, MINEHEAD, SOMERSET TA24 5QG
TEL: 01643 703229 FAX: 01643 708925 E-MAIL: channel.house@virgin.net

OWNERS: Jackie and Brian Jackman
CHEFS: Jackie and Brian Jackman

S: £62–£82
D: £99–£124
(including dinner)

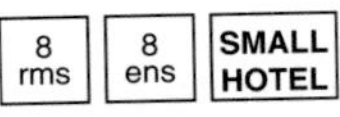

The owners pride themselves on offering their guests the gracious living of the Edwardian era in which the house was built. This is evident from the warm and personal welcome received on arrival and the first impressions of the tasteful furnishings. This warm and friendly atmosphere pervades throughout the whole hotel.

On the lower slopes of Minehead's picturesque North Hill, the hotel is secluded within award-winning gardens where visitors can enjoy magnificent views of the sea and Exmoor.

All eight bedrooms are furnished to a high standard and beautifully decorated in soft pastel shades which, with the views they enjoy, gives one the feeling of total peace. All have en suite bathrooms which are excellently appointed.

The restaurant continues this beautiful ambience; it is furnished in soft pinks with sparkling crystal, shining silver and Royal Doulton china. The cuisine is of the highest quality and is created with great care by the owners using only the finest of local produce. Everything is prepared and cooked on the premises, including the bread. Channel House is ETB Highly Commended.
Places of interest nearby: Knightshayes Court, West Somerset Steam Railway and Exmoor National Park.
Directions: On reaching Minehead follow signs to the sea front then turn left into Blenheim Road. Take first right up Northfield Road. Church Path is on the left and first right is into Channel House.

The Old Rectory

103 YARMOUTH ROAD, THORPE ST ANDREW, NORWICH, NORFOLK NR7 OHF
TEL: 01603 700772 FAX: 01603 300772 E-MAIL: Rectorytl@aol.com

OWNERS: Chris and Sally Entwistle

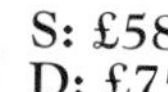

S: £58–£63
D: £75–£85

Chris and Sally Entwistle extend a warm and hospitable welcome and the promise of fine personal service to guests at the Old Rectory. Dating back to 1754, their delightful Grade II listed Georgian home, clad with Wisteria and Virginia Creeper, stands in an acre of mature gardens on the outskirts of Norwich overlooking the River Yare.

The spacious and well-furnished bedrooms, both in the hotel and the adjacent Coach House, offer quality, comfort and every modern amenity. After a busy day, guests may unwind over a pre-dinner drink in the elegant Drawing Room, enhanced by a roaring log fire during the winter and choose from a table d'hôte menu. The tempting dishes are changed daily and are freshly prepared to order.

The Wellingtonia Room and the Conservatory, overlooking the sun terrace and gardens, are excellent venues for business meetings and private luncheons or dinners.

Places of interest nearby: Within easy reach of the city centre and the Norfolk Broads, The Old Rectory is an ideal base from which to explore the historic city of Norwich, the beautiful Broadland countryside and the Norfolk coast.

Directions: Follow the A47 Norwich bypass towards Great Yarmouth. Take the A1042 exit and follow the road into Thorpe St Andrew. Bear left onto the A1242 and the hotel is approximately 50 yards on the right after the first set of traffic lights.

For hotel location, see maps on pages 263–269

NOTTINGHAM (Ruddington)

THE COTTAGE COUNTRY HOUSE HOTEL

EASTHORPE STREET, RUDDINGTON, NOTTINGHAM NG11 6LA
TEL: 01159 846882 FAX: 01159 214721

OWNERS: Christina and Tim Ruffell
CHEF: Christina Ruffell

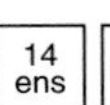

S: from £75
D: from £95
Suites: £115

Roses and honeysuckle ramble over the walls of The Cottage Country House Hotel, a unique restoration of 17th century cottages; it lies tucked away in the village of Ruddington, yet only a few minutes drive from the bustling city of Nottingham. It is the imaginative concept of the designer proprietors and with its private, gated courtyard and delightful walled garden it has won three major awards, including the Conservation Award for the best restoration of an old building in a village setting.

Christina and Tim Ruffell are proud of their attention to detail and they engaged local leading craftsmen to renovate and refurbish the hotel in keeping with its original features. Their aim was to provide quality, style and comfort in tranquil surroundings. They have succeeded in every way.

All the hotel's rooms are individually designed and furnished to reflect the needs of discerning guests. The bedrooms are all en suite, with thoughtful extra touches, and each room is individually named. The hotel offers two superb honeymoon suites. The excellent restaurant serves contemporary international cuisine and fine wines, there are two guest sitting rooms, one with an original inglenook fireplace. The terrace bar overlooks the enclosed courtyard and fountain, and there is a second terrace leading into the garden. Golf, tennis and water sports are within easy reach. **Directions: Ruddington is three miles south of Nottingham on the A60 Loughborough road. The hotel is situated at the heart of the village.**

For hotel location, see maps on pages 263–269

Langar Hall

LANGAR, NOTTINGHAMSHIRE NG13 9HG
TEL: 01949 860559 FAX: 01949 861045 e-mail: langarhall–hotel@ndirect.co.uk

OWNER: Imogen Skirving

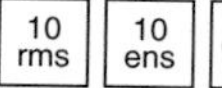

S: £75–£95
D: £95–£150
Suite: £175

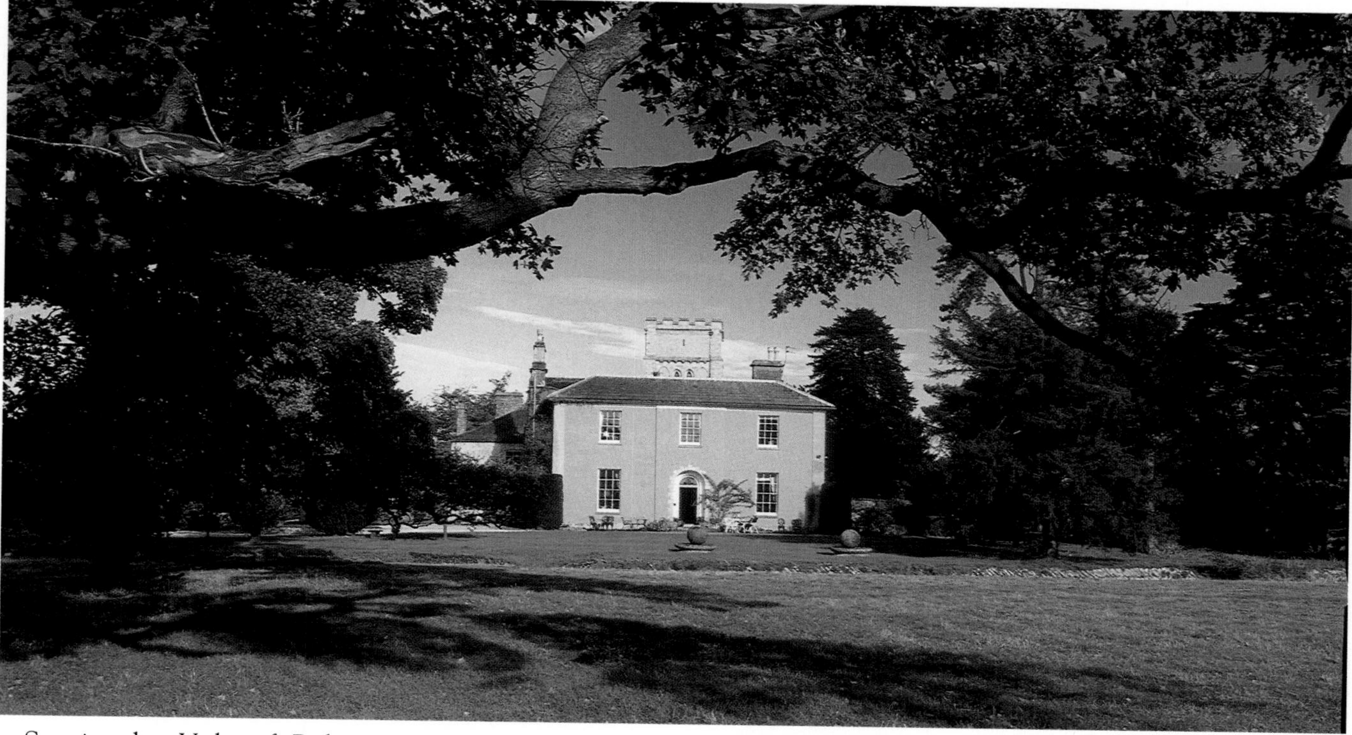

Set in the Vale of Belvoir, mid-way between Nottingham and Grantham, Langar Hall is the family home of Imogen Skirving. Epitomising "excellence and diversity" it combines the standards of good hotel-keeping with the hospitality and style of country house living. Having received a warm welcome, guests can enjoy the atmosphere of a private home that is much loved and cared for.

The en suite bedrooms are individually designed and comfortably appointed. The public rooms feature fine furnishings and most rooms afford beautiful views of the garden, park and moat. Imogen and her kitchen team collaborate to produce an excellent, varied menu of modern British food. This is an ideal venue for exclusive 'House party' bookings and private dinner parties. Celebrations may include a choice of in–house entertainment, opera, theatre, music or a murder mystery dinner. Dogs can be accommodated by arrangement.
Places of interest nearby: Langar Hall is an ideal venue for small boardroom meetings. It is also an ideal base from which to visit Belvoir Castle, to see cricket at Trent Bridge, to visit students at Nottingham University and to see Robin Hood's Sherwood Forest. **Directions: Langar is accessible via Bingham on the A52, or via Cropwell Bishop from the A46 (both signposted). The house adjoins the church and is hidden behind it.**

Pen-Y-Dyffryn Country Hotel

RHYDYCROESAU, NR OSWESTRY, SHROPSHIRE SY10 7JD
TEL: 01691 653700 FAX: 01691 653700

OWNERS: Miles and Audrey Hunter
CHEFS: Paul Thomasson and Audrey Hunter

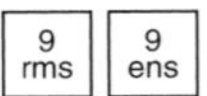   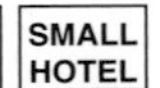

S: £50–£56
D: £80–£88

Pen-y-Dyffryn Country Hotel is a haven of peace and quiet, set in five acres of grounds in the unspoilt Shropshire hills, midway between Shrewsbury and Chester. And while civilisation is close at hand, buzzards, peregrine falcons, badgers and foxes regularly delight the guests with their unscheduled appearances. The stream in front of the hotel marks the border with neighbouring Wales.

All the bedrooms have modern amenities and overlook the attractively terraced hotel gardens. In the cooler months, log fires burning in the two homely lounges help to create a cosy and informal atmosphere in which to relax and forget the pressures of everyday life. The best of British cuisine is served in the hotel's renowned restaurant. Adventurous menus offer dishes using the finest fresh, local ingredients and traditional English puddings are a speciality. The hotel is fully licensed and has an extensive wine list.

Although Pen-y-Dyffryn provides the perfect setting for total relaxation, for more active guests there are facilities for hill-walking and riding on the doorstep, six 18-hole golf courses within 15 miles and a trout pool just yards away.

Places of interest nearby: Four major National Trust properties; Powys and Chirk Castles, Erddig and Attingham. Historic towns of Shrewsbury and Chester. Excursions to Snowdonia. **Directions: From Oswestry town centre take B4580 Llansilin road for 3 miles due West. After sharp bend turn left in village.**

For hotel location, see maps on pages 263–269

VENN OTTERY BARTON

VENN OTTERY, NR OTTERY ST MARY, DEVON EX11 1RZ
TEL: 01404 812733 FAX: 01404 814713 E-MAIL: VOBH@compuserve.com

OWNERS: Shân Merritt and Dan Fishman
CHEF: Andy & Annette Witheridge

S: £37–£47
D: £70–£95

Venn Ottery Barton is a superb country house hotel built in 1530 and extended in Georgian and modern times. Set in the midst of unspoilt East Devon, it boasts an old world charm while providing every creature comfort.

The bedrooms are tasteful, roomy and simple and there is an oak-beamed residents' lounge in which to relax and unwind. Next door is the Bar, with its enormous open fireplace making it a warm and inviting place to enjoy a drink.

Imaginative English food is the order of the day in the restaurant. Tempting main courses include dishes such as duck breast served pink with red berry glaze; fillet of salmon in a pool of saffron and vermouth sauce; and chargrilled aubergine and cream cheese quiche. A choice of delicious home-made desserts follows.

The hotel is an excellent base for touring the Devon Heritage Coast, Exeter and beyond to the South Hams and Dartmoor. For the golfing enthusiast, there are at least six excellent courses close by, including the famous Budleigh Salterton links. Antique-hunters will enjoy browsing around the South-West's nearby antique centres of Honiton and Topsham.

Places of interest nearby: Killerton and Bicton Gardens, Aylesbeare Bird Sanctuary. **Directions: From M5 junction 30 join A3052 towards Sidmouth. On approaching Newton Poppleford turn left at signpost to Venn Ottery. The hotel driveway is a mile along this lane on left at bottom of hill.**

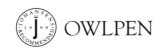

Owlpen Manor

NR ULEY, GLOUCESTERSHIRE GL11 5BZ
TEL: 01453 860261 FAX: 01453 860819 E-MAIL: Nicky@owlpen.demon.co.uk

OWNERS: Nicholas and Karin Mander
CHEF: Karin Mander

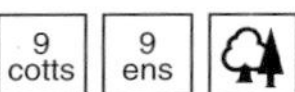

From:
£50-£150
(minimum stay conditions may apply)

Set in its own remote and picturesque wooded valley in the heart of the South Cotswolds, Owlpen Manor is one of the country's most romantic Tudor manor houses. It is steeped in peace and timeless English beauty with the surrounding estate leading the wildlife lover through miles of private woodland paths. Scattered along the valley are distinctive historic cottages, sleeping from two to eight and managed in the style of a country house hotel. There are snug medieval barns and byres, a watermill first restored in 1464, the Court House of the 1620s, weavers' and keepers' cottages and even a modern farmhouse.

All are equipped with every home-from-home comfort, from antiques and chintzes to prints and plants. They are individually furnished in traditional English style and stand in their own secluded gardens. Some have open fireplaces or four-poster beds. An atmospheric restaurant in the medieval cyder house serves seasonal produce from the estate. For sporting visitors fly-fishing and shooting can be arranged. Riding, gliding and golf are nearby.
Places of interest nearby: Owlpen Manor, Uley Tumulus, Westonbirt Arboretum, Berkeley Castle and the Wildfowl Trust at Slimbridge. **Directions: From the M4, exit at junction 18, or M5 junctions 13 or 14, and head for the B4066 to Uley. Owlpen is signposted from the Old Crown opposite the church, or follow the brown signs.**

For hotel location, see maps on pages 263–269

FALLOWFIELDS

KINGSTON BAGPUIZE WITH SOUTHMOOR, OXON OX13 5BH
TEL: 01865 820416 FAX: 01865 821275 E-MAIL: stay@fallowfields.com

OWNERS: Peta and Anthony Lloyd

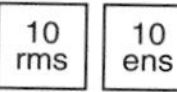

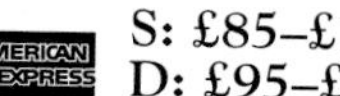

S: £85–£105
D: £95–£145

Fallowfields, once the home of Begum Aga Khan, dates back more than 300 years. It has been updated and extended over past decades and today boasts a lovely early Victorian Gothic southern aspect. The house is set in two acres of gardens, surrounded by ten acres of grassland.

The guests' bedrooms, which offer a choice of four poster or coroneted beds, are large and well appointed and offer every modern amenity to ensure maximum comfort and convenience. The house is centrally heated throughout and during the winter months, there are welcoming log fires in the elegant main reception rooms.

Home-cooked cuisine is imaginative in style and presentation and there is a good choice of menus available. The walled kitchen garden provides most of the vegetables and salads for the table and locally grown organic produce is otherwise used wherever possible. Weekend house parties are ever popular and additional accommodation can be arranged.

Places of interest nearby: Fallowfields is close to Stratford, the Cotswolds, Stonehenge, Bath and Bristol to the west, Oxford, Henley on Thames, the Chilterns and Windsor to the east. Heathrow airport is under an hour away. **Directions: Take the Kingston Bagpuize exit on the A420 Oxford to Swindon. Fallowfields is at the west end of Southmoor.**

Cross House Hotel

CHURCH STREET, PADSTOW, CORNWALL PL28 8BG
TEL: 01841 532391 FAX: 01841 533633

OWNERS: Cross House Hotel Limited
MANAGER: Nichola Gidlow

9 rms | 9 ens

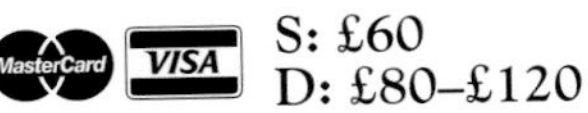

S: £60
D: £80–£120

Tucked away in the quiet and serene area of Padstow, the Cross House Hotel is a delightful Georgian Grade II listed house. Luxury and comfort are important criteria and the décor is distinctly elegant with beautiful fabrics and tasteful paintings. The bedrooms, four of which are in the annexe adjacent to the hotel, are individually furnished and offer every modern amenity as well as extra touches such as air-conditioning and videos. With large fluffy towels, soft bathrobes and fine toiletries, the en suite facilities are both stylish and well-equipped.

Guests often frequent the lounge during the afternoon and enjoy reading or playing a board game in front of the cosy, glowing fire. With its comfortable furnishings and elegant chandeliers, the bar is the ideal place to recline during the evening and enjoy an apéritif. There is a choice of either Full English or Continental breakfast and the fresh pastries are delicious. Many fine restaurants are recommended nearby.

Beautiful walks along the Cornish coast, sea-fishing, cycling and trying the various water sports offered at the Estuary are some of the many pastimes available nearby. Golf enthusiasts will be delighted with the challenging courses.

Places of interest nearby: Prideaux House and Deer Park, the Camel Estuary and the picturesque town of Wadebridge are all within easy reach. **Directions: On approaching Padstow from A30, take 3rd turn on the right, following signs to the parish church. The hotel is 50 yards on the left.**

For hotel location, see maps on pages 263–269

Temple Sowerby House Hotel

TEMPLE SOWERBY, PENRITH, CUMBRIA CA10 1RZ
TEL: 017683 61578 FAX: 017683 61958 FREE PHONE: 0800 146157

OWNERS: Geoffrey and Cécile Temple

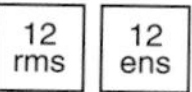

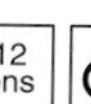

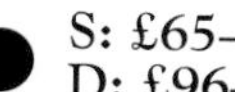

S: £65–£75
D: £96–£116

Temple Sowerby House looks over at Cross Fell, the highest peak in the Pennines, noted for its spectacular ridge walk. This old Cumbrian farmhouse is set in two acres of gardens and guests are assured of peace and quiet. Geoffrey and Cécile Temple offer a warm, hospitable and friendly family service upon which the hotel prides itself. Awarded an AA Rosette, the restaurant has two dining rooms – the panelled room with its cosy atmosphere and the Garden Room. Delicious, home-cooked dishes might include a starter of a pithiviers of creamed wild mushrooms served with crisp salad leaves in a truffle and olive oil dressing, followed by tuna fillet served on a purée of spiced rhubarb with poppy seed vinegar, rounded off with iced chocolate parfait served with a white chocolate sauce. The individually furnished bedrooms all have private bathrooms. Four of the rooms are situated in the Coach House, just yards from the main house. During the winter, apéritifs are taken by the fireside, while in the summer, guests can sip drinks on the terrace and enjoy views across the fells. Private fishing, with tuition if required, takes place on the River Eden, two miles away. Fishing breaks available.

Places of interest nearby: Lakes Ullswater and Derwentwater, the Borders, Scottish Lowlands, Hadrian's Wall and Yorkshire Dales are within easy reach by car. **Directions: Temple Sowerby lies on the A66, seven miles from exit 40 of the M6, between Penrith and Appleby. (Special breaks available).**

For hotel location, see maps on pages 263–269

LANGRISH HOUSE

LANGRISH, NR PETERSFIELD, HAMPSHIRE GU32 1RN
TEL: 01730 266941 FAX: 01730 260543

OWNERS: Nigel and Robina Talbot-Ponsonby
GENERAL MANAGER: Philip H. Vernall MHCIMA
CHEF: Mary Madeleine Lambert

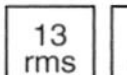

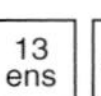

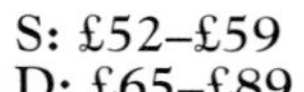

S: £52–£59
D: £65–£89

Standing in 12 acres of beautiful mature grounds including a picturesque lake, Langrish House combines the welcoming ambience of a traditional country house with the facilities expected from a modern hotel. Extended by the present owners' forbears in 1842, it opened as a hotel in 1979 and remains very much a family home. Today, new life is being breathed into the house by Nigel and Robina Talbot-Ponsonby whose family portraits and heirlooms once again adorn the rooms.

Each of the bedrooms overlooks the grounds, giving guests ample opportunity to savour Langrish's peace and tranquillity. All are fully equipped with en suite bathrooms, direct dial telephones, colour televisions and many thoughtful touches.

The recently refurbished Cellar Restaurant and Dungeon Bar are now complemented by the addition of a the Garden Room Restaurant, which affords glorious views of the lawns. Fresh regional produce features in the fine cuisine. Langrish House is an ideal venue for wedding receptions and business conferences and offers dining facilities for up to 120 people. **Places of interest nearby:** This is an excellent base for touring the Hampshire countryside and the New Forest. Gilbert White's Selbourne, Jane Austen's Chawton, Goodwood and Cowdray Park are also close by. **Directions: Follow A272 from the M3/A31 at Winchester (16 miles) or from A3 at Petersfield (3 miles). Langrish House is signposted from the village on the road to East Meon.**

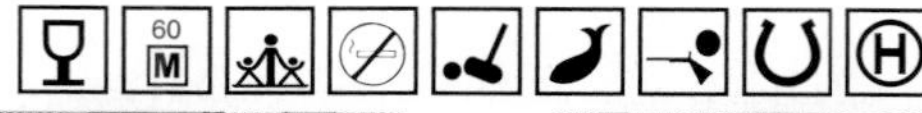

For hotel location, see maps on pages 263–269

THE COTTAGE HOTEL

PORLOCK WEIR, PORLOCK, SOMERSET TA24 8PB
TEL: 01643 863300 FAX: 01643 863311 E-MAIL: cottage@netcomuk.co.uk

OWNERS: Christopher and Ann Baker
CHEF: Ann Baker

5 rms | 5 ens | SMALL HOTEL

MasterCard VISA S: £55–£95
D: £65–£110

Guests will be enchanted by the lovely location of The Cottage Hotel, overlooking a tiny harbour where Exmoor meets the rugged coastline and sea. It is wonderful walking country abounding in history and scenic delights. With origins dating back to the 18th century, the hotel is surrounded by colourful, terraced gardens where visitors can relax in summer shade and breathe in sweet floral scents.

Owners Christopher and Ann Baker offer a very friendly welcome and excellent value for money. The bedrooms are a delight, comfortable, beautifully decorated and well-equipped with all modern necessities.

Drinks can be taken in the attractively draped lounge with its deep, soft sofas and chairs before dining in the elegant restaurant where delightfully presented meals are served using the finest local produce, including lamb, venison, fish and cheeses. Sunday and Monday light meals by arrangement.

Places of interest nearby: Dunster's Norman castle, the smallest church in England at Culbone, Lynmouth's picturesque harbour, Minehead, the scenic, wild delights and attractive stone cottage villages of Exmoor. **Directions: From the M5, exit at junctions 23 or 24 and join the A39 towards Minehead, Porlock and Porlock Weir.**

For hotel location, see maps on pages 263–269

TYE ROCK HOTEL

LOE BAR ROAD, PORTHLEVEN, NR HELSTON, SOUTH CORNWALL TR13 9EW
TEL/FAX: 01326 572695

OWNERS: Richard and Pat Palmer

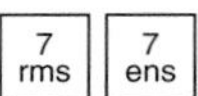
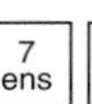

S: £46.50–£56
D: £66–£80

This family-run hotel, with its magnificent location, offers a wonderful warm, relaxing and welcoming atmosphere as you walk in the door. Whether you choose self-catering or hotel accommodation, you can be sure that Tye Rock's superb elevated position, with views extending from The Lizard to Land's End, will be hard to surpass. Set in 3½ acres surrounded by National Trust land, Tye Rock has an air of seclusion yet the village of Porthleven is just steps away.

The hotel's seven en suite bedrooms all have sea views. Relax and enjoy a traditional, home-cooked meal served in the dining room, offering magnificent views of Mounts Bay. In the hotel grounds there are also eight apartments which offer guests the independence of their own front door.

In a sheltered sun-trap at the bottom of the garden is the large, outdoor heated swimming pool. The pool, open from May to September, subject to availability, is built into the cliff top and is unusually large for a small hotel. Thanks to the mild Cornish climate, spring starts early here and the warm days last well into the autumn. Open all year, the hotel offers out of season, Christmas and theme weekends and breaks. 3 Crowns Commended ETB.
Places of interest nearby: St Michael's Mount, Land's End, Goonhilly Earth Satellite Station and many Cornish gardens. **Directions: From Helston take the Porthleven road, then follow signs for Loe Bar; take first left, first right and left at the T-junction.**

For hotel location, see maps on pages 263–269

THE BEAUFORT HOTEL

71 FESTING ROAD, SOUTHSEA, PORTSMOUTH PO4 ONQ
TEL: 01705 823707 FAX: 01705 870270 FREEPHONE: 0800 919237 E-MAIL: enquiries@beauforthotel.co.uk

OWNERS Anthony and Penelope Freemantle
CHEF: Michael Freyne

18 rms | 18 ens | SMALL HOTEL

S: from £48
D: from £78

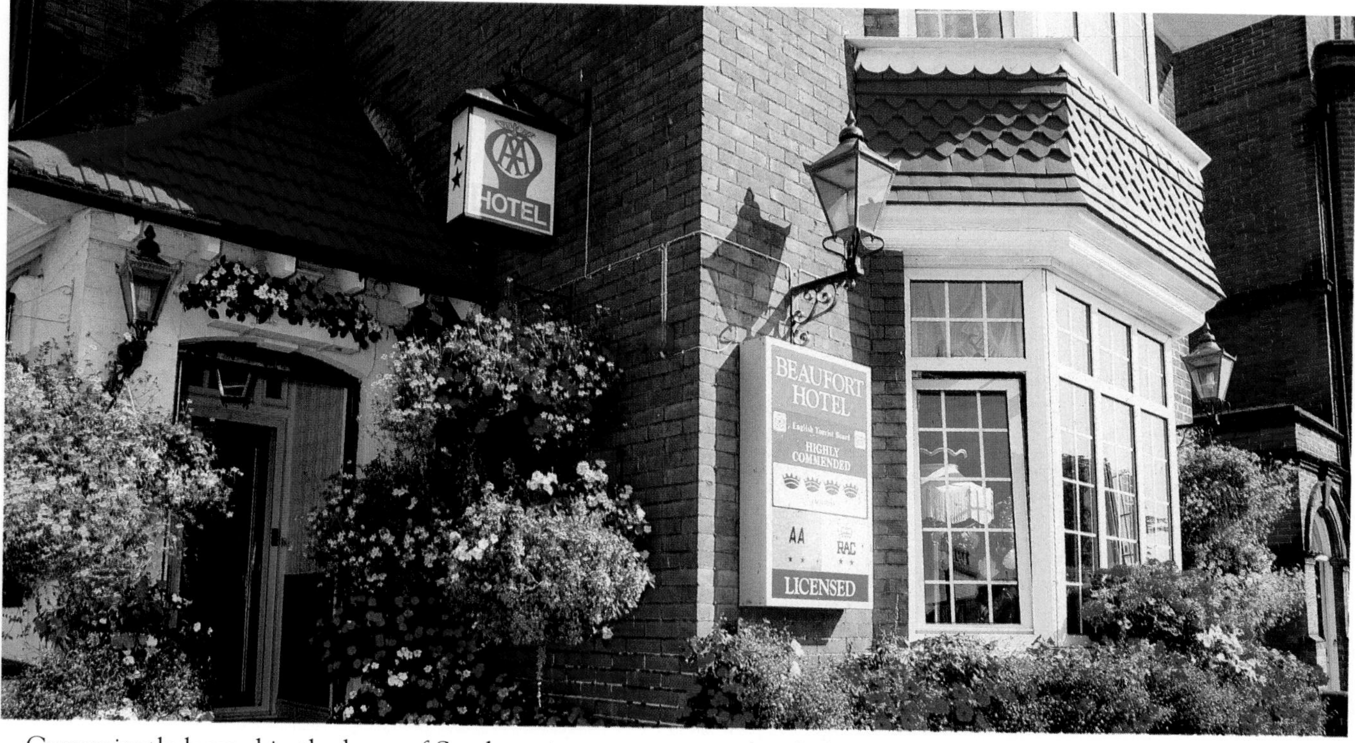

Conveniently located in the heart of Southsea, just one minute's walk from the sea, lies The Beaufort Hotel. A relaxed and friendly atmosphere pervades this comfortable and spotless hotel, creating an ideal setting for relaxation. Owners Penny and Tony Freemantle and their staff pride themselves on providing guests with a personal service that is second to none.

The 18 bedrooms have all been designed to give them individual character, from the magnificent Oxford Room, decorated in royal blue and gold, to the bright and sunny Cambridge Room which is tastefully decorated in Burgundy and overlooks the Canoe lake. All the attractive bathrooms feature porcelain and gold fittings and include a selection of luxurious toiletries.

A comfortable cocktail bar is the ideal place to enjoy a pre-dinner drink before moving on to the charming restaurant. The Beaufort is proud to hold the highest percentage rating by the AA of any hotel in Portsmouth. **Places of interest nearby:** The Mary Rose, H.M.S Warrior, H.M.S Victory and the Royal Naval Museum provide a fascinating insight into life on board Britain's most famous warships. The Isle of Wight and Le Havre and Cherbourg in France are all within easy cruising distance. **Directions: Festing Road is off St Helen's Parade at the eastern end of the seafront.**

PULBOROUGH

CHEQUERS HOTEL

CHURCH PLACE, PULBOROUGH, WEST SUSSEX RH20 1AD
TEL: 01798 872486 FAX: 01798 872715

OWNER: John Searancke
CHEFS: Kevin Chatfield and Matt Sharp

S: £49.50–£59.50
D: £82–£97

A warm welcome awaits visitors to this historic hotel built in 1548 and Grade II listed. Situated on a sandstone ridge, Chequers has enviable views across the beautiful Arun Valley to the South Downs beyond.

Mindful of the needs of today's traveller, owner John Searancke has ensured that modern amenities have been carefully blended with old world charm and comforts. The hotel has recently enjoyed a programme of refurbishment further to enhance its appeal. All 11 bedrooms have private facilities, 10 of which are en suite. There are 4 bedrooms on the ground floor and three family rooms. Public rooms are comfortably furnished, with a log fire in the lounge on winter evenings.

In warmer weather, guests may linger over an apéritif on the patio or in the secluded garden, before dining in the restaurant, where the traditional English menu changes daily. The hotel is set in the heart of the local conservation area and its nine acre adjacent meadow is an ideal spot for walking your dog.

Places of interest nearby: Chequers Hotel is conveniently placed for the Roman city of Chichester, Goodwood, Arundel Castle and the Sussex coast. Packed lunches can be provided. ETB 4 Crowns Highly Commended, 2 RAC Merit Awards and 2 AA Rosettes. **Directions: At the top of the hill, at the northern end of the village, the hotel is opposite the church.**

For hotel location, see maps on pages 263–269

THE OLD RECTORY

IPSLEY LANE, IPSLEY, REDDITCH, WORCESTERSHIRE B98 0AP
TEL: 01527 523000 FAX: 01527 517003

OWNERS: The Moore Family
MANAGERS: Greg Underwood and Elaine Biddlestone

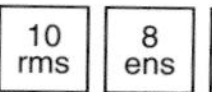

S: £55–£70
D: £80–£90

The Old Rectory at Redditch dates back to the 15th century, although well before that the Romans built Icknield Street which forms one boundary of the grounds. The house was substantially modernised in 1812 by the great grandson of Sir Christopher Wren, who lived in the house for 40 years.

In this historic setting surrounded by beautiful and secluded gardens you will find an atmosphere of peace, tranquillity and comfort.

The bedrooms are of different shapes and sizes: some with exposed beams, one with a barrel ceiling, and are all tastefully decorated. In the 17th century connecting stable block is the working mechanism of the 100 year old clock.

Meals are served in the conservatory. The surroundings are delightful in the early morning sun whilst you enjoy fresh fruit juices, cereals and your light or full English breakfast. The three-course evening meal (which should be ordered by 1pm), followed by coffee in the lounge, will have been specially prepared for you that day in the large farmhouse kitchen.

Places of interest nearby: Stratford-upon-Avon, Warwick, Leamington Spa, the Cotswolds, Oxford, Worcester, the NEC and Birmingham. **Directions: Arriving in Redditch, follow the signs for 'All Other Redditch Districts' to Ipsley. Ipsley Lane is off Icknield Street Drive.**

For hotel location, see maps on pages 263–269

Moortown Lodge

244 CHRISTCHURCH ROAD, RINGWOOD, HAMPSHIRE BH24 3AS
TEL: 01425 471404 FAX: 01425 476052

OWNERS: Bob and Jilly Burrows-Jones
CHEF: Jilly Burrows-Jones

6 rms | 6 ens | SMALL HOTEL

MasterCard VISA AMERICAN EXPRESS S: £40–£50 D: £60–£80

The busy market town of Ringwood stands on the edge of the vast and beautiful New Forest with its abundance of woodland, wildlife and enchanting walks. Moortown Lodge is a perfect base from which to explore this rolling and historic countryside. Dating back to the 1760s this charming, family-run hotel stands just outside the town on the main road to Christchurch and is renowned for its warm and welcoming ambiance. Owners Bob and Jilly Burrows-Jones are justly proud to have been one of the first recipients of an AA Courtesy and Care Award for hospitality.

All the hotel's rooms are well-proportioned and enlivened with furnishing, fabrics and colourings to create a restful atmosphere. There are six en suite double and twin-bedded rooms, including one with a luxury four-poster. All have every amenity and facility to make visitors feel at home.

The intimate restaurant is the ideal place to enjoy some of the finest food in the area. Jilly's menus are varied and she uses local produce whenever possible. Her high standard of cuisine has won two AA Rosettes and has been acclaimed as excellent yet delightfully uncomplicated.

Places of interest nearby: Broadlands, the old home of Lord Mountbatten, Beaulieu, Breamore House and the New Forest. Bournemouth, Poole, Southampton and Salisbury are within easy reach. **Directions: Enter Ringwood from the A31 and follow the signs for the B3347. Moortown Lodge is approximately 1½ miles south of the town.**

For hotel location, see maps on pages 263–269

The St Enodoc Hotel

ROCK, NR WADEBRIDGE, CORNWALL PL27 6LA
TEL: 01208 863394 FAX: 01208 863970 E-MAIL: enodoc@aol.com

OWNERS: K G Hotels Ltd
MANAGER: Mark Gregory

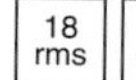

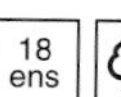

S: £50–£80
D: £70–£120
Suite: £90–£150

Owned by the Marler family and designed by Emily Todhunter, the St Enodoc Hotel makes the best use of its spectacular coastal location to provide a truly relaxed atmosphere in its own distinctive style. Everywhere, in day rooms and bedrooms alike, wonderful views of the Camel estuary and Cornish countryside are enhanced by abundant fresh flowers and interesting modern art to create the feeling of space and tranquillity.

The 15 double bedrooms and three two-bedroom suites are all individually decorated in lush fabrics and soft furnishings that afford comfort and luxury. Flagstone floors and open wood-burning fires lend a rustic feel. The hotel includes the Porthilly Bar and Grill whose split-level restaurant opens on to an attractive dining terrace with panoramic views.It's Pacific Rim cuisine strikes a modern idiom with seafood and vegetable tempura, Caesar salad and filled ciabatta for lunchtime snacks progressing to dinner menus featuring fillets of local sole with olive oil mashed potato and rack of lamb with puy lentils and polenta.

The hotel has it's own outdoor swimming pool, gym and billiard room. Two delightful 18 hole links golf courses adjoin the hotel, with sailing, surfing, and sea fishing nearby.

Places of interest nearby: Many historic houses and gardens, coastal walks, St. Enodoc Church, Padstow and the Camel Trail. **Directions: At Wadebridge follow B3314 for 3 miles turning left at the sign for Rock.**

For hotel location, see maps on pages 263–269

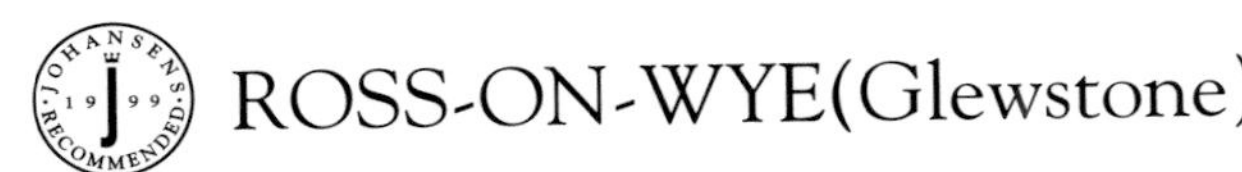

GLEWSTONE COURT

NR ROSS-ON-WYE, HEREFORDSHIRE HR9 6AW
TEL: 01989 770367 FAX: 01989 770282

OWNERS: Bill and Christine Reeve-Tucker

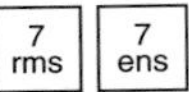
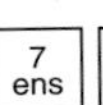

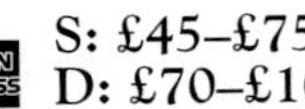

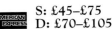

S: £45–£75
D: £70–£105

Glewstone Court is set in three acres of orchards, lawns and flower-beds. Although secluded, it is only three miles from Ross-on-Wye. Furnishings and décor reflect the hospitable personality of the owners and the variety of prints, antiques and bric-à-brac always excites curiosity.

Most country pursuits can be arranged, including canoeing, hot-air ballooning, fishing and riding. This is marvellous country for walking – or just lazing around, too!

Christine's food is always innovative and both the restaurant and extensive bar menus feature local recipes using only the freshest of ingredients. Dishes are both traditional and unusual and are always prepared and served with care and attention to detail. Now in their thirteenth year, accolades awarded are a rosette for good food from the AA and the Which? Hotel Guide Hotel of the Year for Hereford and Worcester. The restaurant and the drawing room bar feature log fires and like the rest of the hotel, are furnished for comfort.

The bedrooms are large and comfortable too. Each has en suite facilities, a hospitality tray, direct dial phone and colour television. Closed Christmas Day and Boxing Day. **Places of interest nearby:** Ross-on-Wye, Hay-on-Wye, the Welsh Marches, Hereford Cathedral and the Brecon Beacons. **Directions: From M50 junction 4 follow A40 signposted Monmouth. One mile past Wilton roundabout turn right to Glewstone; the Court is 1/2 mile on left.**

For hotel location, see maps on pages 263–269

WHITE VINE HOUSE

HIGH STREET, RYE, EAST SUSSEX TN31 7JF
TEL: 01797 224748 FAX: 01797 223599

MANAGER: Irene Cheetham

6 rms | 6 ens | SMALL HOTEL

S: £35–£60
D: £60–£100

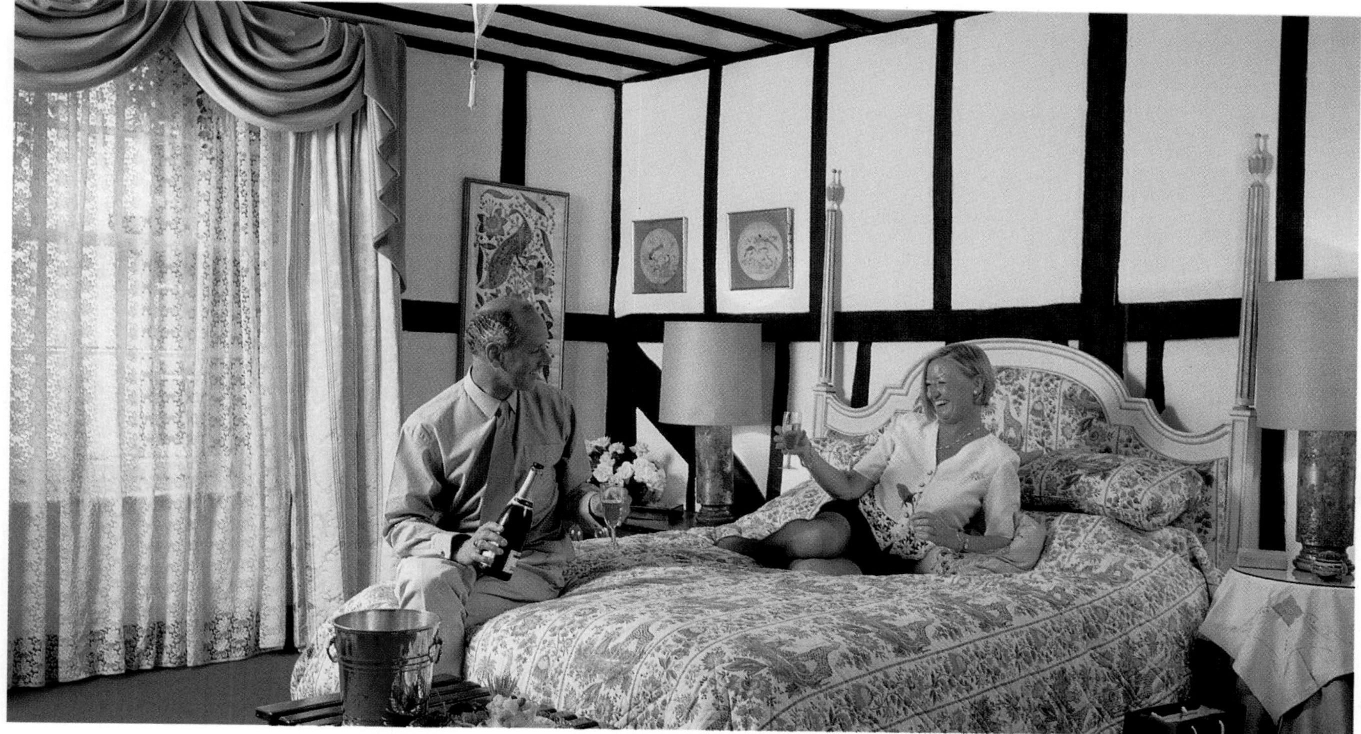

Despite its Georgian exterior this fine timber framed house is much older. Originally built around a courtyard that now forms the reception hallway, the hotel stands over Medieval cellars on the site of the ancient Whyte Vyne Inn. At the hub of the daytime bustle of this fascinating little market town, the house retains a unique character and restful atmosphere.

There are six comfortable bedrooms – of the five doubles, two have four-poster beds. Each is individually styled and well provided with every amenity.

In the morning guests can savour the pleasant surroundings while enjoying breakfast in the Dining Room or The Parlour. Lunch is served daily with an interesting selection of dishes from light options to the more traditional, complemented by a range of good value wines. Small meetings and private dining are offered in the beautifully oak panelled Elizabethan Room. Staff will happily recommend good restaurants from the many within strolling distance of the hotel door and make dinner reservations on behalf of guests to match individual preferences.

Places of interest nearby: Rye is a town of great historical interest and boasts many art galleries, potteries, antique dealers and book sellers. **Directions: Take the A21 to Flimwell, then the A268 to Rye. Telephone first for parking advice.**

For hotel location, see maps on pages 263–269

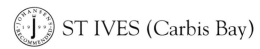

Boskerris Hotel

BOSKERRIS ROAD, CARBIS BAY, ST IVES, CORNWALL TR26 2NQ
TEL: 01736 795295 FAX: 01736 798632 E-MAIL: s.monk@easynet.com.uk

OWNERS: Marie and Spencer Monk
CHEF: Colin Williams

18 rms | 18 ens

S: 53.55–£63.80
D: £97.10–£117.80
(including dinner)

Standing high and gleaming white on a spectacular stretch of coastline, Boskerris Hotel offers magnificent panoramic views over Carbis Bay stretching from the Godrevy Head lighthouse to the picturesque little harbour and narrow cobbled streets of the artists' haven of St Ives. The golden sands of Carbis are a short walk away whilst St Ives is just a cliff-path stroll or a three-minute train journey.

Boskerris is as attractive to visitors who want to relax in comfort as it is to those seeking a more active break. The beautifully light bedrooms are attractively furnished and have every facility from remote control television to baby listening. A friendly atmosphere pervades the hotel with the lounges and cocktail bar particularly inviting.

This corner of Cornwall is a larder of good wholesome produce of which chef Colin Williams makes full use in his table d'hôte menus which have earned the hotel three AA Stars. A comprehensive wine list adds to the pleasure of dining in a room with spectacular views. Guests can enjoy the many surrounding walks, sea fishing and sailing. The hotel has arrangements with West Cornwall Golf Club and 15 others throughout the county. Closed January–February. **Places of interest nearby:** St Ives Tate Gallery, Caerhays Castle, numerous historical sites and many outstanding gardens. **Directions: From A30 take the first junction to St Ives. On entering Carbis Bay take the third turning on the right into Boskerris Road.**

For hotel location, see maps on pages 263–269

THE COUNTRYMAN AT TRINK HOTEL AND RESTAURANT

OLD COACH ROAD, ST IVES, CORNWALL TR26 3JQ
TEL: 01736 797571 FAX: 01736 797571

OWNERS: Howard and Cathy Massey

S: £38
D: £60–£70

Five minutes drive from the quaint town of St Ives is the Countryman Hotel and Restaurant at Trink. St Ives has become a mecca for artists and one of the latest attractions is the new Tate Gallery with its collection of modern paintings and contemporary exhibits. Cornwall has a wealth of interesting things to see not least its dramatic coastline ideal for lovers of nature and walkers.

The Countryman dates from the 17th century. Today the small hotel has been renovated to meet the needs of the modern visitor, all rooms have en suite shower and toilet, colour television and tea making facilities.

The atmosphere of the hotel is friendly and inviting, the emphasis being on cheerful service and good value for money. This is a totally no smoking hotel. In the restaurant, Howard Massey, the chef-patron, likes cooking to order from his varied and interesting menu containing Cornish fish supported by a sensibly priced wine-list. St Ives has always had a tradition for generous hospitality. A former mayor, the legendary John Knill, bequeathed £10 for an annual banquet. Prices may have altered a little but the high quality of the local cooking has not changed. **Places of interest nearby:** Tate Gallery, Lands End. Barbara Hepworth's house, St Michael's Mount. Golf, riding and the sea. **Directions: A30, A3074 to St Ives, then B3311 for about two miles.**

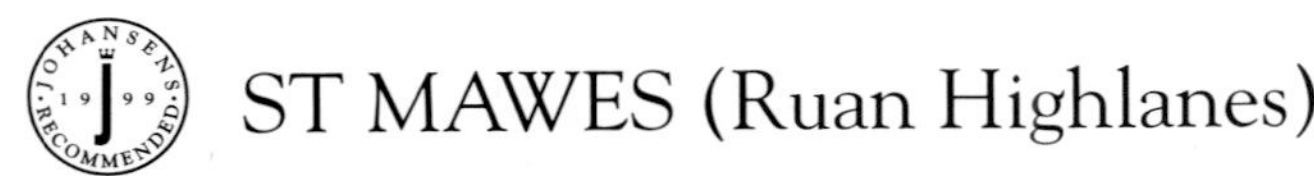

ST MAWES (Ruan Highlanes)

The Hundred House Hotel

RUAN HIGHLANES, NR TRURO, CORNWALL TR2 5JR
TEL: 01872 501336 FAX: 01872 501151

OWNERS: Mike and Kitty Eccles

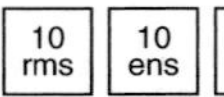

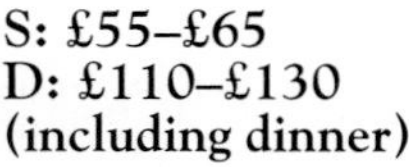

S: £55–£65
D: £110–£130
(including dinner)

Situated on Cornwall's beautiful Roseland Peninsula is The Hundred House Hotel, an 18th century Cornish country house set in three acres of gardens. It commands panoramic views over the countryside and is close to the sea and the lovely Fal estuary.

Once inside the wide hall with its handsome Edwardian staircase, there is the feeling of an elegant English home. Mike and Kitty Eccles have created a delightful hotel where guests can relax in the pretty sitting room, furnished with antiques and browse among the books of local interest. On cooler days they can enjoy a Cornish cream tea by a log fire and in the summer a game of croquet on the lawn. Each bedroom is individually decorated and has full en suite bath or shower room.

Guests regularly return to enjoy the delicious imaginative dinners and the hearty Cornish breakfast prepared by Kitty Eccles who has been awarded a Red Rosette by the AA. She uses fresh seasonal ingredients and specialities include baked avocado, fillet of lemon sole with a salmon mousse and a honey and lavender ice cream.

Places of interest nearby: Picturesque fishing villages, superb cliff walks and sandy beaches. Cornwall Gardens Festival, mid March to 31 May. Boat trips on Fal Estuary. Lanhydrock House (NT). Cathedral city of Truro 12 miles away. **Directions: A390 from St Austell, left on B3278 to Tregony, then A3078 to St Mawes. Hotel is then 4 miles on.**

For hotel location, see maps on pages 263–269

Broom Hall

RICHMOND ROAD, SAHAM TONEY, THETFORD, NORFOLK IP25 7EX
TEL: 01953 882125 FAX: 01953 882125

OWNERS: Nigel and Angela Rowling
MANAGER: Simon Rowling

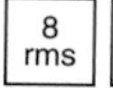

SMALL HOTEL

S: £40
D: £60–£95

Situated in 15 acres of mature gardens and parkland Broom Hall is a charming Victorian country house offering peace and tranquillity. Airy and spacious bedrooms each individually furnished and most offering lovely views provide guests with both comfort and a range of modern amenities.

A feature of the public rooms are the ornate ceilings and in the lounge a large open fire can be enjoyed in the winter months. An indoor heated swimming pool and full size snooker table are available for guests' use.

Fresh vegetables, from Broom Hall's own garden when in season, and many old fashioned desserts ensure that dinner in the dining room overlooking the garden is an enjoyable occasion. Small conferences can be arranged and the entire house can be 'taken over' for your family reunion or celebration.

Places of interest nearby: Norwich, Cambridge, Ely and Bury St Edmunds are within easy reach. Sandringham and many National Trust properties, Thetford Forest, Norfolk Broads and coastline offering nature reserves and bird sanctuaries are also close by. **Directions: Half mile north of Watton on B1077 towards Swaffham.**

THE LYNDHURST HOTEL

BONAVENTURE ROAD, SALCOMBE, SOUTH DEVON TQ8 8BG
TEL: 01548 842481 FAX: 01548 842481

OWNERS: Tina and Phil Towner
CHEF: Philip Figg

8 rms | 8 ens | SMALL HOTEL

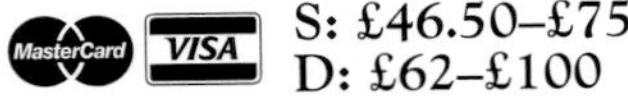

S: £46.50–£75
D: £62–£100

This former harbour-master's residence is close to the centre of the popular resort of Salcombe, and from its elevated position it commands a wonderful view of the harbour, the estuary and surrounding countryside. Salcombe's sandy coves lie close by as well as the ferry across the estuary leading to exploration of South Devon's National Trust coastline.

Under the new ownership of Phil and Tina Towner, the hotel is undergoing an ambitious refurbishment programme and offers double, twin and family rooms of style for those who like to create their own holiday experience. All the bedrooms have shower rooms en suite, colour television, radio and complimentary beverage facilities, and the best of them enjoy a fair share of the view. The comfortable and scenic lounge bar is an ideal spot to enjoy an early evening drink in anticipation of the nightly-changing table d'hôte dinner. Figley's Restaurant, awarded an AA Rosette and an RAC Cuisine/Restaurant Merit Award, has a smart new look and dinner is designed and prepared for your pleasure by Philip Figg. A wide choice of local fish and seafood dishes is balanced by other traditional favourites.

Places of interest nearby: The towns of Kingsbridge and Dartmouth, the Dart Valley Railway, houses and gardens at Buckland, Buckfast and Castle Drago are close by. **Directions: Salcombe is 6 miles from Kingsbridge on A382. On entering Salcombe, take Onslow Road, St Dunstan's Road and then Raleigh Road leading into Bonaventure Road.**

For hotel location, see maps on pages 263–269

Preston House Hotel

SAUNTON, BRAUNTON, NORTH DEVON EX33 1LG
TEL: 01271 890472 FAX: 01271 8990555

OWNERS: Andrew and Timothy Flaherty
CHEF: Timothy Flaherty

S: £45–£65
D: £60–£105

Miles of flat, golden sands and white-capped Atlantic rollers greet guests seeking peace, quiet and relaxation at Preston House, standing high on the glorious coastline of North Devon.Terraced, lawned gardens sweep down to the sea and an atmosphere of undisturbed continuity and tranquillity surrounds and influences the hotel which dates back to the Victorian era. The views are spectacular.

Eleven of the twelve en suite bedrooms face seawards. All are individually decorated, tastefully furnished and contain all modern amenities from colour television and direct dial telephone to tea and coffee facilities. Some have a four-poster bed, balcony and the added luxury of a Jacuzzi.

A spacious and comfortable lounge provides the perfect relaxed environment. Breakfast can be leisurely enjoyed in the hotel's conservatory which overlooks the garden, sands and ocean and chef Timothy Flaherty serves delicious and imaginative cuisine in the elegant restaurant or overlooking the magnificent view in the conservatory. **Places of interest nearby:** Lynton, Lynmouth, Exmoor and many National Trust properties. **Directions: From the M5, exit at junction 27 and take the A361 towards Barnstaple. Continue on to Braunton and when there turn left at the traffic lights towards Croyde. The hotel is on the left after approximately two miles.**

For hotel location, see maps on pages 263–269

THE PHEASANT HOTEL

SEAVINGTON ST MARY, NR ILMINSTER, SOMERSET TA19 0HQ
TEL: 01460 240502 FAX: 01460 242388

OWNERS: Mark and Tania Harris
CHEF: Danny Kilpatrick

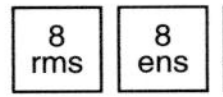 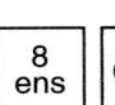  

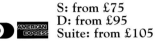

S: from £75
D: from £95
Suite: from £105

Visitors to The Pheasant are immediately captivated by the distinctive charm and character of this sumptuously furnished old-world style hotel and restaurant. Set in the heart of glorious Somerset countryside and surrounded by landscaped lawns and delightful gardens, it has an intimacy and warmth of welcome that make it the perfect 'escape' for both pleasure and business. The luxurious suites and charming bedrooms are individually styled and very tastefully appointed.

Sympathetic décor and furnishings complement the traditional character of both the cosy bar with its vast inglenooks and the beautiful oak-beamed restaurant where Head Chef, Danny Kilpatrick, using the very best of fresh local produce, presides over an imaginative menu with a range of exciting dishes to suit all tastes.

Places of interest nearby: Being situated near the Somerset border close to both Dorset and Devon, there are many attractions to suit all age groups, including Montacute House, the abbey town of Sherborne, the Fleet Air Museum at Yeovilton and Cricket St Thomas, where the BBC television series *To The Manor Born* was filmed. **Directions: Leave the A303 at South Petherton roundabout by Ilminster bypass. Take the left spur, (Seavington St Michael), followed by Seavington exit at the next roundabout. Left by the Volunteer Public House and The Pheasant is 200 yards further on the right.**

For hotel location, see maps on pages 263–269

STAINDROP HOTEL & RESTAURANT

LANE END, CHAPELTOWN, SHEFFIELD, SOUTH YORKSHIRE S35 3UH
TEL: 0114 284 6727 FAX: 0114 284 6783 E-MAIL: staindrop@obelus.co.uk

OWNERS: David Johnson and Jeffrey Crockett
MANAGER: Catherine Slack

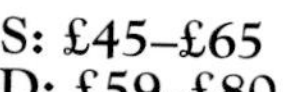

S: £45–£65
D: £59–£80

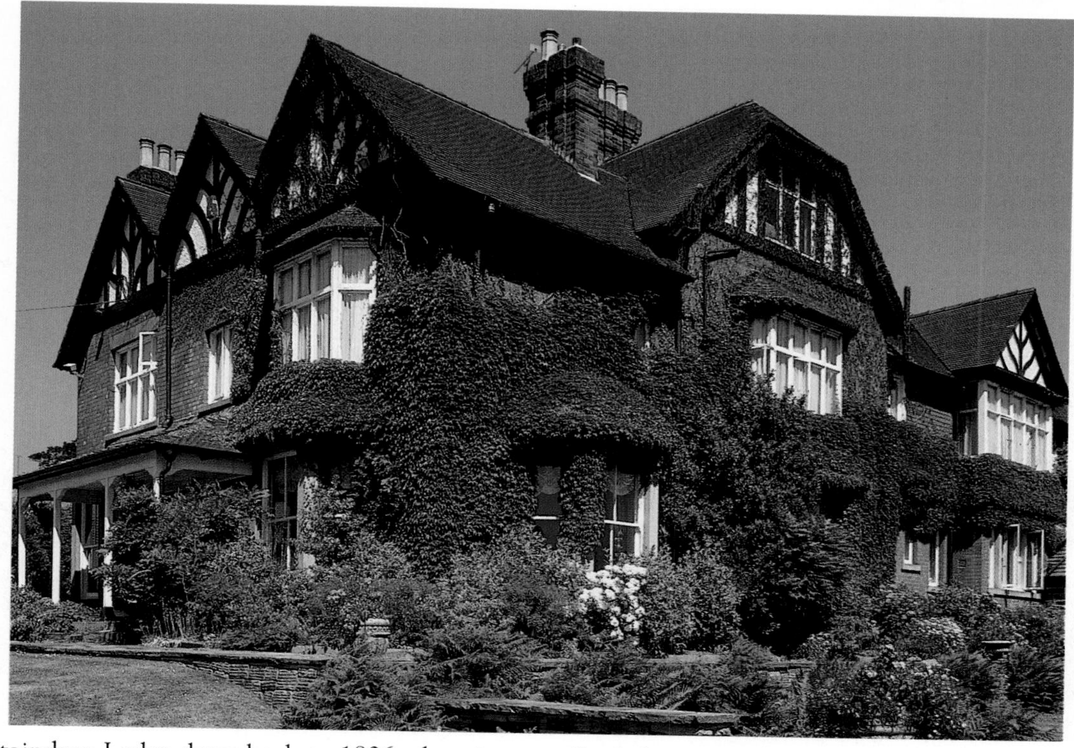

Ivy-clad Staindrop Lodge dates back to 1806 when it was built as the family home of George Newton, a founding father of the famous Yorkshire firm Newton Chambers. Now it has been sympathetically converted into a country hotel with all 20th century facilities. Surrounded by secluded mature gardens on the north side of Sheffield the hotel is five minutes from the M1 and only a few minutes drive from the city centre and within easy reach of Derbyshire's Peak District.

Each of the 13 en suite bedrooms is individually designed, tastefully furnished and has every comfort. The light, pastel coloured restaurant with its fine, flowing drapes has a reputation for good modern English cuisine blended with traditional and classical French influences. Apéritifs can be enjoyed in a small cocktail bar or in the conservatory style lounge. The Thorncliffe Suite is ideal for weddings, dances and business meetings. Special weekend breaks available. **Places of interest nearby:** Sheffield Arena and the Meadowhall shopping centre are just a short car journey away. 20 minutes from the Peak District National Park and Chatsworth is within easy reach. **Directions: From the M1, exit at junction 35 and take the A629 for one mile to Chapeltown. Turn right at the second roundabout into Loundside Road and the hotel is on the right after half-a-mile.**

For hotel location, see maps on pages 263–269

THE EASTBURY HOTEL

LONG STREET, SHERBORNE, DORSET DT9 3BY
TEL: 01935 813131 FAX: 01935 817296

OWNERS: Tom and Alison Pickford

15 rms | 15 ens | SMALL HOTEL

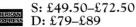

S: £49.50–£72.50
D: £79–£89

The Eastbury Hotel is a traditional town house which was built in 1740 during the reign of George II. During its recent refurbishment great care was taken to preserve its 18th century character. In fine weather guests can enjoy the seclusion of the hotel's private walled garden, which encompasses an acre of shrubs and formal plants and a noteworthy listed walnut tree.

Bedrooms are individually named after well-known English garden flowers and each is equipped with a full range of modern comforts and conveniences. The Eastbury is ideal for parents visiting sons or daughters who board at the Sherborne schools.

Traditional English cooking is a feature of the Eastbury restaurant and the dishes are complemented by an extensive list of the world's fine wines.

Places of interest nearby: Sherborne is rich in history and has a magnificent 15th century Perpendicular Abbey Church and two castles, in one of which Sir Walter Raleigh founded the national smoking habit. At Compton is a silk farm and a collection of butterflies. Beyond Yeovil is Montacute House (NT) and at Yeovilton is the Fleet Air Arm Museum. **Directions: Long Street is in the town centre, south of and parallel to the A30. Parking is at the rear of the hotel.**

For hotel location, see maps on pages 263–269

THE SHAVEN CROWN HOTEL

HIGH STREET, SHIPTON-UNDER-WYCHWOOD, OXFORDSHIRE OX7 6BA
TEL: 01993 830330 FAX: 01993 832136

OWNERS: Mr and Mrs Robert Burpitt

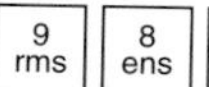   

S: £53
D: £75–£100

Built of honey-coloured stone around an attractive central courtyard, The Shaven Crown Hotel dates back to the 14th century, when it served as a monks' hospice. The proprietors have preserved the inn's many historic features, such as the medieval hall with its ancient timbered roof. This is now the residents' lounge. Each of the bedrooms has en suite facilities and has been sympathetically furnished in a style befitting its own unique character. Rooms of various style and sizes are available, including a huge family room and ground-floor accommodation. Dining in the intimate, candlelit room is an enjoyable experience, with meals served at the tables beautifully laid with fine accessories. The best ingredients are combined to create original dishes with a cosmopolitan flair. The table d'hôte menu offers a wide and eclectic choice with a daily vegetarian dish among the specialities. An imaginative selection of dishes is offered every lunchtime and evening in the Monks Bar.

Places of interest nearby: The Shaven Crown is ideal for day trips to the Cotswolds, Oxford, Stratford-upon-Avon and Bath. There are three golf courses and tennis courts close by. Trout fishing and antique-hunting are popular activities in the area. **Directions: Take the A40 Oxford–Cheltenham road. At Burford follow the A361 towards Chipping Norton. The inn is situated directly opposite the village green in Shipton-under-Wychwood.**

SIMONSBATH HOUSE HOTEL

SIMONSBATH, EXMOOR, SOMERSET TA24 7SH
TEL: 01643 831259 FAX: 01643 831557

OWNERS: Mike and Sue Burns

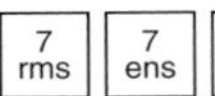

S: £50–£56
D: £84–£96

Simonsbath House was built by James Boevey, Warden of the Forest of Exmoor, in 1654, on rising ground facing due south across the beautiful valley of the River Barle. You are welcomed with log fires in the oak-panelled lounge and with mineral water, fresh fruit and flowers in the bedrooms. A relaxing atmosphere pervades throughout the house, which is still essentially a home, with welcoming owners and caring staff to pamper you with old-fashioned hospitality.

The bedroom windows overlook beech forests of everchanging hue, a crystal river bubbling through the valley and fold after fold of heather-clad hills. Guests can saddle up and gallop off to Exmoor's highest point – Dunkery Beacon – or set out on foot. The surrounding forests are ideal for strollers; hikers will enjoy the challenge of the high moorlands. Sue Burns is the chef and she uses only fresh local produce. Vegetarian meals by arrangement. Closed during December and January.

Places of interest nearby: The cathedral cities of Exeter and Wells; Glastonbury, Bath and Devon's beautiful coast. **Directions: Simonsbath is on the B3223, situated within the village, nine miles south of Lynton.**

For hotel location, see maps on pages 263–269

MARSH HALL COUNTRY HOUSE HOTEL

SOUTH MOLTON, NORTH DEVON EX36 3HQ
TEL: 01769 572666 FAX: 01769 574230

OWNERS: Tony and Judy Griffiths

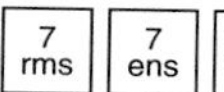   

S: £50–£70
D: £80–£100

Marsh Hall is the perfect place for a refreshing and relaxing holiday and is also ideal for business travellers who require a special overnight stay.

Tony and Judy Griffiths took over ownership of the hotel in 1993 and have created a friendly and informal atmosphere that has guests returning time after time.

The hotel is set in three acres of attractive gardens and was reputedly built by the local squire for his mistress. Here guests can relax in either the elegant chandelier-lit lounge or the friendly bar, both of which have log fires burning during winter. The large hall and stairway light the gallery which leads to the seven en suite bedrooms, all of which are individually furnished and have country views.

The highlight at Marsh Hall is the food. In the delightful award winning restaurant great attention is paid to the quality of the cuisine with the four-course table d'hôte menu changing daily. The finest fresh local produce is used together with vegetables, herbs and fruit from the hotel's kitchen gardens. Special diets are catered for. **Places of interest nearby:** Exmoor National Park, beaches and cliffs of North Devon, many houses and gardens open to the public. **Directions: Leave the M5 at junction 27 and take the A361 to North Devon, continue for 25 miles then turn right at junction signposted North Molton, after ½ mile turn right then sharp right into hotel drive.**

For hotel location, see maps on pages 263–269

KINGSTON HOUSE

STAVERTON, TOTNES, DEVON TQ9 6AR
TEL: 01803 762 235 FAX: 01803 762 444 E-MAIL: kingston–estate.demon.co.uk

OWNERS: Michael and Elizabeth Corfield
CHEF: Sarah George

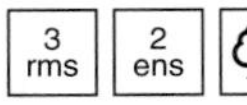

S: £75–£85
D: £110
Suite: £120–£130

The Kingston Estate nestles amongst the rolling hills and valleys of the South Hams region of Devon, bounded by Dartmoor and the sea, with the focal point, Kingston House, commanding sweeping views of the moor.

The Mansion, together with the superb self-catering cottages, have been sympathetically restored by the Corfield family to their former glory and now offer some of the highest standard accommodation to be found in the South West. The House boasts three period suites, (reached by way of the finest example of a marquetry staircase in England), which are hung with authentic wall papers and fabrics and include a 1735 Angel tester bed and an 1830 four-poster.

Dinner guests dine by candlelight in the elegant dining room at tables set with sparkling crystal, shining silver and starched linen. In winter, log fires crackle in the hearths, whilst in the summer pre-dinner drinks may be taken on the terrace overlooking the formal 18th century gardens. For every visitor to Kingston, hospitality and comfort are assured in this magnificent historic setting.

Places of interest nearby: Dartington Hall, Dartmouth, Totnes, Dartmoor & Devon's famous coastline.

Directions: Take A38 from Exeter or Plymouth, at Buckfastleigh take A384 Totnes road for two miles. Turn left to Staverton. At Sea Trout Inn, take left fork to Kingston and follow signs.

For hotel location, see maps on pages 263–269

Redcoats Farmhouse Hotel and Restaurant

REDCOATS GREEN, NEAR HITCHIN, HERTS SG4 7JR
TEL: 01438 729500 FAX: 01438 723322 E-MAIL: info@redcoats.co.uk

OWNERS: The Butterfield Family
CHEF: John Ruffell

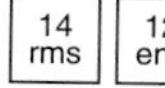   

   S: £70–£85
D: £80–£95

This 15th century farmhouse has been in the Butterfield family's possession for generations and in 1971 Peter and his sister converted it into a hotel. They preserved its traditional character of original beams, exposed brickwork and inglenook fireplaces and furnished it in a comfortable and inviting fashion.

It is set in tranquil gardens – one of the larger rooms has its own garden – in the middle of rolling countryside, not far from A1(M). There are 14 rooms, 12 with en suite bathrooms, diverse in character: those in the main house retaining period charm and those in the stable block more modern.

Meals are served in four dining rooms: the Oak Room and the Old Kitchen, log fire cosiness; the Victorian Room, elegant and formal and the Conservatory, garden room atmosphere. Redcoats has a good reputation for its cuisine, which uses much local produce and a wine list which is as wide ranging geographically as it is in prices.

Places of interest nearby: Redcoats is close to several historic houses including Knebworth House, Hatfield House, Luton Hoo and Woburn. The Roman city of St Albans, the traditional market town of Hitchin and Cambridge University are all within a 30 minute drive. **Directions: Leave the A1(M) at junction 8 for Little Wymondley. At mini-roundabout turn left. At T-Junction go right, hotel is on left.**

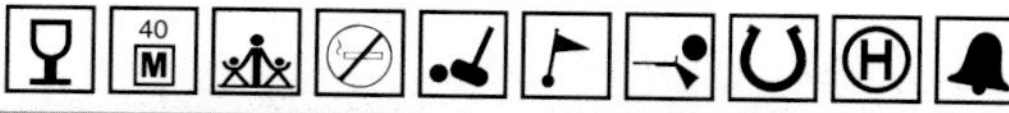

For hotel location, see maps on pages 263–269

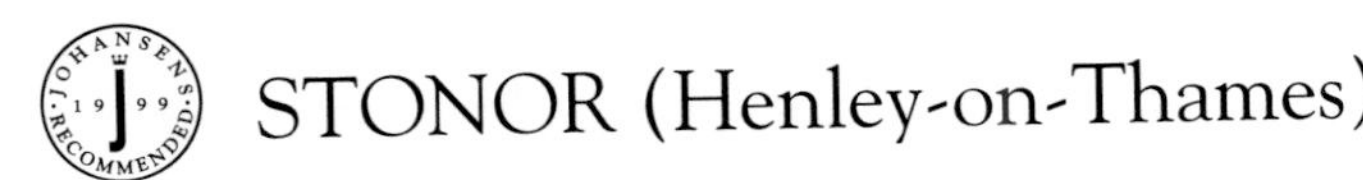

The Stonor Arms

STONOR, NR HENLEY-ON-THAMES, OXFORDSHIRE RG9 6HE
TEL: 01491 638866 FAX: 01491 638863

OWNERS: Stonor Hotels Ltd
MANAGER: Sophia Williams

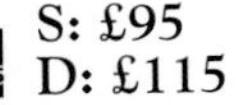

S: £95
D: £115

This small hotel is not too far from London and perfectly located for those going to Henley or Ascot. It is in a pretty village on the edge of Stonor Park and restoration has not diminished its 18th century elegance.

The interior of the hotel has been beautifully decorated in the style of that era, combining grace with comfort. The bedrooms are enchanting, very spacious, furnished with French and English antiques and colourful yet harmonious fabrics.

The hotel has won a high reputation for its first-class food. The restaurant consists of a formal dining area and a conservatory where the atmosphere is more relaxed. The cooking is traditional English and French. Snacks are served in Blades, the flagstoned bar where rowing memorabilia adorn the walls. **Places of interest nearby:** Windsor and Oxford are easily accessible and sporting activities nearby include boating and golf or walking in the countryside. **Directions: Leave the M40 at junction 6, following B4009 to Watlington, then turn left onto B480 through Stonor.**

For hotel location, see maps on pages 263–269

Conygree Gate Hotel

KINGHAM, OXFORDSHIRE OX7 6YA
TEL: 01608 658389 FAX: 01608 659467

OWNER: Judy Krasker
CHEF: Andrew Foster

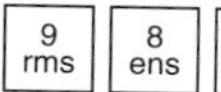  

S: £27.50–£37.50
D: £65–£85

This beautiful Cotswold stone, Grade II listed building began life as a 17th century farmhouse. Situated in the centre of the peaceful village of Kingham, it is an ideal retreat from the hustle and bustle of the modern world.

All the bedrooms are individually decorated and several feature original leaded light windows and window seats. A number open directly onto the walled garden where afternoon tea and evening drinks are served.

Leading off the flagstoned hall are two lounges with log fires, original beams and cosy armchairs – perfect for reading and relaxing.

The young chef, Andrew Foster, winner of the 1997 Académie Culinaire Annual Award of Excellence, prepares the delicious dishes offered on the four or five course menu. Served in the spectacularly decorated dining room, the meals include starters such as terrine of smoked salmon and anchovy butter with sauce gribiche and main dishes including loin of lamb baked in an olive bread with a beetroot jus and fillet of salmon on a bed of saffron risotto with a white wine sauce. Awarded 2 AA Rosettes.

Places of interest nearby: Burford, Bourton-on-the-Water and many other typical Cotswold towns and villages are all close by. Blenheim Palace, Stratford-upon-Avon and Oxford are also within easy reach. **Directions: The hotel is in the centre of Kingham, which lies between the B4450 and A436 to the east of Stow.**

For hotel location, see maps on pages 263–269

STRATFORD-UPON-AVON (Loxley)

GLEBE FARM HOUSE

LOXLEY, WARWICKSHIRE CV35 9JW
TEL/FAX: 01789 842501 E-MAIL: scorpiolimited@msn.com

OWNER: Kate McGovern

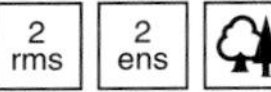

S: £69.50
D: £85

The pleasure of staying at this delightful country house is like that of visiting a private home. Just three miles from historic Stratford-upon-Avon and eight miles from Warwick, Glebe Farm is surrounded by a superb expanse of secluded lawned garden which opens on to 30 acres of beautiful farmland where one can ramble and enjoy the sounds and sights of local wildlife.

Owner Kate McGovern is an accomplished cook and her dinners, served in the attractive surroundings of a conservatory overlooking the gardens, will tempt every palate. Whenever possible fresh produce from the kitchen garden are used. Kate is a talented water colour artist and many of her paintings adorn the walls throughout the house which is furnished and decorated with immaculate taste.

There are two pretty en suite bedrooms with four-poster beds and television and tea and coffee facilities. From both bedrooms and the lounge there are splendid views of the countryside. Local sporting activities include golf, shooting and riding.

Places of interest nearby: The hotel is an ideal base for visiting Shakespeare's Stratford-upon-Avon, Warwick's imposing castle, Ragley Hall, the Heritage Motor Museum and the Cotswolds. **Directions: From the M40, exit at junction 15. Join the A429 and follow the signs to Wellsbourne and then Loxley. Glebe Farm is on the right as you leave Loxley.**

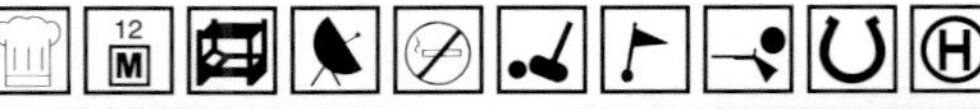

For hotel location, see maps on pages 263–269

UPPER COURT

KEMERTON, NR TEWKESBURY, GLOUCESTERSHIRE GL20 7HY
TEL: 01386 725351 FAX: 01386 725472 E-MAIL: uppercourt@compuserve.com

OWNERS: Bill and Diana Herford

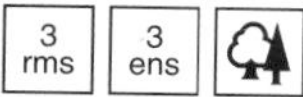

S: £65
D: £80–£120

Upper Court is an outstanding Georgian manor with flower filled Coaching yard with holiday cottages. Guests are warmly welcomed whether staying in the manor or in one of the cottages. The four-poster or twin bedrooms all en suite, furnished in traditional English Country house style with lovely chintzes, needlework and linens.

The main feature of The National Garden Scheme garden is the lake, a 2 acre haven for a variety of wildfowl and for those who seek peace. The idyllic grounds also have a Doomsday watermill and a dovecote.

Kemerton is a splendid location on Bredon Hill with views of 5 counties, and a stroll down the lane is the excellent Crown Inn. Weekend use of the holiday cottages costs £150, please enquire for availability.

Places of interest nearby: Stratford, Sudeley and Warwick Castles, Hidcote, Snowshill Manor, Oxford, Bath, Cheltenham and Broadway. **Directions: From Cheltenham north on A435/B4079. One mile after A46 crossroads sign to Kemerton on the right. Turn off main road at War Memorial. House behind church. From M5 junction 9, go east on A46 to the B4079 crossroads, then left and one mile as above.**

For hotel location, see maps on pages 263–269

TREBREA LODGE

TRENALE, TINTAGEL, CORNWALL PL34 0HR
TEL: 01840 770410 FAX: 01840 770092

OWNERS: John Charlick and Sean Devlin

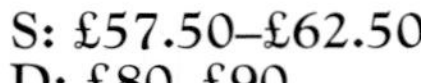

S: £57.50–£62.50
D: £80–£90

Winner of the Johansens 1994 Country House Award, Trebrea Lodge overlooks the beauty and grandeur of the North Cornish coast and is set in 4½ acres of wooded hillside. This Grade II listed house was built on land granted to the Bray family by the Black Prince in the 14th century and has been lived in and improved by successive generations of the Brays for almost 600 years.

All the bedrooms are individually decorated with traditional and antique furniture and they offer uninterrupted views across open fields to the Atlantic Ocean. The elegant first-floor drawing room also boasts spectacular views, while there is a comfortable smoking room downstairs with an open log fire.

A full English breakfast and four-course dinner are served in the oak-panelled dining room and the menu changes daily. The cooks use the finest local ingredients, including sea trout and wild salmon from the River Tamar and they have been awarded an AA Rosette.

Places of interest nearby: Tintagel Island and Boscastle. Bodmin Moor, Lanhydrock House and gardens, Pencarrow House and extensive coastal walks.

Directions: From Launceston take Wadebridge–Camelford road. At A39 follow Tintagel sign – turn left for Trenale ½ mile before reaching Tintagel.

For hotel location, see maps on pages 263–269

THE ROYAL HOTEL

LEMON STREET, TRURO, CORNWALL, TR1 2QB
TEL: 01872 270345 FAX: 01872 242453

OWNER: Lynn Manning
MANAGER: Martin Edwards
CHEF: Bryan Hatton

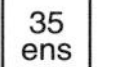

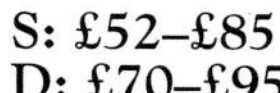

S: £52–£85
D: £70–£95

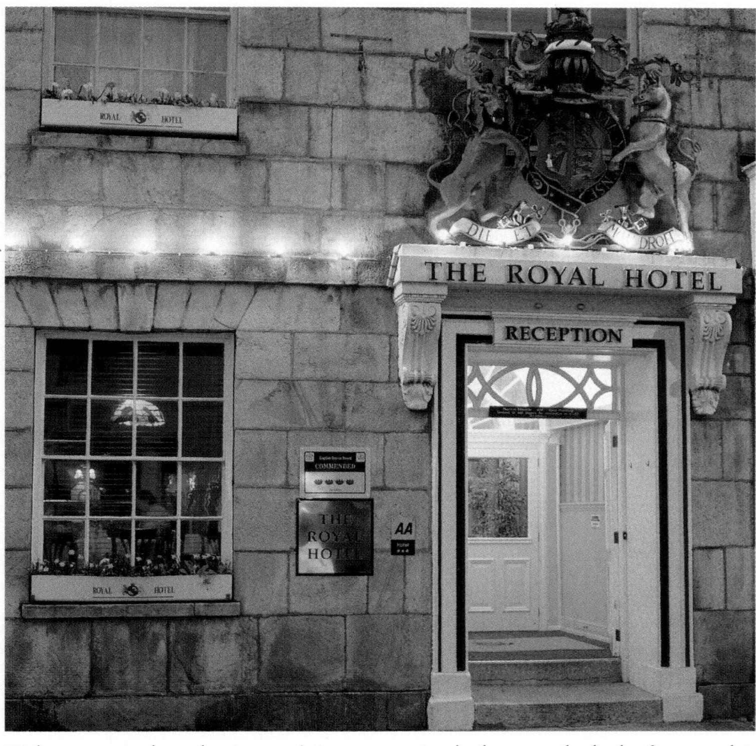

Visitors to this elegant, 17th century hotel, situated in the heart of the cathedral city of Truro, cannot but be impressed by the king-size royal coat of arms above the entrance door and the rich, deep blue carpet enhanced with large red and gold crowns in the reception area. These commemorate a visit to the hotel by Queen Victoria's husband, Prince Albert, in 1846.

The Royal Hotel regally exemplifies some of the most dignified and best preserved examples of Georgian architecture in Britain that surround it. It has style, character and comfort. The carefully appointed bedrooms are all fully en suite and have everything expected from a quality hotel. Business facilities in executive bedrooms include a work desk, fax machine and datapoint phone.

Superb international cuisine is imaginatively created and presented. Guests wishing to work off a heavy meal and stay trim can take advantage of a mirrored fitness studio.

Places of interest nearby: Falmouth, St Ives, the Seal Sanctuary at Gweek, several heritage sites and many magnificent gardens and National Trust properties.

Directions: From the A30 turn left at Carland Cross towards the city centre dual carriageway. Go all the way round the second roundabout to drive back up the dual carriageway. Take the first left and the hotel is ahead of you.

Hooke Hall

HIGH STREET, UCKFIELD, EAST SUSSEX TN22 1EN
TEL: 01825 761578 FAX: 01825 768025

OWNERS: Alister and Juliet Percy

9 rms | 9 ens | SMALL HOTEL

S: from £55
D: from £80

Uckfield lies on the borders of Ashdown Forest, near the South Downs and resorts of Brighton and Eastbourne and 40 minutes from Gatwick Airport. Hooke Hall is an elegant Queen Anne town house, the home of its owners, Juliet and Alister Percy, who have carried out extensive renovations.

The comfortable bedrooms are individually decorated to a high standard with private facilities. In the panelled study guests can relax by the open fire before having dinner at 'La Scaletta' known for its high quality North Italian regional cuisine. The food has earned 2 AA Rosettes and small lunch and dinner parties are arranged in other rooms and are looked after by Juliet, herself a Cordon Bleu chef.

Places of interest nearby: Within easy reach are Leeds, Hever and Bodiam Castles, Penshurst Place and Battle Abbey. The gardens of Sissinghurst, Nymans, Great Dixter, Sheffield Park, Wakehurst Place and Leonardslee are no distance nor is Batemans, Rudyard Kipling's home. Glyndebourne Opera is only 15 minutes by car. There are several English vineyards nearby to be visited. Closed for Christmas. **Directions: From M25 take the exit for East Grinstead and continue South on the A22 to Uckfield. Hooke Hall is at the northern end of the High Street.**

For hotel location, see maps on pages 263–269

TREHELLAS HOUSE & MEMORIES OF MALAYA RESTAURANT

WASHAWAY, BODMIN, CORNWALL PL30 3AD
TEL: 01208 72700 FAX: 01208 73336

OWNERS: Robin and Lee Boyle
CHEF: Lee Boyle

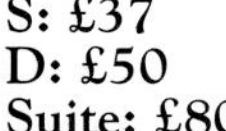

S: £37
D: £50
Suite: £80

This early 18th century former posting inn, steeped in history, is surrounded by two acres of grounds. The bedrooms are charming, varying in size, with five in the main house and others in the former coach house and barn. Following a recent refurbishment, the rooms are enhanced by the comfortable furnishings including patchwork quilts, iron bedsteads and en suite facilities.

The Memories of Malaya restaurant, with its beautifully preserved slate floor and elegant décor, serves a unique style of cuisine known as Nonya. Originating from the Pacific Rim, the dishes are authentically reproduced and flavoured with aromatic herbs and spices. Cornish breakfasts are served with locally produced organic bacon, sausages and free-range eggs.

Guests may wish to stroll in the pleasant gardens or enjoy the heated swimming pool. There are ample parking facilities.

Places of interest nearby: Pencarrow House and Lanhydrock House and Gardens are both within easy reach. The village of Rock is a popular base for sailing and fishing whilst cyclists and ramblers will enjoy the trails to Padstow and the Bodmin Moor. **Directions: Washaway is located on the A389 half-way between the towns of Bodmin and Wadebridge. Approaching from Bodmin, Trehellas House is situated to the right, set back from the main road and accessed by a slip road.**

For hotel location, see maps on pages 263–269

WAREHAM (East Stoke)

KEMPS COUNTRY HOUSE HOTEL AND RESTAURANT

EAST STOKE, WAREHAM, DORSET BH20 6AL
TEL: 01929 462563 FAX: 01929 405287

OWNERS: Jill and Paul Warren

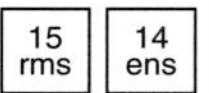  

15 rms | 14 ens | SMALL HOTEL

S: £55–£75
D: £80–£126

This small and welcoming country house hotel, surrounded by unspoilt Dorset countryside, overlooks the Frome Valley and offers lovely views of the Purbeck Hills. The house was originally a Victorian Rectory and its tasteful extension was undertaken with great care to preserve Victorian atmosphere.

There are five bedrooms in the main house, while the Old Coach House has been converted to include four en suite rooms. More recently, six spacious new bedrooms have been added in an annexe, all facing the Purbecks. Decorated and furnished to equally high standards, one of these rooms has a traditional four-poster bed and a whirlpool bath. The bar features the ornate wallpaper and heavy hangings of the Victorian period. The comfortable dining room extends into the conservatory, from which there are picturesque views of the hills. Kemps restaurant, which has been awarded an AA Rosette, enjoys an excellent local reputation for first-rate cuisine. The table d'hôte menu changes daily and there is also an à la carte menu. Food is prepared to order, everything possible is home-made.

Places of interest nearby: Lulworth and Corfe Castles, Athelhampton House and gardens. **Directions: In its own grounds on the A352 between Wareham and Wool.**

60 M

For hotel location, see maps on pages 263–269

THE ARDENCOTE MANOR HOTEL AND COUNTRY CLUB

LYE GREEN ROAD, CLAVERDON, WARWICKSHIRE CV35 8LS
TEL: 01926 843111 FAX 01926 842646 E-MAIL: hotel@ardencote.com

MANAGER: Paul Williams
CHEF: Jonathan Stallard

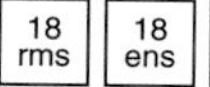   

   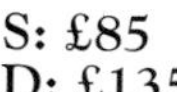

S: £85
D: £135

Situated deep in the Warwickshire countryside yet just minutes from the motorway network, this charming, historic gentleman's residence is a tranquil retreat with an extensive range of sports and leisure facilities. There is an indoor swimming pool with Jacuzzi, solarium and steam rooms, two fully equipped gymnasia, two all-weather tennis courts, four glass-backed squash courts, 3 acre trout lake and 9-hole golf course..

Alternatively, guests can pamper themselves with one of the range of head-to-toe beauty treatments in the hotel's Health and Beauty Suite.

The en suite bedrooms are spacious and tastefully furnished. A creatively designed table d'hôte menu is served in the large, stylish conservatory which opens onto the gardens and has an adjacent cocktail bar and dance area. More intimate dining can be enjoyed in the gourmet Oak Room restaurant with its elegant country house atmosphere.

A traditional log cabin Sports Lodge overlooking a large, trout filled lake and incorporating a separate and informal bar restaurant, nestles gracefully within the 40 acres of immaculate landscaped grounds, gardens and waterways. **Places of interest nearby:** Birmingham's city attractions and Warwick's imposing castle. Stratford-upon-Avon is within easy reach. **Directions: From M40 follow signs to Henley-in-Arden, taking the A4189 to Claverdon/ Warwick.**

For hotel location, see maps on pages 263–269

Beryl

WELLS, SOMERSET BA5 3JP
TEL: 01749 678738 FAX: 01749 670508

OWNERS: Eddie and Holly Nowell

S: £50–£65
D: £65–£85

This nineteenth century Gothic mansion is tastefully furnished with antiques. It also offers hospitality of the highest order.

The host is a famous antique dealer, with a long established shop in Wells, his gardening talents are reflected in the 13 acres of parkland which he has restored with great skill.

His wife is a charming and talented hostess, evident in the attention paid to detail and an excellent cook. Dinner is served by arrangement in the elegant dining room, with a set menu and house wines, pre-dinner and after-dinner drinks are available. It is possible to have small conferences or private celebrations. The en suite bedrooms have interesting views, with all the requisites for modern comfort.

Places of interest nearby: Wells Cathedral (1 mile), The Roman Baths at Bath, Glastonbury Abbey, Longleat House, Stourhead, Farleigh Castle, theatres in Bath and Bristol and many more fascinating places. For more active guests, there is marvellous golf, fishing, riding, excellent walking and a nearby leisure centre. **Directions: Leave Wells on Radstock Road B3139. Opposite the B.P. garage turn left into Hawkers Lane, Beryl is signed at the top with a leafy 500 yard drive to the main gate.**

For hotel location, see maps on pages 263–269

Coxley Vineyard

COXLEY, WELLS, SOMERSET BA5 1RQ
TEL: 01749 670285 FAX: 01749 679708

OWNERS: William Jones and Anita England
CHEF: Simon Jackson

10 rms | 10 ens | SMALL HOTEL

S: £65
D: from £70

Built around a suntrap courtyard in the heart of four acres of grapevines, this small, charming hotel has a Mediterranean ambience. Pastel décor, terracotta tiled flooring, pine furniture and ceilings enhance the continental family atmosphere created by owners Bill Jones and Anita England.

Coxley Vineyard is a hotel providing excellent service and hospitality, where guests can completely relax and enjoy the delights of their surroundings. The ten bedrooms are luxuriously en suite and have every home comfort and facility. Two, including the Bridal/Master room, have large four-posters. Children are very welcome and cots and baby monitoring services are available if required.

A superbly prepared selection of lunch and dinner table d'hôte and à la carte dishes are served in the large, newly refurbished restaurant. Chef Simon Jackson uses the best local produce and his cuisine can be complemented by wine from an extensive list. This includes the hotel's own vintage which is renowned for its distinctive fruity flavour. On warm summer evenings guests can dine in the attractive courtyard.

The hotel has recently had a swimming pool and two tennis courts installed in the grounds, has its own fishing ponds on the moors and can arrange fishing and shooting excursions. **Places of interest nearby:** Wells Cathedral, Glastonbury Abbey, Longleat House, Stourhead, the Cheddar Gorge and caves, Wookey Hole, Stonehenge and Bristol. **Directions: Two miles from Wells on A39 road to Glastonbury.**

For hotel location, see maps on pages 263–269

GLENCOT HOUSE

GLENCOT LANE, WOOKEY HOLE, NR WELLS, SOMERSET BA5 1BH
TEL: 01749 677160 FAX: 01749 670210

OWNER: Jenny Attia

 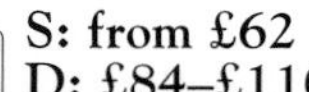

S: from £62
D: £84–£110

Idyllically situated in 18 acres of sheltered gardens and parkland with river frontage, Glencot House is an imposing Grade II listed Victorian mansion built in grand Jacobean style. It has been sensitively renovated to its former glory to provide comfortable country house accommodation and a homely atmosphere.

This elegantly furnished hotel has countless beautiful features: carved ceilings, walnut panelling, mullioned windows, massive fireplaces, antiques and sumptuous chandeliers. The bedrooms are decorated and furnished with period pieces. All have full en suite facilities and splendid views. Many have four-poster or half tester beds.

Guests can enjoy pleasant walks in the garden, trout fishing in the river, snooker, table tennis, a sauna or a dip in the jet-stream pool. The small, intimate bar has a balcony overlooking the grounds and diverse and delicious fare is served in the restaurant, enriched by beautiful glassware, silver and china.

Places of interest nearby: The caves at Wookey Hole, the cathedral town of Wells, the houses and gardens of Longleat, Stourhead and Montacute, Glastonbury, Bath, the Mendip Hills and the Cheddar Gorge. **Directions: From the M4, exit at junction 18. Take the A46 to Bath and then follow the signs to Wells and Wookey Hole. From the M5, exit at junction 22. Join the A38 and then the A371 towards Wells and Wookey Hole.**

For hotel location, see maps on pages 263–269

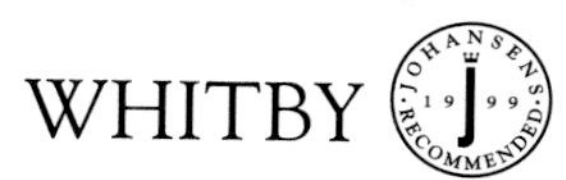

DUNSLEY HALL

DUNSLEY, WHITBY, NORTH YORKSHIRE YO21 3TL
TEL: 01947 893437 FAX: 01947 893505

OWNERS: Bill and Carol Ward
CHEF: Rob Green

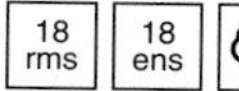   

S: £65–£90
D: £105–£158

Stately Dunsley Hall stands in 4 acres of landscaped gardens in North Yorkshire National Park and has survived almost unaltered since being built at the turn of the century. The oak panelling and some of the original carpets and furnishings are still in fine condition.

Each of the bedrooms is individually furnished and some have views to the sea which is only a few minutes walk away. Two of the bedrooms have four-poster beds.

Guests can relax over a drink in the Pyman Bar or Library Bar whose restful features include mellowed oak panelling, a handsome carved fireplace and stained glass windows. Each evening guests dine in the Oak Room or Terrace Dining Room with its picture window view over the garden.

For exercise and health there is a fully-equipped fitness room, a sauna and large indoor swimming pool. Outside is a hard tennis court, a 9-hole putting green and a croquet lawn. Dogs are allowed by arrangement only. Special break rates available.

Places of interest nearby: Castle Howard, Robin Hood's Bay, the Pickering Steam Railway and the birthplace of Captain Cook. Reduced green fees at Whitby Golf Course.

Directions: From the A171 Whitby-Teeside road, turn right at signpost for Newholme, three miles north of Whitby. Dunsley is the first turning on the left. Dunsley Hall is one mile further on the right.

For hotel location, see maps on pages 263–269

BEECHLEAS

17 POOLE ROAD, WIMBORNE MINSTER, DORSET BH21 1QA
TEL: 01202 841684 FAX: 01202 849344

OWNER: Josephine McQuillan

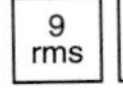

S: £69–£89
D: £89–£99

Beechleas is a delightful Georgian Grade II listed town house hotel. It has been carefully restored and offers guests comfortable accommodation in beautifully furnished quality en suite bedrooms.

The hotel's own charming restaurant, which overlooks a pretty walled garden, is bright and airy in the summer and warmed by cosy log fires in the winter. The carefully prepared menu is changed daily and offers dishes using natural produce wherever possible along with the finest fresh ingredients available from the local market.

Sailing trips are available from Poole Harbour, where guests may choose to go fishing. They can play golf on one of the many local courses. It takes just five minutes to walk into the centre of Wimborne, a historic market town with an interesting twin tower church built on the site of its old Saxon Abbey during the 12th and 13th centuries.

The hotel, which is closed from 24 December to mid January, has been awarded two Red Stars by the AA and two Rosettes for its restaurant along with a Blue Ribbon from the RAC.

Places of interest nearby: There are many National Trust properties within easy reach, including Kingston Lacy House, Badbury Rings and Corfe Castle. Bournemouth and Poole are a 20 minute drive away. **Directions: From London take M3, M27, A31 and then B3073 to Wimborne.**

For hotel location, see maps on pages 263–269

HOLBROOK HOUSE HOTEL

WINCANTON, SOMERSET BA9 8BS
TEL: 01963 32377 FAX: 01963 32681

OWNER: John and Pat McGinley
HOUSE MANAGER: Claire Evans
EXECUTIVE CHEF: Craig Brookes

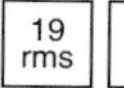

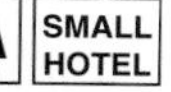

S: from £50
D: from £75

The history of Holbrook dates back to Saxon times, with the earliest records of a property on the site having been drawn up during the reign of Edward III. Today's house lies two miles west of Wincanton at the edge of the low hills that fringe the Blackmore Vale.

Set in 17 acres of mature grounds, the hotel, recently refurbished, delights in providing its guests with a wealth of good food, home comforts and friendly service.

The Holbrook Restaurant serves fresh meat from animals, traditionally reared, with venison and game selected from local shoots on estates and fresh fish which is delivered daily.

Open from May to September, the hotel's swimming pool is located next to a tranquil little orchard plantation and is overlooked by an ancient dovecote.

Other sports presently on offer include tennis, squash and croquet whilst the hotel's Spa and Leisure/Conference facilities are due for completion in early 1999.

By the side of the main building hovers a 'Cedar of Lebanon' dating back to the 1490, indeed a fine feature of the grounds!

Places of interest nearby: The Fleet Air Arm Museum and the great houses and gardens of Montacute, Longleat and Stourhead. **Directions: Leave A303 at Wincanton slip Road and join A371 towards Castle Cary at the first roundabout. Over three more roundabouts and the hotel driveway is on the right immediately after the third.**

FAYRER GARDEN HOUSE HOTEL

LYTH VALLEY ROAD, BOWNESS-ON-WINDERMERE, CUMBRIA LA23 3JP
TEL: 015394 88195 FAX: 015394 45986 E-MAIL: lakescene@fayrergarden.com

OWNERS: Iain and Jackie Garside

18 rms | 18 ens | SMALL HOTEL

MasterCard VISA AMERICAN EXPRESS

S: £65–£95
D: £95–£190
(including dinner)

Overlooking Lake Windermere in spacious gardens and grounds this lovely Victorian House is a very comfortable hotel where guests enjoy the spectacular views over the water, a real welcome and marvellous value for money.

The delightful lounges and bar and the superb air-conditioned restaurant all enjoy Lake views. There is an excellent table d'hôte menu in the award-winning restaurant changing daily using local produce where possible, fish, game and poultry and also a small à la carte choice. The wine list is excellent and very reasonably priced.

Many of the attractive bedrooms face the Lake, some having four- poster beds and whirlpool baths en suite. There are also ground floor rooms suitable for the elderly or infirm.

The nearby Parklands Leisure Complex has an indoor pool, sauna, steam room, badminton, snooker and squash complimentary to hotel residents. Special breaks available. **Places of interest nearby:** The Windermere Steamboat Museum, Boating from Bowness Pier and golf at Windermere Golf Club and The Beatrix Potter Attraction are all close by. **Directions: Junction 36 off the M6, A590 past Kendal. Take B5284 at the next roundabout, turn left at the end and the hotel is 350 yards on the right.**

For hotel location, see maps on pages 263–269

QUARRY GARTH COUNTRY HOUSE HOTEL AND RESTAURANT

WINDERMERE, CUMBRIA LA23 1L7
TEL: 015394 88282 FAX: 015394 46584

OWNER: Ken MacLean
MANAGER: Steve MacLean

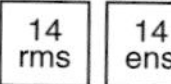
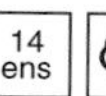

S: £50–£60
D: £70–£118

This mellow Edwardian house enjoys an idyllic setting in eight acres of peaceful woodland gardens near Lake Windermere. Ken MacLean and his staff invite guests to come and sample Quarry Garth's high standards of comfort and hospitality.

The individually designed bedrooms are all en suite some with four-poster or king-size beds. The elegant lounge with its deep soft sofas, open log fire and cocktail bar is the ideal location for relaxation and pre-dinner drinks. The award-winning restaurant 'Le Louvre', which overlooks the tumbling beck and landscaped gardens, serves the finest Anglo-French cuisine prepared using fresh game, fish and locally-produced vegetables. Soft lighting and candles evoke the unique ambience of a country house hotel.

Secluded some 50 yards from the main hotel stands the Quarry Lodge, containing three en suite bedrooms on the ground floor (two with spa baths) and a large lounge dining room on the first floor.

A woodland trail within the grounds offers a relaxing 15 minute walk among rich wildlife. A sauna and spa bathroom is available for use by guests.

Places of interest nearby: The beautiful lakes, the homes of Wordsworth and Beatrix Potter and many historic home and gardens. **Directions: From exit 36 of M6, take A590 for 3 miles then A591 to Windermere. Continue on A591 for 2 miles and the entrance is on the right.**

For hotel location, see maps on pages 263–269

STORRS HALL

WINDERMERE, CUMBRIA LA23 3LG
TEL: 015394 47111 FAX: 015394 47555

OWNER: Richard Livock

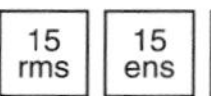  

   **Rooms from £150**

Surrounded on three sides by the lake itself, Storrs Hall stands in 15 acres of landscaped grounds and gardens on a peninsula jutting out into Lake Windermere. This 18th century listed Georgian manor house, once frequented by Wordsworth, Southey and Scott has been purchased by Richard Livock, a fine art dealer, who has magnificently restored the hall to its former glory and furnished it throughout with antiques and objets d'art.

Opened as a hotel in July 1998, the 15 bedrooms have been imaginatively restored and sumptuously furnished. Most have unparalleled views of the lake, the whole of which was once the property of the Hall. Equally splendid views can be enjoyed from the day rooms which incorporate an exquisite lounge, stylish library and a cosy bar. For gentle relaxation there is a garden with croquet lawn and half a mile of lakeside frontage to explore. In the Terrace Restaurant, the lunch and dinner menus reflect the grandeur of the setting, with local specialities such as smoked wild salmon and Cartmel duckling presented alongside oysters, lobster and beef tournedos in classical guises.

Places of interest nearby: These include the Wordsworth Museum at Grasmere, Dove Cottage, Beatrix Potter's Hill Top Farm and many historic houses and gardens. At Bowness is the Steamboat Museum, at Windermere boating and golf.

Directions: Storrs Hall is on Lake Windermere, on A592 two miles south of Bowness; five miles north of Newby Bridge.

For hotel location, see maps on pages 263–269

THE OLD VICARAGE COUNTRY HOUSE HOTEL

CHURCH ROAD, WITHERSLACK, NR GRANGE-OVER- SANDS, CUMBRIA LA11 6RS
TEL: 015395 52381 FAX: 015395 52373 E-MAIL: hotel@old–vic.demon.co.uk

OWNERS: Roger and Jill Brown, Stan and Irene Reeve
CHEF: James Brown

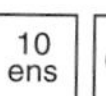

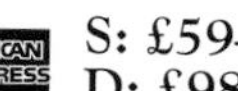

S: £59–£79
D: £98–£138

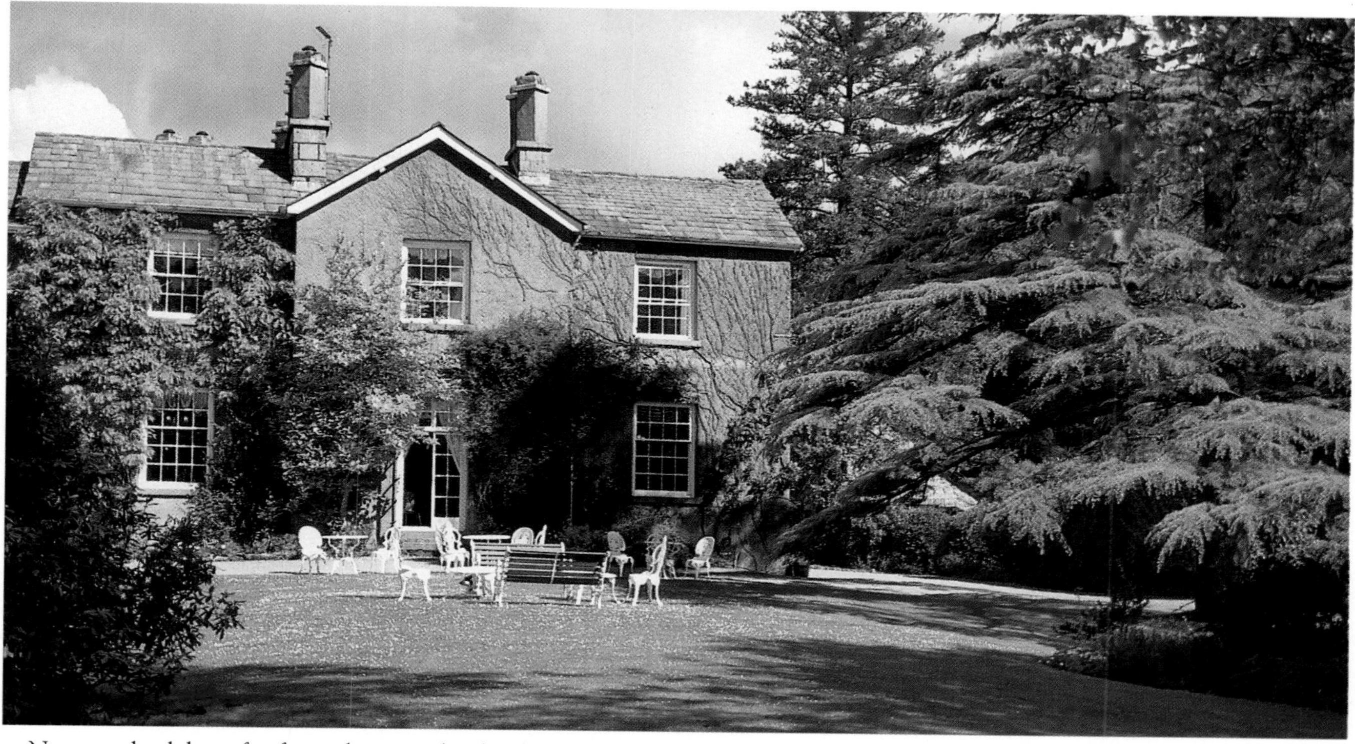

Near to the lakes...far from the crowds, this lovely old, family-run historic house offers the tranquil timeless atmosphere that reflects the calm and beauty of the surrounding countryside.

The delightful, mature garden is stocked with many interesting plants and part of it is left natural for wild flowers, unusual orchids, butterflies, dragonflies and birds. An all-weather tennis court in a delightful setting is for guests' use. Guests also have free use of the nearby Cascades Leisure Club.

In the old house, each of the comfortable bedrooms has its own particular character yet with all the modern facilities. The Orchard House, close by, is set beside an ancient damson orchard and has particularly well-equipped, spacious rooms each with its own woodland terrace. With top culinary awards, the well-planned menus include interesting, good quality locally-produced specialities. Diets can, of course, easily be catered for. **Places of interest nearby:** The Lake District National Park, Windermere, Wordsworth Heritage and Sizergh Castle (a member of The National Trust) are all within easy reach. Nature enthusiasts will be delighted to visit the famous topiary gardens at Levens Hall. **Directions: From M6 junction 36, follow A590 to Barrow. After 6 miles turn right into Witherslack, then first left after the telephone box.**

Wood Hall Hotel Country Club

SHOTTISHAM, WOODBRIDGE, SUFFOLK IP12 3EG
TEL: 01394 411283 FAX: 01394 410007

OWNERS: Harvey and Carole Storch
MANAGERS: Kevin and Samantha Jobson

  SMALL HOTEL

S: £75
D: £75–£95
Suite: £105

Three miles from Woodbridge, on the Deben estuary, this Elizabethan manor house has been transformed into a secluded and luxurious hotel. A walled garden and lake are just part of the magnificent grounds surrounding Wood Hall – which is approached by a long tree lined drive.

The historic background is evident, the reception rooms having fine panelled walls, ornate ceilings and big, open fireplaces, extremely welcoming on dull afternoons.

The bedrooms are romantic, each with its own colour scheme reflected in lovely fabrics. Antiques vie with modern comforts and the bathrooms are wonderfully equipped.

Guests enjoy cocktails at the bar and a choice of three restaurants with appetising menus that include exotic and traditional dishes, grills and local fish. The wine list is excellent and reasonably priced. Additionally there is a magnificent banqueting suite, ideal for conferences and seminars, with appropriate equipment available.

Places of interest nearby: Residents have complimentary membership of the Wood Hall Country Club, which has squash, tennis, croquet, a heated outdoor pool, sauna and solarium. Local attractions include ten golf courses, good sailing off the Suffolk Coast at Woodbridge, fishing and shooting, bird sanctuaries, Aldeburgh Music Festival. **Directions: A12 towards Lowestoft, then A1152 through Melton, next roundabout B1083 towards Bawdsey, after 3 miles hotel is on right.**

For hotel location, see maps on pages 263–269

Findon Manor

HIGH STREET, FINDON, NR WORTHING, WEST SUSSEX BN14 0TA
TEL: 01903 872733 FAX: 01903 877473 E-MAIL: findon@dircon.co.uk

OWNERS: Mike and Jan Parker-Hare
CHEF: Stanley Ball

11 rms | 11 ens

S: from £47.50
D: from £65

Formerly a 16th century rectory, Findon Manor stands at the heart of a picturesque village whose attractive cottages with colourful, flint walled gardens preserve much of the historic downland character. It is a welcoming and friendly hotel whose grounds are fringed with shady, mature trees and evergreens.

Inside are all the comforts of a country house with recent refurbishments providing every facility for the visitor. Original features have been retained, including the 16th century beams in the traditionally furnished lounge.

All 11 bedrooms are en suite, individually decorated and named after well known racehorses who have been trained in the village, some of the bedrooms have four-posters with a jacuzzi. Chef Stanley Ball produces excellent, award winning cuisine in the beautiful dining room which opens onto the secluded gardens.

The hotel is ideally placed for outside interests, from racing at Brighton, Fontwell and Goodwood to golf at Worthing and Ham Manor, flying at Shoreham, sailing and windsurfing at Ferring and walking the South Downs Way. **Places of interest nearby:** Cissbury Ring, the ramparts of a 60 acre site built in the Iron Age and refortified in the 4th century against the Saxons, is close by. Chanctonbury Ring, the Devil's Dyke and the Roman Villa at Bignor are within easy reach. **Directions: Findon lies in a curve of A24 just above the junction with the A27.**

For hotel location, see maps on pages 263–269

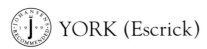

THE PARSONAGE COUNTRY HOUSE HOTEL

ESCRICK, YORK, NORTH YORKSHIRE YO19 6LF
TEL: 01904 728111 FAX: 01904 728151

OWNERS: Paul and Karan Ridley
MANAGER: Frank McCarten

22 rms | 22 ens | SMALL HOTEL

S: £75–£98
D: £110–£140

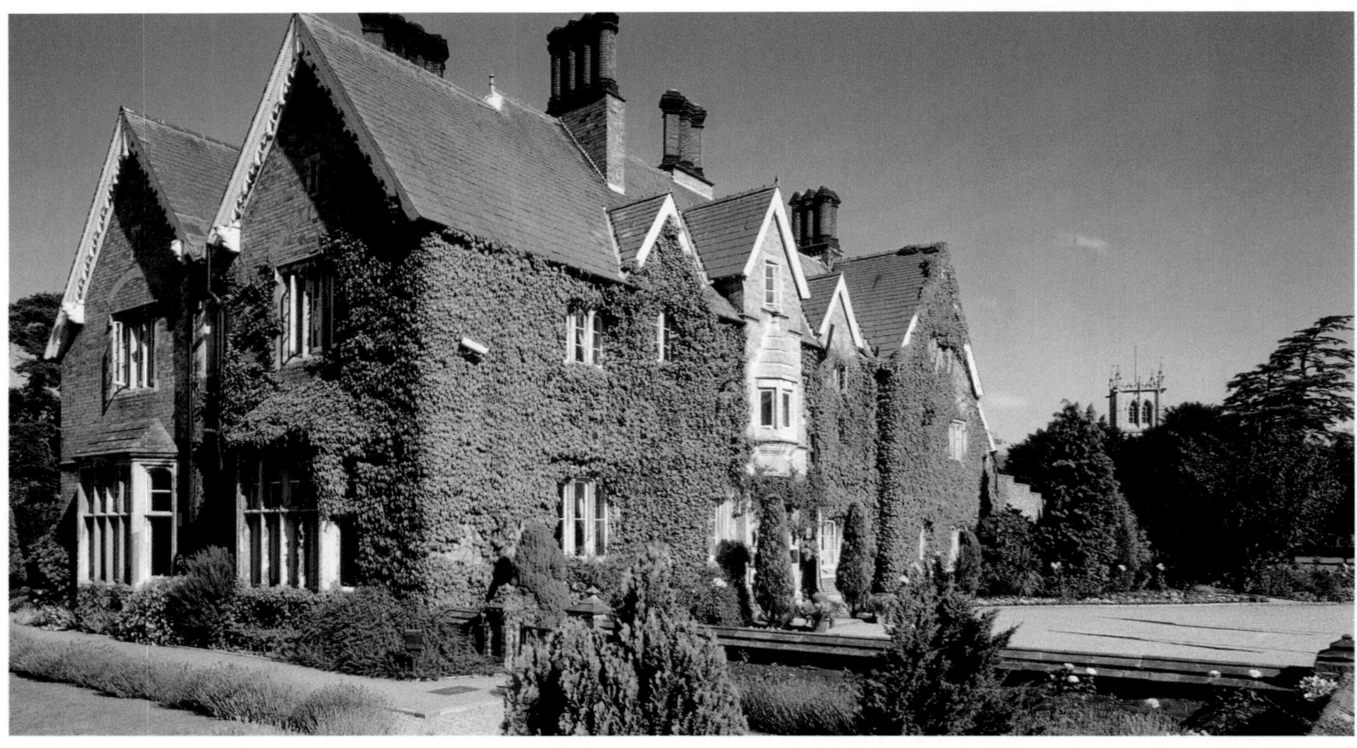

Surrounded by wide expanses of lawn, formal gardens and wild woodland, The Parsonage Country House Hotel provides an oasis of comfort and tranquillity. In the nearby breathtakingly beautiful hills and valleys are hidden ancient hamlets and villages still immersed in the old way of life.

The Parsonage has been passed down through various noble families and baronies from Count Alan of Brittany in the early 11th century, to the de Lascelles, the Knyvetts, Thompsons, Lawleys and finally the Forbes Adams retaining all of its charm and many original features.

Each bedroom has been furnished with comfort and luxury in mind and features a full range of modern facilities. Two of the larger rooms contain magnificent four poster beds. The two new conference suites in the coach house make an ideal venue for executive meetings or conferences.

A highly appetising selection of Anglo-French dishes is created by the chef, who uses only the freshest, high quality local ingredients. A varied and carefully selected wine list is available to complement any meal.

Places of interest nearby: The Parsonage is a perfect base from which to visit York and Harrogate, the estates of Castle Howard, the three Cistercian Abbeys, the Yorkshire coastline or the Yorkshire Dales. **Directions: Escrick is on the A19 a few miles south of York.**

For hotel location, see maps on pages 263–269

Glangrwyney Court

GLANGRWYNEY, NR CRICKHOWELL, POWYS NP8 1ES
TEL: 01873 811288 FAX: 01873 810317

OWNERS: Warwick and Christina Jackson

5 rms | 4 ens

S: £35–£40
D: £65–£75

This graceful Georgian mansion is set in four acres of secluded mature gardens on the Monmouthshire–Powys borders. There is a walled garden and in summer visitors can sit in perfect peace enjoying the views of the rolling hills. The house is furnished with antiques, fine porcelain and paintings. The delightful drawing room and dining room are exclusive to guests. The music room has a grand piano and other instruments. Guests are ensured of a warm welcome.

Hospitality offered includes a traditional breakfast and, by prior discussion, a delicious four-course dinner based on the seasonal fresh produce available.

All the bedrooms have been individually decorated and furnished and the Romantic West Room is especially popular with honeymooners. Four rooms are en suite – The Master room has a steam shower and luxuriously deep bath. The twin room has its own private Jacuzzi. Credit cards are not accepted at Glangrwyney Court.

Places of interest nearby: In summer, guests play croquet, tennis and boules or relax in the garden. If agreed beforehand, dogs are welcome. Golf, pony trekking, and fishing are nearby, also the Brecon Beacons National Park for walkers. Hereford Cathedral and the market towns of Abergavenny and Crickhowell are close by, as are the spectacular Talybont and Gwryne Fawr Reservoirs. **Directions: The Court is signed from Crickhowell on the A40 between Brecon and Abergavenny.**

LLANWENARTH HOUSE

GOVILON, ABERGAVENNY, MONMOUTHSHIRE NP7 9SF
TEL: 01873 830289 FAX: 01873 832199

OWNERS: Bruce and Amanda Weatherill

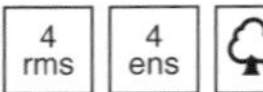

S: £54–£64
D: £74–£82

Llanwenarth House overlooks the Vale of Usk and stands in its own beautiful grounds within the Brecon Beacons National Park. It was built from local rose-grey limestone in the 16th century by the Morgan family, ancestors of Sir Henry Morgan, privateer and Lieutenant Governor of Jamaica. The house has been carefully restored over the years, ensuring that it has retained all of its character, while not compromising on the highest levels of comfort. Guests are personally looked after by the family, who offer comfortable accommodation in period furnished rooms. Many of the elegant spacious bedrooms offer lovely views of the grounds and surrounding countryside. Fine cuisine is prepared by Amanda, a Cordon Bleu cook who makes full use of local game, fish, home-produced meat, poultry and organically grown fruit and vegetables from their own kitchen garden. Dinner is served by candlelight in the beautiful Georgian dining room. Credit cards not accepted.

Sporting activities include trout and salmon fishing on the River Usk, pony-trekking, climbing and golf, the nearest course being 3 miles away. Wales is Host Nation for the 1999 Rugby World Cup and the house is well-located for access to the National and other stadia, where games will be played. **Places of interest nearby:** Chepstow and Raglan Castles and Tintern Abbey. **Directions: From the roundabout 1 mile east of Abergavenny follow A465 towards Merthyr Tydfil for 3 miles to the next roundabout. Take first exit to Govilon, the ½ mile driveway is 150 yards on the right.**

For hotel location, see maps on pages 263–269

PENYCLAWDD COURT

LLANFIHANGEL CRUCORNEY, ABERGAVENNY, GWENT NP7 7LB
TEL: 01873 890719 FAX: 01873 890848

OWNERS: Julia Horton Evans and Ken Peacock
CHEF: Julia Horton Evans

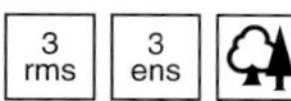

S: £50
D: from £74

Winner of Johansens 1996 Most Excellent Country House Award, Penyclawdd Court is a Grade I Listed Tudor Manor House, situated at the foot of Bryn Arw mountain in the Brecon Beacons National Park. The authentic restoration of the house has been recognised by an accolade from H.R.H. the Prince of Wales. In the grounds is a Norman motte and bailey – a scheduled ancient monument. There is also a traditional herb garden and a walled knot garden. The Court has its own free-range hens and a flock of prize-winning pedigree Jacob sheep.

Featured regularly in magazines and on television and radio, the house is furnished with antiques and there are huge stone fireplaces, flagstone floors and exposed beams. Because of its age, there are many steps, stairs and sloping floors to negotiate, which sadly means that the house is not best suited to everybody.

Four-course dinners are provided by prior arrangement using home produced or local ingredients. Groups can enjoy researched 15th to 17th century feasts. **Places of interest nearby:** Situated as it is in a National Park, the surrounding area offers some wonderful walks. Pony-trekking and golf are available locally. **Directions: Penyclawdd Court is ½ mile off A465 Abergavenny –Hereford road signposted Pantygelli.**

For hotel location, see maps on pages 263–269

TAN-Y-FOEL

CAPEL GARMON, NR BETWS-Y-COED, CONWY LL26 0RE
TEL: 01690 710507 FAX: 01690 710681

OWNERS: Peter and Janet Pitman
CHEF: Janet Pitman

SMALL HOTEL

S: £65–£90
D: £95–£150

This exquisite house, recently described as "a jewel box of colour", has won many accolades as an outstanding small country hotel, a fine example of country elegance at its best. Set in breathtaking surroundings, it commands magnificent views of the verdant Conwy Valley and the rugged peaks of Snowdonia.

Once inside Tan-y-Foel a "no smoking" policy prevails. There are seven extremely comfortable bedrooms, each with their own strikingly individual style, warm colours and rich decorations. Thoughtful small touches add to their charm and the bathrooms are delightfully appointed.

Celebrated for her impeccable cuisine, Janet sources the best local produce – fresh fish, Welsh Black beef, organically-grown vegetables – for her creatively composed nightly menus which have been recognised with 3 AA Rosettes. The distinguished wine list offers over 90 carefully chosen vintages.

The personal welcome which perfectly complements the nature of the Pitmans' fine house has further resulted in RAC Blue Ribbon and AA 2 Red Star accolades. The popularity of their two-night Special Offer Breaks thus comes as no surprise. **Places of interest nearby:** Great Little Trains of Wales, Bodnant Gardens, Conwy Castle and Snowdonia. **Directions: From Chester, A55 to Llandudno, the A470 towards Betws-y-Coed. 2m outside Llanrwst fork left towards Capel Garmon-Nebo. Tan-y-Foel is just over a mile up the hill on the left.**

For hotel location, see maps on pages 263–269

Old Gwernyfed Country Manor

FELINDRE, THREE COCKS, BRECON, POWYS LD3 0SU
TEL: 01497 847376 FAX: 01497 847376

OWNERS: Roger and Dawn Beetham

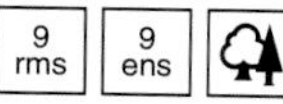

  S: £42–£47
D: £62–£100

Old Gwernyfed is a historian's delight – its passage through the ages has been carefully documented and its antiquated features well preserved. Set in 13 acres in the foothills of the Black Mountains, it was built circa 1600 as a manor house of great importance in its day.

Over the years, Roger and Dawn Beetham have lavished much attention on the building to restore it to its former glory. They have made no attempt to disguise the age of the building, preferring to enhance its original characteristics.

One of the lounges, which is oak panelled from floor to ceiling, is overlooked by the splendid balustraded minstrels gallery. Most of the bedrooms enjoy outstanding views and there is a good choice of four-poster, half-tester and canopied beds. Traffic noise is non-existent.

The dining room is dominated by its cavernous 12 foot fireplace, only rediscovered in recent years. A small table d'hôte menu is changed daily and all dishes are cooked freshly using produce from the garden or local suppliers. Closed mid-December to mid-March.

Places of interest nearby: Hay-on-Wye and the market town of Brecon. Local activities include canoeing, sailing, pony-trekking and gliding. **Directions: From Brecon turn off A438 after the Three Cocks Hotel. Take every turning to right for 1¾ miles. Go through Felindre and Old Gwernyfed is 200 yards on right.**

For hotel location, see maps on pages 263–269

Ty'n Rhos Country House

SEION LLANDDEINIOLEN, CAERNARFON, GWYNEDD LL55 3AE
TEL: 01248 670489 FAX: 01248 670079 E-MAIL: tynrhos@netcomuk.co.uk

OWNERS: Lynda and Nigel Kettle
CHEF: Carys Davies and Lynda Kettle

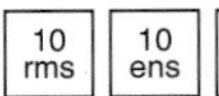

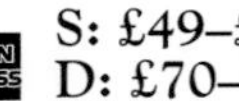

S: £49–£70
D: £70–£96

Award-winning Ty'n Rhos is not the typical country house hotel. The creation of Lynda and Nigel Kettle, it is a 72 acre farm still, but has undergone a magnificent transformation resulting in an immaculate small hotel based on the original farmhouse and former outbuildings.

The ten en suite bedrooms are beautifully appointed with all the comforts of a stylish hotel. Uncompromising standards are offered in the elegant lounge and the West-facing conservatory that enjoys serene views over Caernarfon and the Menai Straits.

Ty'n Rhos's special appeal is based on a unique fusion of personal service and the highest professional standards: perhaps the most important single element is its restaurant food. This former Taste of Wales Restaurant of the Year sources the finest, fresh local ingredients for its seasonal menus: fine spring lamb; home-grown vegetables; fresh local fish and Anglesey scallops. The Welsh breakfasts are notable for farm-cured bacon, freshly baked rolls and home-made preserves and yogurt. To it's hard-earned reputation for food, service and value for money, Ty'n Rhos adds its enviable location between Snowdonia and the sea.

Places of interest nearby: The hotel is within easy touring distance of all of North Wales. **Directions: Situated in the hamlet of Seion off the B4366 and B4547. Reached from the East by A5 or A55.**

For hotel location, see maps on pages 263–269

THE PEMBROKESHIRE RETREAT

RHOS-Y-GILWEN MANSION, CILGERRAN, NR CARDIGAN, PEMBROKESHIRE SA43 2TW
TEL/FAX: 01239 841387 E-MAIL: enquiries@retreat.co.uk

OWNERS: Mr and Mrs Glen Peters
CHEF/MANAGER: Mr R Wilson

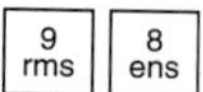

S: £40–£60
D: £75–£110

A long, wide, curving drive brings visitors to the arched entrance of Rhosygilwen Mansion, set in 55 acres of gardens, orchards and walks. Dating from 1850, this listed, grey-stoned building has been carefully restored to maintain period integrity and houses the Retreat, a place of reflection and diversion.

Rhosygilwen Mansion is a family home aiming to offer hospitality and attention at a level that many formal hotels cannot achieve. Spacious rooms include a large panelled drawing room with its log fire, the Library and Conservatory. Eight of the rooms are en suite and all have modern comforts and views over the surrounding countryside and Preseli hills.

Guests can discuss all their dietary requirements in advance with the resident chef, who prepares a nightly set menu using organic vegetables and free-range produce wherever possible.

The mansion provides a tennis court, cricket nets, croquet lawn, table tennis room, cycle paths and woodland walks. Archery, falconry and laser shooting can be arranged on site.

Surrounded by the famous Pembrokeshire Coast National Park, an area of designated natural beauty, there are outstanding walks, riding, golf and other outdoor pursuits nearby. The coast of Pembrokeshire is a superb place for sighting dolphins and seals. **Places of interest nearby:** Cilgerran Castle, Skomer & Skokholm Nature Reserve Islands and St David's Cathedral City. **Directions: From A487 Aberystwyth–Fishguard road take A478 from Cardigan. After 2 miles turn left to Cilgerran at Pen-Y-Bryn, then right from village centre for 1½ miles.**

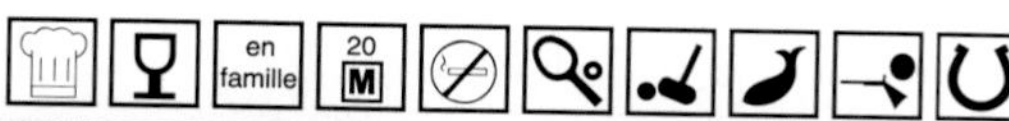

For hotel location, see maps on pages 263–269

Berthlwyd Hall Hotel

LLECHWEDD, NR CONWY, GWYNEDD LL32 8DQ
TEL: 01492 592409 FAX: 01492 572290

OWNERS: Brian and Joanna Griffin

7 rms | 7 ens | SMALL HOTEL

S: £59.50–£66
D: £62–£85
Suite: £120

Only one and a half miles from historic Conwy, on the edge of the Snowdonia national park, in sight of its famous castle, is Berthlwyd Hall Hotel, a charming Victorian and much loved landmark of the Conwy Valley. Many of the Victorian characteristics have been preserved, such as the splendid oak panelling in the entrance hall, a wide staircase sweeping up to an impressive galleried landing, elaborately carved fireplaces and stained-glass windows. The hotel has been furnished with an attention to detail giving the impression of a luxurious private house in the grand style. Each of the seven en suite bedrooms has been individually styled and comfortably appointed. Recent refurbishments include a snooker room and a function conference room seating up to 20 persons plus a Victorian kitchen where 2 day cookery demonstrations take place.

Resident proprietors Brian and Joanna Griffin spent some years in the Périgord region of south-west France, renowned for its gastronomic heritage and the inspiration for their restaurant, 'Truffles', acclaimed as one of the finest restaurants in North Wales.

Places of interest nearby: Snowdonia, the Welsh coast, Anglesey and Bodnant Gardens. **Directions: A55 into Conwy town, round one way system turning left after Lancaster Square into Sychant Pass Road, after 1 mile look for hotel sign on left. Turn left and continue for ½ mile. The Hall is approached through a small private chalet park.**

For hotel location, see maps on pages 263–269

The Old Rectory

LLANRWST ROAD, LLANSANFFRAID GLAN CONWY, COLWYN BAY, CONWY LL28 5LF
TEL: 01492 580611 FAX: 01492 584555 E-MAIL: OldRect@aol.com

OWNERS: Michael and Wendy Vaughan

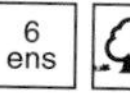 

 **S: £99–£109**
D: £99–£149

Enjoy dramatic Snowdonian vistas, breathtaking sunsets and views of floodlit Conwy Castle from this idyllic country house set in large gardens overlooking Conwy Bird Reserve. Awarded 2 AA Red Stars for 'outstanding levels of comfort, service and hospitality and 3 Rosettes for food.'

Wendy, a 'Master Chef of Great Britain' features in Egon Ronay and all good food guides. Her gourmet four-course dinners combine a lightness of touch and delicacy of flavour with artistic presentation. Welsh mountain lamb, locally reared Welsh black beef and fish landed at Conwy are on her menu. An award-winning wine list complements her fine cuisine. Most diets are catered for.

Antiques and Victorian watercolours decorate the interiors. The luxury en suite bedrooms have draped beds, bathrobes, ironing centres, fresh fruit and flowers.

Michael is happy to share his knowledge of Welsh history, language and culture and always has time to assist in planning touring routes. Relax in the garden and watch the River Conwy ebb and flow and you will see why this elegant Georgian home is a 'beautiful haven of peace'.

Places of interest nearby: Bodnant Gardens, Historic Conwy, Victorian Llandudno Spa, Betws-Y-Coed, Snowdonia. Walk the Roman road to Aber Falls, Chester, Caernarfon and Angelsey 40 mins. **Directions: On the A470, 1/2 mile south of the A55 junction, two miles from Llandudno Junction Station. 3hours from London Euston.**

DOLGELLAU (Ganllwyd)

PLAS DOLMELYNLLYN

GANLLWYD, DOLGELLAU, GWYNEDD LL40 2HP
TEL: 01341 440273 FAX: 01341 440640

OWNERS: Jon Barkwith and Joanna Reddicliffe
CHEF: Joanna Reddicliffe

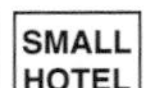

SMALL HOTEL

S: £45–£60
D: £80–£120

The approach to Plas Dolmelynllyn, which is entirely non-smoking, set in the amazing scenery of south Snowdonia, leads through a winding, beech-lined drive that brings guests to the doorway. A house has stood on the site since the 1500s, extended in the 18th and 19th centuries. Bedrooms are individually decorated and comfortably furnished. Joanna Reddicliffe, the daughter of the house, prepares an interesting and varied menu with several choices in each course including vegetarian dishes.

There is a conservatory bar and a large sitting room with full-length windows overlooking the valley. Dogs are allowed in two of the bedrooms only.

The hotel is surrounded by three acres of formal gardens, bounded by a swiftly running stream which flows into a small lake. Guests can take advantage of the hotel's fishing on 10 miles of river and three local lakes.

Places of interest nearby: Adjoining the grounds are 1,200 acres of mountains, meadow and forest, where it is possible to walk all day without seeing a car or crossing a road. Castles, slate caverns, waterfalls and a gold mine can all be visited nearby, but the theme here is relaxation amid wonderful surroundings, comfort and only the gentlest of activities. **Directions: Plas Dolmelynllyn is off the main A470 Dolgellau– Llandudno road, just north of Dolgellau. Dinner, bed and breakfast, combined rates and short breaks are available.**

For hotel location, see maps on pages 263–269

THE CROWN AT WHITEBROOK – RESTAURANT WITH ROOMS

WHITEBROOK, MONMOUTHSHIRE NP5 4TX
TEL: 01600 860254 FAX: 01600 860607

OWNERS: Roger and Sandra Bates

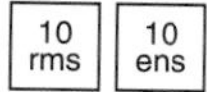   

S: £75
D: £130–£144
(including 3 course dinner)

A romantic auberge nestling deep in the Wye Valley, a designated area of outstanding natural beauty, The Crown is ideally situated for those seeking peace and tranquillity, with its two and three night breaks providing particularly good value for money.

Located up the wooded Whitebrook Valley on the fringe of Tintern Forest and only one mile from the River Wye, this is a place where guests can enjoy spectacular scenery. Roger and Sandra Bates offer their guests a genuinely friendly welcome amid the tranquil comforts of the cosy lounge and bar.

Sandra Bates' cooking has earned the Restaurant 3 AA Rosettes and numerous prestigious awards for excellence. Dishes include local Welsh lamb and Wye salmon cooked with a classical French influence, followed by a choice of delicious home-made puddings and a selection of British farm cheeses. Most dietary requirements can be catered for as all food is freshly cooked to order. The extensive wine list is the work of a true enthusiast.

Places of interest nearby: Tintern Abbey, Chepstow Castle and the Brecon Beacons National Park are all within easy reach. **Directions: Whitebrook is situated between the A466 and the B4293 approximately five miles south of Monmouth.**

For hotel location, see maps on pages 263–269

Plas Bodegroes

NEFYN ROAD, PWLLHELI, GWYNEDD, WALES LL53 5TH
TEL: 01758 612363 FAX: 01758 701247

OWNERS: Gunna Chown
CHEF: Shaun Mitchell

10 rms | 10 ens

S: £70–£90
D: £140–£200
(including dinner)

Towering beech trees and magnificent purple rhododendrons frame this splendid Georgian hotel situated close to Pwllheli on the historic Lleyn Peninsular. It is an ideal retreat for those wishing to explore an area quite unlike the rest of North Wales. Distant horizons are broken by dramatic mountains falling sheer to the sea. There are rocky coves, wide bays, enticing beaches, whitewashed cottages on top of round-backed hills and charming fishing villages.

Plas Bodegroes is the ideal base from which to begin any exploratory journey and a warm, friendly haven to return to after a day's experiences. Owner Gunna Chown oversees a delightfully relaxing country house where peace, tranquillity and comfort abound. When the pure Welsh air has taken effect a good night's sleep is ensured in the en suite bedrooms which have every facility to help make guests feel at home.

Crisp table linen and gleaming cutlery set the scene for excellent meals in the hotel restaurant. With three AA Rosettes the cuisine is an integral part of the hotel's services and chef Shaun Mitchell's menus will satisfy the most discerning diner.

Places of interest nearby: The ancient town of Nefyn, the colourful harbour of Abersoch and the offshore islands of St Tudwall, famous for sea birds and deep sea caves. Criccieth Castle and, on the lowest of the triple peaks of Yr Eifl, the Town of Giants, an Iron Age encampment are also close by.

Directions: On the A497 road just west of Pwllheli.

For hotel location, see maps on pages 263–269

WATERWYNCH HOUSE HOTEL

WATERWYNCH BAY, TENBY, PEMBROKESHIRE SA70 8JT
TEL: 01834 842464 FAX: 01834 845076

OWNERS: Bette and Geoff Hampton

S: £38–£50
D: £52–£80
Suite: £64–£100

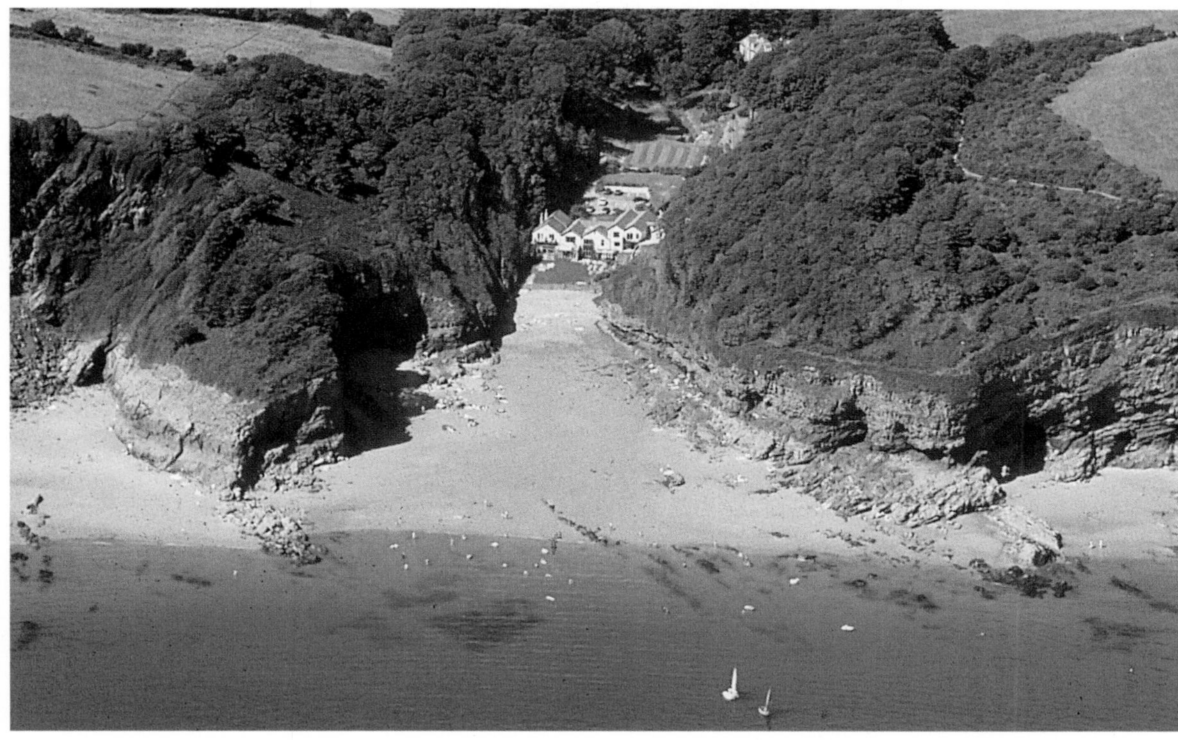

Waterwynch House is a uniquely secluded retreat nestling in a pretty little cove on the beautiful shores of Carmathen Bay. Surrounded by the Pembrokeshire Coastal National Park and 27 acres of its own woodland and gardens, it is a quiet, intimate hotel with an enviable reputation for friendly hospitality and personal service.

Dating from 1820 when it was built as a family home for Tenby based artist Charles Norris, the hotel retains its peaceful charm of the past. It is an ideal base from which to enjoy coastal walks, the wildlife and superb scenery, or just to relax on the private beach.

The 16 tastefully furnished and decorated bedrooms offer every modern comfort. Some have balconies and sea views, others overlook the gardens. An ample selection of table d'hôte and à la carte menus caters for the most discerning connoisseur in the dining room with its panoramic view over the bay. As well as some unusual speciality dishes there are a good selection of fish courses. The hotel is closed from November to February.

Places of interest nearby: Superb walking along the adjacent Pembrokeshire coastal path, bird-watching, painting, fishing, golf and croquet, bowls and putting.

Directions: Off the A478 Kilgetty to Tenby road. Signposted on the left half a mile after the New Hedges roundabout.

Parva Farmhouse and Restaurant

TINTERN, CHEPSTOW, MONMOUTHSHIRE NP6 6SQ
TEL: 01291 689411 FAX: 01291 689557

OWNERS: Dereck and Vickie Stubbs
CHEF: Dereck Stubbs

9 rms | 9 ens

S: £48
D: £66–£76

Surrounded by the glorious, wooded hillsides of the beautiful lower Wye Valley and just a mile from 12th century Tintern Abbey, one of the finest relics of Britain's monastic age, Parva Farmhouse is a homely haven where visitors can relax and forget the pressures of their daily world. For country lovers there is no more ideal spot. The salmon and trout teeming River Wye flows just 50 yards from the hotel's small, flower-filled garden, there is an abundance of wildlife and hundreds of tempting walks.

Built during the 17th century, Parva today provides every comfort. The bedrooms are well-furnished and most have pretty views across the River Wye. The beamed lounge with its log-burning fireplace, "Honesty Bar" and deep Chesterfield sofas and chairs is the perfect place to relax and chat over the day's happenings.

The crowning glory of Parva is the excellent food (AA Rosette), home-cooked by chef-patron Dereck Stubbs and served in the Inglenook Restaurant before a 14-foot beamed fireplace. Golf, shooting and riding are close by and there is horse-racing at Chepstow.

Places of interest nearby: Tintern Abbey, castles at Abergavenny and Chepstow, Offa's Dyke, the Royal Forest of Dean, many old ruins and ancient monuments.

Directions: From the M48, exit at junction 2 and join the A466 towards Monmouth. The hotel is on the north edge of Tintern Village.

For hotel location, see maps on pages 263–269

BUTTINGTON HOUSE

BUTTINGTON, NR WELSHPOOL, POWYS, WALES SY21 8HD
TEL: 01938 553351 FAX: 01686 640604

OWNERS: Brian and Jean Thomas

S: £50
D: £70

Buttington House stands in 2 acres of informal gardens that include an orchard and an ornamental pond. The late Georgian/Regency former gentleman's residence, once a vicarage, has been lovingly restored by resident owners Brian and Jean Thomas.

From its entrance hall with wood-block flooring and scatter rugs an open staircase leads to the wide landing whose skylighting and muted décor give the house its unique atmosphere.

The two guest bedrooms complete with hand-picked furniture, including Louis XIV-style and Victorian brass bedsteads, have immaculately fitted en suite bathrooms replete with modern accessories and top quality toiletries.

Downstairs rooms include a supremely comfortable residents lounge full of recreational books and magazines and a more formal dining room. While evening meals can be provided by prior arrangement, a wider choice of fare is available at the Thomases' delightful country inn, The Lion at Berriew, which is less than 15 minutes' drive away. **Places of interest:** Convenient for Shrewsbury, Powis Castle and the Welsh Borders, this elegant period residence has lovely views of the Severn Valley and stands adjacent to the Offa's Dyke path which passes within yards of the garden. **Directions: From the roundabout at the junction of A483 and A458 to Shrewsbury take 1st turning right by church, house 1st on right.**

HIGHLAND.
An almost feminine charm and character all of its own. Light and aromatic, the Gentle Spirit is rich in body with a soft heather honey finish.

ISLE OF SKYE.
Assertive but not heavy. Fully flavoured with a pungent, peaty ruggedness. It explodes on the palate and lingers on. Well balanced. A sweetish seaweedy aroma.

SPEYSIDE.
Finely balanced with a dry, rather delicate aroma, good firm body and a smoky finish. A pleasantly austere malt of great distinction with a character all its own.

WEST HIGHLAND.
Oban is the West Highland malt. A singular, rich and complex malt with the merest suggestion of peat in the aroma, slightly smoky with a long smooth finish.

ISLE OF ISLAY.
Seaweed, peat, smoke and earth are all elements of the assertive Islay character. Pungent, an intensely dry 16 year old malt with a firm robust body and powerful aroma.

LOWLAND.
Typically soft, restrained and with a touch of sweetness. An exceptionally pale smooth malt which, experts agree, reaches perfection at 10 years maturity.

DALWHINNIE
15 YEARS OLD
HIGHLAND

TALISKER
10 YEARS OLD
SKYE

CRAGGANMORE
12 YEARS OLD
SPEYSIDE

OBAN
14 YEARS OLD
WEST HIGHLAND

LAGAVULIN
16 YEARS OLD
ISLAY

GLENKINCHIE
10 YEARS OLD
LOWLAND

Les grands crus de Scotland.

In the great wine-growing regions, there are certain growths from a single estate that are inevitably superior.

For the Scots, there are the single malts. Subtle variations in water, weather, peat and the distilling process itself lend each single malt its singular character. The Classic Malts are the finest examples of the main malt producing regions. To savour them, one by one, is a rare journey of discovery.

SIX OF SCOTLAND'S FINEST MALT WHISKIES

You'll also find that when your customers taste The Classic Malts, their appreciation will almost certainly increase your sales of malt whisky – in itself a discovery worth making.

To find out more, contact our Customer Services team on 0345 444 111, or contact your local wholesaler.

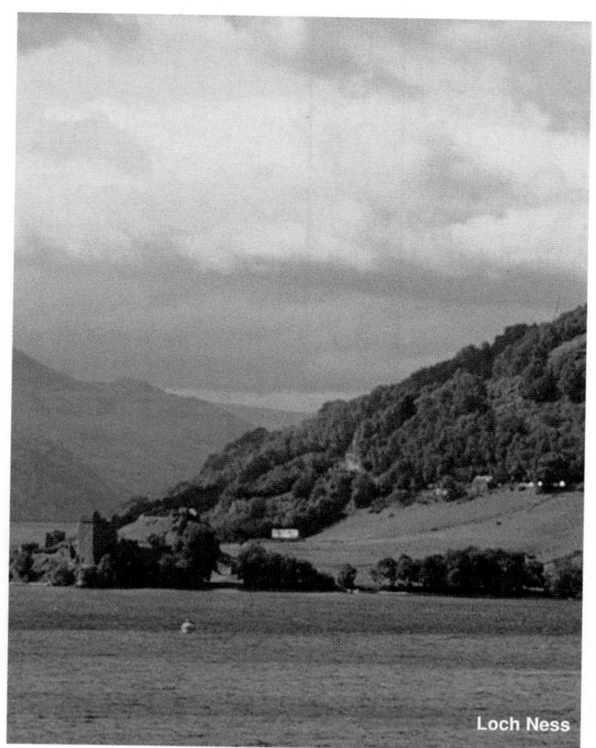

Johansens Recommended Country Houses & Small Hotels in Scotland

Myths and mountains, lochs and legends – Scotland's stunning scenic splendour acts as a magnet for visitors from all over the globe. Superb as it is, Scotland's charismatic charm is more than just visual.

There's little doubt that Scotland's stunning scenery is the most often cited reason for visiting Northern Britain, and it's easy to see why.

This is a domain laced with lochs and threaded with roaring rivers and bubbling burns. Mountains and glens form its waft and weft, while legends weave a note of mystery and romance into the landscape.

From the rolling Border hills to the highest Highland 'Munro', you'll find enticing views and vistas that will surely stay with you for ever.

Superlatives trip off the tongue, like malt from an open bottle, the minute you try to put into words the sheer emotional power and visual pleasure that this land inspires, but Scotland is a country with a lot more to offer.

Steeped in history and populated by a proud and hospitable people with a strong sense of their own identity and cultural heritage, Scotland repays those who look beyond the picture postcard countryside and experience city life too.

Scotland's cities certainly rival the best in the world. Edinburgh, its grand capital, is graceful and alluring. Scotland's Festival City, Edinburgh is world-famous for its International Festival and Fringe, which has caught the public's imagination as no other for more than 50 years.

Whatever time of year you visit, you'll find a festival to interest you. And if not, the city's wonderful array of child-friendly attractions, such as Edinburgh Castle and Edinburgh Zoo, will tempt you from the comfort of your recommended hotel, country house or inn.

The National Museum of Scotland, opening in November 1998, will join the city's extensive list of exhibitions, museums and art galleries, and in April 1999, a new permanent and innovative exhibition – Dynamic Earth – will open at the foot of Edinburgh's Royal Mile.

Situated next to the Palace of Holyroodhouse, where construction is already underway on Scotland's New Parliament, Dynamic Earth is the largest new visitor attraction in Scotland. The development cost of £34 million – a King's ransom – has been made possible with £15 million from the Millennium Commission Fund of the National Lottery.

Edinburgh's Royal connections ripple on in 1999 with the permanent berthing of the former Royal Yacht Britannia at her new home in Leith Docks. Coupled with Edinburgh's colourful heritage and wealth of historic landmarks, Edinburgh becomes a 'must' on anyone's Scottish itinerary, but if you're thinking of joining the city's huge Millennium Hogmanay celebrations, book early!

Across the country, Glasgow is also gearing up for an exciting year. Perhaps, not surprisingly for the city that boasts Charles Rennie MacIntosh's greatest buildings, Glasgow takes on the mantle of 'City of Architecture and Design 1999'. A fitting title for a city that has evolved from ecclesiastical and academic beginnings through a long and successful period of commerce and industry to its present reincarnation as Scotland's style capital – now a Mecca for shoppers and for those with an appetite for classy cosmopolitan culture.

And it's not just a 'tale of two cities' – Aberdeen, Dundee, Inverness, Perth and Stirling can also offer a superb short break holiday, conference venue or incentive destination.

The new Food Festival in Inverness coincides with the popular Highland Festival. Its programme of arts and crafts, music and dance celebrating the unique cultural tradition of the Highlands of Scotland, takes place throughout the region in village halls and rural schools as well as town and city locations.

Sporting events continue to pull in the crowds. Golf, one of Scotland's most popular exports, is high on the sporting calendar in 1999. The championship links course at Nairn (near Inverness) has the privilege of hosting the Walker Cup, while further down the coast between Dundee and Arbroath, The British Open returns to Carnoustie – the first time since 1975.

Scotland's hills and mountains are a natural magnet for walkers and climbers, and the fretted coastline and hundreds of islands create a maritime playground for sailors, fishermen, divers, surfers and anyone who simply loves messing around on or in the water. And, of course, wherever you go and whatever you do, it will be against a magnificent backdrop.

Getting around is easy and most of the islands are accessible by car-ferry. The problem will be deciding where to start, what to see and do and just how long to spend in this gloriously diverse country with its magical mix of rural wilderness and cosmopolitan charm!

For further information on Scotland, please contact:

The Scottish Tourist Board
23 Ravelston Terrace
Edinburgh EH4 3BU
Tel: 0131 332 2433

BALLATER (Royal Deeside)

BALGONIE COUNTRY HOUSE

BRAEMAR PLACE, BALLATER, ROYAL DEESIDE, ABERDEENSHIRE AB35 5NQ
TEL: 013397 55482 FAX: 013397 55482

OWNERS: John and Priscilla Finnie

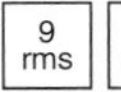

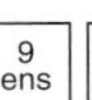

S: £63
D: £105

In the heart of one of Scotland's most unspoilt areas, on the outskirts of the village of Ballater, lies Balgonie House. Winner of the 1997 Johansens Country House Award for Excellence. This Edwardian-style building is set within four acres of mature gardens and commands wonderful views over the local golf course towards the hills of Glen Muick beyond. Balgonie's nine bedrooms are each named after a fishing pool on the River Dee. They are individually decorated and furnished and most offer lovely outlooks from their windows. Amenities include private bathrooms, colour television and direct-dial telephones. At the heart of the hotel is the dining room, offering superb Scottish menus: including fresh salmon from the Dee, succulent local game, high quality Aberdeen Angus beef and seafood from the coastal fishing ports and vintage wine chosen from an excellent list. Balgonie has won the coveted Taste of Scotland Prestige Award for its cuisine, also 2 AA Red Star and 2 Rosettes. **Places of interest nearby:** The village of Ballater, a five minute walk away, is a thriving community. As suppliers to the Queen, many of its shops sport Royal Warrant shields. This is an ideal centre for golf, hillwalking, sightseeing and touring. Balmoral Castle is within easy reach, as are both the Malt Whisky Trail and Castle Trail. **Directions: Upon entering Ballater from Braemar on the A93, Balgonie House is signposted on the right.**

For hotel location, see maps on pages 263–269

LONGACRE MANOR

ERNESPIE ROAD, CASTLE DOUGLAS, DUMFRIES AND GALLOWAY DG7 1LE
TEL: 01556 503576 FAX: 01556 503886 E-MAIL: BALL.Longacre@btinternet.com

OWNERS: Charles and Elma Ball
MANAGER: Charles Ball
CHEF: Elma Ball

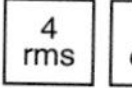
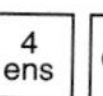

S: £35–£45
D: £60–£80

An impressive drive skirted by woodland gardens overlooking rich green fields leads visitors up to the oak panelled reception hall of this solid, red-roofed country hotel which stands peacefully in the heart of one of the loveliest areas of Southern Scotland. Built by a local businessman in 1920 it is an ideal base from which to tour one of the last unspoilt areas of Britain. All around are towns with rows of 18th century streets, ruined castles, mysterious earthworks and the legacy of prehistory.

Good food and the elegant comfort of deep, soft sofas and chairs, antique furniture, warm fabrics and a subdued décor are the welcoming ingredients provided under the personal supervision of owners Charles and Elma Ball.

The four bedrooms are spacious, well equipped and have delightful views over the gardens. One of the bedrooms has a king-size double four-poster bed, another room has two single four-poster beds. Breakfast is served at one long antique table and dinner can be ordered by arrangement. The hotel has been awarded four stars by the Scottish Tourist Board.

Places of interest nearby: The area has some fine beaches, more than 20 golf courses and excellent salmon and trout fishing. Logan Botanic Gardens and Threave Gardens, the National Trust School of Gardening, the ruined 14th century Threave Castle on an islet in the River Dee. **Directions: Castle Douglas is approximately 17 miles south west of Dumfries approached via the A75 road to Stranraer.**

The Royal Hotel

MELVILLE SQUARE, COMRIE, PERTHSHIRE PH6 2DN
TEL: 01764 679200 FAX: 01764 679219 E-MAIL: reception@royalhotel.co.uk

OWNER: Great Northern Hotels Ltd
MANAGEMENT: The Royal Hotel Company (UK) Ltd
CHEF: Trevor Johnson

S: £65–£85
D: £130–£170
Suite: £190

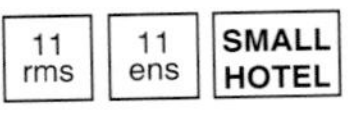

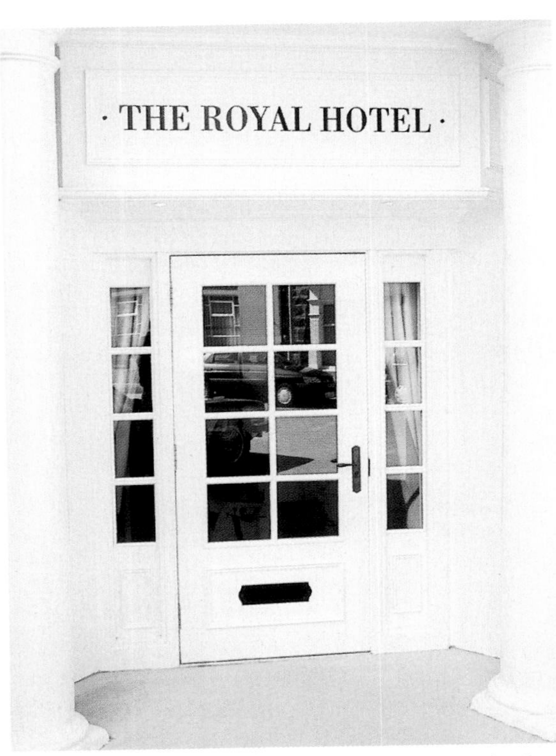

Following a careful and extensive restoration, this glorious country house hotel, set in the Highland village of Comrie, offers a fusion of comfort and opulence. Log fires, period furnishings and fine fabrics adorn the public rooms creating a cosy yet elegant ambience.

The 11 bedrooms are the essence of luxury and have been individually appointed by local craftsmen. Those wishing to be pampered will be delighted with the many thoughtful extras such as scented toiletries, soft bathrobes and private safes.

Natural, local produce including Scotch beef, game, salmon, trout and shell fish is used by the talented chef and his team. Guests may dine informally in the Brasserie or by candlelight in the formal, grand Dining Room. Tasty snacks and beverages may be enjoyed in the Public Bar whilst alfresco diners are seated in the attractive walled garden. This is an ideal residence for golf and fishing enthusiasts as there are some fine courses and rivers nearby.

Places of interest nearby: Day trips to Glenturret Distillery, Comrie's Earthquake House, Auchingarrich Wildlife centre and Stuart Crystal Centre are popular with the hotel's guests. There are many places of historic interest nearby and these include Drummond Castle Gardens, Scone Palace and Fortingall, the birthplace of Roman Governor Pontius Pilate. **Directions: The hotel is situated in the centre of Comrie on the A85, Perth to Fort William Road.**

For hotel location, see maps on pages 263–269

POLMAILY HOUSE HOTEL

DRUMNADROCHIT, LOCH NESS, INVERNESS-SHIRE IV3 6XT
TEL: 01456 450343 FAX: 01456 450813

OWNERS: John and Sonia Whittington-Davies

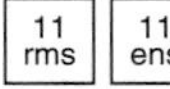 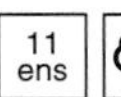   

S: £45–£65
D: £90–£110
Suite: £84–£122

The mysterious Loch Ness lies just below this stylish Edwardian house from which there are views of the slopes of Glen Urquhart and the peaks of Glen Afric. Soaring eagles, deer, wild cat and salmon abound and guests enjoy the 18 acres of garden, woodland and trout pond

A family run hotel making other families especially welcome and the safe facilities for youngsters help parents relax and appreciate their surroundings. With an indoor and outdoor play area and separate children's dinner, Polmaily House is unique in country house facilities for families.

The owners are proud of their kitchen and guests can start the day with a full Highland breakfast. Dinner, served in the spacious and elegant dining room, reflects the local game, beef, fish and garden produce stocking the larder. Carefully chosen wines are reasonably priced.

The delightful bedrooms are all en suite, with one ground floor room ideal for elderly and disabled guests. The family rooms have videos!

Places of interest nearby: On the estate there are ponies, a hard tennis court, heated indoor swimming pool, sauna, solarium, gym and a croquet lawn. Nearby there is superb golf, skiing, fishing with tuition available and stalking.

Directions: By car from Inverness, follow the A82 signposted to Fort William, after 16 miles at Drumnadrochit turn onto A831 signposted to Glen Afric and the hotel is on this road after two miles.

TRIGONY HOUSE HOTEL

CLOSEBURN, THORNHILL, DUMFRIESSHIRE DG3 5EZ
TEL: 01848 331211 FAX: 01848 331303

OWNERS: Robin and Thelma Pollock
CHEF: Janette Brownrigg

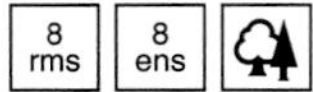

S: £40–£50
D: £70–£90

Trigony was once the home of the oldest woman in Scotland, Miss Frances Shakerley, who lived to be 107. A small, pink sandstone Edwardian house, it stands elegantly in over four acres of secluded gardens and woodlands in the lovely Nithsdale valley of Dumfries. It is an ideal base for discovering and exploring the Land of Burns and the outstanding natural beauty of its unspoilt rolling countryside.

Good food and homely comfort are the ingredients provided under the personal supervision of owners Robin and Thelma Pollock from the moment visitors step into the welcoming hall with its large York stone fireplace and magnificent open stairway. The immaculate en suite bedrooms are comfortable and well equipped and the highest standard of food is served in the charming restaurant, which overlooks the garden. Local produce is extensively used. Taste of Scotland Recommended. Golf, pheasant shooting, horse-riding, and salmon fishing can be arranged locally.

Places of interest nearby: Drumlanrig Castle, home of the Duke of Buccleuch, Maxwelton House, home of Annie Laurie (1682-1764), the Leadhills Mining Museum and historic Dumfries where Robert Burns lived from 1791 until his death in 1796. **Directions: Trigony House is situated off the A76, 13 miles north of Dumfries and one mile south of Thornhill.**

For hotel location, see maps on pages 263–269

The Pend

5 BRAE STREET, DUNKELD, PERTHSHIRE PH8 0BA
TEL: 01350 727586 FAX: 01350 727173 E-MAIL: react@sol.co.uk

OWNERS: Peter and Marina Braney
CHEF: Marina Braney

6 rms

S: £40–£50
D: £80–£90
(including dinner)

Set in the heart of Perthshire, this charming Georgian house has preserved most of its original features while displaying many modern amenities.

The six bedrooms are decorated in a tasteful manner and are complemented by antique furniture. By Spring 1999, two of the four family rooms will incorporate en suite facilities. Two bathrooms are currently available for the guests' use.

The elegant sitting room is enhanced by a beautiful fireplace and soft furnishings. Continental cuisine and traditional Scottish fare are served in the room at breakfast and dinner. Three or four-course dinners of uncompromising standards are offered accompanied by the small but interesting wine list

The range of activities available nearby is extensive and includes many outdoor pursuits. Guests wishing to indulge in the breathtaking Scottish landscape will enjoy abseiling, mountaineering, rock-climbing or simply rambling. For the less adventurous, there are castles, museums, theatres and shops to visit or peruse. Personal itineraries and quotations are designed to suit the needs of the group or individual.
Places of interest nearby: The town of Dunkeld and its cathedral, Scone Palace and Blair Castle. The reserve, close to Dunkeld, is maintained by the Scottish Wildlife Trust and is home to many animals and birds, particularly the Osprey.
Directions: From A9, turn off into Dunkeld. Brae Street is off the Main Street.

For hotel location, see maps on pages 263–269

No 22 Murrayfield Gardens

22 MURRAYFIELD GARDENS, EDINBURGH, LOTHIAN EH12 6DF
TEL: 0131 337 3569 FAX: 0131 337 3803 E-MAIL: NO22FORBANDB@DIAL.PIPEX.COM

OWNERS: Tim and Christine MacDowel

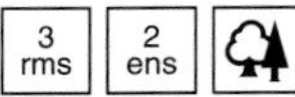

S: £40–£45
D: £70–£80

This large Victorian town house is situated in one of Edinburgh's most prestigious residential areas. Surrounded by its own delightful gardens, featuring attractive ornamental trees and shrubs, it provides panoramic views of the distant hills. Owners Tim and Christine MacDowel have taken great care to create a delightfully relaxed and friendly atmosphere for their guests.

The attractive accommodation at first floor level comprises three distinctly individual rooms; two double and one twin. Each is furnished traditionally, but has an individuality in style and décor. There is a spacious and comfortable drawing room and, for breakfast, a delightful sun-drenched dining room overlooking the gardens.

Although this is primarily a bed and breakfast establishment, dinner can be provided if 24 hours notice is given. Private driveway and street parking in an unrestricted area is available.

The house is well located for Edinburgh Airport, The Forth Road Bridge and the motorway network.

Places of interest nearby: No 22 Murrayfield Gardens is well placed for guests wishing to explore the various attractions of Edinburgh, including its Castle, the National Gallery, Palace of Holyrood House and a host of historic houses. The Highlands are within one hour's drive. **Directions: No 22 is 1 mile due west of Princes Street, just off Corstorphine Road.**

For hotel location, see maps on pages 263–269

CULCREUCH CASTLE HOTEL & COUNTRY PARK

FINTRY, LOCH LOMOND, STIRLING & TROSSACHS, STIRLINGSHIRE G63 0LW
TEL: 01360 860555; FAX: 01360 860556

OWNER: Laird Andrew Haslam

8 rms | 8 ens

S: £40–£54
D: £80–£130

Less than 20 miles from the bustle of Glasgow, Culcreuch Castle stands among the moors, lochs, glens and pinewooded wilds of Stirlingshire, close to Loch Lomond. Built in 1296, this grand ancestral seat of the once-feared Galbraith clan today overlooks 1,600 acres of superb parkland between the Campsie Fells and the Fintry Hills.

The owners, the Haslams, have renovated Culcreuch as a first-class country hotel while preserving its august past in antiques, oil paintings and old, worn steps. All eight bedrooms are en suite, some with four-poster beds. Their names – The Napier Suite, The Keep Room, or The Speirs' Room – help piece together the Castle's history.

Stay a night in the Chinese Bird Room, with its 18th century hand-painted wallpaper. After dark the Phantom Piper sometimes roams and plays. Dinner prepared by award-winning chef William Finneaty is served by candlelight in the panelled dining room; a four-course meal prepared from fresh, local produce costs £23.50 and there is a cellar of fine wines. Self-catering accommodation is also available.

Places of interest nearby: Fishing, walking in the Endrick Valley, visiting Loch Lomond, the village of Fintry and Stirling, to the east. Glasgow and Edinburgh airports are a 55 minute drive. **Directions: Exit M9 junction 10. A84 east towards Stirling. First right, then first right again and join A811. Go 10 miles west to junction with B822 at Kippen. Turn left, go via Kippen to Fintry.**

For hotel location, see maps on pages 263–269

NAVIDALE HOUSE HOTEL

HELMSDALE, SUTHERLAND KW8 6JS
TEL: 01431 821258 FAX: 01431 821531

OWNERS: Navidale House Ltd
CHEF: Tommy Bird

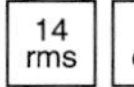 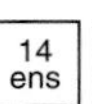  

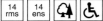

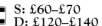

S: £60–£70
D: £120–£140

Originally built as a hunting lodge for the Dukes of Sutherland in the 1830s, Navidale retains the atmosphere of a country retreat, with the added advantage of enjoying spectacular views over the waters of the Moray Firth and Ord of Caithness.

This small, solidly built hotel stands in six acres of woodland and garden which ramble down to the foreshore. The bar, lounge and drawing room have open fires and soft, relaxing chairs and sofas. Nine bedrooms are situated in the main hotel and five are in the adjacent, single storey lodge which has special facilities for disabled guests. All are en suite and have every home-from-home comfort. The majority have glorious sea views.

Chef Tommy Bird takes full advantage of local produce. Freshly caught hake, monkfish, salmon, trout, lobster, crab and oysters, along with Caithness beef, lamb and venison, feature on his extensive menus. For the fishing enthusiast, there are salmon and sea trout in the renowned Helmsdale and Brora rivers and wild brown trout in the Helmsdale Loch system. The hotel has rod and drying rooms and visitors catches can be packed and frozen. Stalking, shooting and golf are also available locally. Closed November, December and January. **Directions: Navidale House Hotel is ½ mile north of Helmsdale on the main A9 coastal road.**

For hotel location, see maps on pages 263–269

THE OLD MANSE OF MARNOCH

BRIDGE OF MARNOCH, BY HUNTLY, ABERDEENSHIRE AB54 5RS
TEL: 01466 780873 FAX: 01466 780873

OWNERS: Patrick and Keren Carter
CHEF: Keren Carter

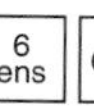 

 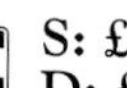

S: £60
D: £94

Dating back to the late 1700s, The Old Manse of Marnoch is set in four acres of mature gardens on the banks of the River Deveron. Designed to create a unique and welcoming atmosphere for guests, this stylish country house is ideal for those seeking peace and quiet in an idyllic setting. The luxurious en suite bedrooms are superbly appointed, tastefully decorated and furnished with antiques. The lounge and dining room echo their striking and individual décor.

Generous Scottish breakfasts and award-winning food are notable features of this delightful establishment. The kitchen garden provides the fresh vegetables and fruit which contribute to the mouth-watering cuisine, with other ingredients supplied locally. Vegetarian and special diets can be catered for without fuss. Along with the better known clarets, Burgundies and Rhône wines, there is a selection of unusual wines to tempt more adventurous palates and to complement the imaginative dishes.

Every country sport is available locally and golfers can choose between parkland or links courses. Spectacular coastal scenery and sandy beaches are within easy reach and the area offers a wealth of lovely walks.

Places of interest nearby: Huntly Castle, Elgin Cathedral and the major cultural centres of Aberdeen and Inverness.

Directions: The Old Manse is on the B9117 less than a mile off the A97 midway between Huntly and Banff.

For hotel location, see maps on pages 263–269

Culduthel Lodge

14 CULDUTHEL ROAD, INVERNESS, INVERNESS-SHIRE IV2 4AG
TEL/FAX: 01463 240089

OWNERS: David and Marion Bonsor

12 rms | 12 ens | SMALL HOTEL

MasterCard VISA S: £45
D: £80–£95

This beautifully appointed hotel, just a few minutes walk from the town centre, is a Grade II Georgian residence set in its own grounds and offering splendid views of the River Ness and surrounding countryside. Great emphasis is placed on providing good food, comfort and a quiet, friendly atmosphere.

On arrival in their rooms, guests are greeted with fresh fruit, flowers and a small decanter of sherry. Each bedroom is individually decorated and furnished to a high standard of comfort and provides every modern amenity including a CD/cassette player.

Delicious, freshly prepared food is presented by a table d'hôte menu which offers choices at each course, including Scottish fare and local produce. A carefully selected range of wines is available to complement the appetising and nourishing meals.

Places of interest nearby: Inverness is a good base for guests wishing to tour the Highlands and the north and west coasts. The Isle of Skye, Royal Deeside and the splendours of the Spey Valley are within a day's travel.

Directions: Take the B851 out of Inverness. Culduthel Road is a continuation of Castle Street and the Lodge is less than half a mile from the city centre on the right.

For hotel location, see maps on pages 263–269

ARDVOURLIE CASTLE

AIRD A MHULAIDH, ISLE OF HARRIS, WESTERN ISLES HS3 3AB
TEL: 01859 502307 FAX: 01859 502348

OWNER: Derek Martin

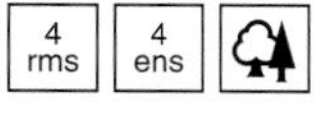

S: £75–£90
D: £150–£160
(including dinner)

Despite its name, this was a hunting lodge built in 1863 by the Earl of Dunmore now restored recently to its full glory. Some rooms have gas and oil lamps, and fire-grates from the original period: mahogany-panelled baths with brass fittings add to the luxurious setting. With just four guest rooms, visitors are guaranteed a warm welcome and personal service from brother and sister team Derek and Pamela Martin. Each room has a private bathroom.

The castle stands on the shores of Loch Seaforth: further on are the sandy beaches of the west coast and the rocky wilderness of South Harris. Otters and seals frequent the bay and golden eagles can be seen over the hills.

The menu at Ardvourlie is based upon local produce wherever possible, including salmon, trout, island lamb, Scottish cheeses and Stornaway oatcakes. Vegetarian meals are available by arrangement. The food is Taste of Scotland, Michelin and Good Hotel Guide recommended. Ardvourlie Castle has a residents' licence and a self-service bar.

Places of interest nearby: Hill-walking (it is advisable to bring suitable clothing), beaches of the West Coast, Callanish Stones, Rodel Church. Salmon and trout fishing on Harris. **Directions: The castle stands on the shores of Loch Seaforth 24 miles from Stornoway and 10 miles from Tarbert.**

For hotel location, see maps on pages 263–269

ISLE OF MULL (Tobermory)

HIGHLAND COTTAGE

BREADALBANE STREET, TOBERMORY, ISLE OF MULL, ARGYLL PA75 6PD
TEL: 01688 302030 FAX: 01688 302727

OWNERS: David and Josephine Currie

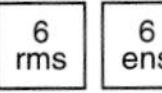

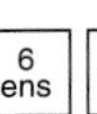

S: £50–£55
D: £74–£90

Situated in Tobermory, the "capital" of the Isle of Mull with frequent access from Oban by modern drive–on car ferry, Highland Cottage stands amidst the quiet elegance of the upper town's Conservation Area – quite literally above the town and yet just a few minute's walk from the hustle and bustle of Main Street and fisherman's harbour.

Comfort is an important criterion in this beautifully appointed hotel featuring period décor and stylish ornaments. The bedrooms are furnished with flair and imagination in bright and pleasant shades and are complemented by the fine bathrooms. All bedrooms are fully-equipped, some contain four-poster beds and others are suitable for the disabled.

Guests recline and enjoy a board game or relax with a drink in the comfortable lounge. Traditional cuisine, made with fresh local produce, is served in the intimate dining room.

The Executive Retreat Package comprises luxury accommodation, all meals for each delegate, exclusive use of the cottage and excellent meeting facilities.

Places of interest: Outdoor pursuits include fishing, sailing and golf whilst many organised day trips are offered around the scenic region of Mull including Staffa and Iona.

Directions: From the car ferries at Craignure or Fishnish, at roundabout on approach to Tobermory, carry straight on across the narrow bridge and turn immediately right signposted "Tobermory–Breadalbane Street". Follow the road round and Highland Cottage is on the right.

For hotel location, see maps on pages 263–269

KILLIECHRONAN

KILLIECHRONAN, ISLE OF MULL, ARGYLL PA72 6JU
TEL: 01680 300403 FAX: 01680 300463

OWNERS: The Leroy Family
MANAGERS: Margaret and Patrick Freytag

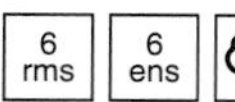

S: £73–£87
D: £61–£76
(including dinner)

An original Highland lodge, built in 1846, now a superb country house hotel, ideally located at the head of Loch na Keal. The owners already have an established reputation in Scotland with The Manor House Hotel at Oban and The Lake Hotel at Port of Menteith.

This, their third hotel, is their own family home and contains a magnificent collection of antiques and pictures. Most of the rooms face south, overlooking the sheltered grounds, part of the 5,000 acre estate.

Bringing the chef from the Manor House has ensured those high standards in the restaurant, awarded 2 AA rosettes that one associates with the Leroy family and there is a fine wine list to complement the menu.

There are just six bedrooms, all en suite, with telephone and other modern comforts.

The area is renowned for its outstanding beauty. Visit Fingal's Cave, the white beach at Calgary, Duart Castle, the herring village of Tobermory and Torosay set in Italianate gardens. There is fishing, sailing, golf, pony treking and a fairly easy walk to the summit of Ben More. **Directions: Mull is reached by the ferry from Oban (40 minute crossing) or Lochalin. Take A849 to Salen. Left on B8035. House on right 2 miles after.**

For hotel location, see maps on pages 263–269

ISLE OF SKYE (Portree)

BOSVILLE HOTEL & CHANDLERY SEAFOOD RESTAURANT

BOSVILLE TERRACE, PORTREE, ISLE OF SKYE, SCOTLAND IV51 9DG
TEL: 01478 612846 FAX: 01478 613434 E-MAIL: bosville@macleodhotels.co.uk

OWNERS: Donald W MacLeod
CHEF: Craig Rodger

15 rms | 15 ens | SMALL HOTEL

S: £60–£70
D: £76–£96

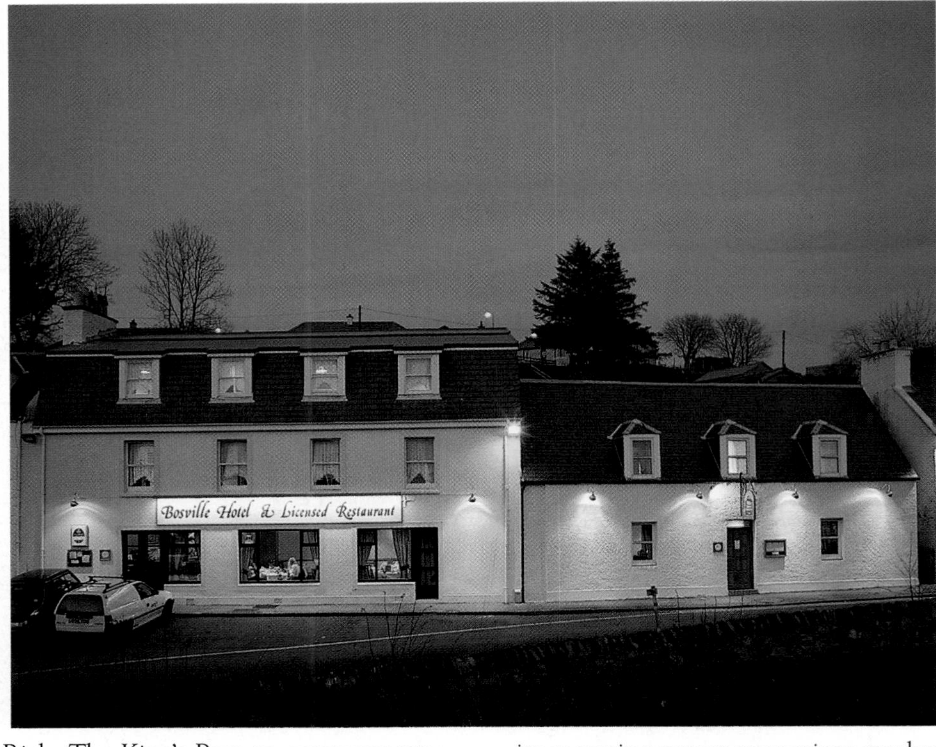

Named Port an Righ, The King's Port, to commemorate the visit of King James V of Scotland in 1540, there is a strong Celtic feel to Portree whose ubiquitous bilingual signs still indicate a thriving Gaelic language on the island.

A warm welcome and Celtic hospitality mark out the Bosville Hotel, just a step back from the waterfront and overlooking the harbour with Raasay and Ben Tianavaig beyond. There is a convivial feel to the bar and lounge and all the bedrooms have been carefully refurbished to a high standard. Modern luxuries such as telephones and satellite television have recently been added and en suite bathrooms are brightly lit and equally well-appointed.

With no part of Skye more than four miles from the sea, its recurring presence receives marked attention in The Chandlery Seafood Restaurant. Masterminded by chef Craig Rodger the menu features the finest Scottish produce, and the restaurant has been recognised by the AA with one Rosette for food quality. Highland game and venison, Aberdeen Angus beef and West Coast seafood all feature prominently, as do Scottish hand-made cheeses, oatcakes and traditional Cranachan and Clootie Dumplings.

Places of interest nearby: Portree is ideal for exploring the unrestricted countryside with its unspoiled landscapes and abundant wildlife. Fishing and pony trekking can be arranged. **Directions: Take A87 from Kyle of Lochalsh toll bridge to Portree. Bosville Hotel overlooks the harbour.**

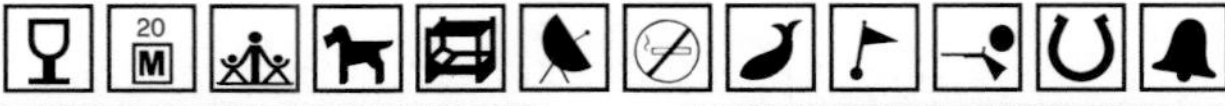

For hotel location, see maps on pages 263–269

Ardsheal House

KENTALLEN OF APPIN, ARGYLL PA38 4BX
TEL: 01631 740227 FAX: 01631 740342 E-MAIL: ardsheal@aol.com

OWNERS: Neil and Philippa Sutherland

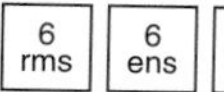

  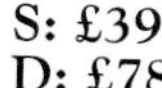

S: £39
D: £78

A long private drive winds alongside lovely Loch Linnhe and through ancient woodland to this magnificent 18th century granite and stone manor which stands high on a natural promontory of pink marble with magnificent views over the loch and the mountains of Morvern. The scenery is breathtaking even for the West Highlands.

Set in 800 acres of hills, woods, gardens and shore front, Ardsheal House has a charming country house ambience and a friendly welcome is extended to all visitors by the resident owners.

The reception hall is particularly attractive, with warm polished oak panelling, an imposing open fire and a unique barrel window. Family antiques and bright fabrics are to be found in all the individually furnished bedrooms.

Philippa Sutherland serves memorable, daily changing four-course dinners in the attractive dining room. Vegetables, herbs and fruit from the garden and home-made jellies, jams and preserves form the basis for her innovative set meals.

Places of interest nearby: Islands, castles, lochs and glens, Oban's Cathedral of the Isles and ruined 13th century castle. **Directions: Ardsheal House is on the A828 five miles south of the Ballachulish Bridge between Glencoe and Appin on the way to Oban. From Glasgow and Edinburgh, follow the signs to Crianlarich and take the A82 north to Ballachulish.**

For hotel location, see maps on pages 263–269

KILLIECRANKIE (By Pitlochry)

THE KILLIECRANKIE HOTEL

KILLIECRANKIE, BY PITLOCHRY, PERTHSHIRE PH16 5LG
TEL: 01796 473220 FAX: 01796 472451 E-MAIL: killiecrankie.hotel@btinternet.com

OWNERS: Colin and Carole Anderson

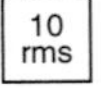 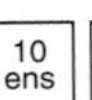 

S: £57–£84
D: £114–£168
(including dinner)

The Killiecrankie Hotel is peacefully situated in four acres of landscaped gardens overlooking the Pass of Killiecrankie and River Garry. It was here, in 1689, that the Jacobites clashed with William of Orange's men in a battle to gain supremacy over the crowns of England and Scotland – an event which illustrates the area's rich heritage.

Guests will find a friendly welcome and a relaxed, informal style. There are ten charming bedrooms, including two on the ground floor. All are very comfortably furnished and decorated to a high standard. There is a cosy residents' sitting room with a patio in the garden in fine weather.

With two AA Rosettes, the Dining Room has a very good reputation. Fresh ingredients indigenous to Scotland are used and presented with flair and imagination. Menus offer a good, balanced choice: start perhaps with Grilled Isle of Gigha Goats Cheese with Asparagus Salad or Ballottine of Duck, before going to a main course of Chargrilled Monkfish with Basil and Pinenut Pesto or Braised Fillet of Pork in an Ale and Caraway Sauce with Herb Dumplings. In the bar, a superb range of bar meals is served at lunch and supper time. Closed January and February. 3 night breaks at Christmas/New Year – also in Spring and Autumn.

Places of interest nearby: Blair Castle, Pitlochry Festival Theatre – golfing, fishing, shooting and hill-walking.

Directions: Turn off the main A9 at sign for Killiecrankie.

For hotel location, see maps on pages 263–269

The Kinlochbervie Hotel

KINLOCHBERVIE, BY LAIRG, SUTHERLAND IV27 4RP
TEL: 01971 521275 FAX: 01971 521438 E-MAIL: klbhotel@aol.com

OWNERS: Stewart and Val McHattie
MANAGERS: Jill and Linda McHattie
CHEF: Joan Harvey

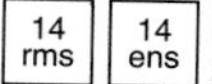
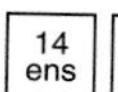

D: £90–£110

The Kinlochbervie Hotel stands amongst the awesome beauty of the Atlantic coastline just below Cape Wrath, once the turning point for marauding Viking longships. It overlooks the little fishing port and lochs and offers magnificent views over the open sea whose depths and roaring waves attract divers and surfers from miles around.

The Kinlochbervie incorporates all that visitors would expect from a quality three-star hotel. The lounges and bars are comfortably relaxing, the bedrooms warm and cosy and the restaurant imparts exactly the right atmosphere in which to savour the Scottish delights of the Kinlochbervie's kitchens and cellars. In addition to local lamb and venison, delicious fish figures prominently on the menus, as the daily arrival of deep-sea trawlers to the local market ensures a plentiful supply of shellfish, monkfish, turbot and sole. Excellent wines complement the fine cooking. Ornithologists and naturalists will revel in the abundance of wildlife, golfers will find a challenge on the the most northerly course in Britain, just a short drive away. Fly and sea fishing can be arranged.

Places of interest nearby: Europe's highest waterfall at Kylesku, Handa Island bird sanctuary, Cape Wrath and the sandy stretches of Oldshoremore, Polin and Sheigra. **Directions: Take the A836 and then the A838 north west from Lairg. At Rhiconich, turn left onto the B801 which runs alongside Loch Inchard to Kinlochbervie.**

NIVINGSTONE COUNTRY HOUSE

CLEISH, NR KINROSS, KINROSS-SHIRE, KY13 7LS
TEL: 01577 850216 FAX: 01577 850238 E-MAIL: centuryhousehotel@compuserve.com

OWNER: Allan Deeson
CHEF: Tom McConnell

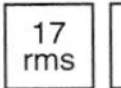

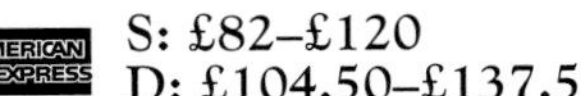

S: £82–£120
D: £104.50–£137.50

Peacefully set in 12 acres of landscaped gardens at the foot of the Cleish Hills, this comfortable old country house and its celebrated restaurant offer the warmest of welcomes. Standing more or less half-way between Edinburgh and Perth the original 1725 building has benefited from several architectural additions and it is now further enlarged and refurbished with all the characteristics of an up-to-date hotel.

Nivington House, personally managed by Kevin Kenny, is particularly well known for its fine food, prepared from traditional Scottish produce such as Perthshire venison and locally caught salmon. The restaurant has regularly been commended in leading guides and deservedly it has "Taste of Scotland" status and an AA Rosette. The menus are changed daily. The attractive en suite bedrooms are decorated in soft, subtle colours, with Laura Ashley fabrics and wallpapers. In the grounds there is a putting green and practice net for keen golfers. Sporting facilities within easy reach include the famous golf courses at St Andrews, Murrayshall and countless others of lesser renown.

Places of interest nearby: Loch Leven is popular for trout fishing and there are boat trips to Loch Leven Castle. **Directions: From M90 take exit 5 onto B9097 towards Crook of Devon. Cleish is 2 miles from motorway. Price guide: Single £75–£100; double/twin £95–£125.**

For hotel location, see maps on pages 263–269

THE DRYFESDALE HOTEL

LOCKERBIE, DUMFRIESSHIRE DG11 2SF
TEL: 01576 202427 FAX: 01576 20418

MANAGER: Angela Dunbobbin
CHEF: Michael Dunbobbin

15 rms 15 ens

S: £55–£65
D: £84–£87

The Dryfesdale Hotel, a former manse, is situated in one of the most beautiful settings in the area of Annandale. Built in 1782, it was converted into a country house hotel in the early 1950s.

The Dunbobbin family acquired the hotel in 1995 and have striven to enhance the ambience and standards of old. The lounges and bar are comfortably relaxing whilst the individually decorated bedrooms are warm and cosy.

Recently awarded an AA Rosette for the quality of food and service, the popular restaurant serves traditional cuisine, made with the best of regional produce.

Places of interest nearby: Amongst the many attractions in the surrounding area are Sammyling Tibetan centre and Temple at Eskdalemuir, Drumlanrigg Castle near Thornhill and the beautiful Galloway coastline passing Shambellie House museum at New Abbey, Gem Rock museum at Cree Town and Threave gardens near Castle Douglas. Dumfries is situated 20 minutes drive to the west of Lockerbie, the home of Robbie Burns monument and museum, historic buildings and shopping centre. A 20 minute drive to the south of Lockerbie takes you to the historic city of Carlisle. Cathedral and the Lanes shopping centre. The beautiful Cumbrian lakes and mountains are also within driving distance from the hotel as are the Scottish cities of Glasgow and Edinburgh. **Directions: The Dryfesdale Hotel is situated on junction 17 of the M74, approximately 27 miles north of Carlisle.**

For hotel location, see maps on pages 263–269

WELL VIEW HOTEL

BALLPLAY ROAD, MOFFAT, DUMFRIESSHIRE DG10 9JU
TEL: 01683 220184 FAX: 01683 220088

OWNERS: John and Janet Schuckardt

6 rms 6 ens

S: £45–£55
D: £64–£90

This delightful Victorian house on the edge of Moffat has been in excellent hands for the last ten years – the host being elected to the Academy of Wine Service and the hostess a member of the Craft Guild of Chefs, giving master classes on special occasions.

Guests enjoy an apéritif and canapé in the elegant lounge while studying the menu, or, after dinner, relax with home-made sweets accompanying the coffee – and maybe, an excellent malt whisky. Dinner in the charming, non-smoking, dining room, is six courses – including a sorbet – cooked with great flair and beautifully presented. Vegetarian dishes are available by prior request. The Cellar holds many fine wines from all parts of the world.

The bedrooms are all en suite and extremely comfortable, reflecting the high standards of hospitality throughout the hotel.

Places of interest nearby: Moffat is surrounded by mountains: Glasgow is reached over Beattock Summit, Edinburgh over the Devil's Beef Tub. St Mary's Loch and the Border Abbeys are also within driving distance.

Directions: Moffat is three miles from the M74/A74 trunk road between Carlisle and Glasgow. Leave the centre of the town on A708 (Selkirk) and turn left at crossroads into Ballplay Road. The hotel is a short distance on the right.

For hotel location, see maps on pages 263–269

Boath House

AULDEARN, NAIRN, INVERNESS IV12 5TE
TEL: 01667 454896 FAX: 01667 455469 E-MAIL: wendy@Boath–house.demon.co.uk

OWNERS: Don and Wendy Matheson
CHEF: Charles Lockley

6 rms | 6 ens

S: £55–£85
D: £65–£110

This classic Georgian country mansion, set in 20 acres of grounds, has been described as the most beautiful Regency house in Scotland. It was built in 1825 for the Dunbar family, replacing 'the great stone house' mentioned in a court circular from Mary Queen of Scots' time.

Over the years the house passed through various hands and fell into disrepair. In the early 1990s, it was bought by the present owners and sympathetically restored to recreate its original splendour. The six en suite bedrooms, which have all been decorated according to individual themes, are spacious and well furnished. The reception rooms match their high standard of comfort.

The award-winning restaurant offers excellent views over the lake and menus are chosen daily, dependent on fresh local produce available from the kitchen garden and local suppliers. Vegetarian and healthy options menus are also available.

A small but well-equipped gymnasium complements the beauty and hairdressing salon and a leisure area complete with sauna and heated whirlpool.

Places of interest nearby: Cawdor Castle, Elgin Cathedral, Culloden Battlefield and Brodie Castle.

Directions: Well signposted off the A96 Aberdeen to Inverness Road at Auldrean, 2 miles east of Nairn.

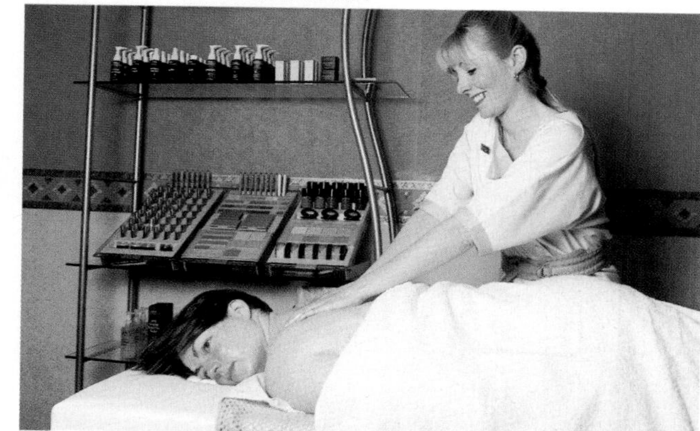

For hotel location, see maps on pages 263–269

Dungallan House Hotel

GALLANACH ROAD, OBAN, ARGYLL PA34 4PD
TEL: 01631 563799 FAX: 01631 566711

OWNERS: George and Janice Stewart

  S: £35–£45
D: £70–£90

Peacefully set in five acres of gardens and lawns and with sloping woodland front and rear this impressive old Victorian house offers the warmest of welcomes. Although just a 15 minutes walk away from the bustling main centre of Oban, Dungallan has a restful country atmosphere and enjoys magnificent panoramic views over Oban Bay to the Island of Mull, Lismore and the spectacular Hills of Morvern.

Built in 1870 by the Campbell family, Dungallan House has undergone a major programme of upgrading to provide full facilities for today's visitor and to enhance the elegance of the building. Most bedrooms have a wonderful outlook and are harmoniously decorated reflecting the high standards of hospitality throughout the hotel.

In the spacious dining room guests can savour superb traditional Scottish meals prepared with the best of local produce by Janice Stewart who, with owner and husband George now run Dungallan House. A carefully chosen wine list complements the menu. Sporting activities locally include fishing, sailing and golf.

Places of interest nearby: Oban is Scotland's main ferry port for the Western Isles and the many day trips are a splendid way of discovering this beautiful area. **Directions: The Hotel is on the southern outskirts of Oban beyond the ferry terminal and then follow signs for Gallanach.**

For hotel location, see maps on pages 263–269

The Manor House Hotel

GALLANACH ROAD, OBAN, ARGYLL PA34 4LS
TEL: 01631 562087 FAX: 01631 563053

OWNERS: The Leroy Family

11 rms | 11 ens | SMALL HOTEL

S: £64–£110
D: £90–£160
(including dinner)

Late Georgian in style, The Manor House was built in 1780 as the principal residence of the Duke of Argyll's Oban estate. Today it is a hotel where great care has been taken to preserve the elegance of its bygone days. The Manor House occupies a prime position overlooking Oban Bay, the islands and the mountains of Movern and Mull.

In the dining room guests can enjoy a fine blend of Scottish and French cooking, with the emphasis on local seafood and game in season. The table d'hôte menus take pride of place and are changed daily to offer a choice of starters, intermediate fish course or soup, home-made sorbet, choice of main courses, choice of puddings, and to round off, coffee and mints. The restaurant menu is partnered by a cellar of wines and selection of malt whiskies.

The bedrooms have twin or double beds, all with en suite bathrooms, TV and tea-making facilities. The Manor House Hotel is quietly located on the outskirts of Oban, yet within easy walking distance of the town. Special mini-breaks are available for stays of two nights or more. Closed Mondays and Tuesday from mid-November to February. Special Christmas and Hogmanay breaks available.
Places of interest nearby: Oban is Scotland's main ferry port for trips to the Western Isles and the many day tours are a splendid way of discovering this beautiful area.
Directions: The Manor House Hotel is situated on the western outskirts of Oban beyond the ferry boat pier.

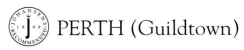

NEWMILN COUNTRY HOUSE

NEWMILN ESTATE, GUILDTOWN, PERTH, PERTHSHIRE PH2 6AE
TEL: 01738 552364 FAX: 01738 553505

OWNERS: James and Elaine McFarlane
CHEF: J. Paul Burns

7 rms 5 ens

S: £70–£130
D: £125–£200

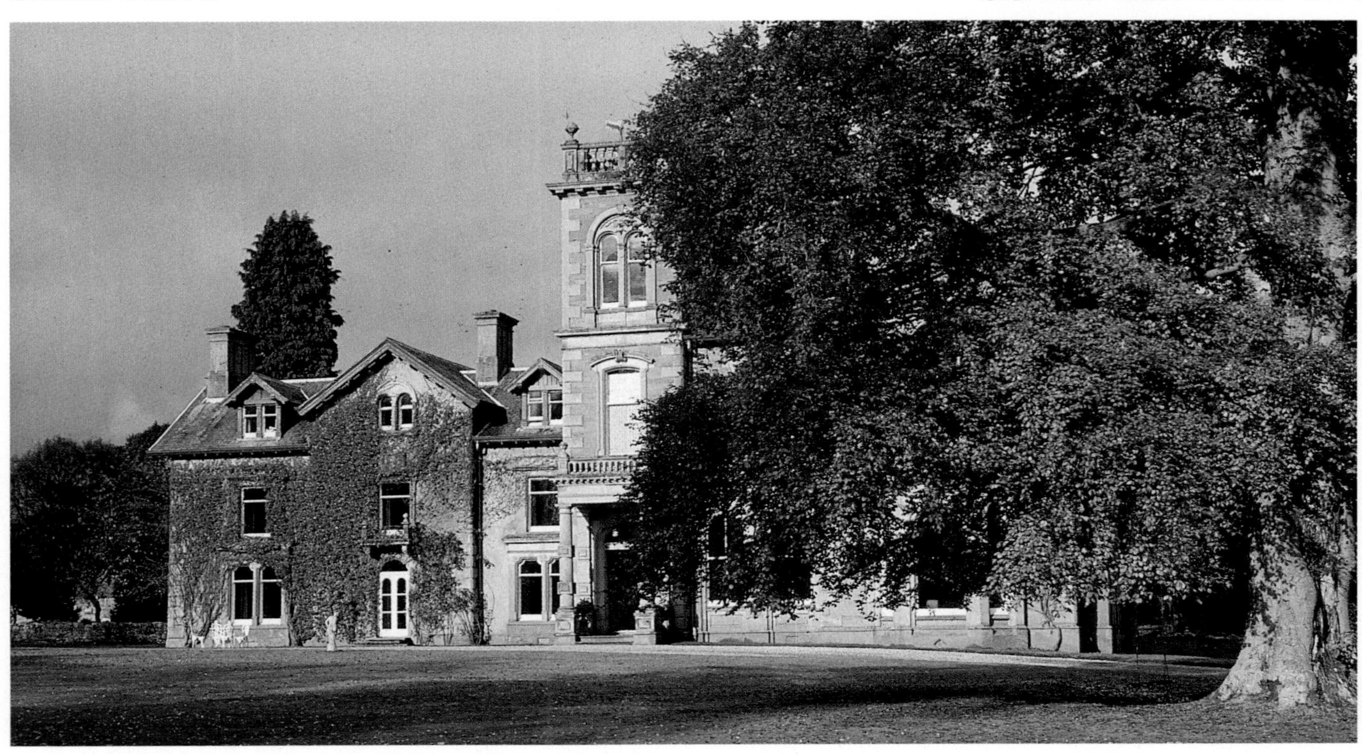

A rich but homely style of hospitality awaits guests at Newmiln Country House. This superb 18th century mansion is set within a 700-acre sporting estate and offers breathtaking views of the surrounding natural woodlands and waterfalls. With its warm and friendly atmosphere, the house is ideal for romantic weekends, family celebrations or a simply peaceful break away.

The beautifully proportioned public rooms, with their cosy log fires and intricate wood panelling, are ideal settings for a quiet read or drink, while the immaculate bedrooms boast the highest standards of comfort. Each of the two bedrooms which are not en suite have their own private bathroom.

The talented chef creates sumptuous cuisine featuring the best local produce; prime fillet of Perthshire beef on onion and toasted pine-nut marmalade, pigeon oven roasted presented with salad leaves and redcurrant jus and east coast Lobster Thermidor. Immaculately presented dishes are complemented with a fine selection of wines. There is no smoking in the dining room. Awarded 3 AA Rosettes for food and was MaCallan 'Taste of Scotland Country Hotel of the Year Awards 1997' runner up. Special winter rates. Horses are available on site for experienced riders. For golf St Andrews, Gleneagles and Carnoustie are an easy drive away. **Places of interest nearby:** Scone Palace, Blair Castle and Perth Racecourse. **Directions: A93 Blairgowrie road out of Perth. 3 miles after Scone Palace on left.**

For hotel location, see maps on pages 263–269

DUNFALLANDY HOUSE

LOGIERAIT ROAD, PITLOCHRY, PERTHSHIRE PH16 5NA
TEL: 01796 472648 FAX: 01796 472017 E-MAIL: dunfalhse@aol.com

OWNERS: Michael and Jane Bardsley

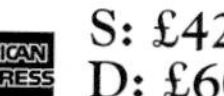

S: £42–£52
D: £60–£76

Dunfallandy House is a secluded Georgian Mansion House built in 1790 and now lovingly restored and converted into a fine small Country House Hotel.

In an elevated position, in three and a half acres of grounds, within the Dunfallandy Estate, surrounded by the splendour of the Tummel Valley, it stands above the highland town of Pitlochry. The House retains many historic features, yet it has all been sympathetically modernised to provide year round comfort including central heating.

The bedrooms are designed and furnished to a high standard. All double/twin rooms have en suite shower/bath, toilet and washbasin. Some have four-poster beds. All are equipped with colour televisions, clock radios, tea and coffee making facilities, hairdryers and trouser presses.

Full Scottish or light continental breakfasts are served in the Georgian dining room, where guests can later enjoy a delicious dinner – vegetarian dishes available. Before or after dining guests can relax in front of the open fire in the Green Room, where they may select a good book and enjoy a fine malt whisky from the oak-panelled bar.

Places of interest nearby: Golf, fishing, shooting and riding. Pitochry Theatre and the famous salmon ladder.

Directions: From Pitlochry, take road signposted Pitlochry Festival Theatre, cross river, turn left on road signposted Dunfallandy, hotel is 500 yards on the right.

For hotel location, see maps on pages 263–269

DRUIMNEIL

PORT APPIN, ARGYLLSHIRE PA38 4DQ
TEL & FAX: 01631 730228

OWNER: Janet Glaisher
CHEF: Janet Glaisher

3 rms | 3 ens

S: £35
D: £70

Twenty miles north of Oban lies Druimneil, a grand mid-Victorian country house overlooking the lovely Sound of Shuna and Loch Linnhe, which stretches inland from the sea towards Loch Lochy. Wildlife is abundant. Rare birds of prey, deer, otters and seals can often be seen.

The hotel is owned and run by Janet Glaisher, who goes out of her way to ensure that guests enjoy their stay. It is excellent in every way and is the ideal base for touring the jagged coastline and surrounding mountain ranges.

In the dining room guests enjoy traditional country house meals with the emphasis on local seafood and fruit from the kitchen garden. The downstairs rooms are spacious and elegant with antique family furniture, fine pictures and porcelain, while the three upstairs en suite bedrooms have all modern comforts. The hotel's boat "Tiddely-Wee" is available for fishing and viewing the nearby seal colony.

Places of interest nearby: Oban's Cathedral of the Isles and ruined 13th century castle. This is Scotland's main ferry port for trips to the Western Isles and the many day tours are a splendid way of discovering this beautiful area. **Directions: Take the A85 and A828 coastal roads north from Oban to Tynribbie. Then turn west for Port Appin.**

For hotel location, see maps on pages 263–269

THE LAKE HOTEL

PORT OF MENTEITH, PERTHSHIRE FK8 3RA
TEL: 01877 385258 FAX: 01877 385671

OWNERS: The Leroy Family

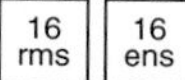

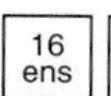

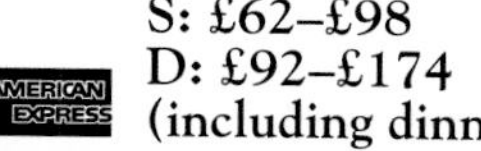

S: £62–£98
D: £92–£174
(including dinner)

The Lake Hotel is set in a splendid sheltered position on the banks of the Lake of Menteith in the Trossachs. Its lawn runs down to the edge of the lake, which in winter months often freezes over. When this happens, it is not unusual for locals to bring out their skates for a skim over the ice.

Guests are assured of all the amenities of an STB 4 Crown Highly Commended hotel. A programme of refurbishment has been completed, so the interiors have fresh decoration and furnishings. All bedrooms have en suite facilities and the details that will make your stay comfortable. There is an elegant lounge and a large conservatory from which the vista of lake and mountains is stunning.

The à la carte and table d'hôte menus present a varied choice of imaginatively prepared dishes. The table d'hôte menus are particularly good value: start with chicken & herb terrine with sun dried tomato dressing, followed by sorbet, then after a main course of grilled halibut with spinach,saffron potatoes and an orange & aniseed sauce, enjoy a Drambuie parfait with raspberry coulis before your coffee and home-made petits fours. Special rates are available for mini-breaks of two nights or more.
Places of interest nearby: Inchmahome Priory – haven for both Mary, Queen of Scots and Robert the Bruce – Loch Lomond and Stirling Castle. **Directions: Situated on the A81 road, south of Callander and east of Aberfoyle, on the northern banks of the Lake of Menteith.**

For hotel location, see maps on pages 263–269

ALDONAIG

RHU, ARGYLL & BUTE G84 8NH
TEL: 01436 820863 FAX: 01436 821618

OWNER: Mark and Connie Webster

3 rms | 2 ens

S: £39–£44
D: £60–£70

Aldonaig stands gleamingly white amongst lush, mature gardens on the eastern side of Gare Loch. The surrounding mountain scenery is magnificent with the twin peaks of Doune Hill (2,408ft and 2,298ft) dominating the wild hills and Glens. Just five miles away is Loch Lomond, the largest and one of the loveliest lochs in Scotland, whose 23 miles length is studded with 30 islands and historic sites.

Originally built in the 18th century, the oldest part of Aldonaig is believed to have been a malt barn of a distillery. Today the house offers visitors beautiful furnishings and many fine antiques, whilst offering every comfort and modern facilities.

The hotel is owned and run by Connie Webster, who goes out of her way to ensure guests enjoy their stay. It is excellent in every way and is an ideal base for exploring and enjoying the Highlands and Islands of the West Coast of Scotland. Two of the bedrooms are en suite with the third having a private bathroom. All are beautifully decorated and have superb views over the lawns to the loch and hills beyond. Dinner by arrangement. Connie serves traditional country house meals with the emphasis on fresh local produce.

Places of interest nearby: Loch Lomond, Loch Long, The Trossacks and Glencoe are close by whilst being conveniently situated for Glasgow Airport (25 mins). **Directions: From Glasgow, take A82 northwest, then join A814. Aldonaig can be found on leaving the village of Rhu.**

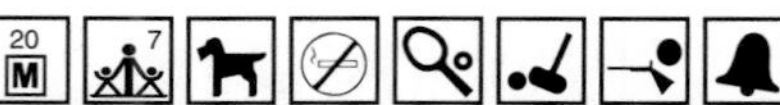

For hotel location, see maps on pages 263–269

Clint Lodge

ST BOSWELLS, MELROSE, ROXBURGHSHIRE TD6 0DZ
TEL: 01835 822027 FAX: 01835 822656 E-MAIL: Clintlodge@aol.com

PROPRIETORS/CONTACT: Bill and Heather Walker

 S: £25–£40
D: £50–£80

Clint Lodge stands square and solid in the heart of the Borders with magnificent views over the River Tweed to the distant Cheviot hills. Surrounded by a spacious lawned garden it was built in 1869 by Lord Polworth as the family's shooting home and is now owned by the Duke of Sutherland. The Lodge retains many of its original features – large open fireplaces, wooden and tiled floors – and has been carefully refurbished and modernised to provide year round comfort.

The bedrooms are furnished and decorated to a high standard. Three are en suite, two with original deep-fill baths, and one of the double rooms has a private bathroom. There is also an adjacent, self-catering cottage with three bedrooms, lounge, kitchen and bathroom.

Guests can relax during colder months before an open log fire in the Lodge's spacious drawing room and on warmer days enjoy the rural views from an adjoining sun lounge which opens onto a small patio. Heather Walker provides excellent, traditional meals and caters for all diets.

Sporting and leisure pursuits are close by, including salmon and trout fishing, grouse, pheasant and clay pigeon shooting. There are 12 golf courses within a half hour's drive.

Places of interest nearby: Scott's View, Dryburgh Abbey and Melrose Abbey. **Directions: Take B6404 from St Boswells and after two miles turn left onto B6356, signposted Scott's View and Earlston. Clint Lodge is on the right, one mile beyond Clint Mains village.**

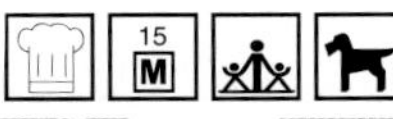

QUEEN'S VIEW HOTEL

STRATHTUMMEL, BY PITLOCHRY, PERTHSHIRE PH16 5NR
TEL: 01796 473291 FAX: 01796 473515 E-MAIL: queensviewhotel@compuserve.com

OWNERS: Richard and Norma Tomlinson
CHEF: Norma Tomlinson

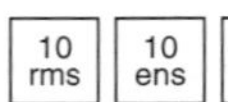

S: £60–£95
D: £100–£160
(including dinner)

Queen's View Hotel stands high and majestically overlooking the shimmering waters of Loch Tummel, close to the little town of Pitlochry and just a few miles from the ancient city of Perth. All around are the splendours of the Tummel Valley and the good things that Scotland has to offer. Despite its stunning location, the hotel has been a well-kept secret for many years. Owners Richard and Norma Tomlinson have now sympathetically renovated it to provide relaxing comfort and modern facilities.

The bedrooms, including a family suite, are furnished to a high standard and have magnificent views over the loch 150 feet below. All but one of the bedrooms are en suite.

There is an attractive and well-furnished lounge, a comfortable bar where you can enjoy a fine malt whisky and out of the ordinary lunchtime food and there is also a very pleasant restaurant with a growing reputation for its innovative and tasty cuisine. Many theatre-goers like to take two courses before the performance returning for a drink or coffee and pudding afterwards. The hotel is closed from mid January to early March.

Places of interest nearby: Pitlochy has its own theatre. Fishing within the grounds. Golf, riding and curling can be arranged. Blair Castle, Bruar Falls, Scone Palace and Balmoral are close. **Directions: A9 to Pitlochry then B8079 north. Turn left onto B8019 for Tummel Bridge and the hotel is three miles miles further on.**

For hotel location, see maps on pages 263–269

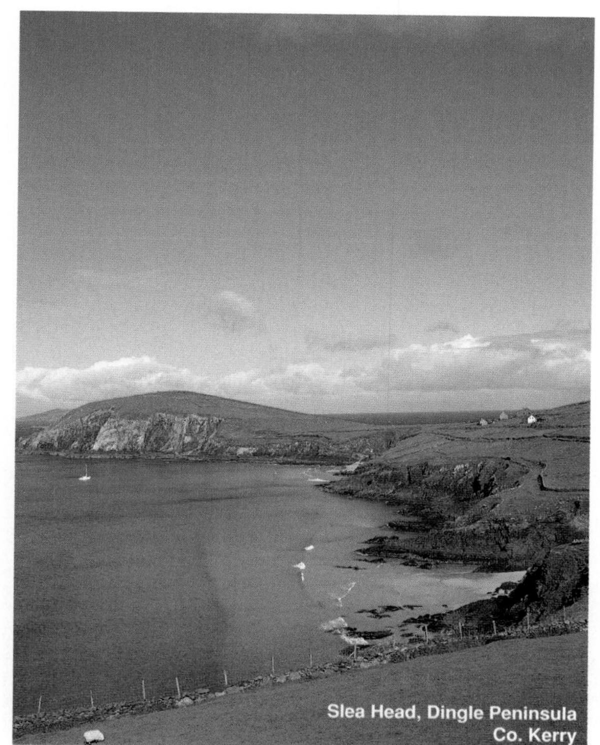
Slea Head, Dingle Peninsula
Co. Kerry

Johansens Recommended Country Houses & Small Hotels in
Ireland

Celtic treasures and legends, medieval architecture, racecourses and golf courses, great art collections and a richness of literature are all to be found amongst the green landscapes of Ireland.

The range of visitor attractions, facilities and all-weather specialist pursuits which is now available throughout Ireland is at its most comprehensive to date. Following a 12-year nation-wide programme of investment in infrastructure, the quality and choice on offer to Ireland's annually increasing international visitor numbers reflect standards of excellence, which are not only hard to match in other national destinations, but neither are they so readily discoverable there.

With well over 300 golf courses dotted around the country – parkland and links alike – often offering world class challenges, and all of them welcoming visitors, it is no surprise that Ireland is now internationally referred to as the 'golfing Mecca' of Europe. Equally, angling, sailing and equestrian enthusiasts indulge their particular passion in the Emerald Isle's friendly atmosphere and pristine environment at a standard rarely to be found elsewhere.

An integral part of any visit is the cultural and social encounter involved. In Ireland the unique blend of Celtic, Scandinavian and Anglo-Norman heritage, which has formed the national character, nowadays finds vigorous expression in theatre and literature, music and sport as well as in the everyday life of the people. Indeed, the Irish life experience is one which is now happily shared with millions of leisure travellers every year and for many of them a single visit to Ireland is not enough.

Not to be outdone, Irish food has reached new creative heights in recent years, and with the innovative use of the finest local ingredients, the unsuspecting are pleasantly surprised with memorable dining experiences encountered alike in city, town, village and rural retreat.

People who have never been to Northern Ireland think it is somehow different from the rest of the island. In some ways, that is true, but in most ways it is just as 'Irish' as anywhere else. People are genuinely friendly to visitors as they don't see too many of them – and appreciative of anyone who wants to see the 'real' Northern Ireland for themselves.

Lough Erne is one of the most beautiful waterways in Europe, but there are so few boats on it that you can cruise for hours without seeing another craft. Lower Lough Erne is a large lake stretching for 26 miles with numerous small islands, while Upper Lough Erne is more like a river winding through a maze of islands. The town of Enniskillen stands on an isthmus between Lower and Upper, with green hills forming a dramatic backdrop.

Northern Ireland has dramatic seascapes as well as lakes and mountains and the drive north from the port of Larne to Ballycastle is unforgettable. While in Ballycastle you can visit remote Rathlin Island, and you can sail to Ballycastle directly on the summer-only ferry from Campbeltown on the Mull of Kintyre in Scotland.

West of Ballycastle you will find some of Northern Ireland's top attractions, and if you have gone easy on the poteen, then sway along Carrick-a-Rode rope bridge made to help fishermen reach their boats. Little villages including Ballintoy and Portballintrae are worth discovering, but the sight you must not miss is the Giant's Causeway.

Formed of 40,000 basalt columns stretching out into the sea, this natural wonder is steeped in mythology. The giant Finn McCool is said to have built the causeway to bring his lover from the Hebrides, and while fighting with a Scottish giant he flung a huge piece of earth across the sea. The hole it left is now Lough Neagh; but the missile fell short and now forms the Isle of Man.

Close to the Giant's Causeway you can also tour the distillery at Bushmills – where the produce is legal! See the clifftop ruins of Dunluce Castle, and enjoy the seaside resorts of Portrush and Portstewart, famed for their wide, white sands. One of Ireland's top golf courses, Royal Portrush, is nearby.

One of the great things about Northern Ireland is that everywhere is within easy reach, as it is only the same size as Yorkshire. You could base yourself in Belfast to enjoy city attractions, and make day trips to the Causeway Coast, the Mountains of Mourne, historic Armagh and the scenic Ards peninsula.

Belfast has come alive over the last few years, and the nightlife is particularly good along the 'Golden Mile' from the Grand Opera House to historic Queen's University. You can take a guided walking tour of Belfast pubs and one 'must' is the Crown Bar with beautifully preserved Victorian decor. Old and new come together in Belfast, with the turn-of-the-century City Hall contrasting with the Waterfront Hall, opened in 1997 to give Northern Ireland a world-class concert venue.

For more information about Ireland and Northern Ireland please contact:

The Irish Tourist Board
Bord Failte
Baggot Street Bridge
Dublin 2
Tel: 00 353 1 602 4000

Northern Ireland Tourist Board
St Anne's Court
59 North Street
Belfast BT1 1NB
Tel: 01232 246609

Ballylickey Manor House

BALLYLICKEY, BANTRY BAY, CO. CORK, IRELAND
TEL: 00 353 27 50071 FAX: 00 353 27 50124 E-MAIL: ballymh@tinet.ie

OWNERS: Christian and George Graves

12 rms | 12 ens

S: IR£100
D: IR£130–IR£220

Built some 300 years ago as a shooting lodge by Lord Kenmare, Ballylickey Manor House was totally restored and splendidly refurbished to open as a hotel in 1950. Its latter-day creator was George Graves whose uncle, the poet, Robert Graves was a regular visitor here, and whose mother Kitty laid out the sumptuous gardens.

Furnished in perfect taste with heirlooms and antiques, the main house with its five spacious suites has impressive views overlooking majestic Bantry Bay. Within the ten acres of grounds that surround the house is a charming outdoor swimming pool and seven chalets with en suite facilities.

An informal lunch and dining venue, Le Rendezvous, borders the pool. Within the Manor House the dining room is more formal and open to residents only. Christian Graves supervises a stylish and classically-based cuisine expertly cooked by the French chef. Bantry Bay crab and lobster feature on a menu which relies strongly on seafood, local lamb and garden produce. Pâté de foie gras to start with and desserts such as crème caramel and strawberry gratin reinforce the emphatically French accent.

Places of interest nearby: The River Ouvane runs past the house. Fishing and hunting are popular pastimes. Nearby there are two golf courses and facilities for horse-riding. This is a good base for touring the Ring of Kerry. **Directions: Ballylickey stands on the main N71 road between Bantry and Glengariff. The hotel is signposted on the road.**

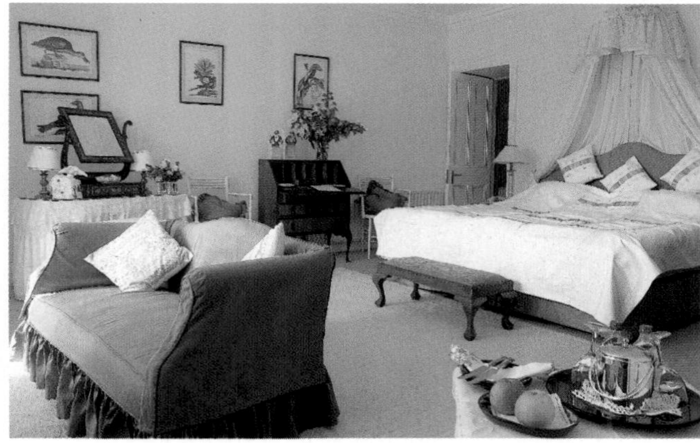

For hotel location, see maps on pages 263–269

ARD-NA-SIDHE

CARAGH LAKE, CO KERRY, IRELAND
TEL: 00 353 66 69105 FAX: 00 353 66 69282

OWNERS: Killarney Hotels Ltd.

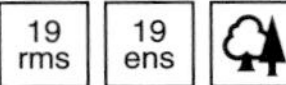

S: £70–£110
D: £125–£158

This romantic Victorian former country house was built in 1880 by an English lady who called it the 'House of Fairies'. Surrounded by a magnificent park, it is situated at Caragh Lake, 17 miles from Killarney. The house is furnished with valuable antiques and still retains the atmosphere of a private residence. Its tastefully decorated and furnished bedrooms, along with the comfortable reception rooms, offer guests luxurious surroundings in which to relax and unwind.

Simple but delicious cuisine is served in the elegant restaurant. A sample menu might include cockle and mussel broth with pesto, followed by grilled sirloin steak with onion and mustard crust, buttered carrots and leeks and rosemary potatoes. For dessert try the peach and mint ragout with lemon sorbet, baby pineapple with strawberry ice and fresh fruits, or cheese selection. The hotel has twice won first prize in the National Gardens Competition. This is an idyllic setting in which to read, paint, walk and explore. Boating and fishing are available on Caragh Lake and the facilities of sister hotels The Europe and Dunloe Castle in Killarney can be used by Ard Na Sidhe guests. Some of Ireland's most beautiful golf courses are just a few minutes away by car. Closed 2nd October to 1st May.

Places of interest nearby: The picturesque town of Killarney, surrounded by lakes and mountains, just a few miles from the Atlantic coast. **Directions: West of Killorglin off N70 on the side of Caragh Lake.**

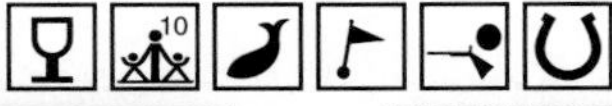

Caragh Lodge

CARAGH LAKE, CO KERRY

TEL: 00 353 66 9769115 FAX: 00 353 66 9769316 E-MAIL: caraghl@IOL.IE

OWNER: Mary Gaunt

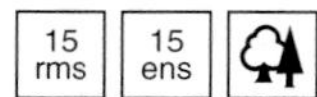

S: IR£66
D: IR£99–IR£132
Suite: IR£198

The breathtaking slopes of Ireland's highest mountain range, McGillycuddy Reeks, rise majestically above this elegant Victorian hotel whose award-winning gardens run gently down to the shore of Caragh Lake. Less than a mile from the spectacular Ring of Kerry, Caragh Lodge offers an unsurpassed blend of luxury, heritage, tranquillity, hospitality and service. It is excellent in every way and an ideal base for the sightseeing, golfing and fishing enthusiast.

All the en suite bedrooms are decorated with period furnishings and antiques, with the converted garden rooms looking over magnificent displays of magnolias, camellias, rhododendrons, azaleas and rare subtropical shrubs. The exquisite dining room overlooks the lake and Mary Gaunt personally prepares menus of the finest Irish food, including freshly caught salmon, succulent Kerry lamb, garden grown vegetables and home-baked breads. Open 23 Apr–17 Oct '99.

Caragh Lodge's gardens conceal an all-weather tennis court and sauna chalet. Salmon and trout swim in the lake and two boats are available for angling guests. Ghillies or permits for fishing in the two local rivers can be arranged. There are also local golf courses, where tee off times can be organised. **Places of interest nearby:** The Ring of Kerry, Dingle Peninsula, Gap of Dunloe, Killarney and Tralee. **Directions: From Killorglin travel on N70 towards Glenbeigh and take second road signposted for Caragh Lake. At lake turn left, Caragh Lodge is on your right.**

For hotel location, see maps on pages 263–269

Cashel Palace Hotel

MAIN STREET, CASHEL, CO TIPPERARY
TEL: 00 353 62 62707 FAX: 00 353 62 61521 E-MAIL: cphotel@ibm.net

OWNERS: Silkestan Ltd
PROPRIETORS: Patrick and Susan Murphy

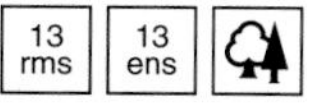

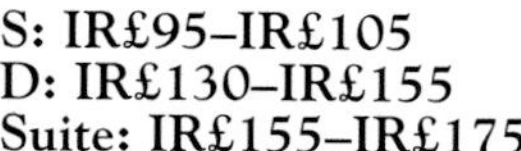

S: IR£95–IR£105
D: IR£130–IR£155
Suite: IR£155–IR£175

This magnificent and luxurious 18th century hotel stands in the shadow of the famous Rock of Cashel at the heart of a heritage town surrounded by a wealth of historical sites. Built in 1730 as a palace for Archbishop Theophilus Bolton it is a jewel of late Queen Anne and early Georgian style. Described as "A place of notable hospitality" in Loveday's Tour of 1732, the Cashel Palace Hotel's beauty is complemented by 22 acres of walled gardens which include a private walk to the Rock of Cashel and two mulberry trees planted in 1702 to commemorate the coronation of Queen Anne.

The hotel has been lovingly restored with great attention given to preserving its character and integrity. Spacious bedrooms echo the style and elegance of the 18th century and are individually furnished to the highest standards. The tradition of fine food continues in the relaxed ambience of the Bishops Buttery which specialises in lighter modern Irish cuisine with classical influences.

Local leisure activities include pony trekking, horse riding, golf, tennis, trout and salmon fishing.

Places of interest nearby: Cashel is an ideal base from which to tour Munster and the South East and is within easy reach of Cahir Castle, the Devil's Bit Mountain and Holy Cross. **Directions: Cashel is on the junction of the N8 and N74.**

For hotel location, see maps on pages 263–269

Ross Lake House Hotel

ROSSCAHILL, OUGHTERARD, CO GALWAY, IRELAND
TEL: 00 353 91 550109 FAX: 00 353 91 550184

OWNERS: Henry and Elaine Reid

S: £50–£70
D: £80–£100
Suite: £90–£120

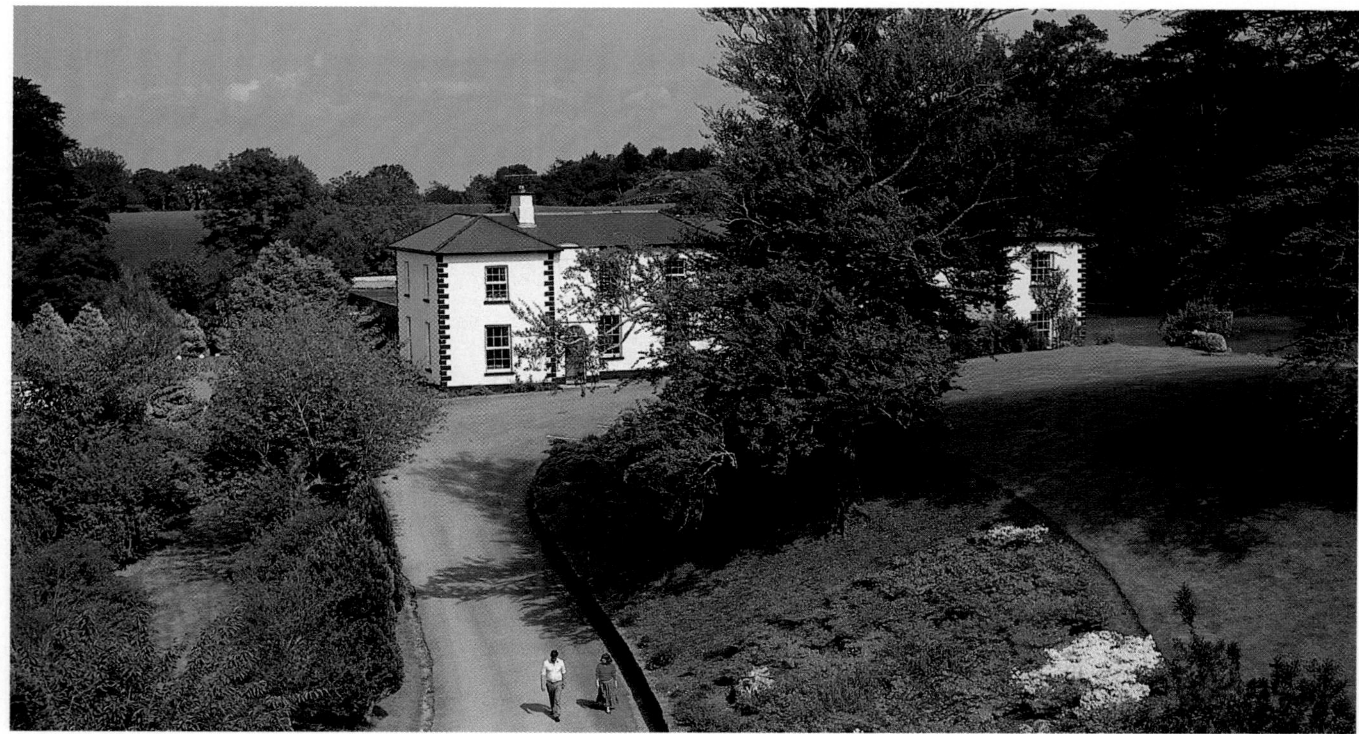

Homeliness and relaxation are the hallmarks of this elegant 18th century hotel situated in the beautiful County Galway countryside unspoilt by the advance of time. It is an attractive old house whose former glory has been carefully and tastefully revived by owners Henry and Elaine Reid.

Surrounded by rambling woods and magnificent lawned gardens studded with colourful flowers and evergreen shrubs, Ross Lake was formerly an estate house of landed gentry who praised it for its serenity. The owners pride themselves that the hotel is a haven of peace where recreation comes naturally and service and hospitality are of the highest order.

Public rooms are spacious and combine the elegance of an earlier age with modern comforts. The drawing room, which is a favourite of all those who enjoy afternoon tea, is particularly attractive. Comfort and good taste are also reflected in the hotel's 12 bedrooms which are all en suite and offer lovely views over the gardens.

Quality Irish food is excellently prepared and presented in the intimate restaurant with dishes enhanced by fresh produce from the Connemara hills, streams and lakes.

For the active there is tennis in the grounds, golfing at the Oughterard 18-hole parkland course, game and course fishing. **Places of interest nearby:** Aughnanure Castle, Kylemore Abbey, Connemara National Park, the Aran Islands, Cliffs of Moher and the Burren. **Directions: Ross Lake House is off N59, 14 miles north west of Galway.**

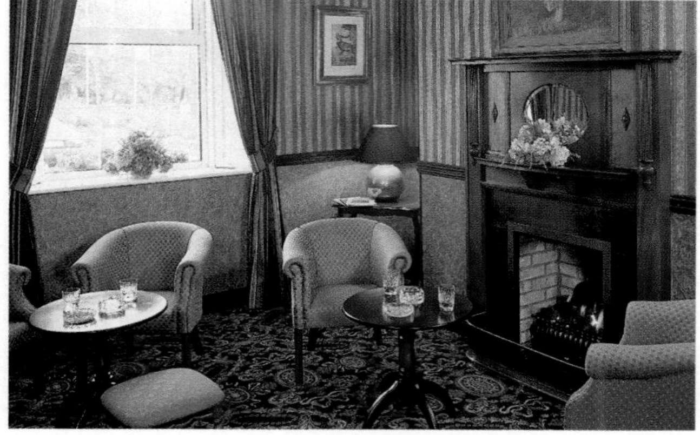

For hotel location, see maps on pages 263–269

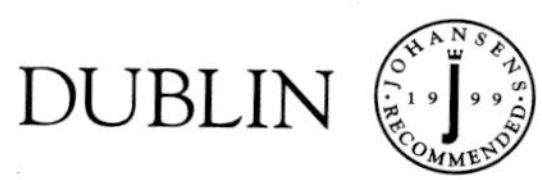

ABERDEEN LODGE

53-55 PARK AVENUE, OFF AILESBURY ROAD, DUBLIN 4
TEL: 00 353 1 2838155 FAX: 00 353 1 2837877 E-MAIL: aberdeen@iol.ie

OWNER: Pat Halpin

17 rms 17 ens

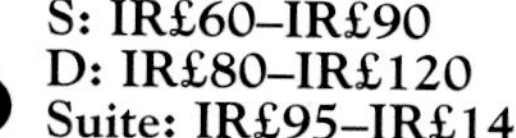

S: IR£60–IR£90
D: IR£80–IR£120
Suite: IR£95–IR£145

This symbol of classical Edwardian architecture has a prime site in a serene tree-lined avenue in what is often called Dublin's Embassy Belt. Set in its own large formal gardens, Aberdeen Lodge provides high quality accommodation, comfort and service accompanied by all the modern luxuries which visitors to a flourishing capital city would expect today.

Every room is an elegant reminder of Edwardian grace and Pat Halpin and his family's renowned hotel experience is evident in the detail of décor and operation. They pride themselves on being able to ensure that the needs of guests are met quickly and efficiently.

Each of the tastefully furnished bedrooms is en suite and designed in complete harmony with the house. The spacious suites feature a Jacuzzi and period style furniture.

The award-winning intimate Breakfast Room is complemented by a special menu served between 11am and 10pm, accompanied by a good selection of fine wines from around the world.

Places of interest nearby: The hotel makes an ideal base from which to explore Dublin and enjoy shopping in the famous Grafton Street. As well as many first-class golf courses there is horse racing and two major marinas along the coast. Lansdowne Road rugby ground is a short walk.

Directions: Off Ailesbury Road, Aberdeen Lodge is 7 minutes from the city centre by D.A.R.T. bus.

For hotel location, see maps on pages 263–269

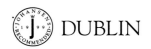

Fitzwilliam Park

NO 5, FITZWILLIAM SQUARE, DUBLIN 2, IRELAND
TEL: 00 353 1 662 8280 FAX: 00 353 662 8281 E-MAIL: info@fitzpark.ie

OWNER: Mary Madden

S: IR£85
D: IR£105
Suite: IR£125

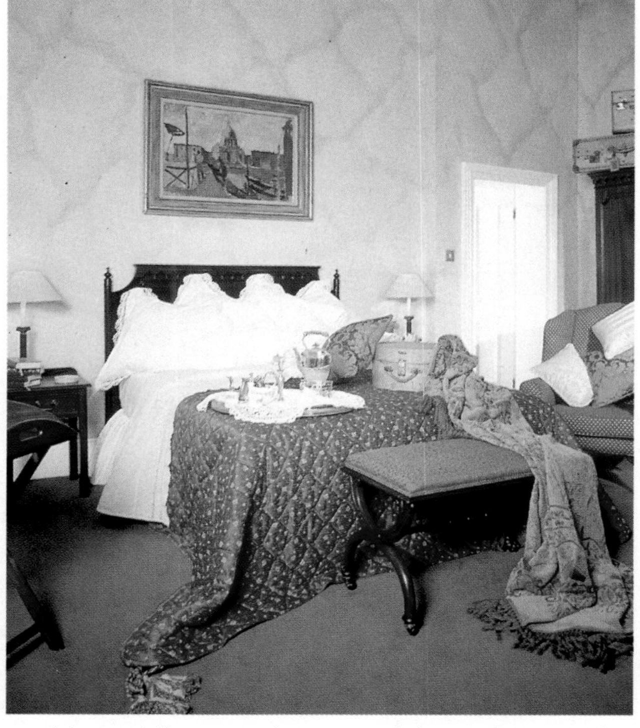

Fitzwilliam Park is a luxurious and beautifully restored town house situated in one of Dublin's most elegant and best preserved Georgian squares just a short stroll from the heart of the city. Built in 1816 on land leased from the 5th Viscount Fitzwilliam it is one of the largest houses on the square and retains many of its original period features. It has a charm of casual country elegance, offering high quality, exquisitely furnished accommodation, comfort and service accompanied by all the modern luxuries which today's visitors to a capital city would expect. Each room, with its high ceiling, decorative friezes, tall windows, fine drapes, pastel décor, gold framed mirrors and pictures, is a stylish reminder of Georgian grace. All 20 bedrooms are en suite and designed in complete harmony with the house. A full Irish breakfast can be enjoyed in the first floor Grand Salon overlooking the park or served in the comfort of your bedroom. Full business facilities are available, including a private boardroom and secretarial services. There is also secure car parking at the rear of the town house.

Places of interest nearby: Fitzwilliam Park is a five minutes' walk from St Stephen's Green and is an ideal base from which to explore Dublin and visit its busy shopping centres, theatres, museums and art galleries. As well as many first-class golf courses there is horse-racing and two marinas along the coast. **Directions: Fitzwilliam Park is situated in the city centre, a short walk from St Stephen's Green.**

For hotel location, see maps on pages 263–269

HALPINS HOTEL AND VITTLE'S RESTAURANT

ERIN STREET, KILKEE, CO CLARE
TEL: 00 353 65 56032 FAX: 00 353 65 56317 E-MAIL: halpins@iol.ie

OWNER: Pat Halpin
MANAGER: Ann Keane
CHEF: Ethel O'Donnell

S: IR£35–IR£50
D: IR£65–IR£90

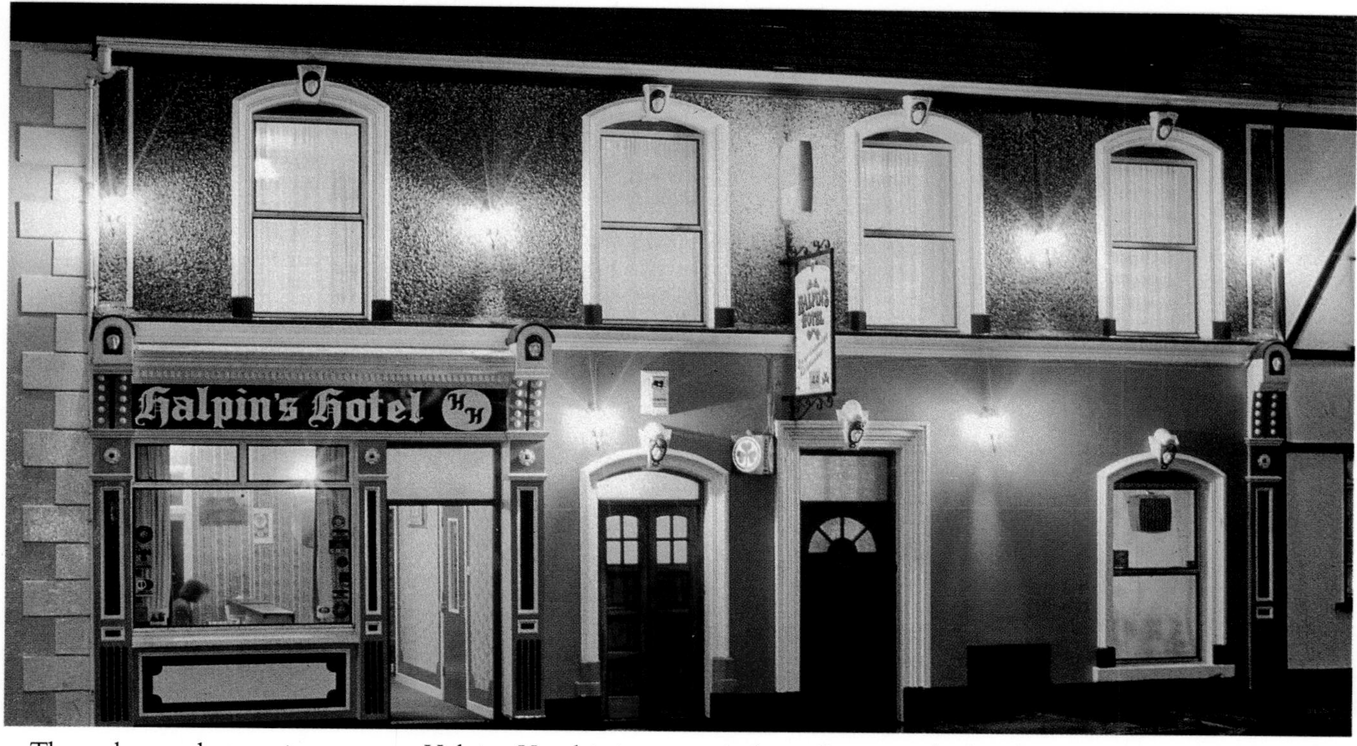

The welcome that awaits guests to Halpins Hotel is in the best traditions of Irish hospitality. Built in 1880, this charming hotel with a unique "shop-style" entrance is situated in a terrace at the heart of a popular resort facing a one mile long semi-circular sweep of sand. Surrounded by fine cliff scenery and reputed to be the safest bathing place in Ireland, Kilkee has attracted distinguished visitors from all over Europe for almost two centuries, among them literary figures such as Alfred Tennyson and Charlotte Brontë. Egon Ronay Commended and RAC Highly Acclaimed.

The Halpin family has owned and run the hotel for 15 years and are proud of its reputation for its friendly style and excellent standards. There are 12 prettily decorated en suite bedrooms, all of which are individually furnished.

The bar and lounge are famous for their old world atmosphere, complemented by quality food and fine wines of the world. The hotel restaurant Vittle's is one of the best in town. Chef Ethel O'Donnell produces wonderful modern Irish cuisine to suit all tastes.

Places of interest nearby: Kilkee Golf Club. The famous cliffs of Moher and Ailwee Caves, Doonbeg castle, Scattery Island's 6th century monastic settlement, Loop Head and the lunar-type landscape of the Burren.

Directions: Kilkee is situated on the N67 road from Galway, just 50 minutes from Shannon airport.

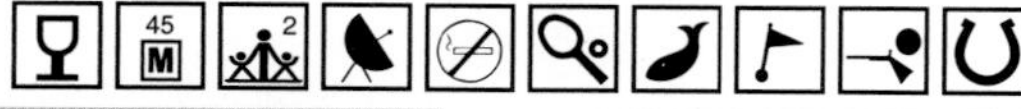

For hotel location, see maps on pages 263–269

KILLADEAS (Irvingstown, Northern Ireland)

THE INISHCLARE RESTAURANT

KILLADEAS, IRVINGSTOWN, CO FERMANAGH BT94 1SF, N. IRELAND
TEL: 01365 628550 FAX: 01365 628552

OWNER: Frank Maguire

10 rms | 10 ens

S: £25–£30
D: £40–£45

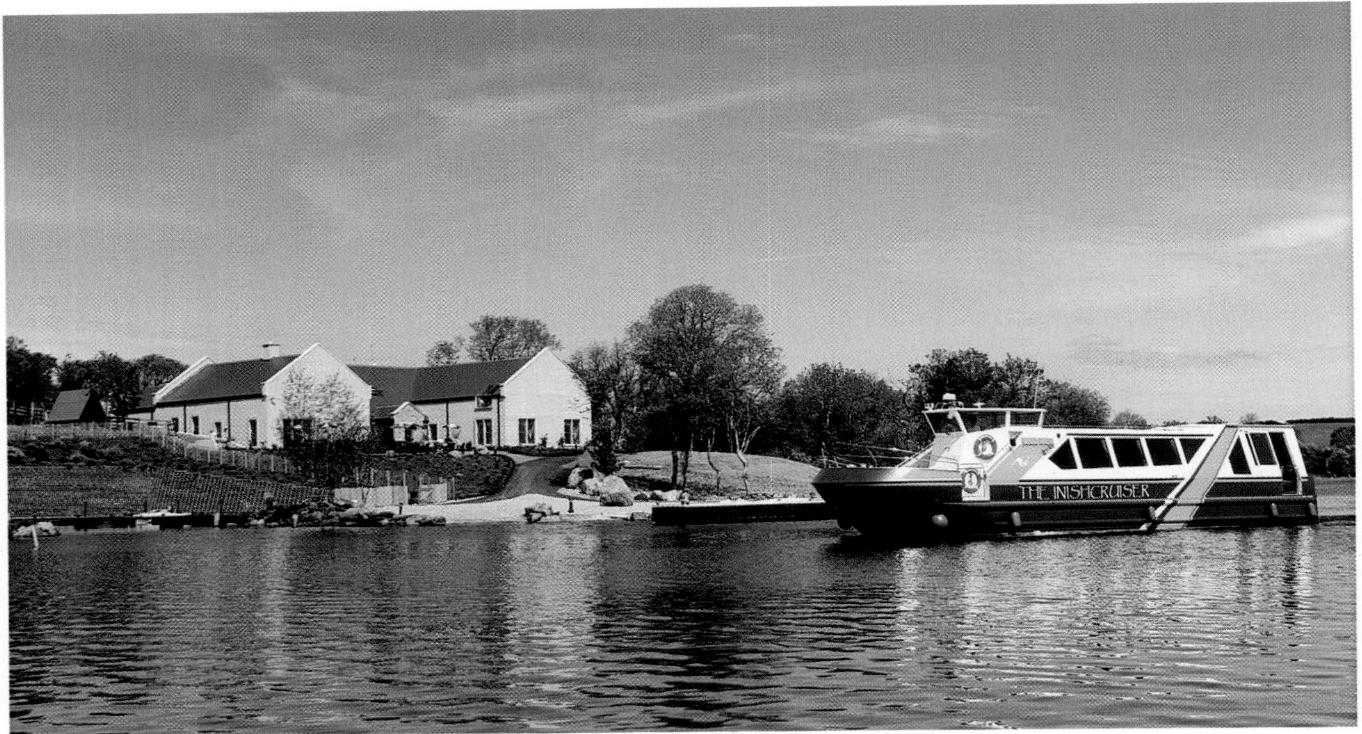

The Inishclare Restaurant nestles peacefully on the shores of lovely Lower Lough Erne offering visitors total relaxation and spectacular views over the island-speckled waters and Fermanagh countryside. Opened in 1997 it features a beamed 90-seater à la carte restaurant, a beautifully designed, three level bistro and bar and a 12 berth marina. The Inishclare serves superb food and provides the best of Irish hospitality. During summer months there are traditional Irish music sessions, barbecues and live entertainment. There are no rooms at the restaurant but guests are welcome at The Cedars, a sister establishment just two miles away. Guests not using their own cars are invited to travel in courtesy buses to and from the restaurant. A charming, family-run country home, The Cedars offers a haven of tranquillity away from the bustle of the outside world. There are ten luxurious, en suite bedrooms with elegant fittings and full amenities. One bedroom has a magnificent four-poster with draping canopies and lavish pine furnishings. All have panoramic views, as has the comfortable and relaxing lounge. The latest addition to the Inishclare is a 35-ton lake cruiser on which guests can dine while enjoying the beauty of Lough Erne. The cruiser has wheelchair access and is ideal for functions and corporate hospitality. Golf, riding, fishing, windsurfing, water and jet skiing are close by. **Directions: On the B82 Enniskillin to Kesh Road.**

Earls Court House

WOODLAWN JUNCTION, MUCKROSS ROAD, KILLARNEY, CO KERRY
TEL: 00 353 64 34009 FAX: 00 353 64 34366 E-MAIL: earls@tinet.ie

OWNERS: Ray and Emer Moynihan

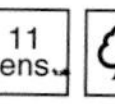

S: IR£45–IR£75
D: IR£65–IR£85

Earls Court House stands elevated and shadowed by tall, whispering trees just a five minutes walk from the bustling town centre of Killarney. It is in the heart of beautiful Co Kerry, surrounded by the 25,000 acres of Killarney National Park with its lakes, mountains and magnificent gardens where giant rhododendrons and tropical plants grow in abundance. Owners Ray and Emer Moynihan pride themselves that the hotel is a haven of tranquillity where relaxation comes naturally and service and hospitality is of the highest standards.

Earls Court is a purpose built, spacious hotel in the country house tradition. Fine antiques, prints and fabrics adorn the rooms throughout. Magnificent carved beds complement the charming, en suite bedrooms which are furnished with all modern amenities. Most of the bedrooms have private balconies with views over the open spaces of Muckross Park.

The hotel is an ideal base from which to tour Kerry, to explore Killarney National Park, or play south west Ireland's premier golf courses. Pony trekking, salmon and trout fishing can be arranged. Dinner is not available, but there are many good restaurants close by. The hotel is closed from November 5 to February 28.

Places of interest nearby: Killarney National Park.
Directions: Earls Court House is close to the centre of Killarney, just off the N71 Muckross Road.

THE OLD RECTORY – KILMEADEN HOUSE

KILMEADEN, CO WATERFORD, IRELAND
TEL: 00 353 51 384254 FAX: 00 353 51 384884

OWNERS: Jerry and Patricia Cronin

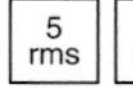  

S: IR£100–IR£120
D: IR£70–IR£80

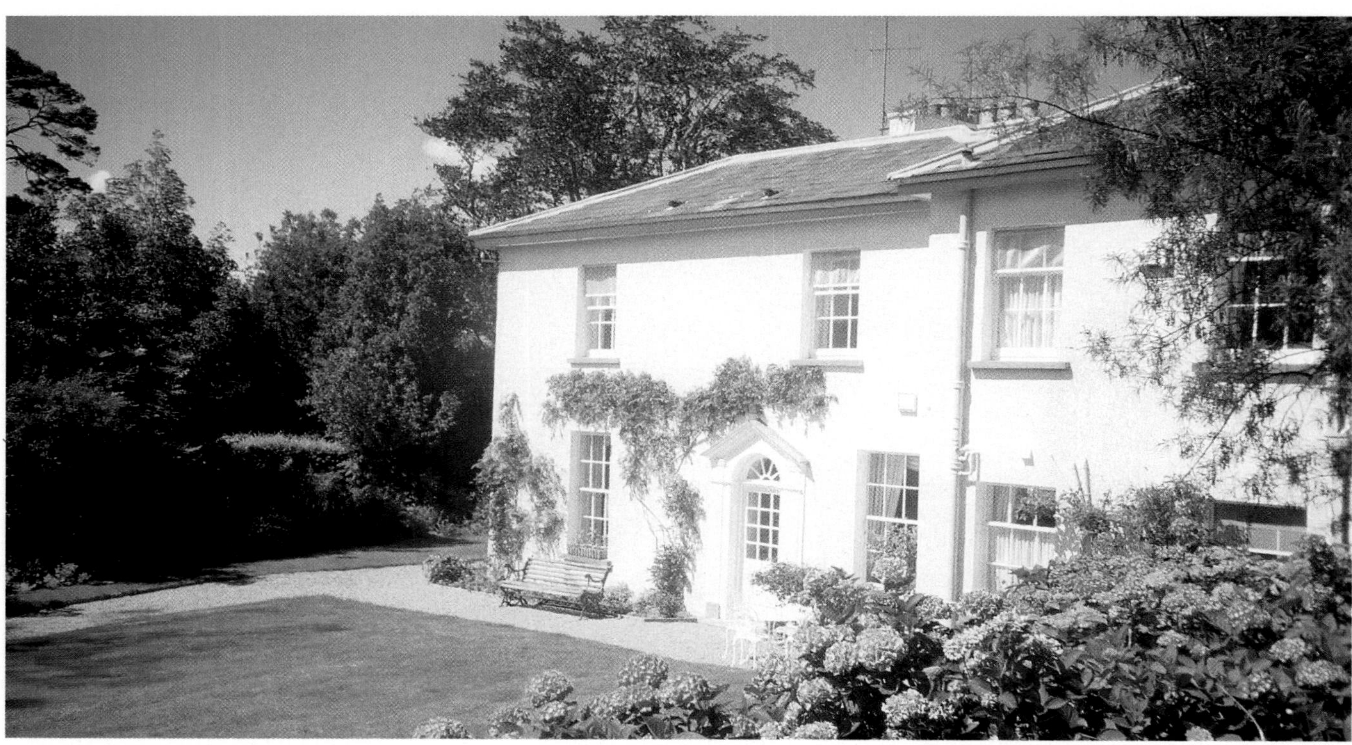

A truly warm and friendly Irish welcome awaits visitors as they arrive at the lovely Old Rectory situated in seclusion in County Waterford's beautiful landscape, capped from the west by the majestic Comeragh and Monavullagh ranges.

Constructed in the mid 19th century, this solidly built house stands serenely and imposingly in 12 acres of paddock, woodland and gardens just a short drive from Waterford City. The vision of the owners, Jerry Cronin, a local surgeon, and his wife Patricia, is to create simple elegance.

The charm of this country house is in its warm and comfortable atmosphere. Each of the tastefully decorated, non-smoking bedrooms is en suite and designed in complete harmony with the house. They are individually furnished with antiques, high ceilings, wooden sash windows and many personal touches to help guests feel at home. Views from their windows over the delightful garden which contains rare and well known plants are particularly delightful.

Light meals are available in the evening; guests must give 24 hours notice.

Places of interest nearby: Dunmore East - a picturesque fishing village, the Comeragh and Monavullagh mountains and Waterford with its busy harbour. There are five major golf courses within easy reach whilst riding and fishing can be enjoyed locally. **Directions: Approximately 10 miles west of Waterford just off N25 road to Cork.**

For hotel location, see maps on pages 263–269

Castle Grove Country House

RAMELTON ROAD, LETTERKENNY, CO DONEGAL
TEL: 00 353 74 51118 FAX: 00 353 74 51384

OWNER: Mary T and Raymond Sweeny

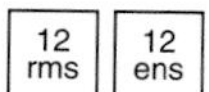

S: IR£45–£50
D: IR£60–IR£100
Suite: IR£130–IR£160

This elegant Georgian House, reached by a mile long avenue through parkland, is in a sheltered position with a spectacular view of Lough Swilly.

True Irish hospitality is offered at this family-owned country residence with its gracious reception rooms and the charming drawing room looking out on the extensive grounds. There is a separate television room.

The dining room is very popular with the people who live in the neighbourhood, so reservations are necessary. The succulent dishes offered on the extensive menu reflecting the marvellous local produce – especially the fish – are served in great style accompanied by wines from a list of the highest calibre. Small corporate lunches are a speciality.

The bedrooms are spacious, all recently refurbished and equipped with modern necessities.

Donegal is famous for its white sand beaches and clean seas. The scenery is superb along the coast roads and in the mountains. Glenveagh National Park is fascinating, with its castle and famous gardens. One can meet Derek Hill at his fine Art Gallery at Churchill. Activities nearby include golf and fishing (lake, river and deep sea). Rough and walked up shoots are available throughout the season. Riding can be arranged on request. **Directions: Castle Grove is three miles from Letterkenny, off the R245.**

For hotel location, see maps on pages 263–269

COOPERSHILL HOUSE

RIVERSTOWN, CO SLIGO
TEL: 00 353 71 65108 FAX: 00 353 71 65466 E-MAIL: ohara@coopershill.com

OWNERS: Brian and Lindy O'Hara

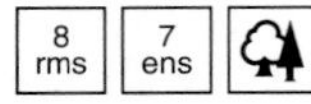

S: IR£60–IR£65
D: IR£100–IR£110

Winner of Johansens 1995 Country House Award, Coopershill is a fine example of a Georgian family mansion. Home to seven generations of the O'Hara family since 1774, it combines the spaciousness and elegance of an earlier age with modern comforts. Public rooms are furnished in period style with gilt-framed portraits, hunting trophies and antiques. Five of the bedrooms have four-poster or canopy beds and all have private bathrooms.

Dinner is served by candlelight in the elegant dining room, where good cooking is complemented by a wide choice of wines. Open log fires and personal attention from owners Brian and Lindy O'Hara help to create the warm atmosphere and hospitality that typify Coopershill. Out of season the house is open to parties of 10 to 16 people at a special rate. Tariffs are reduced if guests stay for three consecutive nights or more.

The River Arrow winds through the 500-acre estate and boating, trout and coarse fishing are available. Shooting is not permitted, leaving the abundant wildlife undisturbed. There is an excellent hard tennis court and also a croquet lawn. There are marvellous mountain and lakeside walks to enjoy in the area. Closed 1st November to mid-March. **Places of interest nearby:** Sligo and Yeats country. **Directions: Leave N4 Sligo–Dublin road at Drumfin follow signs for Coopershill. One mile on, turn left.**

For hotel location, see maps on pages 263–269

LISS ARD LAKE LODGE

SKIBBEREEN, CO CORK
TEL: 00 353 28 40000 FAX: 00 353 28 40001 E-MAIL: lissardlakelodge@tinet.ie

DIRECTORS: Claudia Turske and Gisa Deilmann

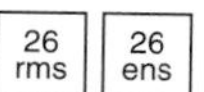

S: IR£120–IR£260
D: IR£200–IR£330

This recently renovated hotel set in the tranquil and beautiful West Cork countryside was originally the summer home of a wealthy Victorian landowner.

Refined and minimalist furnishings are to be found in the excellent bedrooms, each of which is equipped with a television, video, stereo and PC and facsimile points.

A generous and balanced breakfast is available until noon, so there is no rush for late risers! The hotel's restaurant serves light, imaginative, international cuisine, with local meat, fish and vegetables carefully prepared to suit all tastes. An excellent wine list is available.

Guests are invited to stroll through the surrounding Liss Ard Gardens, a unique project which creates ten contemporary landscaped "garden-rooms" out of a 50-acre park. Guests may enjoy a number of spa treatments available at the hotel. Sample the delights of a Woodland Walk, Wild Flower Meadow or Irish Sky Garden. Nearby leisure activities include cycling, fishing in the hotel's lake and water sports. **Places of interest nearby:** Cape Clear, Baltimore, Castletownsend, Mizen Head and Fastnet. **Directions: In Skibbereen, follow the one way system for 400 metres and turn left at roundabout onto L60, direction Castletownsend (Liss Ard signpost 5km). After 3½km you will see Lake Abisdealy on your right. Turn right after lake, direction Tragumna, (Liss Ard signpost 1½km) and follow this road to the Lodge.**

MARKREE CASTLE

COLLOONEY, COUNTY SLIGO, IRELAND
TEL: 00 353 71 67800 FAX: 00 353 71 67840 E-MAIL: markree@iol.ie

OWNER: Charles Cooper

S: IR£62.50
D: IR£105
De luxe: IR£115

Regarded as one of Ireland's major architectural masterpieces, Markree Castle is Sligo's oldest inhabited castle. It has been the home of the Cooper family since 1640, but over the years the house has undergone a number of transformations. Today, the castle retains its family atmosphere and the character of the old building, while providing every modern comfort.

The interior boasts a spectacular oak staircase. This is overlooked by a stained glass window, purportedly tracing the Cooper family tree back to the time of King John of England. There are a variety of notable reception rooms, in addition to the interconnecting dining rooms which feature Louis-Philippe style plasterwork created by Italian craftsmen in 1845. An imaginative menu is provided

The bedrooms vary in character and style, but all offer views over the gardens or surrounding countryside.

Markree is in the heart of "Yeats Country", with magnificent scenery all around. The Rosses Point golf course and the Strandhill course are within a few miles. Trout and salmon fishing can be arranged nearby.

Places of interest nearby: Carrowmore, which has Europe's largest and oldest collection of megalithic remains; Lissadell House; Yeats's grave at Drumcliffe; and the town of Donegal. **Directions: Nine miles from Sligo airport, 125 from Dublin via N4. Collooney is just south of Sligo town.**

For hotel location, see maps on pages 263–269

THE OLD RECTORY

WICKLOW TOWN, CO WICKLOW, IRELAND
TEL: 00 353 404 67048 FAX: 00 353 404 69181 E-MAIL: mail@oldrectory.ie

OWNERS: Paul and Linda Saunders

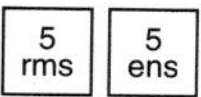

The Old Rectory is situated in secluded gardens on the edge of the harbour town of Wicklow in County Wicklow, "the Garden of Ireland". A peaceful Victorian house, personally run by Paul and Linda Saunders, it combines charming country house accommodation with an elegant gourmet restaurant. The house is freshly decorated throughout and furnished with style. A small Fitness Suite includes aerobic equipment and a relaxing sauna. Individually designed bedrooms offer en suite bathrooms and lots of little extras to make you feel welcome. This special ambience has made it a winner of the coveted AA "Inspector's Selected" award for Ireland. The restaurant is exceptional and featured on television's *"Gourmet Ireland"* and *"Summer Holiday"* series. Set gourmet and à la carte menus use fresh seafood, local and organic produce enhanced with herbs and edible flowers. Vegetarians welcome. In May/June 10-course "floral dinners" are a highlight of the Wicklow Gardens Festival. The Old Rectory also offers a choice of breakfasts which have won the National Breakfast award for Ireland.

Places of interest nearby: Glendalough, Wicklow Mountains, Wicklow Historic Jail, Powerscourt Gardens, Mount Usher Gardens, Russborough House, "Ballykissangel", 20 golf courses including Druids Glen. **Directions: 30m south of Dublin on N11, then 1m south of Rathnew on R750. Entrance has stone walls.**

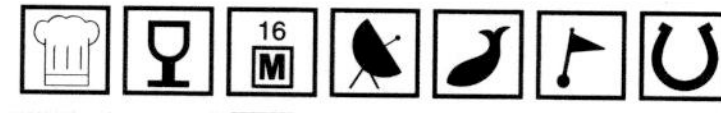

For hotel location, see maps on pages 263–269

By appointment to HRH The Duke of Edinburgh Manufacturers of Toilet Requisites Penhaligon's Limited London

By appointment to HRH The Prince of Wales Manufacturers of Toilet Requisites Penhaligon's Limited London

PENHALIGON'S

PERFUMERS EST. 1870

Exclusively available to leading hotels

Pacific Direct

Tel: +44 (0)1234 347140
Fax: +44 (0)1234 346480
E-mail: sales@pacific-direct.demon.co.uk

USA Office **Tel: (607) 273 1984**
Fax: (607) 273 5148
E-mail: PDirectUSA@aol.com

www.pacificdirect.co.uk

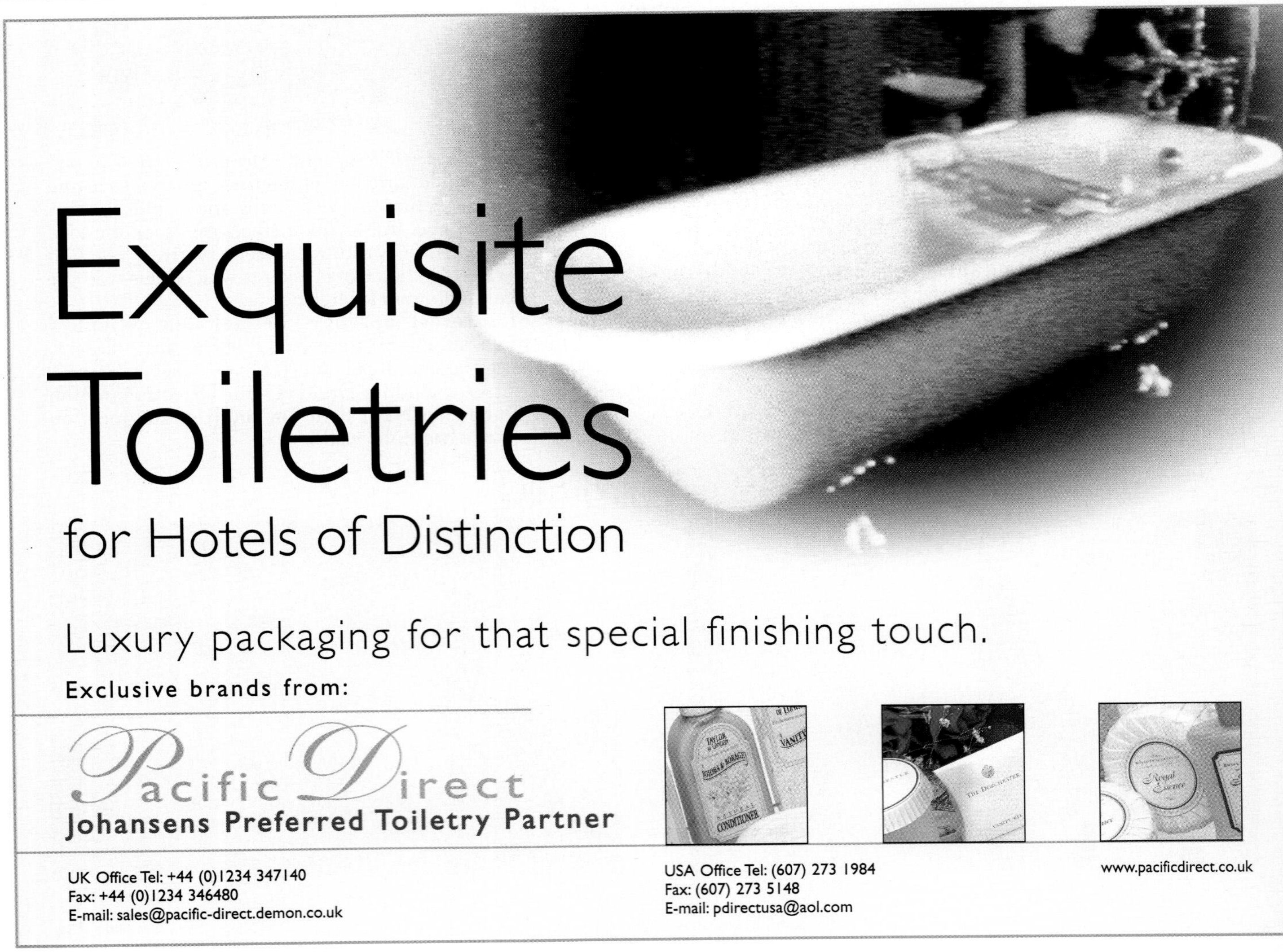

Exquisite Toiletries

for Hotels of Distinction

Luxury packaging for that special finishing touch.

Exclusive brands from:

Johansens Preferred Toiletry Partner

UK Office Tel: +44 (0)1234 347140
Fax: +44 (0)1234 346480
E-mail: sales@pacific-direct.demon.co.uk

USA Office Tel: (607) 273 1984
Fax: (607) 273 5148
E-mail: pdirectusa@aol.com

www.pacificdirect.co.uk

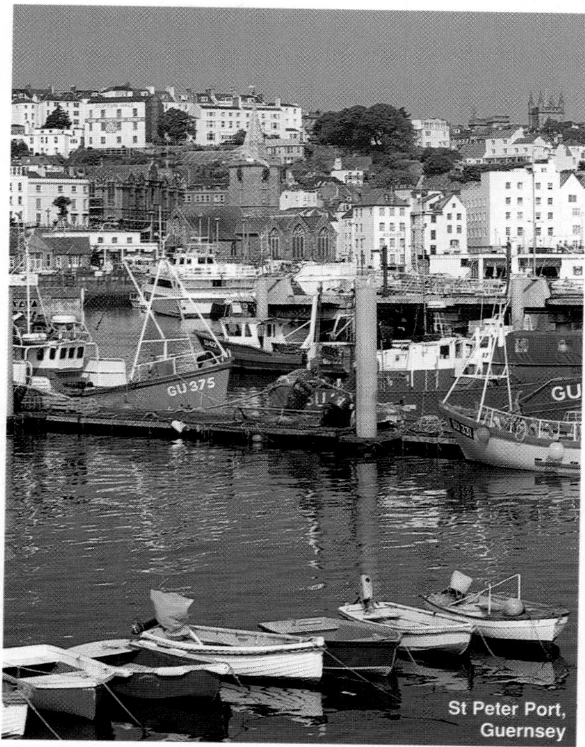

St Peter Port, Guernsey

Johansens Recommended Country Houses & Small Hotels in the Channel Islands

With a wealth of wonderful scenery, magnificent coastlines, historic buildings, natural and man-made attractions plus mouthwatering local produce, the Channel Islands provide a memorable destination that's distinctly different.

ALL OF THE JOHANSENS RECOMMENDED ESTABLISHMENTS IN THE CHANNEL ISLANDS ARE ABLE TO MAKE FAVOURABLE TRAVEL ARRANGEMENTS FOR YOU.

Jersey and Guernsey offer VAT free shopping, the official language is English, passports are not required and both islands can be reached by sea from Poole or any one of about 30 airports in Britain and Europe.

And don't forget the other islands. Herm has dazzling beaches, Sark lives in a rural timewarp without traffic and Alderney's cobbled streets, pretty cottages and Victorian forts are another world again.

JERSEY

The largest and most southerly of the Channel Islands, Jersey, measures only nine miles by five and is just fourteen miles from the French coast. The island slopes from north to south, creating dramatic differences between the high cliffs of the north and broad sandy bays of the south.

Jersey was originally part of Normandy. When William the Conqueror invaded England, it came under English rule until 1204, when King John lost Normandy to France.

The Islanders were given a choice – stay with Normandy or remain loyal to the English Crown. They chose England and gained rights and privileges which to this day are subject not to the British Parliament, but only to the reigning monarch.

The French influence is still strong however, and visitors are often surprised to find the names of streets and villages in French. The granite architecture of the farms and manor houses has a Continental feel too, and in rural areas, you may still hear farmworkers speaking in the local 'patois' or dialect.

Food is also something for which Jersey is renowned. Shellfish and fresh fish are the specialities of the island and lobster, crab, seafood platter, bass and Jersey plaice feature on many menus. The annual Good Food Festival, held in early summer, is a must for food lovers.

History enthusiasts can trace the island's development from prehistory to the present day through a variety of different sites. The Channel Islands were the only part of the British Isles to be occupied by the Germans during World War II and there are reminders all over Jersey.

For a small island, Jersey boasts more than its fair share of museums. The Maritime Museum, which opened in 1997, tells the story of Jersey people's ability to find new ways in which to adapt to the opportunities presented by the sea. Designed as an interactive, hands on museum, it has a strong family focus.

You're never far from Jersey's spectacular coastline – all 50 miles of it – but the interior of the Island is worth exploring too. The largely rural landscape is criss-crossed by a network of narrow country roads, some of which have been designated as 'Green Lanes', where priority is given to walkers, cyclists and horseriders.

But the cultural attractions of Jersey can never eclipse the Island's natural beauty. Every bend in the lane, every turn in the coast path reveals a new view to be savoured and enjoyed.

GUERNSEY

Guernsey, with a total area of only 25 square miles, lies at the centre of a group of even smaller islands which, together, comprise 'The Bailiwick of Guernsey'. Like Jersey, only 20 miles away, Guernsey has its own government – quite independent of that of the United Kingdom – at the head of which is the Bailiff, and within its jurisdiction are the islands of Sark, Alderney, Herm and Jethou. Guernsey, therefore, offers the visitor not only its own varied attractions, but also opportunities to discover these smaller islands, each with its own very distinctive character.

Getting there is easy, with regular flights from many UK and Continental airports, and departures by sea, for both passengers and cars, from the UK and nearby French ports. Arrival by sea at St Peter Port, Guernsey's little capital, provides a memorable introduction to the island as it is one of the prettiest ports in Europe, its distinctive buildings rising in tiers above the quays of the busy harbour where colourful banners of yachts of all nations flutter in the sunshine. It's a friendly town, whose narrow cobbled streets are lined with interesting shops, and where the choice of restaurants is quite outstanding.

Within its small size, Guernsey offers enormous variety. Roughly triangular in shape, the south coast – the base as it were – comprises high cliffs, covered in springtime with a profusion of colourful flowers, at the foot of which nestle lovely little sandy coves. A network of cliff paths provides superb walking all the way from St Peter Port to the extreme south-west corner of the island, a distance of some twenty five miles, one spectacular sea view succeeding another all the way. Inland, high-banked country lanes lead past old granite farmhouses and tiny fields where the world-famous Guernsey cows contentedly graze.

For those interested in the past, Guernsey offers a fascinating choice of subjects to investigate; prehistoric tombs and menhirs, medieval churches and chapels, the remarkable house where the great French writer Victor Hugo lived for fifteen years during his exile from France, elegant Regency architecture and fortifications dating from the 13th century up to the German occupation during World War II. Not to be missed is Castle Cornet, which dominates the entrance to St Peter Port harbour and contains galleries and museums which narrate the Castle's own turbulent history, as well as revealing the island's maritime past.

For further information, please contact:

Jersey Tourism
Liberation Square, St Helier, JE1 IBB
Tel: 01534 500 700

Guernsey Tourist Board
PO Box 23, St Peter Port, Guernsey GY1 3AN
Tel: 01481 723557 (24 hours); 01481 723552

LA FAVORITA HOTEL

FERMAIN BAY, GUERNSEY, CHANNEL ISLANDS GY4 6SD
TEL: 01481 35666 FAX: 01481 35413 E-MAIL: info@favorita.com

OWNERS: Simon and Helen Wood

S: from £41
D: from £76

Once a fine private country house, La Favorita retains all the charm and character of those former days. The hotel is comfortable and fully licensed. Set in its own grounds, a few minutes walk from Guernsey's famous Fermain Bay, it enjoys spectacular views over the sea towards Jersey.

The bedrooms, all non smoking, are comfortable and provide every modern amenity, including colour television, radio and refreshment tray. Guernsey's mild climate means that it has much to offer out of season and the hotel also has a full range of facilities to satisfy the extra needs of spring, autumn and winter guests, including the indoor pool.

La Favorita has an excellent reputation for traditional English cooking and island seafood specialities. The restaurant is strictly no smoking. A coffee shop serves a wide range of lunch dishes and bar suppers for those who enjoy a more informal meal.

St Peter Port is within easy walking distance, whether taking the woodland walk which follows the coastline or the more direct route past Victor Hugo's house.

Places of interest nearby: The coast of Guernsey and all the island's attractions. Boat trips to Jersey, Alderney, Herm and Sark can easily be arranged. **Directions: Fermain Bay is 10 minutes from the airport and five minutes from St Peter Port on the east coast of Guernsey.**

For hotel location, see maps on pages 263–269

BELLA LUCE HOTEL & RESTAURANT

LA FOSSE, ST MARTIN, GUERNSEY, CHANNEL ISLANDS GY4 6EB
TEL: 01481 38764 FAX: 01481 39561

OWNER: Richard Cann
MANAGER: John Cockcroft

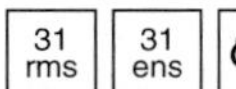
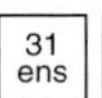

S: From £27
D: From £52

The Bella Luce is one of Guernsey's original Norman manor houses. Set in splendid grounds on the most select side of the island, this perfectly preserved house includes extensions built in the 14th century. Happily the utmost care has been taken to maintain its period character during upgrading, so today's hotel offers excellent accommodation with every modern amenity.

Drinks are served throughout the day in the hotel's lounge bar, which dates back to the 11th century and is the oldest part of the building. Here, under the fine oak beamed ceiling, guests can enjoy a lunch and savour the cheerful and serene old world.

A varied table d'hôte menu, offering a wide range of English and Continental dishes, is provided in the restaurant which enjoys an excellent reputation throughout the island. A comprehensive à la carte menu featuring fresh seafood specialities is also available.

In a sun-trapped corner of the gardens there is a swimming pool surrounded by sun-beds and providing a perfect location for relaxation. Refreshments are served throughout the day and there is a sauna/solarium room nearby.

Places of interest nearby: Within easy reach of the three most beautiful south coast bays of Moulin Huet, Petit Port and Saints. Marine trips operate daily in season to Herm, Sark, Jersey and the nearby coast of France. **Directions: 5 minutes from the airport and St Peter Port.**

For hotel location, see maps on pages 263–269

THE WHITE HOUSE

HERM ISLAND, GUERNSEY, CHANNEL ISLANDS GY1 3HR
TEL: 01481 722159 FAX: 01481 710066

OWNERS: Adrian and Pennie Heyworth
CHEF: Chris Walder

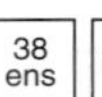

Room rate: from £54.50 per person

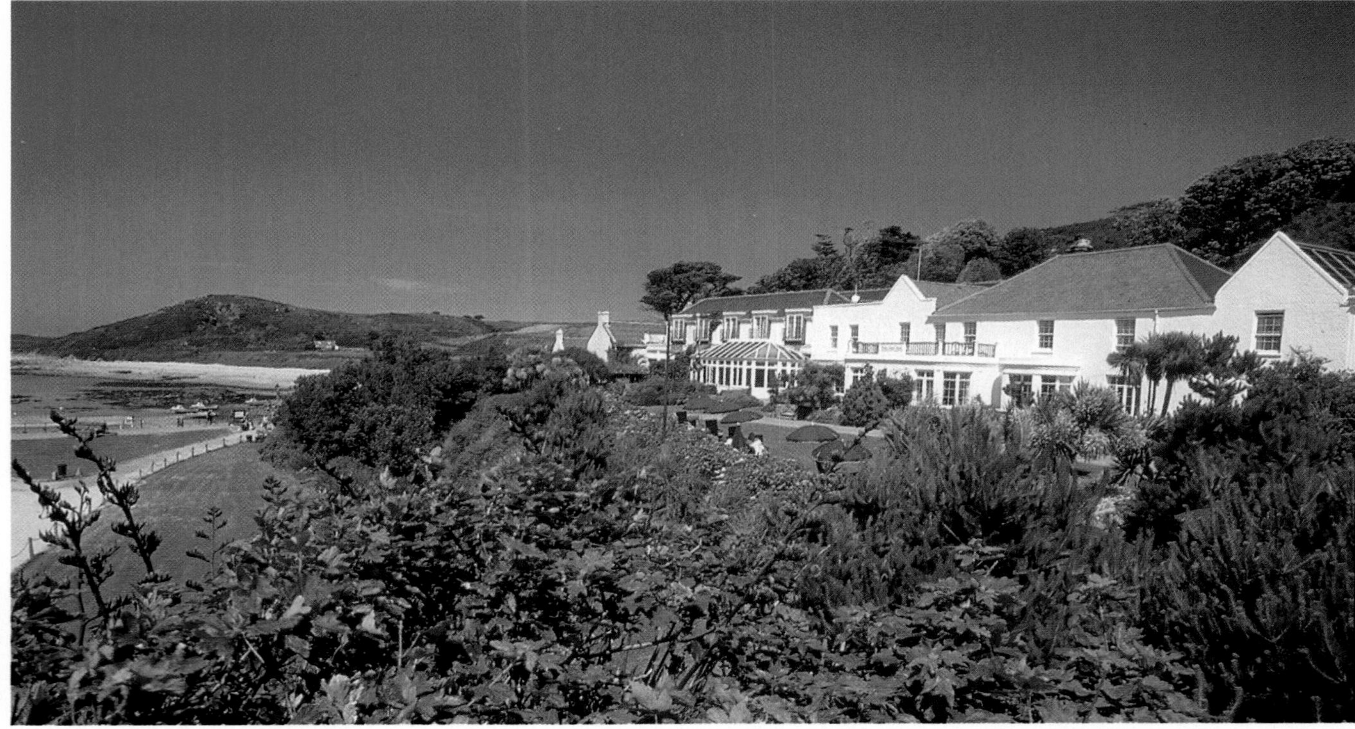

As wards of Herm Island, Adrian and Pennie Heyworth assume responsibility for the well-being of all visitors to their island home which is for all to enjoy at leisure. For an island just 1½ miles long its diversity is remarkable and during a two-hour stroll that takes in its cliff walks, white sandy coves and abundant wildlife no two moments are the same.

The magic starts to work from the moment of arrival at the pretty harbour, for in the absence of cars on Herm a tractor laden with guests' luggage chugs up from the jetty to The White House. Here, relaxation is the key, and guests can enjoy afternoon tea or a drink in its succession of homely lounges, in the bar or on the poolside patio.

In keeping with a cherished tradition there are no televisions, no clocks nor telephones in the hotel's 38 bedrooms, the best of which have balconies and sea views. Appointments are nonetheless faultless and all include spacious up-to-date private bathrooms. Families are made particularly welcome and high tea is a popular event with younger guests.

Seafood plays a prominent part on the menus: the hotel has its own oyster farm. Guernsey plaice, scallops and crab are landed regularly.

Places of interest nearby: There is excellent fishing and snorkelling; yachts and cruisers can be chartered; and there are regular trips to Sark, Guernsey, Jersey and France. **Directions: Herm is reached by boat from Guernsey.**

For hotel location, see maps on pages 263–269

NORTHERN IRELAND
IRELAND
Campbeltown
To Stranraer, Cairnryan
To Liverpool, Douglas
To Liverpool, Holyhead
To Holyhead
To Pembroke Dock
To Swansea
Fishguard
Coleraine
Londonderry
LETTERKENNY
BALLYMENA
Carrickfergus
BELFAST
BELFAST (ALDERGROVE)
KILLADEAS
SLIGO
Armagh
RIVERSTOWN
NEWCASTLE
Newry
Dundalk
CARRICKMACROSS
CONNAUGHT
CONNEMARA
CONG
Drogheda
Galway
FURBO
DUBLIN
Dun Laoghaire
Bray
Gort
RATHNEW
WICKLOW
KILTEGAN
NEWMARKET-ON-FERGUS
KILKEE
SHANNON
Limerick
ADARE
Kilkenny
GOREY
CASHEL
Tralee
Clonmel
KILMEADAN
Waterford
Wexford
ROSSLARE
CARAGH LAKE
KILLARNEY
MALLOW
PARKNASILLA
KENMARE
Cork
CORK
BANTRY
SKIBBEREEN
CLONAKILTY
JOHANSENS RECOMMENDED HOTEL
JOHANSENS RECOMMENDED INN OR RESTAURANT
JOHANSENS RECOMMENDED COUNTRY HOUSE
0 20 40 60 80 100 Kilometres
0 10 20 30 40 50 Miles

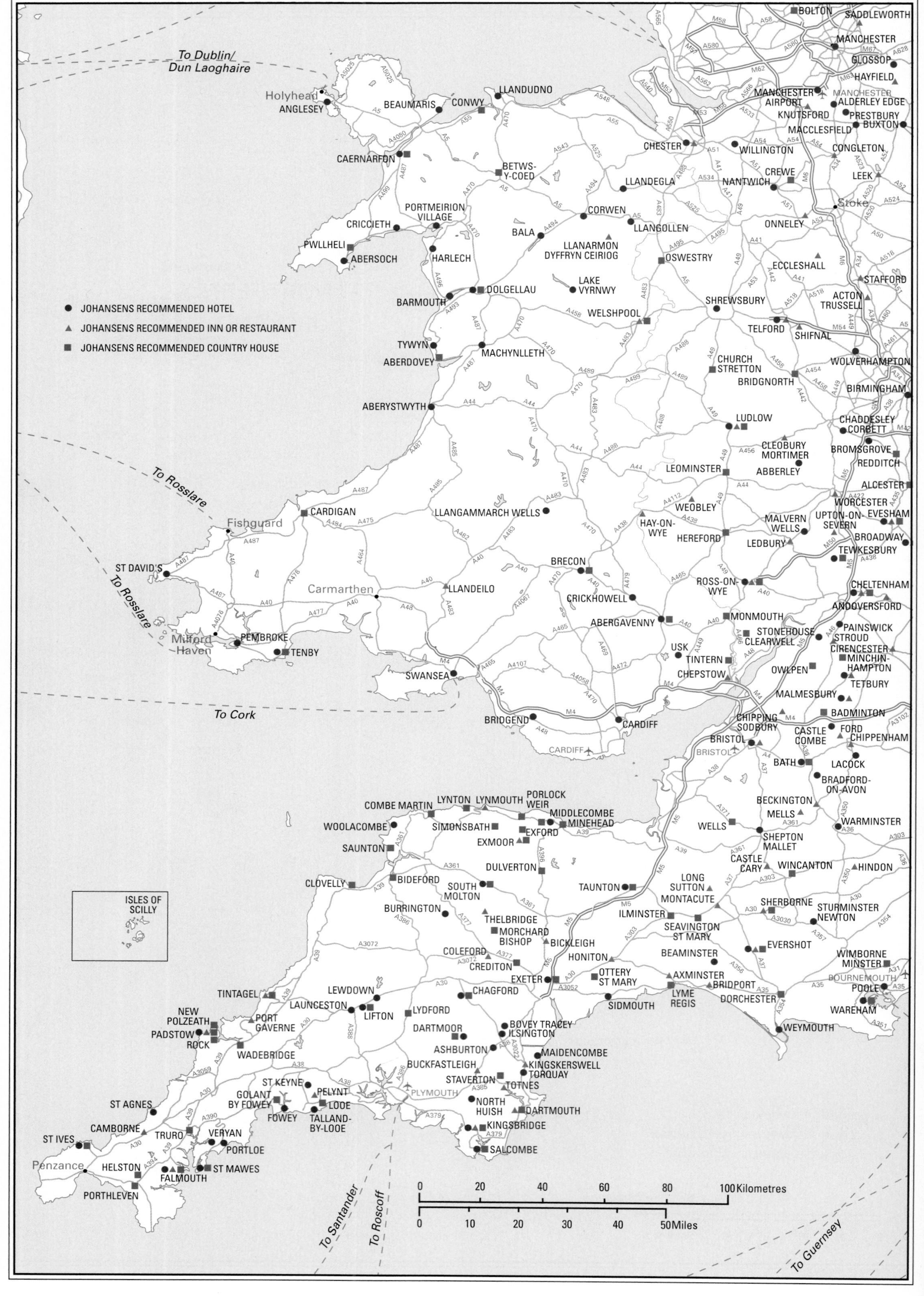

JOHANSENS RECOMMENDED HOTEL
JOHANSENS RECOMMENDED INN OR RESTAURANT
JOHANSENS RECOMMENDED COUNTRY HOUSE
To Dublin/
Dun Laoghaire
Holyhead
ANGLESEY
BEAUMARIS
CONWY
LLANDUDNO
CAERNARFON
BETWS-Y-COED
PORTMEIRION VILLAGE
CRICCIETH
PWLLHELI
ABERSOCH
HARLECH
BALA
CORWEN
LLANGOLLEN
LLANARMON DYFFRYN CEIRIOG
LLANDEGLA
CHESTER
WILLINGTON
NANTWICH
CREWE
OSWESTRY
LAKE VYRNWY
BARMOUTH
DOLGELLAU
WELSHPOOL
SHREWSBURY
TELFORD
SHIFNAL
TYWYN
ABERDOVEY
MACHYNLLETH
CHURCH STRETTON
BRIDGNORTH
ABERYSTWYTH
LUDLOW
CLEOBURY MORTIMER
ABBERLEY
LEOMINSTER
BOLTON
SADDLEWORTH
MANCHESTER
GLOSSOP
HAYFIELD
MANCHESTER AIRPORT
ALDERLEY EDGE
KNUTSFORD
PRESTBURY
MACCLESFIELD
BUXTON
CONGLETON
LEEK
Stoke
ONNELEY
ECCLESHALL
STAFFORD
ACTON TRUSSELL
WOLVERHAMPTON
BIRMINGHAM
CHADDESLEY CORBETT
BROMSGROVE
REDDITCH
ALCESTER
WORCESTER
UPTON-ON-SEVERN
EVESHAM
MALVERN WELLS
BROADWAY
LEDBURY
TEWKESBURY
CHELTENHAM
ANDOVERSFORD
To Rosslare
Fishguard
CARDIGAN
LLANGAMMARCH WELLS
WEOBLEY
HAY-ON-WYE
HEREFORD
ST DAVID'S
Carmarthen
LLANDEILO
BRECON
CRICKHOWELL
ROSS-ON-WYE
ABERGAVENNY
MONMOUTH
Milford Haven
PEMBROKE
TENBY
USK
TINTERN
CHEPSTOW
STONEHOUSE
CLEARWELL
PAINSWICK
STROUD
CIRENCESTER
MINCHINHAMPTON
OWLPEN
TETBURY
MALMESBURY
SWANSEA
To Cork
BRIDGEND
CARDIFF
CHIPPING SODBURY
BADMINTON
CASTLE COMBE
FORD
CHIPPENHAM
BRISTOL
BATH
LACOCK
BRADFORD-ON-AVON
COMBE MARTIN
LYNTON
LYNMOUTH
PORLOCK WEIR
MIDDLECOMBE
MINEHEAD
WOOLACOMBE
SIMONSBATH
EXFORD
EXMOOR
SAUNTON
BECKINGTON
MELLS
WELLS
SHEPTON MALLET
WARMINSTER
DULVERTON
CLOVELLY
BIDEFORD
SOUTH MOLTON
TAUNTON
LONG SUTTON
MONTACUTE
CASTLE CARY
WINCANTON
HINDON
ISLES OF SCILLY
BURRINGTON
THELBRIDGE
MORCHARD BISHOP
BICKLEIGH
ILMINSTER
SEAVINGTON ST MARY
SHERBORNE
STURMINSTER NEWTON
COLEFORD
CREDITON
HONITON
BEAMINSTER
EVERSHOT
WIMBORNE MINSTER
TINTAGEL
LEWDOWN
CHAGFORD
EXETER
OTTERY ST MARY
AXMINSTER
BRIDPORT
BOURNEMOUTH
POOLE
LAUNCESTON
LIFTON
LYDFORD
SIDMOUTH
LYME REGIS
DORCHESTER
WAREHAM
NEW POLZEATH
PADSTOW
ROCK
PORT GAVERNE
DARTMOOR
BOVEY TRACEY
ILSINGTON
WEYMOUTH
WADEBRIDGE
ASHBURTON
MAIDENCOMBE
BUCKFASTLEIGH
KINGSKERSWELL
TORQUAY
ST KEYNE
PELYNT
STAVERTON
TOTNES
PLYMOUTH
ST AGNES
GOLANT BY FOWEY
LOOE
NORTH HUISH
DARTMOUTH
FOWEY
TALLAND-BY-LOOE
CAMBORNE
TRURO
VERYAN
KINGSBRIDGE
ST IVES
PORTLOE
SALCOMBE
Penzance
HELSTON
FALMOUTH
ST MAWES
PORTHLEVEN
To Santander
To Roscoff
To Guernsey
0 20 40 60 80 100 Kilometres
0 10 20 30 40 50 Miles

SADDLEWORTH
MANCHESTER
PENISTONE
GLOSSOP
HAYFIELD
HOPE
SHEFFIELD
MANCHESTER
GRINDLEFORD
HATHERSAGE
ALDERLEY EDGE
PRESTBURY
CALVER
DRONFIELD
BUXTON
BASLOW
MACCLESFIELD
ASHFORD-IN-THE-WATER
BAKEWELL
CONGLETON
MATLOCK
LEEK
BIGGIN BY HARTINGTON
Stoke
BELPER
ASHBOURNE
NOTTINGHAM
DERBY
EAST MIDLANDS
BURTON UPON TRENT
LOUGHBOROUGH
STAFFORD
ACTON TRUSSELL
COALVILLE
LICHFIELD
ROTHLEY
LEICESTER
ATHERSTONE
FENNY DRAYTON
WOLVERHAMPTON
BIRMINGHAM
BIRMINGHAM
COVENTRY
CHADDESLEY CORBETT
HOCKLEY HEATH
RUGBY
BROMSGROVE
REDDITCH
WARWICK
DAVENTRY
BADBY
ALCESTER
STRATFORD-UPON-AVON
WORCESTER
UPTON-ON-SEVERN
EVESHAM
CHIPPING CAMPDEN
BROADWAY
BLOCKLEY
BANBURY
TEWKESBURY
MORETON-IN-MARSH
ADDERBURY
KINGHAM
DUNS TEW
UPPER SLAUGHTER
CHELTENHAM
STOW-ON-THE-WOLD
ANDOVERSFORD
BOURTON-ON-THE-WATER
SHIPTON-UNDER-WYCHWOOD
LOWER SLAUGHTER
WOODSTOCK
PAINSWICK
BURFORD
STROUD
BIBURY
OXFORD
CIRENCESTER
CLANFIELD
MINCHIN-HAMPTON
TETBURY
MALMESBURY
SWINDON
WALLINGFORD
DORCHESTER-ON-THAMES
STONOR
BADMINTON
FORD
CHIPPENHAM
GORING-ON-THAMES
STREATLEY-ON-THAMES
HENLEY-ON-THAMES
MARLOW-ON-THAMES
MAIDENHEAD
SONNING-ON-THAMES
READING
LACOCK
MARLBOROUGH
NEWBURY
BINFIELD
WARMINSTER
BASINGSTOKE
HARTLEY WINTNEY
ANDOVER
MIDDLE WALLOP
HINDON
SALISBURY
WINCHESTER
ROMSEY
FORDINGBRIDGE
SOUTHAMPTON
Southampton
LYNDHURST
RINGWOOD
WIMBORNE MINSTER
BROCKENHURST
BEAULIEU
LYMINGTON
BOURNEMOUTH
POOLE
BOURNEMOUTH
WAREHAM
Cowes
YARMOUTH
ISLE OF WIGHT
PORTSMOUTH
CHICHESTER
PETERSFIELD
MIDHURST
GRAYSHOTT
HASLEMERE
LIPHOOK
LINCOLN
GRANTHAM
GRIMSTHORPE
STAPLEFORD
OAKHAM
STAMFORD
RUTLAND WATER
UPPINGHAM
PETERBOROUGH
OUNDLE
ST IVES
HUNTINGDON
BUCKDEN
Northampton
CASTLE ASHBY
BEDFORD
MILTON KEYNES
WOBURN
STEVENAGE
LUTON
LUTON
AYLESBURY
ALDBURY
TRING
HEMEL HEMPSTEAD
ST ALBANS
HADLEY WOOD
ENFIELD
HAMPSTEAD VILLAGE
London
LONDON CITY
SLOUGH
BRAY-ON-THAMES
ETON
HEATHROW
RICHMOND-UPON-THAMES
WINDSOR
ASCOT
EGHAM
WEYBRIDGE
HAMPTON COURT
OTTERSHAW
COBHAM
EPSOM
GUILDFORD
REDHILL
GATWICK
RUSPER
GATWICK
HORSHAM
HANDCROSS
CUCKFIELD
PETWORTH
PULBOROUGH
STORRINGTON
AMBERLEY
ARUNDEL
WORTHING
BRIGHTON
Newhaven
LEWES
UCKFIELD
ALFRISTON
EASTBOURNE
FOREST ROW
CROWBOROUGH
BUXTED
TICEHURST
BATTLE
RYE
NEW ROMNEY
TENTERDEN
ASHFORD
Folkestone
DOVER
CANTERBURY
Ramsgate
MAIDSTONE
SEVENOAKS
EDENBRIDGE
TUNBRIDGE WELLS
FAWKHAM
DARTFORD
Sheerness
CHELMSFORD
WARE
BISHOP'S STORTFORD
STANSTED
STANSTED
CLAVERING
COLCHESTER
DEDHAM
Harwich
Felixstowe
IPSWICH
WOODBRIDGE
FAKENHAM
SUDBURY
LONG MELFORD
LAVENHAM
CLARE
HAVERHILL
CAMBRIDGE
NEWMARKET
BURY ST EDMUNDS
THORNHAM MAGNA
DISS
SOUTHWOLD
WALBERSWICK
YOXFORD
ALDEBURGH
KING'S LYNN
NORWICH
SAHAM TONEY
WROXHAM
NORTH WALSHAM
THORPE MARKET
HOLT
GREAT SNORING
BURNHAM MARKET
THORNHAM
BLAKENEY
To Zeebrugge
To Rotterdam
To Gothenburg/Esbjerg/Hamburg
To Hook of Holland
To Zeebrugge
To Dunkerque
To Oostende
To Calais
Channel Tunnel
To Boulogne
To Boulogne
To Dieppe
To Le Havre
To Caen
To Cherbourg
To St Malo
To Cherbourg
To Jersey
To Bilbao
THE CHANNEL ISLANDS
GUERNSEY
HERM ISLAND
GUERNSEY
SARK
JERSEY
JERSEY

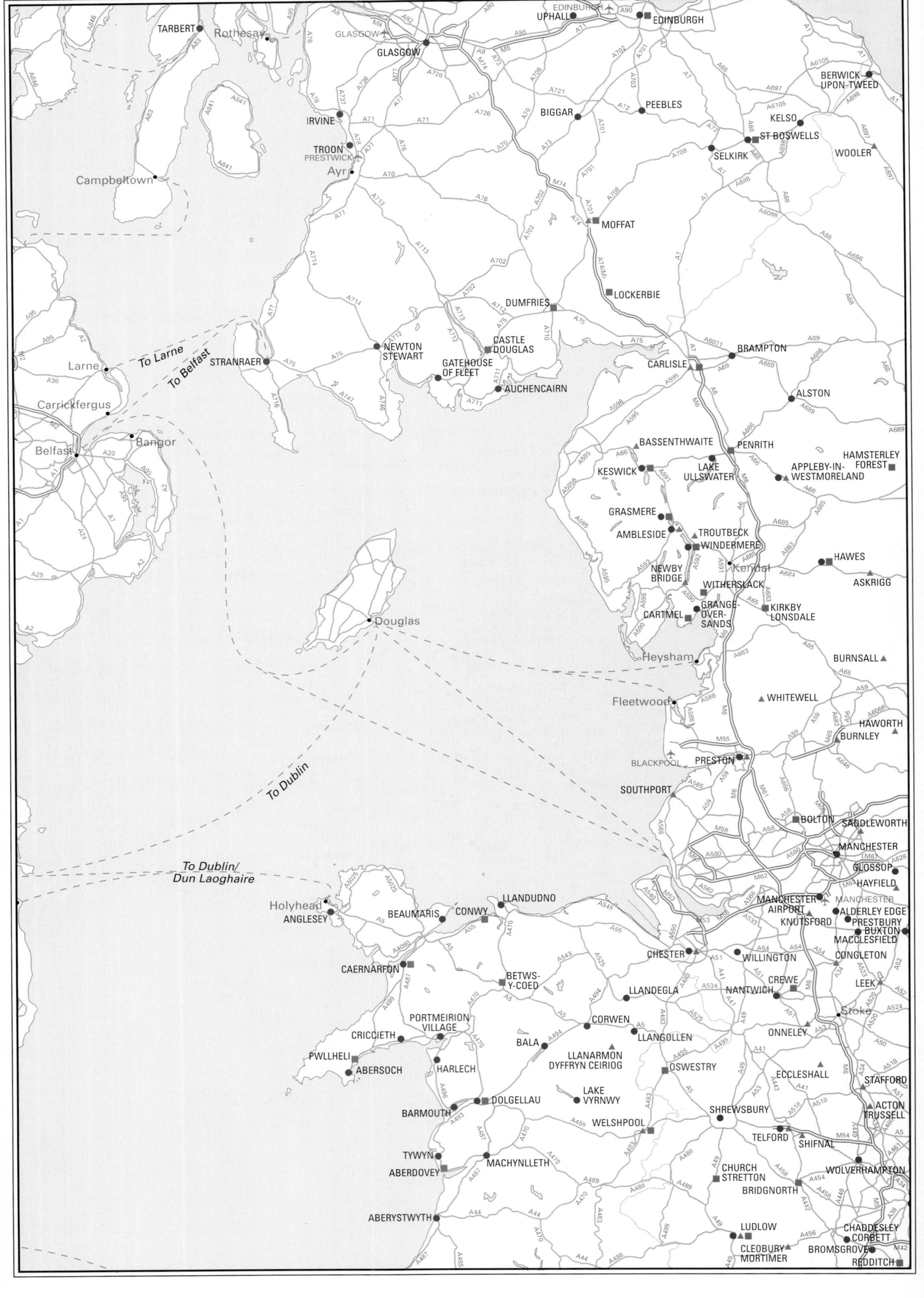
EDINBURGH
UPHALL
EDINBURGH
TARBERT
Rothesay
GLASGOW
GLASGOW
BERWICK-UPON-TWEED
PEEBLES
BIGGAR
IRVINE
KELSO
ST BOSWELLS
TROON
PRESTWICK
WOOLER
SELKIRK
Ayr
Campbeltown
MOFFAT
LOCKERBIE
DUMFRIES
To Larne
NEWTON STEWART
CASTLE DOUGLAS
Larne
STRANRAER
To Belfast
GATEHOUSE OF FLEET
BRAMPTON
CARLISLE
AUCHENCAIRN
Carrickfergus
ALSTON
Bangor
Belfast
BASSENTHWAITE
PENRITH
HAMSTERLEY FOREST
KESWICK
LAKE ULLSWATER
APPLEBY-IN-WESTMORELAND
GRASMERE
AMBLESIDE
TROUTBECK
WINDERMERE
HAWES
NEWBY BRIDGE
Kendal
ASKRIGG
WITHERSLACK
CARTMEL
GRANGE-OVER-SANDS
KIRKBY LONSDALE
Douglas
Heysham
BURNSALL
Fleetwood
WHITEWELL
HAWORTH
BURNLEY
BLACKPOOL
PRESTON
To Dublin
SOUTHPORT
BOLTON
SADDLEWORTH
MANCHESTER
GLOSSOP
To Dublin/
Dun Laoghaire
HAYFIELD
MANCHESTER AIRPORT
MANCHESTER
LLANDUDNO
Holyhead
ALDERLEY EDGE
BEAUMARIS
CONWY
KNUTSFORD
PRESTBURY
ANGLESEY
BUXTON
MACCLESFIELD
CHESTER
WILLINGTON
CONGLETON
CAERNARFON
BETWS-Y-COED
CREWE
LLANDEGLA
NANTWICH
LEEK
Stoke
PORTMEIRION VILLAGE
CORWEN
CRICCIETH
LLANGOLLEN
ONNELEY
BALA
LLANARMON DYFFRYN CEIRIOG
PWLLHELI
ABERSOCH
HARLECH
OSWESTRY
ECCLESHALL
STAFFORD
LAKE VYRNWY
DOLGELLAU
ACTON TRUSSELL
BARMOUTH
SHREWSBURY
WELSHPOOL
TELFORD
SHIFNAL
TYWYN
MACHYNLLETH
WOLVERHAMPTON
ABERDOVEY
CHURCH STRETTON
BRIDGNORTH
ABERYSTWYTH
LUDLOW
CHADDESLEY CORBETT
CLEOBURY MORTIMER
BROMSGROVE
REDDITCH

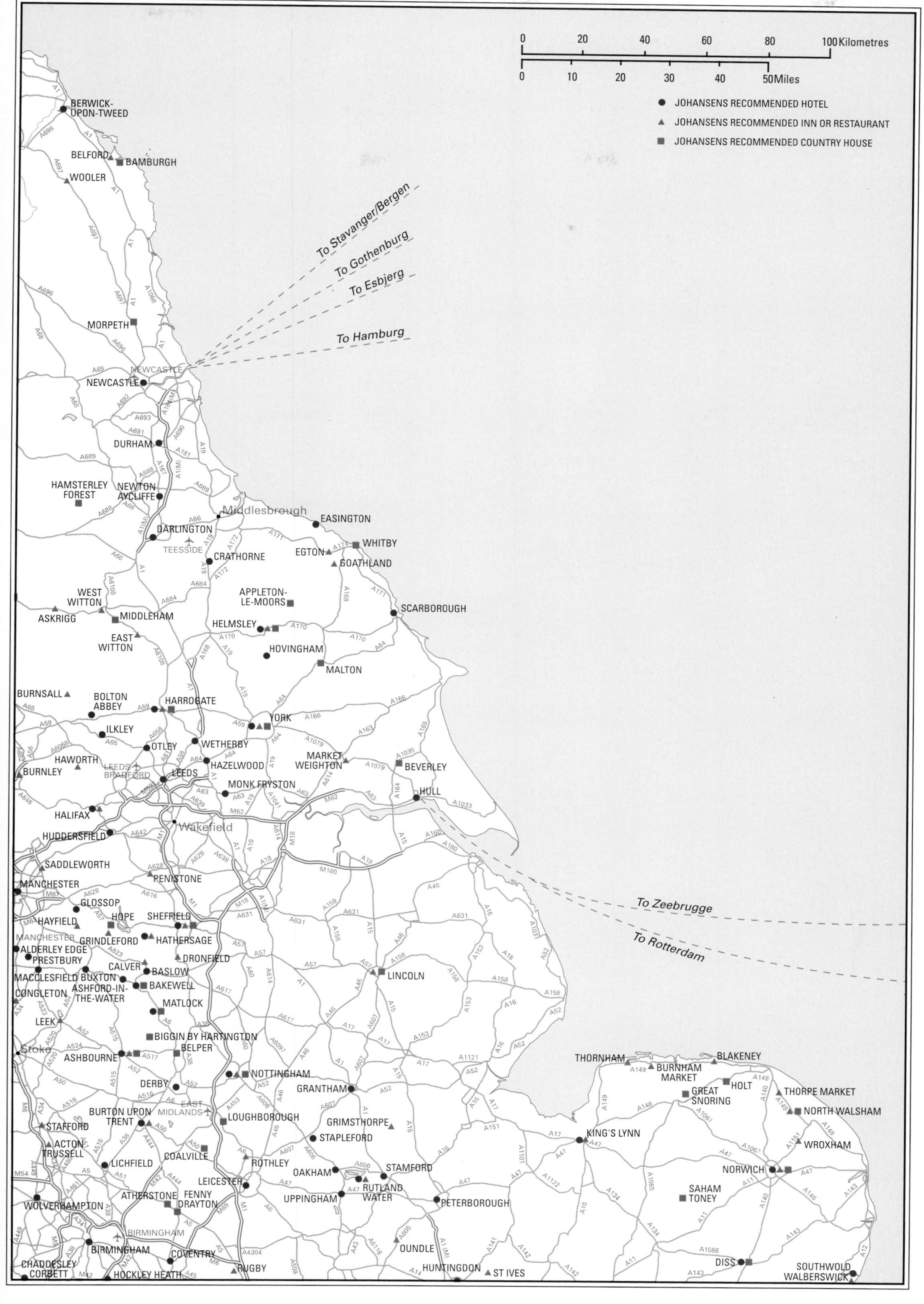
0 20 40 60 80 100 Kilometres
0 10 20 30 40 50 Miles
JOHANSENS RECOMMENDED HOTEL
JOHANSENS RECOMMENDED INN OR RESTAURANT
JOHANSENS RECOMMENDED COUNTRY HOUSE
To Stavanger/Bergen
To Gothenburg
To Esbjerg
To Hamburg
To Zeebrugge
To Rotterdam
BERWICK-UPON-TWEED
BELFORD
BAMBURGH
WOOLER
MORPETH
NEWCASTLE
NEWCASTLE
DURHAM
HAMSTERLEY FOREST
NEWTON AYCLIFFE
Middlesbrough
EASINGTON
DARLINGTON
TEESSIDE
CRATHORNE
EGTON
WHITBY
GOATHLAND
APPLETON-LE-MOORS
SCARBOROUGH
WEST WITTON
ASKRIGG
MIDDLEHAM
HELMSLEY
EAST WITTON
HOVINGHAM
MALTON
BURNSALL
BOLTON ABBEY
HARROGATE
YORK
ILKLEY
OTLEY
WETHERBY
HAWORTH
MARKET WEIGHTON
BEVERLEY
BURNLEY
LEEDS BRADFORD
LEEDS
HAZELWOOD
MONK FRYSTON
HULL
HALIFAX
Wakefield
HUDDERSFIELD
SADDLEWORTH
PENISTONE
MANCHESTER
GLOSSOP
HAYFIELD
HOPE
SHEFFIELD
MANCHESTER
GRINDLEFORD
HATHERSAGE
ALDERLEY EDGE
PRESTBURY
DRONFIELD
CALVER
BASLOW
MACCLESFIELD
BUXTON
ASHFORD-IN-THE-WATER
BAKEWELL
CONGLETON
MATLOCK
LINCOLN
LEEK
BIGGIN BY HARTINGTON
Stoke
BELPER
ASHBOURNE
THORNHAM
BLAKENEY
BURNHAM MARKET
HOLT
NOTTINGHAM
DERBY
GRANTHAM
GREAT SNORING
THORPE MARKET
NORTH WALSHAM
BURTON UPON TRENT
EAST MIDLANDS
LOUGHBOROUGH
STAFFORD
GRIMSTHORPE
STAPLEFORD
KING'S LYNN
WROXHAM
ACTON TRUSSELL
LICHFIELD
COALVILLE
ROTHLEY
OAKHAM
STAMFORD
NORWICH
LEICESTER
RUTLAND WATER
UPPINGHAM
SAHAM TONEY
ATHERSTONE
FENNY DRAYTON
PETERBOROUGH
WOLVERHAMPTON
BIRMINGHAM
OUNDLE
BIRMINGHAM
COVENTRY
CHADDESLEY CORBETT
HOCKLEY HEATH
RUGBY
HUNTINGDON
ST IVES
DISS
SOUTHWOLD
WALBERSWICK

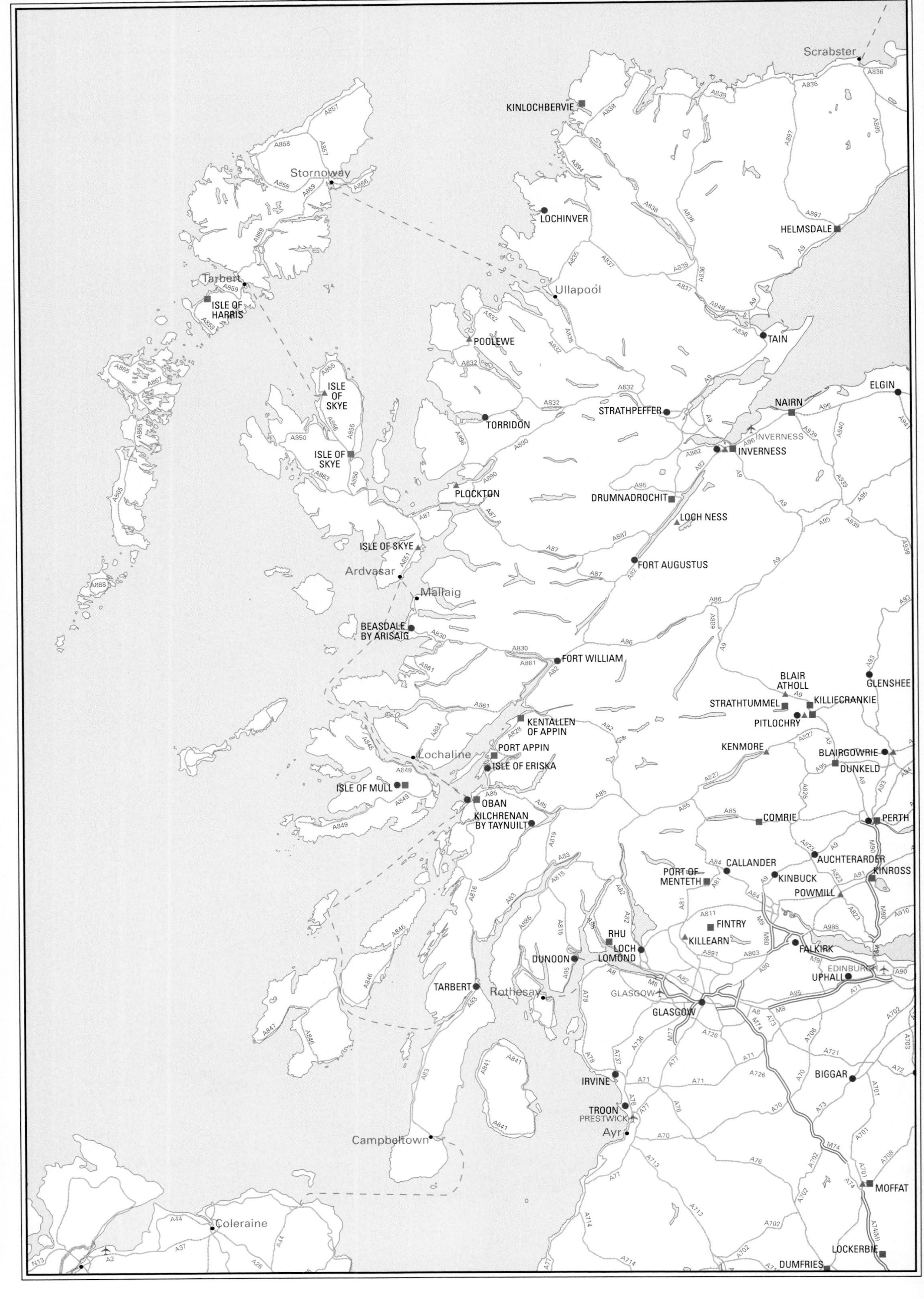
Scrabster
KINLOCHBERVIE
Stornoway
LOCHINVER
HELMSDALE
Tarbert
ISLE OF HARRIS
Ullapool
POOLEWE
TAIN
ISLE OF SKYE
ELGIN
NAIRN
STRATHPEFFER
TORRIDON
INVERNESS
INVERNESS
ISLE OF SKYE
PLOCKTON
DRUMNADROCHIT
LOCH NESS
ISLE OF SKYE
FORT AUGUSTUS
Ardvasar
Mallaig
BEASDALE BY ARISAIG
FORT WILLIAM
BLAIR ATHOLL
GLENSHEE
STRATHTUMMEL
KILLIECRANKIE
PITLOCHRY
KENTALLEN OF APPIN
KENMORE
BLAIRGOWRIE
PORT APPIN
Lochaline
ISLE OF ERISKA
DUNKELD
ISLE OF MULL
OBAN
KILCHRENAN BY TAYNUILT
COMRIE
PERTH
AUCHTERARDER
CALLANDER
PORT OF MENTETH
KINBUCK
KINROSS
POWMILL
FINTRY
KILLEARN
RHU
LOCH LOMOND
FALKIRK
DUNOON
EDINBURGH
UPHALL
TARBERT
Rothesay
GLASGOW
GLASGOW
IRVINE
BIGGAR
TROON
PRESTWICK
Ayr
Campbeltown
MOFFAT
Coleraine
LOCKERBIE
DUMFRIES

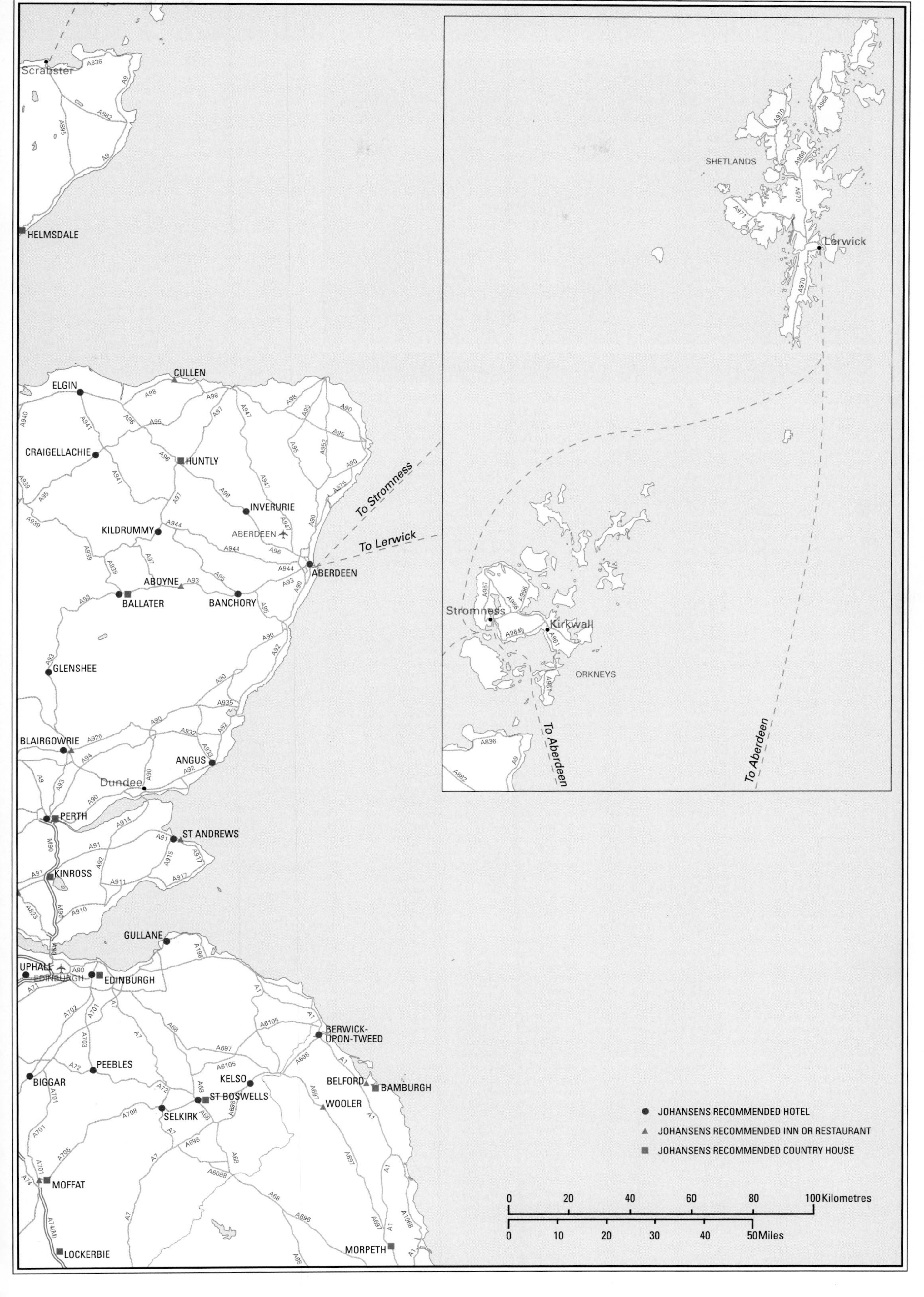
Scrabster
HELMSDALE
SHETLANDS
Lerwick
CULLEN
ELGIN
CRAIGELLACHIE
HUNTLY
INVERURIE
KILDRUMMY
ABERDEEN
ABOYNE
BALLATER
BANCHORY
ABERDEEN
To Stromness
To Lerwick
Stromness
Kirkwall
ORKNEYS
To Aberdeen
To Aberdeen
GLENSHEE
BLAIRGOWRIE
ANGUS
Dundee
PERTH
ST ANDREWS
KINROSS
GULLANE
UPHALL
EDINBURGH
EDINBURGH
BERWICK-
UPON-TWEED
PEEBLES
BIGGAR
KELSO
ST BOSWELLS
SELKIRK
BELFORD
BAMBURGH
WOOLER
MOFFAT
LOCKERBIE
MORPETH
JOHANSENS RECOMMENDED HOTEL
JOHANSENS RECOMMENDED INN OR RESTAURANT
JOHANSENS RECOMMENDED COUNTRY HOUSE
0 20 40 60 80 100 Kilometres
0 10 20 30 40 50 Miles

To enable you to use your 1999 Johansens Recommended Country Houses and Small Hotels Guide more effectively, the following five pages of indexes contain a wealth of useful information about the establishments featured in the Guide. As well as listing them alphabetically, by region and by county, the indexes also show which Country Houses and Small Hotels offer certain specialised facilities.

The indexes are listed as follows:

- Alphabetically by region
- By county
- With a swimming pool
- With tennis
- With fishing nearby
- With shooting facilities
- With conference facilities for 30 delegates or more
- Double rooms for £50 or less
- Country Houses accepting Johansens Privilege Card
- Johansens Preferred Partners

1999 Johansens Recommended Country Houses listed alphabetically by region

ENGLAND

Abbots Oak ..... Coalville 56
Allhays Country House ..... Looe 104
Appleton Hall ..... Appleton-Le-Moors ... 13
Apsley House ..... Bath 21
The Ardencote Manor Hotel . Warwick 171
Arrow Mill Hotel ..... Alcester 12
Ashelford ..... Combe Martin 57
Ashwick Country House Hotel .. Dulverton 68
Aynsome Manor Hotel ..... Cartmel 46
Bath Lodge Hotel ..... Bath 22
The Beacon Country House ... Exmoor 75
The Beaufort Hotel ..... Portsmouth 141
The Beeches Farmhouse ..... Ashbourne 15
The Beeches Hotel & Victorian Gardens ..... Norwich 126
Beechleas ..... Wimborne Minster .. 176
Beechwood Hotel ..... North Walsham 125
Bel Alp House ..... Dartmoor 60
Beryl ..... Wells 172
Bibury Court ..... Bibury 32
Biggin Hall ..... Biggin-By-Hartington 34
Bloomfield House ..... Bath 23
Boskerris Hotel ..... St. Ives 148
The Bowens Country House .. Hereford 90
Broom Hall ..... Saham Toney 151
Broome Court ..... Dartmouth 61
Burleigh Court ..... Minchinhampton 119
Burpham Country House Hotel .. Arundel 14
Catton Old Hall ..... Norwich 127
Chalk Lane Hotel ..... Epsom 70
Channel House Hotel ..... Minehead 120
Chapel House ..... Atherstone 16
Charlton Kings Hotel ..... Cheltenham 48
Chase Lodge ..... Hampton Court 84
Chequers Hotel ..... Pulborough 142
Chippenhall Hall ..... Diss 64
Collin House Hotel ..... Broadway 39
Conygree Gate Hotel ..... Stow-On-The-Wold 163
Coombe Farm ..... Looe 105
Coombe House Country Hotel . Crediton 58
The Cormorant Hotel ..... Golant by Fowey 80
The Cornish Cottage Hotel & Gourmet Restaurant ..... New Polzeath 123
The Cottage Country House Hotel ..... Nottingham 130
The Cottage Hotel ..... Porlock Weir 139
The Countryman At Trink Hotel & Restaurant ..... St Ives 149
Coxley Vineyard ..... Wells 173
Crosby Lodge Country House Carlisle 45
Cross House Hotel ..... Padstow 136
Cross Lane House Hotel ..... Bridgnorth 37
Crouchers Bottom Country Hotel ..... Chichester 50
The Crown Hotel ..... Exford 74
Dale Head Hall Lakeside Hotel .. Keswick 96
Dannah Farm Country Guest House ..... Belper 30
Delbury Hall ..... Ludlow 107
Duke's Hotel ..... Bath 24
Dunsley Hall ..... Whitby 175
Eagle House ..... Bath 25
East Lodge Country House ..... Bakewell 18
The Eastbury Hotel ..... Sherborne 156
Easton Court Hotel ..... Chagford 47
Eshott Hall ..... Morpeth 122
Fallowfields ..... Oxford 135
Fayrer Garden House Hotel ... Windermere 178
Felbrigg Lodge ..... Holt 92
Findon Manor ..... Worthing 183
Foxdown Manor ..... Clovelly 55
Glebe Farm House ..... Stratford-upon-Avon . 164
Glencot House ..... Wells 174
Glewstone Court ..... Ross-On-Wye 146
The Granville ..... Brighton 38
Grove House ..... Hamsterley Forest 85
Halewell ..... Cheltenham 49
Hewitt's Hotel ..... Lynton 112
Hipping Hall ..... Kirkby Lonsdale 99
Holbrook House Hotel ..... Wincanton 177
Hooke Hall ..... Uckfield 168
Hope House ..... Yoxford 185
The Hundred House Hotel ..... St Mawes 150
Kemps Country House Hotel . Wareham 170
Kingston House ..... Staverton 160
Langar Hall ..... Nottingham 131
Langrish House ..... Petersfield 138
Lavenham Priory ..... Lavenham 100
Little Offley ..... Luton 109
The Lord Haldon Hotel ..... Exeter 73
Lower Bache House ..... Leominster 101
Lower Brook House ..... Blockley 35
The Lyndhurst Hotel ..... Salcombe 152
The Malt House ..... Chipping Campden ... 52
The Manor Farmhouse ..... Matlock 115
The Manor House ..... Beverley 31
Marsh Hall Country House ..... South Molton 159
Melbourn Bury ..... Cambridge 44
The Mill At Harvington ..... Evesham 72
Millers House Hotel ..... Middleham 118
Moor View House ..... Lydford 110
Moortown Lodge ..... Ringwood 144
Mynd House Hotel ..... Church Stretton 53
Nansloe Manor ..... Helston 89
Newstead Grange ..... Malton 114
Nonsuch House ..... Dartmouth 62
Norfolk Mead Hotel ..... Norwich 128
Oak Lodge Hotel ..... Enfield 69
The Old Manor Hotel ..... Loughborough 106
The Old Rectory ..... Great Snoring 82
The Old Rectory ..... Redditch 143
The Old Rectory ..... Broadway 40
The Old Rectory ..... Norwich 129
The Old Rectory ..... Ilminster 94
The Old Vicarage Country House . Witherslack 181
Oldfields ..... Bath 26
Overton Grange Hotel ..... Ludlow 108
Owlpen Manor ..... Owlpen 134
Paradise House ..... Bath 27
The Parsonage Country House . York 184
The Peacock Hotel at Rowsley . Bakewell 19
Pear Tree Lake Farms ..... Crewe 59
Pen-y-Dyffryn Country Hotel Oswestry 132
Periton Park Hotel ..... Middlecombe 117
Petty France ..... Badminton 17
The Pheasant Hotel ..... Seavington St Mary . 154
Preston House Hotel ..... Saunton 153
Prince Hall Hotel ..... Dartmoor 63
The Priory ..... Bury St. Edmunds 43
Quarlton Manor Farm ..... Bolton 36
Quarry Garth Country House . Windermere 179
Rectory House ..... Evershot 71
Redcoats Farmhouse Hotel ..... Stevenage 161
Romney Bay House ..... New Romney 124
Rookhurst Georgian Country House Hotel ..... Hawes 87
The Royal Hotel ..... Truro 167
Ryedale Country Lodge ..... Helmsley 88
Rylstone Manor ..... Isle of Wight 95
Sandringham Hotel ..... Hampstead Village 83
The Shaven Crown Hotel ..... Shipton-Under-Wychwood . 157
Sheriff Lodge Hotel ..... Matlock 116
Simonsbath House Hotel ..... Simonsbath 158
The St Enodoc Hotel ..... Rock 145
Staindrop Hotel & Restaurant .. Sheffield 155
Stanhill Court Hotel ..... Gatwick 79
The Steppes ..... Hereford 91
The Stonor Arms ..... Stonor 162
Storrs Hall ..... Windermere 180
Swinside Lodge Hotel ..... Keswick 97
Tanyard ..... Maidstone 113
Temple Sowerby House Hotel . Penrith 137
Thatch Lodge Hotel ..... Lyme Regis 111
The Thatched Cottage Country Hotel ..... Lifton 102
Thatched Cottage Hotel ..... Brockenhurst 41
Trebrea Lodge ..... Tintagel 166
Trehellas House & Memories of Malaya Restaurant ..... Wadebridge 169
Trelawne Hotel -The Hutches Restaurant ..... Falmouth 77
Tudor Farmhouse Hotel ..... Clearwell 54
Tye Rock Hotel ..... Porthleven 140
Underleigh House ..... Hope 93
Upper Court ..... Tewkesbury 165
Venn Ottery Barton ..... Ottery St. Mary 133
Vere Lodge ..... Fakenham 76
Wallett's Court ..... Dover 66
Waren House Hotel ..... Bamburgh 20
Washingborough Hall ..... Lincoln 103
The White House ..... Harrogate 86
The White House ..... Kingsbridge 98
White Moss House ..... Grasmere 81
White Vine House ..... Rye 147
White Wings ..... Fenny Drayton 78
Whitley Ridge & Country House Hotel ..... Brockenhurst 42
Widbrook Grange ..... Bath 28
Wigham ..... Morchard Bishop 121
Wood Hall Hotel ..... Woodbridge 182
Woodstock House Hotel ..... Chichester 51
The Woodville Hall ..... Dover 67
Woolverton House ..... Bath 29
Yalbury Cottage Hotel ..... Dorchester 65
Yeoldon House Hotel ..... Bideford 33

WALES

Berthlwyd Hall Hotel ..... Conwy 196
Buttington House ..... Welshpool 203
The Crown At Whitebrook ... Monmouth 199
Glangrwyney Court ..... Abergavenny 189
Llanwenarth House ..... Abergavenny 190
Old Gwernyfed Country Manor . Brecon 193
The Old Rectory ..... Conwy 197
Parva Farmhouse and Restaurant . Tintern 202
The Pembrokeshire Retreat ... Cardigan 195
Penyclawdd Court ..... Abergavenny 191
Plas Bodegroes ..... Pwllheli 200
Plas Dolmelynllyn ..... Dolgellau 198
Plas Penhelig Country House . Aberdovey 188
Tan-y-Foel ..... Betws-y-Coed 192
Ty'n Rhos Country House ..... Caernarfon 194
Waterwynch House Hotel ..... Tenby 201

SCOTLAND

Aldonaig ..... Rhu 234
Ardsheal House ..... Kentallen Of Appin . 221
Ardvourlie Castle ..... Isle Of Harris 217
Balgonie Country House ..... Ballater 206
Boath House ..... Nairn 227
Bosville Hotel & Chandlery Seafood Restaurant ..... Isle of Skye 220
Clint Lodge ..... St. Boswell By Melrose . 235
Culcreuch Castle Hotel ..... Fintry 213
Culduthel Lodge ..... Inverness 216
Druimneil ..... Port Appin 232
The Dryfesdale Hotel ..... Lockerbie 225
Dunfallandy House ..... Pitlochry 231
Dungallen House Hotel ..... Oban 228
Highland Cottage ..... Isle of Mull 218
Killiechronan ..... Isle Of Mull 219
The Killiecrankie Hotel ..... Killiecrankie 222
The Kinlochbervie Hotel ..... Kinlochbervie 223
The Lake Hotel ..... Port Of Menteith 233
Longacre Manor ..... Castle Douglas 207
The Manor House Hotel ..... Oban 229
Navidale House Hotel ..... Helmsdale 214
Newmiln Country House ..... Perth 230
Nivingston Country House ..... Kinross 224
No 22 Murrayfield Gardens ..... Edinburgh 212
The Old Manse of Marnoch ..... By Huntly 215
The Pend ..... Dunkeld 211
Polmaily House Hotel ..... Drumnadrochit 209
Queen's View Hotel ..... Strathtummel 236
The Royal Hotel ..... Comrie 208
Trigony House Hotel ..... Dunfries 210
Well View Hotel ..... Moffat 226

IRELAND

Aberdeen Lodge ... Dublin ... 243
Ard-na-Sidhe ... Caragh Lake Co Kerry 239
Ballylickey Manor House ... Bantry ... 238
Caragh Lodge ... Caragh Lake Co Kerry 240
Cashel Palace Hotel ... Cashel Co Tipperary . 241
Castle Grove Country House . Letterkenny ... 249
Coopershill House ... Riverstown,Co Sligo . 250
Earls Court House ... Killarney Co Kerry ... 247
Fitzwilliam Park ... Dublin ... 244
Halpins Hotel &
Vittles Restaurant ... Kilkee, Co Clare ... 245
The Inishclare Restaurant ... Killadeas ... 246
Liss Ard Lake Lodge ... Skibbereen, Co.Cork 251
Markree Castle ... Sligo, Co Sligo ... 252
The Old Rectory ... Wicklow, Co Wicklow 253
The Old Rectory
– Kilmeaden House ... Kilmeaden ... 248
Ross Lake House Hotel ... Connemara ... 242

CHANNEL ISLANDS

Bella Luce Hotel ... Guernsey ... 257
Hotel La Tour ... Jersey ... 259
La Favorita Hotel ... Guernsey ... 256
The White House ... Herm Island ... 258

1998 Johansens Recommended Country Houses by county

ENGLAND

Bath/Avon (please refer to Somerset listings)

London
Sandringham Hotel ... Hampstead Village ... 83

B & NE Somerset
Apsley House ... Bath ... 21

Cambridgeshire
Melbourn Bury ... Cambridge ... 44

Cheshire
Pear Tree Lake Farms ... Crewe ... 59

Co.Durham
Grove House ... Hamsterley Forest ... 85

Cornwall
Allhays Country House ... Looe ... 104
Boskerris Hotel ... St. Ives ... 148
Coombe Farm ... Looe ... 105
The Cormorant Hotel ... Golant by Fowey ... 80
The Countryman At
Trink Hotel & Restaurant .. St Ives ... 149
Cross House Hotel ... Padstow ... 136
The Hundred House Hotel ... St Mawes ... 150
Nansloe Manor ... Helston ... 89
The Royal Hotel ... Truro ... 167
The St Enodoc Hotel ... Rock ... 145
Trebrea Lodge ... Tintagel ... 166
Trehellas House & Memories
of Malaya Restaurant ... Wadebridge ... 169
Trelawne Hotel –
The Hutches Restaurant ... Falmouth ... 77

Cumbria
Aynsome Manor Hotel ... Cartmel ... 46
Crosby Lodge Country House Carlisle ... 45
Dale Head Hall Lakeside Hotel . Keswick ... 96
Fayrer Garden House Hotel ... Windermere ... 178
Hipping Hall ... Kirkby Lonsdale ... 99
The Old Vicarage
Country House Hotel ... Witherslack ... 181
Quarry Garth Country House Windermere ... 179
Storrs Hall ... Windermere ... 180
Swinside Lodge Hotel ... Keswick ... 97
Temple Sowerby House Hotel . Penrith ... 137
White Moss House ... Grasmere ... 81

Derbyshire
The Beeches Farmhouse ... Ashbourne ... 15
Biggin Hall ... Biggin-By-Hartington 34
Dannah Farm
Country Guest House ... Belper ... 30
East Lodge Country House ... Bakewell ... 18
The Manor Farmhouse ... Matlock ... 115
The Peacock Hotel at Rowsley . Bakewell ... 19
Sheriff Lodge Hotel ... Matlock ... 116
Underleigh House ... Hope ... 93

Devon
Ashelford ... Combe Martin ... 57
Bel Alp House ... Dartmoor ... 60
Broome Court ... Dartmouth ... 61
Coombe House Country Hotel . Crediton ... 58
Easton Court Hotel ... Chagford ... 47
Foxdown Manor ... Clovelly ... 55
Hewitt's Hotel ... Lynton ... 112
Kingston House ... Staverton ... 160
The Lord Haldon Hotel ... Exeter ... 73
The Lyndhurst Hotel ... Salcombe ... 152
Marsh Hall Country House ... South Molton ... 159
Moor View House ... Lydford ... 110
Nonsuch House ... Dartmouth ... 62
Preston House Hotel ... Saunton ... 153
Prince Hall Hotel ... Dartmoor ... 63
The Thatched Cottage
Country Hotel ... Lifton ... 102
Venn Ottery Barton ... Ottery St. Mary ... 133
The White House ... Kingsbridge ... 98
Wigham ... Morchard Bishop ... 121
Yeoldon House Hotel ... Bideford ... 33

Dorset
Beechleas ... Wimborne Minster .. 176
The Eastbury Hotel ... Sherborne ... 156
Kemps Country House
Hotel & Restaurant ... Wareham ... 170
Rectory House ... Evershot ... 71
Thatch Lodge Hotel ... Lyme Regis ... 111
Yalbury Cottage Hotel ... Dorchester ... 65

East Sussex
The Granville ... Brighton ... 38
Hooke Hall ... Uckfield ... 168
White Vine House ... Rye ... 147

East Yorkshire
The Manor House ... Beverley ... 31

Gloucestershire
Bibury Court ... Bibury ... 32
Burleigh Court ... Minchinhampton ... 119
Charlton Kings Hotel ... Cheltenham ... 48
Halewell ... Cheltenham ... 49
Lower Brook House ... Blockley ... 35
The Malt House ... Chipping Campden ... 52
The Old Rectory ... Broadway ... 40
Owlpen Manor ... Owlpen ... 134
Tudor Farmhouse Hotel ... Clearwell ... 54
Upper Court ... Tewkesbury ... 165

Hampshire
The Beaufort Hotel ... Portsmouth ... 141
Langrish House ... Petersfield ... 138
Moortown Lodge ... Ringwood ... 144
Thatched Cottage Hotel ... Brockenhurst ... 41
Whitley Ridge &
Country House Hotel ... Brockenhurst ... 42

Herefordshire
The Bowens Country House .. Hereford ... 90
Glewstone Court ... Ross-On-Wye ... 146
Lower Bache House ... Leominster ... 101
The Steppes ... Hereford ... 91
Little Offley ... Luton ... 109
Redcoats Farmhouse Hotel ... Stevenage ... 161

Isle of Wight
Rylstone Manor ... Isle of Wight ... 95

Kent
Romney Bay House ... New Romney ... 124
Tanyard ... Maidstone ... 113
Wallett's Court ... Dover ... 66
The Woodville Hall ... Dover ... 67

Lancashire
Quarlton Manor Farm ... Bolton ... 36

Leicestershire
Abbots Oak ... Coalville ... 56
The Old Manor Hotel ... Loughborough ... 106
White Wings ... Fenny Drayton ... 78

Lincolnshire
Washingborough Hall ... Lincoln ... 103

Middlesex
Oak Lodge Hotel ... Enfield ... 69

Norfolk
The Beeches Hotel &
Victorian Gardens ... Norwich ... 126
Beechwood Hotel ... North Walsham ... 125
Broom Hall ... Saham Toney ... 151
Catton Old Hall ... Norwich ... 127
Felbrigg Lodge ... Holt ... 92
Norfolk Mead Hotel ... Norwich ... 128
The Old Rectory ... Great Snoring ... 82
The Old Rectory ... Norwich ... 129
Vere Lodge ... Fakenham ... 76

North Cornwall
The Cornish Cottage Hotel
& Gourmet Restaurant ... New Polzeath ... 123

North Yorkshire
Appleton Hall ... Appleton-Le-Moors ... 13
Dunsley Hall ... Whitby ... 175
Millers House Hotel ... Middleham ... 118
Newstead Grange ... Malton ... 114
The Parsonage Country House . York ... 184
Rookhurst Georgian
Country House Hotel ... Hawes ... 87
Ryedale Country Lodge ... Helmsley ... 88
The White House ... Harrogate ... 86

Northumberland
Eshott Hall ... Morpeth ... 122
Waren House Hotel ... Bamburgh ... 20

Nottinghamshire
The Cottage Country House .. Nottingham ... 130
Langar Hall ... Nottingham ... 131

Oxfordshire
Conygree Gate Hotel ... Stow-On-The-Wold 163
Fallowfields ... Oxford ... 135
The Shaven Crown Hotel ... Shipton-Under-Wychwood . 157
The Stonor Arms ... Stonor ... 162

Shropshire
Cross Lane House Hotel ... Bridgnorth ... 37
Delbury Hall ... Ludlow ... 107
Mynd House Hotel ... Church Stretton ... 53
Overton Grange Hotel ... Ludlow ... 108
Pen-y-Dyffryn Country Hotel .. Oswestry ... 132

Somerset
Ashwick Country House Hotel . Dulverton ... 68
Bath Lodge Hotel ... Bath ... 22
The Beacon Country House ... Exmoor ... 75
Beryl ... Wells ... 172
Bloomfield House ... Bath ... 23
Channel House Hotel ... Minehead ... 120
The Cottage Hotel ... Porlock Weir ... 139
Coxley Vineyard ... Wells ... 173
The Crown Hotel ... Exford ... 74
Duke's Hotel ... Bath ... 24
Eagle House ... Bath ... 25
Glencot House ... Wells ... 174
Holbrook House Hotel ... Wincanton ... 177
The Old Rectory ... Ilminster ... 94
Oldfields ... Bath ... 26
Paradise House ... Bath ... 27
Periton Park Hotel ... Middlecombe ... 117
The Pheasant Hotel ... Seavington St Mary . 154
Simonsbath House Hotel ... Simonsbath ... 158
Woolverton House ... Bath ... 29

South Cornwall
Tye Rock Hotel ... Porthleven ... 140

South Gloucestershire
Petty France ... Badminton ... 17

South Yorkshire
Staindrop Hotel & Restaurant . Sheffield ... 155

Suffolk
Chippenhall Hall ... Diss ... 64
Hope House ... Yoxford ... 185
Lavenham Priory ... Lavenham ... 100
The Priory ... Bury St. Edmunds ... 43
Wood Hall Hotel ... Woodbridge ... 182

Surrey
Chalk Lane Hotel ... Epsom ... 70
Chase Lodge ... Hampton Court ... 84
Stanhill Court Hotel ... Gatwick ... 79

Warwickshire
The Ardencote Manor Hotel . Warwick ... 171
Arrow Mill Hotel ... Alcester ... 12
Chapel House ... Atherstone ... 16
Glebe Farm House ... Stratford-upon-Avon 164

West Sussex
Burpham Country House Hotel . Arundel ... 14
Chequers Hotel ... Pulborough ... 142
Crouchers Bottom Country Hotel .. Chichester ... 50
Findon Manor ... Worthing ... 183
Woodstock House Hotel ... Chichester ... 51

Wiltshire
Widbrook Grange ... Bath ... 28

Worcestershire
Collin House Hotel ... Broadway ... 39
The Mill At Harvington ... Evesham ... 72
The Old Rectory ... Redditch ... 143

WALES

Conwy
The Old Rectory ... Conwy ... 197
Tan-y-Foel ... Betws-y-Coed ... 192

Gwynedd
Berthlwyd Hall Hotel ... Conwy ... 196
Plas Bodegroes ... Pwllheli ... 200
Plas Dolmelynllyn ... Dolgellau ... 198
Plas Penhelig Country House ... Aberdovey ... 188
Ty'n Rhos Country House ... Caernarfon ... 194

Monmouthshire
The Crown At Whitebrook ... Monmouth ... 199
Llanwenarth House ... Abergavenny ... 190
Parva Farmhouse and Restaurant ... Tintern ... 202
Penyclawdd Court ... Abergavenny ... 191

Pembrokeshire
The Pembrokeshire Retreat ... Cardigan ... 195
Waterwynch House Hotel ... Tenby ... 201

Powys
Buttington House ... Welshpool ... 203
Glangrwyney Court ... Abergavenny ... 189
Old Gwernyfed Country Manor ... Brecon ... 193

SCOTLAND

Aberdeenshire
Balgonie Country House ... Ballater ... 206
The Old Manse of Marnoch ... By Huntly ... 215

Argyll & Bute
Aldonaig ... Rhu ... 234

Argyllshire
Ardsheal House ... Kentallen Of Appin ... 221
Druimneil ... Port Appin ... 232
Dungallen House Hotel ... Oban ... 228
Highland Cottage ... Isle of Mull ... 218
Killiechronan ... Isle Of Mull ... 219
The Manor House Hotel ... Oban ... 229

Dumfries & Galloway
Longacre Manor ... Castle Douglas ... 207

Dumfriesshire
The Dryfesdale Hotel ... Lockerbie ... 225
Well View Hotel ... Moffat ... 226
Trigony House Hotel ... Dunfries ... 210

Inverness-shire
Boath House ... Nairn ... 227
Culduthel Lodge ... Inverness ... 216
Polmaily House Hotel ... Drumnadrochit ... 209

Isle of Skye
Bosville Hotel & Chandlery
Seafood Restaurant ... Isle of Skye ... 220

Kinross-shire
Nivingston Country House ... Kinross ... 224

Lothian
No 22 Murrayfield Gardens ... Edinburgh ... 212

Perthshire
Dunfallandy House ... Pitlochry ... 231
The Killiecrankie Hotel ... Killiecrankie ... 222
The Lake Hotel ... Port Of Menteith ... 233
Newmiln Country House ... Perth ... 230
The Pend ... Dunkeld ... 211
Queen's View Hotel ... Strathtummel ... 236
The Royal Hotel ... Comrie ... 208

Roxburghshire
Clint Lodge ... St. Boswell ... 235

Stirling & Trossachs
Culcreuch Castle Hotel ... Fintry ... 213

Sutherland
The Kinlochbervie Hotel ... Kinlochbervie ... 223
Navidale House Hotel ... Helmsdale ... 214

Western Isles
Ardvourlie Castle ... Isle Of Harris ... 217

IRELAND

Dublin
Fitzwilliam Park ... Dublin ... 244

Co Clare
Halpins Hotel &
Vittles Restaurant ... Kilkee ... 245

Co Cork
Ballylickey Manor House ... Bantry ... 238
Liss Ard Lake Lodge ... Skibbereen ... 251

Co Donegal
Castle Grove Country House ... Letterkenny ... 249

Co Galway
Ross Lake House Hotel ... Connemara ... 242

Co Kerry
Ard-na-Sidhe ... Caragh Lake ... 239
Caragh Lodge ... Caragh Lake ... 240
Earls Court House ... Killarney ... 247

Co Fermanagh
The Inishclare Restaurant ... Killadeas ... 246

Co Sligo
Coopershill House ... Riverstown ... 250
Markree Castle ... Sligo ... 252

Co Tipperary
Cashel Palace Hotel ... Cashel ... 241

Co Waterford
The Old Rectory
– Kilmeaden House ... Kilmeaden ... 248

Co Wicklow
The Old Rectory ... Wicklow ... 253

Dublin 4
Aberdeen Lodge ... Dublin ... 243

CHANNEL ISLANDS

Herm Island
The White House ... Herm Island ... 258

Jersey
Hotel La Tour ... Jersey ... 259

Guernsey
Bella Luce Hotel & Restaurant ... Guernsey ... 257
La Favorita Hotel ... Guernsey ... 256

Country Houses with a swimming pool

ENGLAND

The Ardencote Manor Hotel ... Warwick ... 171
The Beacon Country House ... Exmoor ... 75
Beryl ... Wells ... 172
Boskerris Hotel ... St. Ives ... 148
Broom Hall ... Saham Toney ... 151
Burleigh Court ... Minchinhampton ... 119
Chippenhall Hall ... Diss ... 64
Coombe Farm ... Looe ... 105
The Cormorant Hotel ... Golant by Fowey ... 80
The Cornish Cottage Hotel
& Gourmet Restaurant ... New Polzeath ... 123
Coxley Vineyard ... Wells ... 173
Dunsley Hall ... Whitby ... 175
Fallowfields ... Oxford ... 135
Felbrigg Lodge ... Holt ... 92
Foxdown Manor ... Clovelly ... 55
Glencot House ... Wells ... 174
Halewell ... Cheltenham ... 49
Holbrook House Hotel ... Wincanton ... 177
Little Offley ... Luton ... 109
The Mill At Harvington ... Evesham ... 72
Norfolk Mead Hotel ... Norwich ... 128
The Old Rectory ... Norwich ... 129
Preston House Hotel ... Saunton ... 153
The St Enodoc Hotel ... Rock ... 145
Trehellas House & Memories
of Malaya Restaurant ... Wadebridge ... 169
Trelawne Hotel
–The Hutches Restaurant ... Falmouth ... 77
Tye Rock Hotel ... Porthleven ... 140
Vere Lodge ... Fakenham ... 76
Wallett's Court ... Dover ... 66
Washingborough Hall ... Lincoln ... 103
White Wings ... Fenny Drayton ... 78
Widbrook Grange ... Bath ... 28
Wigham ... Morchard Bishop ... 121
Wood Hall Hotel ... Woodbridge ... 182

WALES

Berthlwyd Hall Hotel ... Conwy ... 196

SCOTLAND

Polmaily House Hotel ... Drumnadrochit ... 209

IRELAND

Ballylickey Manor House ... Bantry ... 238

CHANNEL ISLANDS

Bella Luce Hotel & Restaurant ... Guernsey ... 257
La Favorita Hotel ... Guernsey ... 256
The White House ... Herm Island ... 258

Country Houses with tennis

ENGLAND

Abbots Oak ... Coalville ... 56
The Ardencote Manor Hotel ... Warwick ... 171
The Bowens Country House ... Hereford ... 90
Coombe House Country Hotel ... Crediton ... 58
Coxley Vineyard ... Wells ... 173
Delbury Hall ... Ludlow ... 107
Dunsley Hall ... Whitby ... 175
Eagle House ... Bath ... 25
Eshott Hall ... Morpeth ... 122
Fallowfields ... Oxford ... 135
Foxdown Manor ... Clovelly ... 55
Holbrook House Hotel ... Wincanton ... 177
The Mill At Harvington ... Evesham ... 72
The Old Vicarage
Country House Hotel ... Witherslack ... 181
Romney Bay House ... New Romney ... 124
Stanhill Court Hotel ... Gatwick ... 79
Upper Court ... Tewkesbury ... 165
Vere Lodge ... Fakenham ... 76
Wallett's Court ... Dover ... 66
Whitley Ridge &
Country House Hotel ... Brockenhurst ... 42
Wood Hall Hotel ... Woodbridge ... 182
Woolverton House ... Bath ... 29

WALES

Glangrwyney Court ... Abergavenny ... 189
The Pembrokeshire Retreat ... Cardigan ... 195

SCOTLAND

Aldonaig ... Rhu ... 234
Newmiln Country House ... Perth ... 230
Polmaily House Hotel ... Drumnadrochit ... 209

IRELAND

Ard-na-Sidhe ... Caragh Lake ... 239
Caragh Lodge ... Caragh Lake ... 240
Coopershill House ... Riverstown ... 250
Liss Ard Lake Lodge ... Skibbereen ... 251
Ross Lake House Hotel ... Connemara ... 242

CHANNEL ISLANDS

The White House ... Herm Island ... 258

Country Houses with fishing nearby

ENGLAND

Abbots Oak ... Coalville ... 56
Allhays Country House ... Looe ... 104
Apsley House ... Bath ... 21
The Ardencote Manor Hotel ... Warwick ... 171
Arrow Mill Hotel ... Alcester ... 12
Ashelford ... Combe Martin ... 57
Aynsome Manor Hotel ... Cartmel ... 46
Bath Lodge Hotel ... Bath ... 22
The Beacon Country House ... Exmoor ... 75
The Beaufort Hotel ... Portsmouth ... 141
The Beeches Farmhouse ... Ashbourne ... 15
Beechleas ... Wimborne Minster ... 176
Beechwood Hotel ... North Walsham ... 125
Beryl ... Wells ... 172
Bibury Court ... Bibury ... 32
Boskerris Hotel ... St. Ives ... 148
The Bowens Country House ... Hereford ... 90
Broom Hall ... Saham Toney ... 151
Broome Court ... Dartmouth ... 61
Burleigh Court ... Minchinhampton ... 119
Burpham Country House ... Arundel ... 14
Catton Old Hall ... Norwich ... 127
Channel House Hotel ... Minehead ... 120
Chapel House ... Atherstone ... 16
Chequers Hotel ... Pulborough ... 142
Chippenhall Hall ... Diss ... 64
Conygree Gate Hotel ... Stow-On-The-Wold 163
Coombe Farm ... Looe ... 105
Coombe House Country Hotel ... Crediton ... 58
The Cormorant Hotel ... Golant by Fowey ... 80
The Cottage Country House ... Nottingham ... 130
The Cottage Hotel ... Porlock Weir ... 139
The Countryman At
Trink Hotel & Restaurant ... St Ives ... 149
Coxley Vineyard ... Wells ... 173

Take One For
Easy Calling Worldwide.

It's all within your reach.

AT&T

AT&T Direct℠ Service

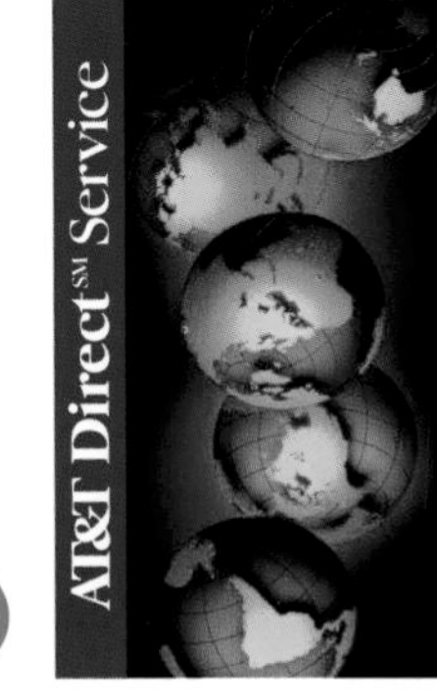

AT&T Access Numbers

Country	Number	Country	Number
Austria○	022-903-011	Germany	0130-0010
Bahrain	800-001	Greece●	00-800-1311
Belgium●	0-800-100-10	Hungary●	00✦800-01111
Croatia▲	99-385-0111	Iceland●	800-9001
Cyprus●	080-90010	Ireland✓	1-800-550-000
Czech Rep.▲	00-42-000-101	Israel	1-800-94-94-949
Denmark	8001-0010	Italy●	172-1011
Egypt●(Cairo)‡	510-0200	Ivory Coast●	00-111-11
Finland●	9800-100-10	Kuwait	800-288
France	0-800-99-0011	Lithuania✦	8✦196

AT&T

AT&T Direct℠ Service

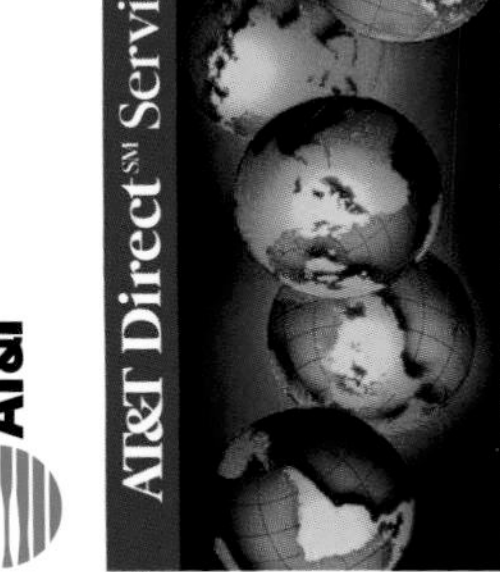

AT&T Access Numbers

Country	Number	Country	Number
Austria○	022-903-011	Germany	0130-0010
Bahrain	800-001	Greece●	00-800-1311
Belgium●	0-800-100-10	Hungary●	00✦800-01111
Croatia▲	99-385-0111	Iceland●	800-9001
Cyprus●	080-90010	Ireland✓	1-800-550-000
Czech Rep.▲	00-42-000-101	Israel	1-800-94-94-949
Denmark	8001-0010	Italy●	172-1011
Egypt●(Cairo)‡	510-0200	Ivory Coast●	00-111-11
Finland●	9800-100-10	Kuwait	800-288
France	0-800-99-0011	Lithuania✦	8✦196

Take One For
Easy Calling Worldwide.

It's all within your reach.

Country	Access Number	Country	Access Number
Luxembourg□	0-800-0111	**South Africa**	0-800-99-0123
Monaco●	800-90-288	**Spain**	900-99-00-11
Netherlands●	0800-022-9111	**Sweden**	020-795-611
Norway	800-190-11	**Switzerland**●	0-800-89-0011
Poland	0◆0-800-111-1111	**Turkey**●	00-800-12277
Portugal▲	05017-1-288	**Ukraine**▲	8◆100-11
Romania●	01-800-4288	U. Arab Emirates●	800-121
Russia●▲(Moscow)◗	755-5042	**U.K.**▲✣	0800-89-0011
Saudi Arabia◇	1-800-10	**U.K.**▲✣	0500-89-0011
Slovakia▲	00-42-100-101	**Zimbabwe**▲	110-98990

FOR EASY CALLING WORLDWIDE

1. Just dial the AT&T Access Number for the country you are calling from.
2. Dial the phone number you're calling. *3.* Dial your card number.

For access numbers not listed ask any operator for **AT&T Direct℠** Service. In the U.S. call 1-800-331-1140 for a wallet guide listing all worldwide AT&T Access Numbers.

Visit our Web site at: **www.att.com/traveler**

Bold faced countries permit country-to-country calling outside the U.S.

- ● Public phones require coin or card deposit.
- ✖ Not available from public phones.
- ▲ May not be available from every phone/public phone.
- ◆ Await second dial tone.
- ◗ Additional charges apply when calling outside of Moscow.
- ǂ Dial "02" first, outside of Cairo.
- ▬ Not yet available from all areas.
- ◇ Calling available to most countries.
- ○ Public phones require local coin payment during call.
- □ Collect calling from public phones.
- ✓ Use U.K. access number in N. Ireland.
- ✣ If call does not complete, use 0800-013-0011.

When placing an international call ***from*** the U.S., dial 1 800 CALL ATT.

Country	Access Number	Country	Access Number
Luxembourg□	0-800-0111	**South Africa**	0-800-99-0123
Monaco●	800-90-288	**Spain**	900-99-00-11
Netherlands●	0800-022-9111	**Sweden**	020-795-611
Norway	800-190-11	**Switzerland**●	0-800-89-0011
Poland	0◆0-800-111-1111	**Turkey**●	00-800-12277
Portugal▲	05017-1-288	**Ukraine**▲	8◆100-11
Romania●	01-800-4288	U. Arab Emirates●	800-121
Russia●▲(Moscow)◗	755-5042	**U.K.**▲✣	0800-89-0011
Saudi Arabia◇	1-800-10	**U.K.**▲✣	0500-89-0011
Slovakia▲	00-42-100-101	**Zimbabwe**▲	110-98990

FOR EASY CALLING WORLDWIDE

1. Just dial the AT&T Access Number for the country you are calling from.
2. Dial the phone number you're calling. *3.* Dial your card number.

For access numbers not listed ask any operator for **AT&T Direct℠** Service. In the U.S. call 1-800-331-1140 for a wallet guide listing all worldwide AT&T Access Numbers.

Visit our Web site at: **www.att.com/traveler**

Bold faced countries permit country-to-country calling outside the U.S.

- ● Public phones require coin or card deposit.
- ✖ Not available from public phones.
- ▲ May not be available from every phone/public phone.
- ◆ Await second dial tone.
- ◗ Additional charges apply when calling outside of Moscow.
- ǂ Dial "02" first, outside of Cairo.
- ▬ Not yet available from all areas.
- ◇ Calling available to most countries.
- ○ Public phones require local coin payment during call.
- □ Collect calling from public phones.
- ✓ Use U.K. access number in N. Ireland.
- ✣ If call does not complete, use 0800-013-0011.

When placing an international call ***from*** the U.S., dial 1 800 CALL ATT.

© 8/98 AT&T

Crosby Lodge Country House Carlisle ... 45
Cross House Hotel ... Padstow ... 136
Cross Lane House Hotel ... Bridgnorth ... 37
Crouchers Bottom Country Hotel Chichester ... 50
The Crown Hotel ... Exford ... 74
Dale Head Hall Lakeside Hotel Keswick ... 96
Dannah Farm Country
Guest House ... Belper ... 30
Delbury Hall ... Ludlow ... 107
Duke's Hotel ... Bath ... 24
Dunsley Hall ... Whitby ... 175
Eagle House ... Bath ... 25
East Lodge Country House ... Bakewell ... 18
The Eastbury Hotel ... Sherborne ... 156
Easton Court Hotel ... Chagford ... 47
Eshott Hall ... Morpeth ... 122
Fallowfields ... Oxford ... 135
Fayrer Garden House Hotel ... Windermere ... 178
Glencot House ... Wells ... 174
Glewstone Court ... Ross-On-Wye ... 146
The Granville ... Brighton ... 38
Halewell ... Cheltenham ... 49
Hewitt's Hotel ... Lynton ... 112
Hipping Hall ... Kirkby Lonsdale ... 99
Holbrook House Hotel ... Wincanton ... 177
Hooke Hall ... Uckfield ... 168
Hope House ... Yoxford ... 185
Kingston House ... Staverton ... 160
Langar Hall ... Nottingham ... 131
Langrish House ... Petersfield ... 138
Lavenham Priory ... Lavenham ... 100
The Lord Haldon Hotel ... Exeter ... 73
Lower Bache House ... Leominster ... 101
Lower Brook House ... Blockley ... 35
The Lyndhurst Hotel ... Salcombe ... 152
The Malt House ... Chipping Campden ... 52
The Manor House ... Beverley ... 31
The Mill At Harvington ... Evesham ... 72
Millers House Hotel ... Middleham ... 118
Moor View House ... Lydford ... 110
Moortown Lodge ... Ringwood ... 144
Nonsuch House ... Dartmouth ... 62
Norfolk Mead Hotel ... Norwich ... 128
Oak Lodge Hotel ... Enfield ... 69
The Old Rectory ... Ilminster ... 94
The Old Vicarage
Country House Hotel ... Witherslack ... 181
Overton Grange Hotel ... Ludlow ... 108
Owlpen Manor ... Owlpen ... 134
Paradise House ... Bath ... 27
The Peacock Hotel at Rowsley . Bakewell ... 19
Pear Tree Lake Farms ... Crewe ... 59
Pen-y-Dyffryn Country Hotel Oswestry ... 132
Periton Park Hotel ... Middlecombe ... 117
Petty France ... Badminton ... 17
Preston House Hotel ... Saunton ... 153
Prince Hall Hotel ... Dartmoor ... 63
Quarry Garth Country House Windermere ... 179
Rectory House ... Evershot ... 71
Romney Bay House ... New Romney ... 124
Ryedale Country Lodge ... Helmsley ... 88
Rylstone Manor ... Isle of Wight ... 95
The Shaven Crown Hotel ... Shipton-Under-Wychwood ... 157
Simonsbath House Hotel ... Simonsbath ... 158
The St Enodoc Hotel ... Rock ... 145
Stanhill Court Hotel ... Gatwick ... 79
The Steppes ... Hereford ... 91
The Stonor Arms ... Stonor ... 162
Storrs Hall ... Windermere ... 180
Swinside Lodge Hotel ... Keswick ... 97
Temple Sowerby House Hotel .. Penrith ... 137
Thatch Lodge Hotel ... Lyme Regis ... 111
The Thatched Cottage
Country Hotel ... Lifton ... 102
Thatched Cottage Hotel ... Brockenhurst ... 41
Trebrea Lodge ... Tintagel ... 166
Trelawne Hotel
–The Hutches Restaurant ... Falmouth ... 77
Tye Rock Hotel ... Porthleven ... 140
Underleigh House ... Hope ... 93
Venn Ottery Barton ... Ottery St. Mary ... 133
Vere Lodge ... Fakenham ... 76
Wallett's Court ... Dover ... 66
Waren House Hotel ... Bamburgh ... 20
Washingborough Hall ... Lincoln ... 103
White Moss House ... Grasmere ... 81
White Wings ... Fenny Drayton ... 78
Whitley Ridge
& Country House Hotel ... Brockenhurst ... 42
Widbrook Grange ... Bath ... 28
Wood Hall Hotel ... Woodbridge ... 182
Woolverton House ... Bath ... 29
Yalbury Cottage Hotel ... Dorchester ... 65
Yeoldon House Hotel ... Bideford ... 33

WALES

Buttington House ... Welshpool ... 203
The Crown At Whitebrook ... Monmouth ... 199
Glangrwyney Court ... Abergavenny ... 189
Llanwenarth House ... Abergavenny ... 190
Old Gwernyfed Country Manor . Brecon ... 193
Parva Farmhouse and Restaurant . Tintern ... 202
The Pembrokeshire Retreat ... Cardigan ... 195
Plas Bodegroes ... Pwllheli ... 200
Plas Dolmelynllyn ... Dolgellau ... 198
Plas Penhelig Country House . Aberdovey ... 188
Ty'n Rhos Country House ... Caernarfon ... 194
Waterwynch House Hotel ... Tenby ... 201

SCOTLAND

Ardvourlie Castle ... Isle Of Harris ... 217
Balgonie Country House ... Ballater ... 206
Boath House ... Nairn ... 227
Bosville Hotel & Chandlery
Seafood Restaurant ... Isle of Skye ... 220
Culcreuch Castle Hotel ... Fintry ... 213
Dunfallandy House ... Pitlochry ... 231
Dungallen House Hotel ... Oban ... 228
Highland Cottage ... Isle of Mull ... 218
Killiechronan ... Isle Of Mull ... 219
The Killiecrankie Hotel ... Killiecrankie ... 222
The Kinlochbervie Hotel ... Kinlochbervie ... 223
The Lake Hotel ... Port Of Menteith ... 233
The Manor House Hotel ... Oban ... 229
Navidale House Hotel ... Helmsdale ... 214
Newmiln Country House ... Perth ... 230
Nivingston Country House ... Kinross ... 224
The Old Manse of Marnoch ... By Huntly ... 215
The Pend ... Dunkeld ... 211
Polmaily House Hotel ... Drumnadrochit ... 209
Queen's View Hotel ... Strathtummel ... 236
The Royal Hotel ... Comrie ... 208
Trigony House Hotel ... Dunfries ... 210

IRELAND

Aberdeen Lodge ... Dublin ... 243
Ard-na-Sidhe ... Caragh Lake ... 239
Ballylickey Manor House ... Bantry ... 238
Caragh Lodge ... Caragh Lake ... 240
Cashel Palace Hotel ... Cashel ... 241
Castle Grove Country House . Letterkenny ... 249
Coopershill House ... Riverstown ... 250
Earls Court House ... Killarney ... 247
Fitzwilliam Park ... Dublin ... 244
Halpins Hotel &
Vittles Restaurant ... Kilkee ... 245
Liss Ard Lake Lodge ... Skibbereen ... 251
Markree Castle ... Sligo ... 252
The Old Rectory ... Wicklow ... 253
The Old Rectory
– Kilmeaden House ... Kilmeaden ... 248
Ross Lake House Hotel ... Connemara ... 242

CHANNEL ISLANDS

Bella Luce Hotel ... Guernsey ... 257
Hotel La Tour ... Jersey ... 259
La Favorita Hotel ... Guernsey ... 256
The White House ... Herm Island ... 258

Country Houses with shooting nearby

ENGLAND

Abbots Oak ... Coalville ... 56
Apsley House ... Bath ... 21
The Ardencote Manor Hotel . Warwick ... 171
Arrow Mill Hotel ... Alcester ... 12
Ashwick Country House ... Dulverton ... 68
Aynsome Manor Hotel ... Cartmel ... 46
Bath Lodge Hotel ... Bath ... 22
The Beacon Country House ... Exmoor ... 75
The Beeches Farmhouse ... Ashbourne ... 15
Beechleas ... Wimborne Minster ... 176
Bibury Court ... Bibury ... 32
The Bowens Country House .. Hereford ... 90
Broom Hall ... Saham Toney ... 151
Burleigh Court ... Minchinhampton ... 119
Catton Old Hall ... Norwich ... 127
Chapel House ... Atherstone ... 16
Charlton Kings Hotel ... Cheltenham ... 48
Chippenhall Hall ... Diss ... 64
Conygree Gate Hotel ... Stow-On-The-Wold 163
Coombe House Country Hotel . Crediton ... 58
The Cottage Country House .. Nottingham ... 130
Coxley Vineyard ... Wells ... 173
Crosby Lodge Country House Carlisle ... 45
Cross Lane House Hotel ... Bridgnorth ... 37
The Crown Hotel ... Exford ... 74
Dale Head Hall Lakeside Hotel .. Keswick ... 96
Dannah Farm Country
Guest House ... Belper ... 30
Delbury Hall ... Ludlow ... 107
Duke's Hotel ... Bath ... 24
The Eastbury Hotel ... Sherborne ... 156
Easton Court Hotel ... Chagford ... 47
Eshott Hall ... Morpeth ... 122
Fallowfields ... Oxford ... 135
Fayrer Garden House Hotel ... Windermere ... 178
Findon Manor ... Worthing ... 183
Foxdown Manor ... Clovelly ... 55
Glebe Farm House ... Stratford-upon-Avon .. 164
Glewstone Court ... Ross-On-Wye ... 146
Hipping Hall ... Kirkby Lonsdale ... 99
Hooke Hall ... Uckfield ... 168
Hope House ... Yoxford ... 185
Kingston House ... Staverton ... 160
Langar Hall ... Nottingham ... 131
Langrish House ... Petersfield ... 138
The Lord Haldon Hotel ... Exeter ... 73
Lower Brook House ... Blockley ... 35
The Malt House ... Chipping Campden ... 52
The Manor House ... Beverley ... 31
The Mill At Harvington ... Evesham ... 72
Millers House Hotel ... Middleham ... 118
Moor View House ... Lydford ... 110
Norfolk Mead Hotel ... Norwich ... 128
Oak Lodge Hotel ... Enfield ... 69
The Old Rectory ... Norwich ... 129
The Old Vicarage Country
House Hotel ... Witherslack ... 181
Owlpen Manor ... Owlpen ... 134
Paradise House ... Bath ... 27
The Parsonage Country House . York ... 184
Pen-y-Dyffryn Country Hotel Oswestry ... 132
Periton Park Hotel ... Middlecombe ... 117
Petty France ... Badminton ... 17
Preston House Hotel ... Saunton ... 153
Prince Hall Hotel ... Dartmoor ... 63
Quarlton Manor Farm ... Bolton ... 36
Rectory House ... Evershot ... 71
Redcoats Farmhouse Hotel ... Stevenage ... 161
Romney Bay House ... New Romney ... 124
Ryedale Country Lodge ... Helmsley ... 88
The Shaven Crown Hotel ... Shipton-Under-Wychwood .. 157
Simonsbath House Hotel ... Simonsbath ... 158
The St Enodoc Hotel ... Rock ... 145
Staindrop Hotel ... Sheffield ... 155
Stanhill Court Hotel ... Gatwick ... 79
The Stonor Arms ... Stonor ... 162
Storrs Hall ... Windermere ... 180
Temple Sowerby House Hotel . Penrith ... 137
Thatched Cottage Hotel ... Brockenhurst ... 41
Upper Court ... Tewkesbury ... 165
Venn Ottery Barton ... Ottery St. Mary ... 133
Wallett's Court ... Dover ... 66
Washingborough Hall ... Lincoln ... 103
White Wings ... Fenny Drayton ... 78
Whitley Ridge &
Country House Hotel ... Brockenhurst ... 42
Widbrook Grange ... Bath ... 28
Wood Hall Hotel ... Woodbridge ... 182
Woolverton House ... Bath ... 29
Yalbury Cottage Hotel ... Dorchester ... 65
Yeoldon House Hotel ... Bideford ... 33

WALES

Berthlwyd Hall Hotel ... Conwy ... 196
Buttington House ... Welshpool ... 203
The Crown At Whitebrook ... Monmouth ... 199
Glangrwyney Court ... Abergavenny ... 189
Llanwenarth House ... Abergavenny ... 190
Old Gwernyfed Country Manor .. Brecon ... 193
Parva Farmhouse ... Tintern ... 202
The Pembrokeshire Retreat ... Cardigan ... 195
Ty'n Rhos Country House ... Caernarfon ... 194

SCOTLAND

Aldonaig ... Rhu ... 234
Balgonie Country House ... Ballater,Royal ... 206
Boath House ... Nairn ... 227
Bosville Hotel & Chandlery
Seafood Restaurant ... Isle of Skye ... 220
Dunfallandy House ... Pitlochry ... 231
Killiechronan ... Isle Of Mull ... 219
The Killiecrankie Hotel ... Killiecrankie ... 222
The Manor House Hotel ... Oban ... 229
Navidale House Hotel ... Helmsdale ... 214
Newmiln Country House ... Perth ... 230

Nivingston Country House ....Kinross 224
The Old Manse of Marnoch...By Huntly 215
The Pend ....Dunkeld..................211
Polmaily House Hotel ....Drumnadrochit 209
The Royal Hotel.....................Comrie 208
Trigony House Hotel..............Dunfries 210

IRELAND

Aberdeen Lodge ....Dublin 243
Ard-na-Sidhe.........................Caragh Lake 239
Caragh Lodge.........................Caragh Lake 240
Cashel Palace Hotel ....Cashel......................241
Castle Grove Country House.Letterkenny 249
Earls Court House..................Killarney..................247
Fitzwilliam Park ....Dublin 244
Halpins Hotel & Vittles Restaurant................Kilkee 245
Markree Castle ....Sligo 252

CHANNEL ISLANDS

La Favorita Hotel ....Guernsey 256

Country Houses with conference facilities for 30 delegates or more

ENGLAND

The Ardencote Manor Hotel.Warwick 171
Arrow Mill Hotel ....Alcester.......................12
The Beacon Country House...Exmoor 75
The Beeches Hotel & Victorian Gardens..............Norwich....................126
Beechwood Hotel ....North Walsham........125
Chalk Lane Hotel...................Epsom 70
Chase Lodge ....Hampton Court 84
Coombe House Country Hotel .Crediton 58
The Cornish Cottage Hotel & Gourmet Restaurant........New Polzeath............123
The Cottage Country House..Nottingham 130
Coxley Vineyard....................Wells 173
Dannah Farm Country Guest House ....Belper 30
Dunsley Hall..........................Whitby......................175
East Lodge Country House.....Bakewell 18
The Eastbury Hotel ....Sherborne 156
Eshott Hall.............................Morpeth 122
Fallowfields............................Oxford 135
Findon Manor........................Worthing 183
Glencot House.......................Wells.........................174
Grove House..........................Hamsterley Forest 85
Hewitt's Hotel ....Lynton 112
Holbrook House Hotel...........Wincanton 177
Kemps Country House Hotel .Wareham 170
Kingston House ....Staverton 160
Langrish House ....Petersfield 138
The Lord Haldon Hotel ....Exeter 73
Melbourn Bury.......................Cambridge 44
Norfolk Mead Hotel..............Norwich 128
The Old Manor Hotel............Loughborough 106
The Old Rectory.....................Norwich 129
Overton Grange Hotel...........Ludlow 108
The Parsonage Country House..York 184
The Priory..............................Bury St. Edmunds.......43
Quarry Garth Country House Windermere.............179
Redcoats Farmhouse Hotel.....Stevenage 161
The St Enodoc Hotel ....Rock 145
Staindrop Hotel......................Sheffield 155
Stanhill Court Hotel ....Gatwick 79
Temple Sowerby House.........Penrith 137
Upper Court ....Tewkesbury 165
Venn Ottery Barton ....Ottery St. Mary 133
Washingborough Hall ....Lincoln 103
The White House...................Harrogate...................86
Widbrook Grange...................Bath 28
Wood Hall Hotel....................Woodbridge 182
Woolverton House ....Bath 29
Yeoldon House Hotel.............Bideford 33

WALES

Berthlwyd Hall Hotel ....Conwy 196
Plas Dolmelynllyn ....Dolgellau 198
Plas Penhelig Country House.Aberdovey 188

SCOTLAND

Balgonie Country House ....Ballater 206
Culcreuch Castle Hotel..........Fintry 213
The Dryfesdale Hotel ....Lockerbie 225
Dungallen House Hotel..........Oban 228
The Kinlochbervie Hotel ....Kinlochbervie 223
The Lake Hotel ....Port Of Menteith......233
Nivingston Country House ....Kinross 224

IRELAND

Cashel Palace Hotel ....Cashel.......................241
Halpins Hotel & Vittles Restaurant...............Kilkee........................245

CHANNEL ISLANDS

La Favorita Hotel ....Guernsey 256

Country Houses with double rooms for £50 per night or less

ENGLAND

Biggin Hall.............................Biggin-By-Hartington 34
Eagle House ....Bath...........................25
Lower Brook House ....Blockley 35
The Manor Farmhouse...........Matlock 115
Owlpen Manor ....Owlpen.....................134
Pear Tree Lake Farms ....Crewe 59
Trehellas House & Memories of Malaya Restaurant..........Wadebridge 169

SCOTLAND

Clint Lodge............................St. Boswell................235

IRELAND

The Inishclare Restaurant......Killadeas 246

CHANNEL ISLANDS

Hotel La Tour........................Jersey 259

Country Houses accepting the Johansens Privilege Card

ENGLAND

Chalk Lane Hotel...................Epsom 70
Channel House Hotel ....Minehead..................120
Charlton Kings Hotel............Cheltenham 48
The Cottage Hotel ....Porlock Weir 139
Dunsley Hall..........................Whitby......................175
The Parsonage Country House .York 184
Simonsbath House Hotel ....Simonsbath 158
The Stonor Arms ....Stonor 162
Waren House Hotel ....Bamburgh 20
Yeoldon House Hotel............Bideford 33

WALES

Parva Farmhouse ....Tintern 202

IRELAND

Earls Court House..................Killarney 247

Johansens Preferred Partners

AT&T Global Services 484
Classic Malts...505
Diners Club International 484
Dunhill Tobacco................................Inside Back Cover
Ercol 11
Knight Frank ....Inside Front Cover
Hildon Ltd ....7 & 9
Honda UK Ltd 513
J&H Marsh & McLennan 491
Moët Hennessy 5
Pacific Direct 506

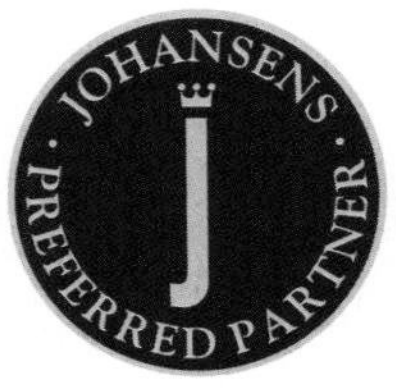

PREFERRED PARTNERS

Preferred partners are those organisations specifically chosen and exclusively recommended by Johansens for the quality and excellence of their products and services for the mutual benefit of Johansens members, readers and independent travellers.

AT&T Global Services

Classic Malts of Scotland

Diners Club International

Dunhill Tobacco

Ercol Furniture Ltd

Hildon Ltd

J&H Marsh & McLennan

Knight Frank International

Honda UK Ltd

Moët Hennessy

NPI

Pacific Direct

ORDER FORM

Call our 24hr credit card hotline FREEPHONE 0800 269 397

Simply indicate which title(s) you require by putting the quantity in the boxes provided. Choose your preferred method of payment and return this coupon (NO STAMP REQUIRED) to: Johansens, FREEPOST (CB264), 43 Millharbour, London E14 9BR. Your FREE gifts will automatically be dispatched with your order. Fax orders welcome on 0171 537 3594

PRINTED GUIDES

	Title	Price	Qty	Total £
A	Hotels – Great Britain & Ireland 1999	£19.95		
B	Country Houses and Small Hotels – Great Britain & Ireland 1999	£10.95		
C	Traditional Inns, Hotels and Restaurants – Great Britain & Ireland 1999	£10.95		
D	Hotels – Europe & The Mediterranean 1999	£14.95		
E	Hotels – North America, Bermuda, Caribbean 1999	£9.95		
F	Historic Houses Castles & Gardens 1999 *published & mailed to you in March '99*	£4.99		
G	Museums & Galleries 1999 *published & mailed to you in April '99*	£8.95		
H	Business Meeting Venues 1999 *published & mailed to you in March '99*	£20.00		
I	Japanese Edition 1999	£9.95		
J	Privilege Card 1999 *You get one free card with you order, please mention here the number of additional cards you require*	£20.00		

TOTAL 1

SPECIAL OFFERS

Save	Offer	Qty	Total £
SAVE £7.85	3 Johansens guides A+B+C ~~£41.85~~ £34		
	In a presentation box set add £5		
SAVE £12.80	4 Johansens guides A+B+C+D ~~£56.80~~ £44		
	In a presentation box set add £5		
SAVE £14.75	5 Johansens guides A+B+C+D+E ~~£66.75~~ £52		
	In a presentation box set add £5		
	+Johansens Suit Cover		FREE
	+P&P		FREE
SAVE £10.90	2 Johansens CD-ROMS K+L ~~£49.90~~ £39		
SAVE £10	Business Meeting Pack H+M ~~£40~~ £30		

TOTAL 3

CD-ROMs

	Title	Price	Qty	Total £
K	The Guide 1999 – Great Britain & Ireland *published and mailed to you in Nov 98*	£29.95		
L	The Guide 1999 – Europe & North America *published and mailed to you in Nov 98*	£19.95		
M	Business Meeting Venues 1999 *published and mailed to you in April '99*	£20.00		

TOTAL 2

Postage & Packing

UK: £4.50 or £2.50 for single orders and CD-ROMs
Ouside UK: Add £5 or £3 for single orders and CD-ROMs.

TOTAL 4

One Privilege Card — FREE
10% discount, room upgrade when available, VIP service at participating establishments

TOTAL 1+2+3+4

Name (Mr/Mrs/Miss)

Address

Postcode

Prices Valid Until 31 August 1999
Please allow 21 days for delivery

Occasionally we may allow other reputable organisations to write to you with offers which may be of interest. If you prefer not to hear from them, tick this box. ☐

☐ **I enclose a cheque for £** ______ **payable to Johansens**
☐ **I enclose my order on company letterheading, please invoice (UK only)**
☐ **Please debit my credit/charge card account (please tick).**
☐ **MasterCard** ☐ **Diners** ☐ **Amex** ☐ **Visa** ☐ **Switch** (Issue Number)

Card No

Signature **Exp date**

J15

ORDER FORM

Call our 24hr credit card hotline FREEPHONE 0800 269 397

Simply indicate which title(s) you require by putting the quantity in the boxes provided. Choose your preferred method of payment and return this coupon (NO STAMP REQUIRED) to: Johansens, FREEPOST (CB264), 43 Millharbour, London E14 9BR. Your FREE gifts will automatically be dispatched with your order. Fax orders welcome on 0171 537 3594

PRINTED GUIDES

	Title	Price	Qty	Total £
A	Hotels – Great Britain & Ireland 1999	£19.95		
B	Country Houses and Small Hotels – Great Britain & Ireland 1999	£10.95		
C	Traditional Inns, Hotels and Restaurants – Great Britain & Ireland 1999	£10.95		
D	Hotels – Europe & The Mediterranean 1999	£14.95		
E	Hotels – North America, Bermuda, Caribbean 1999	£9.95		
F	Historic Houses Castles & Gardens 1999 *published & mailed to you in March '99*	£4.99		
G	Museums & Galleries 1999 *published & mailed to you in April '99*	£8.95		
H	Business Meeting Venues 1999 *published & mailed to you in March '99*	£20.00		
I	Japanese Edition 1999	£9.95		
J	Privilege Card 1999 *You get one free card with you order, please mention here the number of additional cards you require*	£20.00		

TOTAL 1

SPECIAL OFFERS

Save	Offer	Qty	Total £
SAVE £7.85	3 Johansens guides A+B+C ~~£41.85~~ £34		
	In a presentation box set add £5		
SAVE £12.80	4 Johansens guides A+B+C+D ~~£56.80~~ £44		
	In a presentation box set add £5		
SAVE £14.75	5 Johansens guides A+B+C+D+E ~~£66.75~~ £52		
	In a presentation box set add £5		
	+Johansens Suit Cover		FREE
	+P&P		FREE
SAVE £10.90	2 Johansens CD-ROMS K+L ~~£49.90~~ £39		
SAVE £10	Business Meeting Pack H+M ~~£40~~ £30		

TOTAL 3

CD-ROMs

	Title	Price	Qty	Total £
K	The Guide 1999 – Great Britain & Ireland *published and mailed to you in Nov 98*	£29.95		
L	The Guide 1999 – Europe & North America *published and mailed to you in Nov 98*	£19.95		
M	Business Meeting Venues 1999 *published and mailed to you in April '99*	£20.00		

TOTAL 2

Postage & Packing

UK: £4.50 or £2.50 for single orders and CD-ROMs
Ouside UK: Add £5 or £3 for single orders and CD-ROMs.

TOTAL 4

One Privilege Card — FREE
10% discount, room upgrade when available, VIP service at participating establishments

TOTAL 1+2+3+4

Name (Mr/Mrs/Miss)

Address

Postcode

Prices Valid Until 31 August 1999
Please allow 21 days for delivery

Occasionally we may allow other reputable organisations to write to you with offers which may be of interest. If you prefer not to hear from them, tick this box. ☐

☐ **I enclose a cheque for £** ______ **payable to Johansens**
☐ **I enclose my order on company letterheading, please invoice (UK only)**
☐ **Please debit my credit/charge card account (please tick).**
☐ **MasterCard** ☐ **Diners** ☐ **Amex** ☐ **Visa** ☐ **Switch** (Issue Number)

Card No

Signature **Exp date**

J15

Guest Survey Report

Your own Johansens 'inspection' gives reliability to our guides and assists in the selection of Award Nominations

Name/location of hotel: ______________________ Page No: __________

Date of visit: ______________________

Name & address of guest: ______________________

______________________ Postcode: __________

Please tick one box in each category below:	Excellent	Good	Disappointing	Poor
Bedrooms				
Public Rooms				
Restaurant/Cuisine				
Service				
Welcome/Friendliness				
Value For Money				

PLEASE return your Guest Survey Report form!

Occasionally we may allow other reputable organisations to write with offers which may be of interest.
If you prefer not to hear from them, tick this box ☐

To: Johansens, FREEPOST (CB264), 43 Millharbour, London E14 9BR

Guest Survey Report

Your own Johansens 'inspection' gives reliability to our guides and assists in the selection of Award Nominations

Name/location of hotel: ______________________ Page No: __________

Date of visit: ______________________

Name & address of guest: ______________________

______________________ Postcode: __________

Please tick one box in each category below:	Excellent	Good	Disappointing	Poor
Bedrooms				
Public Rooms				
Restaurant/Cuisine				
Service				
Welcome/Friendliness				
Value For Money				

PLEASE return your Guest Survey Report form!

Occasionally we may allow other reputable organisations to write with offers which may be of interest.
If you prefer not to hear from them, tick this box ☐

To: Johansens, FREEPOST (CB264), 43 Millharbour, London E14 9BR

ORDER FORM

Call our 24hr credit card hotline FREEPHONE 0800 269 397

Simply indicate which title(s) you require by putting the quantity in the boxes provided. Choose your preferred method of payment and return this coupon (NO STAMP REQUIRED) to: Johansens, FREEPOST (CB264), 43 Millharbour, London E14 9BR. Your FREE gifts will automatically be dispatched with your order.
Fax orders welcome on 0171 537 3594

PRINTED GUIDES

	Qty	Total £
A Hotels – Great Britain & Ireland 1999 ....£19.95		
B Country Houses and Small Hotels – Great Britain & Ireland 1999 ....£10.95		
C Traditional Inns, Hotels and Restaurants – Great Britain & Ireland 1999 ....£10.95		
D Hotels – Europe & The Mediterranean 1999 ....£14.95		
E Hotels – North America, Bermuda, Caribbean 1999 ....£9.95		
F Historic Houses Castles & Gardens 1999 *published & mailed to you in March '99* £4.99		
G Museums & Galleries 1999 *published & mailed to you in April '99* £8.95		
H Business Meeting Venues 1999 *published & mailed to you in March '99* £20.00		
I Japanese Edition 1999 ....£9.95		
J Privilege Card 1999 ....£20.00 *You get one free card with your order, please mention here the number of additional cards you require*		

TOTAL 1

SPECIAL OFFERS

	Qty	Total £
SAVE £7.85 3 Johansens guides A+B+C ..~~£41.85~~..£34		
In a presentation box set add £5		
SAVE £12.80 4 Johansens guides A+B+C+D ....~~£56.80~~..£44		
In a presentation box set add £5		
SAVE £14.75 5 Johansens guides A+B+C+D+E ....~~£66.75~~..£52		
In a presentation box set add £5		
+Johansens Suit Cover		FREE
+P&P		FREE
SAVE £10.90 2 Johansens CD-ROMS K+L ~~£49.90~~..£39		
SAVE £10 Business Meeting Pack H+M.....~~£40~~..£30		

TOTAL 3

CD-ROMs

	Qty	Total £
K The Guide 1999 – Great Britain & Ireland *published and mailed to you in Nov 98* £29.95		
L The Guide 1999 – Europe & North America *published and mailed to you in Nov 98* ..£19.95		
M Business Meeting Venues 1999 *published and mailed to you in April '99* £20.00		

TOTAL 2

Postage & Packing

UK: £4.50 or £2.50 for single orders and CD-ROMs
Ouside UK: Add £5 or £3 for single orders and CD-ROMs.

TOTAL 4

One Privilege Card — FREE
10% discount, room upgrade when available,
VIP service at participating establishments

TOTAL 1+2+3+4

Name (Mr/Mrs/Miss)

Address

Postcode

Prices Valid Until 31 August 1999
Please allow 21 days for delivery

Occasionally we may allow other reputable organisations to write to you with offers which may be of interest. If you prefer not to hear from them, tick this box. ☐

☐ I enclose a cheque for £ ______ payable to Johansens
☐ I enclose my order on company letterheading, please invoice (UK only)
☐ Please debit my credit/charge card account (please tick).
☐ MasterCard ☐ Diners ☐ Amex ☐ Visa ☐ Switch (Issue Number) ______

Card No

Signature

Exp date

J15

ORDER FORM

Call our 24hr credit card hotline FREEPHONE 0800 269 397

Simply indicate which title(s) you require by putting the quantity in the boxes provided. Choose your preferred method of payment and return this coupon (NO STAMP REQUIRED) to: Johansens, FREEPOST (CB264), 43 Millharbour, London E14 9BR. Your FREE gifts will automatically be dispatched with your order.
Fax orders welcome on 0171 537 3594

PRINTED GUIDES

	Qty	Total £
A Hotels – Great Britain & Ireland 1999 ....£19.95		
B Country Houses and Small Hotels – Great Britain & Ireland 1999 ....£10.95		
C Traditional Inns, Hotels and Restaurants – Great Britain & Ireland 1999 ....£10.95		
D Hotels – Europe & The Mediterranean 1999 ....£14.95		
E Hotels – North America, Bermuda, Caribbean 1999 ....£9.95		
F Historic Houses Castles & Gardens 1999 *published & mailed to you in March '99* £4.99		
G Museums & Galleries 1999 *published & mailed to you in April '99* £8.95		
H Business Meeting Venues 1999 *published & mailed to you in March '99* £20.00		
I Japanese Edition 1999 ....£9.95		
J Privilege Card 1999 ....£20.00 *You get one free card with your order, please mention here the number of additional cards you require*		

TOTAL 1

SPECIAL OFFERS

	Qty	Total £
SAVE £7.85 3 Johansens guides A+B+C ..~~£41.85~~..£34		
In a presentation box set add £5		
SAVE £12.80 4 Johansens guides A+B+C+D ....~~£56.80~~..£44		
In a presentation box set add £5		
SAVE £14.75 5 Johansens guides A+B+C+D+E ....~~£66.75~~..£52		
In a presentation box set add £5		
+Johansens Suit Cover		FREE
+P&P		FREE
SAVE £10.90 2 Johansens CD-ROMS K+L ~~£49.90~~..£39		
SAVE £10 Business Meeting Pack H+M.....~~£40~~..£30		

TOTAL 3

CD-ROMs

	Qty	Total £
K The Guide 1999 – Great Britain & Ireland *published and mailed to you in Nov 98* £29.95		
L The Guide 1999 – Europe & North America *published and mailed to you in Nov 98* ..£19.95		
M Business Meeting Venues 1999 *published and mailed to you in April '99* £20.00		

TOTAL 2

Postage & Packing

UK: £4.50 or £2.50 for single orders and CD-ROMs
Ouside UK: Add £5 or £3 for single orders and CD-ROMs.

TOTAL 4

One Privilege Card — FREE
10% discount, room upgrade when available,
VIP service at participating establishments

TOTAL 1+2+3+4

Name (Mr/Mrs/Miss)

Address

Postcode

Prices Valid Until 31 August 1999
Please allow 21 days for delivery

Occasionally we may allow other reputable organisations to write to you with offers which may be of interest. If you prefer not to hear from them, tick this box. ☐

☐ I enclose a cheque for £ ______ payable to Johansens
☐ I enclose my order on company letterheading, please invoice (UK only)
☐ Please debit my credit/charge card account (please tick).
☐ MasterCard ☐ Diners ☐ Amex ☐ Visa ☐ Switch (Issue Number) ______

Card No

Signature

Exp date

J15

Guest Survey Report

Your own Johansens 'inspection' gives reliability to our guides and assists in the selection of Award Nominations

Name/location of hotel: ______________________ Page No: ________

Date of visit: ______________________

Name & address of guest: ______________________

______________________ Postcode: ________

Please tick one box in each category below:	*Excellent*	*Good*	*Disappointing*	*Poor*
Bedrooms				
Public Rooms				
Restaurant/Cuisine				
Service				
Welcome/Friendliness				
Value For Money				

PLEASE return your Guest Survey Report form!

Occasionally we may allow other reputable organisations to write with offers which may be of interest.
If you prefer not to hear from them, tick this box ☐

To: Johansens, FREEPOST (CB264), 43 Millharbour, London E14 9BR

Guest Survey Report

Your own Johansens 'inspection' gives reliability to our guides and assists in the selection of Award Nominations

Name/location of hotel: ______________________ Page No: ________

Date of visit: ______________________

Name & address of guest: ______________________

______________________ Postcode: ________

Please tick one box in each category below:	*Excellent*	*Good*	*Disappointing*	*Poor*
Bedrooms				
Public Rooms				
Restaurant/Cuisine				
Service				
Welcome/Friendliness				
Value For Money				

PLEASE return your Guest Survey Report form!

Occasionally we may allow other reputable organisations to write with offers which may be of interest.
If you prefer not to hear from them, tick this box ☐

To: Johansens, FREEPOST (CB264), 43 Millharbour, London E14 9BR

ORDER FORM

Call our 24hr credit card hotline FREEPHONE 0800 269 397

Simply indicate which title(s) you require by putting the quantity in the boxes provided. Choose your preferred method of payment and return this coupon (NO STAMP REQUIRED) to: Johansens, FREEPOST (CB264), 43 Millharbour, London E14 9BR. Your FREE gifts will automatically be dispatched with your order. Fax orders welcome on 0171 537 3594

PRINTED GUIDES

	Item	Price	Qty	Total £
A	Hotels – Great Britain & Ireland 1999	£19.95		
B	Country Houses and Small Hotels – Great Britain & Ireland 1999	£10.95		
C	Traditional Inns, Hotels and Restaurants – Great Britain & Ireland 1999	£10.95		
D	Hotels – Europe & The Mediterranean 1999	£14.95		
E	Hotels – North America, Bermuda, Caribbean 1999	£9.95		
F	Historic Houses Castles & Gardens 1999 *published & mailed to you in March '99*	£4.99		
G	Museums & Galleries 1999 *published & mailed to you in April '99*	£8.95		
H	Business Meeting Venues 1999 *published & mailed to you in March '99*	£20.00		
I	Japanese Edition 1999	£9.95		
J	Privilege Card 1999 *You get one free card with you order, please mention here the number of additional cards you require*	£20.00		

TOTAL 1

CD-ROMs

	Item	Price	Qty	Total £
K	The Guide 1999 – Great Britain & Ireland *published and mailed to you in Nov 98*	£29.95		
L	The Guide 1999 – Europe & North America *published and mailed to you in Nov 98*	£19.95		
M	Business Meeting Venues 1999 *published and mailed to you in April '99*	£20.00		

TOTAL 2

SPECIAL OFFERS

Save	Offer	Qty	Total £
SAVE £7.85	3 Johansens guides A+B+C ~~£41.85~~ £34		
	In a presentation box set add £5		
SAVE £12.80	4 Johansens guides A+B+C+D ~~£56.80~~ £44		
	In a presentation box set add £5		
SAVE £14.75	5 Johansens guides A+B+C+D+E ~~£66.75~~ £52		
	In a presentation box set add £5		
	+Johansens Suit Cover		FREE
	+P&P		FREE
SAVE £10.90	2 Johansens CD-ROMS K+L ~~£49.90~~ £39		
SAVE £10	Business Meeting Pack H+M ~~£40~~ £30		

TOTAL 3

Postage & Packing

UK: £4.50 or £2.50 for single orders and CD-ROMs
Ouside UK: Add £5 or £3 for single orders and CD-ROMs.

TOTAL 4

One Privilege Card **FREE**
10% discount, room upgrade when available, VIP service at participating establishments

TOTAL 1+2+3+4

Name (Mr/Mrs/Miss)

Address

Postcode

Prices Valid Until 31 August 1999
Please allow 21 days for delivery

Occasionally we may allow other reputable organisations to write to you with offers which may be of interest. If you prefer not to hear from them, tick this box. ☐

☐ **I enclose a cheque for £** ______ **payable to Johansens**
☐ **I enclose my order on company letterheading, please invoice (UK only)**
☐ **Please debit my credit/charge card account (please tick).**
☐ **MasterCard** ☐ **Diners** ☐ **Amex** ☐ **Visa** ☐ **Switch** (Issue Number)

Card No

Signature **Exp date**

J15

ORDER FORM

Call our 24hr credit card hotline FREEPHONE 0800 269 397

Simply indicate which title(s) you require by putting the quantity in the boxes provided. Choose your preferred method of payment and return this coupon (NO STAMP REQUIRED) to: Johansens, FREEPOST (CB264), 43 Millharbour, London E14 9BR. Your FREE gifts will automatically be dispatched with your order. Fax orders welcome on 0171 537 3594

PRINTED GUIDES

	Item	Price	Qty	Total £
A	Hotels – Great Britain & Ireland 1999	£19.95		
B	Country Houses and Small Hotels – Great Britain & Ireland 1999	£10.95		
C	Traditional Inns, Hotels and Restaurants – Great Britain & Ireland 1999	£10.95		
D	Hotels – Europe & The Mediterranean 1999	£14.95		
E	Hotels – North America, Bermuda, Caribbean 1999	£9.95		
F	Historic Houses Castles & Gardens 1999 *published & mailed to you in March '99*	£4.99		
G	Museums & Galleries 1999 *published & mailed to you in April '99*	£8.95		
H	Business Meeting Venues 1999 *published & mailed to you in March '99*	£20.00		
I	Japanese Edition 1999	£9.95		
J	Privilege Card 1999 *You get one free card with you order, please mention here the number of additional cards you require*	£20.00		

TOTAL 1

CD-ROMs

	Item	Price	Qty	Total £
K	The Guide 1999 – Great Britain & Ireland *published and mailed to you in Nov 98*	£29.95		
L	The Guide 1999 – Europe & North America *published and mailed to you in Nov 98*	£19.95		
M	Business Meeting Venues 1999 *published and mailed to you in April '99*	£20.00		

TOTAL 2

SPECIAL OFFERS

Save	Offer	Qty	Total £
SAVE £7.85	3 Johansens guides A+B+C ~~£41.85~~ £34		
	In a presentation box set add £5		
SAVE £12.80	4 Johansens guides A+B+C+D ~~£56.80~~ £44		
	In a presentation box set add £5		
SAVE £14.75	5 Johansens guides A+B+C+D+E ~~£66.75~~ £52		
	In a presentation box set add £5		
	+Johansens Suit Cover		FREE
	+P&P		FREE
SAVE £10.90	2 Johansens CD-ROMS K+L ~~£49.90~~ £39		
SAVE £10	Business Meeting Pack H+M ~~£40~~ £30		

TOTAL 3

Postage & Packing

UK: £4.50 or £2.50 for single orders and CD-ROMs
Ouside UK: Add £5 or £3 for single orders and CD-ROMs.

TOTAL 4

One Privilege Card **FREE**
10% discount, room upgrade when available, VIP service at participating establishments

TOTAL 1+2+3+4

Name (Mr/Mrs/Miss)

Address

Postcode

Prices Valid Until 31 August 1999
Please allow 21 days for delivery

Occasionally we may allow other reputable organisations to write to you with offers which may be of interest. If you prefer not to hear from them, tick this box. ☐

☐ **I enclose a cheque for £** ______ **payable to Johansens**
☐ **I enclose my order on company letterheading, please invoice (UK only)**
☐ **Please debit my credit/charge card account (please tick).**
☐ **MasterCard** ☐ **Diners** ☐ **Amex** ☐ **Visa** ☐ **Switch** (Issue Number)

Card No

Signature **Exp date**

J15

Guest Survey Report

Your own Johansens 'inspection' gives reliability to our guides and assists in the selection of Award Nominations

Name/location of hotel: ______________________ Page No: ________

Date of visit: ______________________

Name & address of guest: ______________________

______________________ Postcode: ________

Please tick one box in each category below:	Excellent	Good	Disappointing	Poor
Bedrooms				
Public Rooms				
Restaurant/Cuisine				
Service				
Welcome/Friendliness				
Value For Money				

PLEASE return your Guest Survey Report form!

Occasionally we may allow other reputable organisations to write with offers which may be of interest.
If you prefer not to hear from them, tick this box ☐

To: Johansens, FREEPOST (CB264), 43 Millharbour, London E14 9BR

Guest Survey Report

Your own Johansens 'inspection' gives reliability to our guides and assists in the selection of Award Nominations

Name/location of hotel: ______________________ Page No: ________

Date of visit: ______________________

Name & address of guest: ______________________

______________________ Postcode: ________

Please tick one box in each category below:	Excellent	Good	Disappointing	Poor
Bedrooms				
Public Rooms				
Restaurant/Cuisine				
Service				
Welcome/Friendliness				
Value For Money				

PLEASE return your Guest Survey Report form!

Occasionally we may allow other reputable organisations to write with offers which may be of interest.
If you prefer not to hear from them, tick this box ☐

To: Johansens, FREEPOST (CB264), 43 Millharbour, London E14 9BR

ORDER FORM

Call our 24hr credit card hotline FREEPHONE 0800 269 397

Simply indicate which title(s) you require by putting the quantity in the boxes provided. Choose your preferred method of payment and return this coupon (NO STAMP REQUIRED) to: Johansens, FREEPOST (CB264), 43 Millharbour, London E14 9BR. Your FREE gifts will automatically be dispatched with your order. Fax orders welcome on 0171 537 3594

PRINTED GUIDES

	Qty	Total £
A Hotels – Great Britain & Ireland 1999 ....£19.95		
B Country Houses and Small Hotels – Great Britain & Ireland 1999 ....£10.95		
C Traditional Inns, Hotels and Restaurants – Great Britain & Ireland 1999 ......£10.95		
D Hotels – Europe & The Mediterranean 1999 ....£14.95		
E Hotels – North America, Bermuda, Caribbean 1999 ....£9.95		
F Historic Houses Castles & Gardens 1999 *published & mailed to you in March '99* £4.99		
G Museums & Galleries 1999 *published & mailed to you in April '99* £8.95		
H Business Meeting Venues 1999 *published & mailed to you in March '99* £20.00		
I Japanese Edition 1999 ....£9.95		
J Privilege Card 1999 ....£20.00 *You get one free card with you order, please mention here the number of additional cards you require*		

TOTAL 1

SPECIAL OFFERS

	Qty	Total £
SAVE £7.85 3 Johansens guides A+B+C .. ~~£41.85~~ ..£34		
In a presentation box set add £5		
SAVE £12.80 4 Johansens guides A+B+C+D .... ~~£56.80~~ ..£44		
In a presentation box set add £5		
SAVE £14.75 5 Johansens guides A+B+C+D+E .... ~~£66.75~~ ..£52		
In a presentation box set add £5		
+Johansens Suit Cover		FREE
+P&P		FREE
SAVE £10.90 2 Johansens CD-ROMS K+L ~~£49.90~~ ..£39		
SAVE £10 Business Meeting Pack H+M..... ~~£40~~ ..£30		

TOTAL 3

CD-ROMs

	Qty	Total £
K The Guide 1999 – Great Britain & Ireland *published and mailed to you in Nov 98* £29.95		
L The Guide 1999 – Europe & North America *published and mailed to you in Nov 98* ..£19.95		
M Business Meeting Venues 1999 *published and mailed to you in April '99* £20.00		

TOTAL 2

Postage & Packing

UK: £4.50 or £2.50 for single orders and CD-ROMs
Ouside UK: Add £5 or £3 for single orders and CD-ROMs.

TOTAL 4

One Privilege Card — FREE
10% discount, room upgrade when available,
VIP service at participating establishments

TOTAL 1+2+3+4

Name (Mr/Mrs/Miss)

Address

Postcode

Prices Valid Until 31 August 1999
Please allow 21 days for delivery

Occasionally we may allow other reputable organisations to write to you with offers which may be of interest. If you prefer not to hear from them, tick this box. ☐

☐ **I enclose a cheque for £** ______ **payable to Johansens**
☐ **I enclose my order on company letterheading, please invoice (UK only)**
☐ **Please debit my credit/charge card account (please tick).**
☐ **MasterCard** ☐ **Diners** ☐ **Amex** ☐ **Visa** ☐ **Switch** (Issue Number)

Card No

Signature **Exp date**

J15

ORDER FORM

Call our 24hr credit card hotline FREEPHONE 0800 269 397

Simply indicate which title(s) you require by putting the quantity in the boxes provided. Choose your preferred method of payment and return this coupon (NO STAMP REQUIRED) to: Johansens, FREEPOST (CB264), 43 Millharbour, London E14 9BR. Your FREE gifts will automatically be dispatched with your order. Fax orders welcome on 0171 537 3594

PRINTED GUIDES

	Qty	Total £
A Hotels – Great Britain & Ireland 1999 ....£19.95		
B Country Houses and Small Hotels – Great Britain & Ireland 1999 ....£10.95		
C Traditional Inns, Hotels and Restaurants – Great Britain & Ireland 1999 ......£10.95		
D Hotels – Europe & The Mediterranean 1999 ....£14.95		
E Hotels – North America, Bermuda, Caribbean 1999 ....£9.95		
F Historic Houses Castles & Gardens 1999 *published & mailed to you in March '99* £4.99		
G Museums & Galleries 1999 *published & mailed to you in April '99* £8.95		
H Business Meeting Venues 1999 *published & mailed to you in March '99* £20.00		
I Japanese Edition 1999 ....£9.95		
J Privilege Card 1999 ....£20.00 *You get one free card with you order, please mention here the number of additional cards you require*		

TOTAL 1

SPECIAL OFFERS

	Qty	Total £
SAVE £7.85 3 Johansens guides A+B+C .. ~~£41.85~~ ..£34		
In a presentation box set add £5		
SAVE £12.80 4 Johansens guides A+B+C+D .... ~~£56.80~~ ..£44		
In a presentation box set add £5		
SAVE £14.75 5 Johansens guides A+B+C+D+E .... ~~£66.75~~ ..£52		
In a presentation box set add £5		
+Johansens Suit Cover		FREE
+P&P		FREE
SAVE £10.90 2 Johansens CD-ROMS K+L ~~£49.90~~ ..£39		
SAVE £10 Business Meeting Pack H+M..... ~~£40~~ ..£30		

TOTAL 3

CD-ROMs

	Qty	Total £
K The Guide 1999 – Great Britain & Ireland *published and mailed to you in Nov 98* £29.95		
L The Guide 1999 – Europe & North America *published and mailed to you in Nov 98* ..£19.95		
M Business Meeting Venues 1999 *published and mailed to you in April '99* £20.00		

TOTAL 2

Postage & Packing

UK: £4.50 or £2.50 for single orders and CD-ROMs
Ouside UK: Add £5 or £3 for single orders and CD-ROMs.

TOTAL 4

One Privilege Card — FREE
10% discount, room upgrade when available,
VIP service at participating establishments

TOTAL 1+2+3+4

Name (Mr/Mrs/Miss)

Address

Postcode

Prices Valid Until 31 August 1999
Please allow 21 days for delivery

Occasionally we may allow other reputable organisations to write to you with offers which may be of interest. If you prefer not to hear from them, tick this box. ☐

☐ **I enclose a cheque for £** ______ **payable to Johansens**
☐ **I enclose my order on company letterheading, please invoice (UK only)**
☐ **Please debit my credit/charge card account (please tick).**
☐ **MasterCard** ☐ **Diners** ☐ **Amex** ☐ **Visa** ☐ **Switch** (Issue Number)

Card No

Signature **Exp date**

J15

Guest Survey Report

Your own Johansens 'inspection' gives reliability to our guides and assists in the selection of Award Nominations

Name/location of hotel: ______________________ Page No: __________

Date of visit: ______________________

Name & address of guest: ______________________

______________________ Postcode: __________

Please tick one box in each category below:	*Excellent*	*Good*	*Disappointing*	*Poor*
Bedrooms				
Public Rooms				
Restaurant/Cuisine				
Service				
Welcome/Friendliness				
Value For Money				

PLEASE return your Guest Survey Report form!

Occasionally we may allow other reputable organisations to write with offers which may be of interest.
If you prefer not to hear from them, tick this box ☐

To: Johansens, FREEPOST (CB264), 43 Millharbour, London E14 9BR

Guest Survey Report

Your own Johansens 'inspection' gives reliability to our guides and assists in the selection of Award Nominations

Name/location of hotel: ______________________ Page No: __________

Date of visit: ______________________

Name & address of guest: ______________________

______________________ Postcode: __________

Please tick one box in each category below:	*Excellent*	*Good*	*Disappointing*	*Poor*
Bedrooms				
Public Rooms				
Restaurant/Cuisine				
Service				
Welcome/Friendliness				
Value For Money				

PLEASE return your Guest Survey Report form!

Occasionally we may allow other reputable organisations to write with offers which may be of interest.
If you prefer not to hear from them, tick this box ☐

To: Johansens, FREEPOST (CB264), 43 Millharbour, London E14 9BR

ORDER FORM

Call our 24hr credit card hotline FREEPHONE 0800 269 397

Simply indicate which title(s) you require by putting the quantity in the boxes provided. Choose your preferred method of payment and return this coupon (NO STAMP REQUIRED) to: Johansens, FREEPOST (CB264), 43 Millharbour, London E14 9BR. Your FREE gifts will automatically be dispatched with your order. Fax orders welcome on 0171 537 3594

PRINTED GUIDES

	Qty	Total £
A Hotels – Great Britain & Ireland 1999 ....£19.95		
B Country Houses and Small Hotels – Great Britain & Ireland 1999 ....£10.95		
C Traditional Inns, Hotels and Restaurants – Great Britain & Ireland 1999 ....£10.95		
D Hotels – Europe & The Mediterranean 1999 ....£14.95		
E Hotels – North America, Bermuda, Caribbean 1999 ....£9.95		
F Historic Houses Castles & Gardens 1999 *published & mailed to you in March '99* £4.99		
G Museums & Galleries 1999 *published & mailed to you in April '99* £8.95		
H Business Meeting Venues 1999 *published & mailed to you in March '99* £20.00		
I Japanese Edition 1999 ....£9.95		
J Privilege Card 1999 ....£20.00 *You get one free card with you order, please mention here the number of additional cards you require*		

TOTAL 1

SPECIAL OFFERS

	Qty	Total £
SAVE £7.85 3 Johansens guides A+B+C ~~£41.85~~ ..£34		
In a presentation box set add £5		
SAVE £12.80 4 Johansens guides A+B+C+D ....~~£56.80~~ ..£44		
In a presentation box set add £5		
SAVE £14.75 5 Johansens guides A+B+C+D+E ....~~£66.75~~ ..£52		
In a presentation box set add £5		
+Johansens Suit Cover		FREE
+P&P		FREE
SAVE £10.90 2 Johansens CD-ROMS K+L ~~£49.90~~ ..£39		
SAVE £10 Business Meeting Pack H+M..... ~~£40~~ ..£30		

TOTAL 3

CD-ROMs

	Qty	Total £
K The Guide 1999 – Great Britain & Ireland *published and mailed to you in Nov 98* £29.95		
L The Guide 1999 – Europe & North America *published and mailed to you in Nov 98* ..£19.95		
M Business Meeting Venues 1999 *published and mailed to you in April '99* £20.00		

TOTAL 2

Postage & Packing

UK: £4.50 or £2.50 for single orders and CD-ROMs
Ouside UK: Add £5 or £3 for single orders and CD-ROMs.

TOTAL 4

One Privilege Card — FREE
10% discount, room upgrade when available,
VIP service at participating establishments

TOTAL 1+2+3+4

Name **(Mr/Mrs/Miss)**

Address

Postcode

Prices Valid Until 31 August 1999
Please allow 21 days for delivery

Occasionally we may allow other reputable organisations to write to you with offers which may be of interest. If you prefer not to hear from them, tick this box. ☐

☐ **I enclose a cheque for £** ____ **payable to Johansens**
☐ **I enclose my order on company letterheading, please invoice (UK only)**
☐ **Please debit my credit/charge card account (please tick).**
☐ **MasterCard** ☐ **Diners** ☐ **Amex** ☐ **Visa** ☐ **Switch** (Issue Number)

Card No

Signature **Exp date**

J15

ORDER FORM

Call our 24hr credit card hotline FREEPHONE 0800 269 397

Simply indicate which title(s) you require by putting the quantity in the boxes provided. Choose your preferred method of payment and return this coupon (NO STAMP REQUIRED) to: Johansens, FREEPOST (CB264), 43 Millharbour, London E14 9BR. Your FREE gifts will automatically be dispatched with your order. Fax orders welcome on 0171 537 3594

PRINTED GUIDES

	Qty	Total £
A Hotels – Great Britain & Ireland 1999 ....£19.95		
B Country Houses and Small Hotels – Great Britain & Ireland 1999 ....£10.95		
C Traditional Inns, Hotels and Restaurants – Great Britain & Ireland 1999 ....£10.95		
D Hotels – Europe & The Mediterranean 1999 ....£14.95		
E Hotels – North America, Bermuda, Caribbean 1999 ....£9.95		
F Historic Houses Castles & Gardens 1999 *published & mailed to you in March '99* £4.99		
G Museums & Galleries 1999 *published & mailed to you in April '99* £8.95		
H Business Meeting Venues 1999 *published & mailed to you in March '99* £20.00		
I Japanese Edition 1999 ....£9.95		
J Privilege Card 1999 ....£20.00 *You get one free card with you order, please mention here the number of additional cards you require*		

TOTAL 1

SPECIAL OFFERS

	Qty	Total £
SAVE £7.85 3 Johansens guides A+B+C ~~£41.85~~ ..£34		
In a presentation box set add £5		
SAVE £12.80 4 Johansens guides A+B+C+D ....~~£56.80~~ ..£44		
In a presentation box set add £5		
SAVE £14.75 5 Johansens guides A+B+C+D+E ....~~£66.75~~ ..£52		
In a presentation box set add £5		
+Johansens Suit Cover		FREE
+P&P		FREE
SAVE £10.90 2 Johansens CD-ROMS K+L ~~£49.90~~ ..£39		
SAVE £10 Business Meeting Pack H+M..... ~~£40~~ ..£30		

TOTAL 3

CD-ROMs

	Qty	Total £
K The Guide 1999 – Great Britain & Ireland *published and mailed to you in Nov 98* £29.95		
L The Guide 1999 – Europe & North America *published and mailed to you in Nov 98* ..£19.95		
M Business Meeting Venues 1999 *published and mailed to you in April '99* £20.00		

TOTAL 2

Postage & Packing

UK: £4.50 or £2.50 for single orders and CD-ROMs
Ouside UK: Add £5 or £3 for single orders and CD-ROMs.

TOTAL 4

One Privilege Card — FREE
10% discount, room upgrade when available,
VIP service at participating establishments

TOTAL 1+2+3+4

Name **(Mr/Mrs/Miss)**

Address

Postcode

Prices Valid Until 31 August 1999
Please allow 21 days for delivery

Occasionally we may allow other reputable organisations to write to you with offers which may be of interest. If you prefer not to hear from them, tick this box. ☐

☐ **I enclose a cheque for £** ____ **payable to Johansens**
☐ **I enclose my order on company letterheading, please invoice (UK only)**
☐ **Please debit my credit/charge card account (please tick).**
☐ **MasterCard** ☐ **Diners** ☐ **Amex** ☐ **Visa** ☐ **Switch** (Issue Number)

Card No

Signature **Exp date**

J15

Guest Survey Report

Your own Johansens 'inspection' gives reliability to our guides and assists in the selection of Award Nominations

Name/location of hotel: ______________________ Page No: ________

Date of visit: ______________________

Name & address of guest: ______________________

______________________ Postcode: ________

Please tick one box in each category below:

	Excellent	Good	Disappointing	Poor
Bedrooms				
Public Rooms				
Restaurant/Cuisine				
Service				
Welcome/Friendliness				
Value For Money				

PLEASE return your Guest Survey Report form!

Occasionally we may allow other reputable organisations to write with offers which may be of interest.
If you prefer not to hear from them, tick this box ☐

To: Johansens, FREEPOST (CB264), 43 Millharbour, London E14 9BR

Guest Survey Report

Your own Johansens 'inspection' gives reliability to our guides and assists in the selection of Award Nominations

Name/location of hotel: ______________________ Page No: ________

Date of visit: ______________________

Name & address of guest: ______________________

______________________ Postcode: ________

Please tick one box in each category below:

	Excellent	Good	Disappointing	Poor
Bedrooms				
Public Rooms				
Restaurant/Cuisine				
Service				
Welcome/Friendliness				
Value For Money				

PLEASE return your Guest Survey Report form!

Occasionally we may allow other reputable organisations to write with offers which may be of interest.
If you prefer not to hear from them, tick this box ☐

To: Johansens, FREEPOST (CB264), 43 Millharbour, London E14 9BR

ORDER FORM

Call our 24hr credit card hotline FREEPHONE 0800 269 397

Simply indicate which title(s) you require by putting the quantity in the boxes provided. Choose your preferred method of payment and return this coupon (NO STAMP REQUIRED) to: Johansens, FREEPOST (CB264), 43 Millharbour, London E14 9BR. Your FREE gifts will automatically be dispatched with your order. Fax orders welcome on 0171 537 3594

PRINTED GUIDES

	Qty	Total £
A Hotels – Great Britain & Ireland 1999 ....£19.95		
B Country Houses and Small Hotels – Great Britain & Ireland 1999 ....£10.95		
C Traditional Inns, Hotels and Restaurants – Great Britain & Ireland 1999 ......£10.95		
D Hotels – Europe & The Mediterranean 1999 ....£14.95		
E Hotels – North America, Bermuda, Caribbean 1999 ....£9.95		
F Historic Houses Castles & Gardens 1999 *published & mailed to you in March '99* £4.99		
G Museums & Galleries 1999 *published & mailed to you in April '99* £8.95		
H Business Meeting Venues 1999 *published & mailed to you in March '99* £20.00		
I Japanese Edition 1999 ....£9.95		
J Privilege Card 1999 ....£20.00 *You get one free card with you order, please mention here the number of additional cards you require*		
TOTAL 1		

CD-ROMs

	Qty	Total £
K The Guide 1999 – Great Britain & Ireland *published and mailed to you in Nov 98* £29.95		
L The Guide 1999 – Europe & North America *published and mailed to you in Nov 98* ..£19.95		
M Business Meeting Venues 1999 *published and mailed to you in April '99* £20.00		
TOTAL 2		

SPECIAL OFFERS

	Qty	Total £
SAVE £7.85 3 Johansens guides A+B+C ..~~£41.85~~..£34		
In a presentation box set add £5		
SAVE £12.80 4 Johansens guides A+B+C+D ....~~£56.80~~..£44		
In a presentation box set add £5		
SAVE £14.75 5 Johansens guides A+B+C+D+E ....~~£66.75~~..£52		
In a presentation box set add £5		
+Johansens Suit Cover		FREE
+P&P		FREE
SAVE £10.90 2 Johansens CD-ROMS K+L ~~£49.90~~..£39		
SAVE £10 Business Meeting Pack H+M.....~~£40~~..£30		
TOTAL 3		

Postage & Packing

UK: £4.50 or £2.50 for single orders and CD-ROMs
Ouside UK: Add £5 or £3 for single orders and CD-ROMs.

TOTAL 4

One Privilege Card — FREE
10% discount, room upgrade when available, VIP service at participating establishments

TOTAL 1+2+3+4

Name (Mr/Mrs/Miss)

Address

Postcode

Prices Valid Until 31 August 1999
Please allow 21 days for delivery

Occasionally we may allow other reputable organisations to write to you with offers which may be of interest. If you prefer not to hear from them, tick this box. ☐

☐ I enclose a cheque for £ ______ payable to Johansens
☐ I enclose my order on company letterheading, please invoice (UK only)
☐ Please debit my credit/charge card account (please tick).
☐ MasterCard ☐ Diners ☐ Amex ☐ Visa ☐ Switch (Issue Number) ______

Card No

Signature — Exp date

J15

ORDER FORM

Call our 24hr credit card hotline FREEPHONE 0800 269 397

Simply indicate which title(s) you require by putting the quantity in the boxes provided. Choose your preferred method of payment and return this coupon (NO STAMP REQUIRED) to: Johansens, FREEPOST (CB264), 43 Millharbour, London E14 9BR. Your FREE gifts will automatically be dispatched with your order. Fax orders welcome on 0171 537 3594

PRINTED GUIDES

	Qty	Total £
A Hotels – Great Britain & Ireland 1999 ....£19.95		
B Country Houses and Small Hotels – Great Britain & Ireland 1999 ....£10.95		
C Traditional Inns, Hotels and Restaurants – Great Britain & Ireland 1999 ......£10.95		
D Hotels – Europe & The Mediterranean 1999 ....£14.95		
E Hotels – North America, Bermuda, Caribbean 1999 ....£9.95		
F Historic Houses Castles & Gardens 1999 *published & mailed to you in March '99* £4.99		
G Museums & Galleries 1999 *published & mailed to you in April '99* £8.95		
H Business Meeting Venues 1999 *published & mailed to you in March '99* £20.00		
I Japanese Edition 1999 ....£9.95		
J Privilege Card 1999 ....£20.00 *You get one free card with you order, please mention here the number of additional cards you require*		
TOTAL 1		

CD-ROMs

	Qty	Total £
K The Guide 1999 – Great Britain & Ireland *published and mailed to you in Nov 98* £29.95		
L The Guide 1999 – Europe & North America *published and mailed to you in Nov 98* ..£19.95		
M Business Meeting Venues 1999 *published and mailed to you in April '99* £20.00		
TOTAL 2		

SPECIAL OFFERS

	Qty	Total £
SAVE £7.85 3 Johansens guides A+B+C ..~~£41.85~~..£34		
In a presentation box set add £5		
SAVE £12.80 4 Johansens guides A+B+C+D ....~~£56.80~~..£44		
In a presentation box set add £5		
SAVE £14.75 5 Johansens guides A+B+C+D+E ....~~£66.75~~..£52		
In a presentation box set add £5		
+Johansens Suit Cover		FREE
+P&P		FREE
SAVE £10.90 2 Johansens CD-ROMS K+L ~~£49.90~~..£39		
SAVE £10 Business Meeting Pack H+M.....~~£40~~..£30		
TOTAL 3		

Postage & Packing

UK: £4.50 or £2.50 for single orders and CD-ROMs
Ouside UK: Add £5 or £3 for single orders and CD-ROMs.

TOTAL 4

One Privilege Card — FREE
10% discount, room upgrade when available, VIP service at participating establishments

TOTAL 1+2+3+4

Name (Mr/Mrs/Miss)

Address

Postcode

Prices Valid Until 31 August 1999
Please allow 21 days for delivery

Occasionally we may allow other reputable organisations to write to you with offers which may be of interest. If you prefer not to hear from them, tick this box. ☐

☐ I enclose a cheque for £ ______ payable to Johansens
☐ I enclose my order on company letterheading, please invoice (UK only)
☐ Please debit my credit/charge card account (please tick).
☐ MasterCard ☐ Diners ☐ Amex ☐ Visa ☐ Switch (Issue Number) ______

Card No

Signature — Exp date

J15

Guest Survey Report

Your own Johansens 'inspection' gives reliability to our guides and assists in the selection of Award Nominations

Name/location of hotel: ______________________ Page No: __________

Date of visit: ______________________

Name & address of guest: ______________________

______________________ Postcode: __________

Please tick one box in each category below:	*Excellent*	*Good*	*Disappointing*	*Poor*
Bedrooms				
Public Rooms				
Restaurant/Cuisine				
Service				
Welcome/Friendliness				
Value For Money				

PLEASE return your Guest Survey Report form!

Occasionally we may allow other reputable organisations to write with offers which may be of interest.
If you prefer not to hear from them, tick this box ☐

To: Johansens, FREEPOST (CB264), 43 Millharbour, London E14 9BR

Guest Survey Report

Your own Johansens 'inspection' gives reliability to our guides and assists in the selection of Award Nominations

Name/location of hotel: ______________________ Page No: __________

Date of visit: ______________________

Name & address of guest: ______________________

______________________ Postcode: __________

Please tick one box in each category below:	*Excellent*	*Good*	*Disappointing*	*Poor*
Bedrooms				
Public Rooms				
Restaurant/Cuisine				
Service				
Welcome/Friendliness				
Value For Money				

PLEASE return your Guest Survey Report form!

Occasionally we may allow other reputable organisations to write with offers which may be of interest.
If you prefer not to hear from them, tick this box ☐

To: Johansens, FREEPOST (CB264), 43 Millharbour, London E14 9BR